*The Writings of Melanie Klein*

*Under the general editorship of*
Roger Money-Kyrle
*in collaboration with*
Betty Joseph, Edna O'Shaughnessy and Hanna Segal

Volume I

LOVE, GUILT AND REPARATION
AND OTHER WORKS

\*

Volume II

THE PSYCHO-ANALYSIS OF CHILDREN

\*

Volume III

ENVY AND GRATITUDE
AND OTHER WORKS

\*

Volume IV

NARRATIVE OF A CHILD ANALYSIS

# ENVY
# AND GRATITUDE
## and Other Works
### 1946–1963

*by*

MELANIE KLEIN

LONDON
**KARNAC BOOKS**
AND THE INSTITUTE OF PSYCHO-ANALYSIS
1993

First Published by
The Hogarth Press Ltd.
London
1975

Reprinted with their permission
by H. Karnac (Books) Ltd.,
58, Gloucester Road,
London, SW7 4QY.
1993

ISBN 1 85575 059 7

Printed in Great Britain by
BPCC Wheatons Ltd, Exeter

# CONTENTS

# PREFACE

THIS third volume of *The Writings of Melanie Klein* contains all her later work from 1946 until her death in 1960—with the exception of *Narrative of a Child Analysis* which is published separately as Volume IV. Unlike the papers which compose Volume I, *Love, Guilt and Reparation 1921–45* (most of which were originally published in *Contributions to Psycho-Analysis*) the contents of Volume III have never before been collected together. Some of them appeared first in two books, *Developments in Psycho-Analysis* and *New Directions in Psycho-Analysis*, which also included contributions by authors other than Melanie Klein. *Envy and Gratitude* was originally a monograph, and some of the papers were published posthumously in *Our Adult World and Other Essays*. Moreover, written as they were some specifically for psycho-analysts and some for the general reader, they are less homogeneous than are the contents of the other volumes. But they contain writings of the latter and most mature phase of Melanie Klein's working life and so include works which for the Kleinian student are of the very first importance.

As in the case of Volumes I and II there are Explanatory Notes towards the end of the book designed to indicate the position of each main theme in the evolution of Melanie Klein's thought. At the end, one Introduction and two Prefaces written by Ernest Jones for earlier editions are preserved for their historical interest.

R. E. MONEY-KYRLE

# I

# NOTES ON SOME
# SCHIZOID MECHANISMS[1]
## (1946)

### INTRODUCTION

THE present paper is concerned with the importance of early paranoid and schizoid anxieties and mechanisms. I have given much thought to this subject for a number of years, even before clarifying my views on the depressive processes in infancy. In the course of working out my concept of the infantile depressive position, however, the problems of the phase preceding it again forced themselves on my attention. I now wish to formulate some hypotheses at which I have arrived regarding the earlier anxieties and mechanisms.[2]

The hypotheses I shall put forward, which relate to very early stages of development, are derived by inference from material gained in the analyses of adults and children, and some of these hypotheses seem to tally with observations familiar in psychiatric work. To substantiate my contentions would require an accumulation of detailed case material for which there is no room in the framework of this paper, and I hope in further contributions to fill this gap.

At the outset it will be useful to summarize briefly the conclusions regarding the earliest phases of development which I have already put forward.[3]

In early infancy anxieties characteristic of psychosis arise which drive the ego to develop specific defence-mechanisms. In this period the fixation-points for all psychotic disorders are to be found. This hypothesis led some people to believe that I regarded all infants as psychotic; but I have already dealt sufficiently with this misunderstanding on other occasions. The psychotic anxieties, mechanisms

---

[1] [footnote to 1952 version:] This paper was read before the British Psycho-Analytical Society on December 4, 1946, and has been left unchanged and then published, apart from a few slight alterations (in particular the addition of one paragraph and some footnotes).

[2] Before completing this paper I discussed its main aspects with Paula Heimann and am much indebted to her for stimulating suggestions in working out and formulating a number of the concepts presented here.

[3] Cf. my *Psycho-Analysis of Children* (1932), and 'A Contribution to the Psychogenesis of Manic-Depressive States' (1935).

and ego-defences of infancy have a profound influence on development in all its aspects, including the development of the ego, super-ego and object-relations.

I have often expressed my view that object-relations exist from the beginning of life, the first object being the mother's breast which to the child becomes split into a good (gratifying) and bad (frustrating) breast; this splitting results in a severance of love and hate. I have further suggested that the relation to the first object implies its introjection and projection, and thus from the beginning object-relations are moulded by an interaction between introjection and projection, between internal and external objects and situations. These processes participate in the building up of the ego and super-ego and prepare the ground for the onset of the Oedipus complex in the second half of the first year.

From the beginning the destructive impulse is turned against the object and is first expressed in phantasied oral-sadistic attacks on the mother's breast, which soon develop into onslaughts on her body by all sadistic means. The persecutory fears arising from the infant's oral-sadistic impulses to rob the mother's body of its good contents, and from the anal-sadistic impulses to put his excrements into her (including the desire to enter her body in order to control her from within) are of great importance for the development of paranoia and schizophrenia.

I enumerated various typical defences of the early ego, such as the mechanisms of splitting the object and the impulses, idealization, denial of inner and outer reality and the stifling of emotions. I also mentioned various anxiety-contents, including the fear of being poisoned and devoured. Most of these phenomena—prevalent in the first few months of life—are found in the later symptomatic picture of schizophrenia.

This early period (first described as the 'persecutory phase') I later termed 'paranoid position',[1] and held that it precedes the depressive position. If persecutory fears are very strong, and for this reason (among others) the infant cannot work through the paranoid-schizoid position, the working through of the depressive position is in turn impeded. This failure may lead to a regressive reinforcing of persecutory fears and strengthen the fixation-points for severe psychoses (that is to say, the group of schizophrenias). Another outcome of serious difficulties arising during the period of the

---

[1] When this paper was first published in 1946, I was using my term 'paranoid position' synonymously with W. R. D. Fairbairn's 'schizoid position'. On further deliberation I decided to combine Fairbairn's term with mine and throughout the present book [*Developments in Psycho-Analysis*, 1952, in which this paper was first published] I am using the expression 'paranoid-schizoid position'.

depressive position may be manic-depressive disorders in later life. I also concluded that in less severe disturbances of development the same factors strongly influence the choice of neurosis.

While I assumed that the outcome of the depressive position depends on the working through of the preceding phase, I nevertheless attributed to the depressive position a central rôle in the child's early development. For with the introjection of the object as a whole the infant's object-relation alters fundamentally. The synthesis between the loved and hated aspects of the complete object gives rise to feelings of mourning and guilt which imply vital advances in the infant's emotional and intellectual life. This is also a crucial juncture for the choice of neurosis or psychosis. To all these conclusions I still adhere.

### SOME NOTES ON FAIRBAIRN'S RECENT PAPERS

In a number of recent papers[1] W. R. D. Fairbairn has given much attention to the subject-matter with which I am now dealing. I therefore find it helpful to clarify some essential points of agreement and disagreement between us. It will be seen that some of the conclusions which I shall present in this paper are in line with Fairbairn's conclusions, while others differ fundamentally. Fairbairn's approach was largely from the angle of ego-development in relation to objects, while mine was predominantly from the angle of anxieties and their vicissitudes. He called the earliest phase the 'schizoid position': he stated that it forms part of normal development and is the basis for adult schizoid and schizophrenic illness. I agree with this contention and consider his description of developmental schizoid phenomena as significant and revealing, and of great value for our understanding of schizoid behaviour and of schizophrenia. I also think that Fairbairn's view that the group of schizoid or schizophrenic disorders is much wider than has been acknowledged is correct and important; and the particular emphasis he laid on the inherent relation between hysteria and schizophrenia deserves full attention. His term 'schizoid position' would be appropriate if it is understood to cover both persecutory fear and schizoid mechanisms.

I disagree—to mention first the most basic issues—with his revision of the theory of mental structure and instincts. I also disagree with his view that to begin with only the bad object is internalized—a view which seems to me to contribute to the important differences between us regarding the development of object-relations as well as of ego-development. For I hold that the introjected good

[1] Cf. 'A Revised Psychopathology of the Psychoses and Neuroses', 'Endopsychic Structure Considered in Terms of Object-Relationships' and 'Object-Relationships and Dynamic Structure'.

breast forms a vital part of the ego, exerts from the beginning a fundamental influence on the process of ego-development and affects both ego-structure and object-relations. I also differ from Fairbairn's view that 'the great problem of the schizoid individual is how to love without destroying by love, whereas the great problem of the depressive individual is how to love without destroying by hate'.[1] This conclusion is in line not only with his rejecting Freud's concept of primary instincts but also with his underrating the role which aggression and hatred play from the beginning of life. As a result of this approach, he does not give enough weight to the importance of early anxiety and conflict and their dynamic effects on development.

## CERTAIN PROBLEMS OF THE EARLY EGO

In the following discussion I shall single out one aspect of ego-development and I shall deliberately not attempt to link it with the problems of ego-development as a whole. Nor can I here touch on the relation of the ego to the id and super-ego.

So far, we know little about the structure of the early ego. Some of the recent suggestions on this point have not convinced me: I have particularly in mind Glover's concept of ego nuclei and Fairbairn's theory of a central ego and two subsidiary egos. More helpful in my view is Winnicott's emphasis on the unintegration of the early ego.[2] I would also say that the early ego largely lacks cohesion, and a tendency towards integration alternates with a tendency towards disintegration, a falling into bits.[3] I believe that these fluctuations are characteristic of the first few months of life.

We are, I think, justified in assuming that some of the functions which we know from the later ego are there at the beginning. Prominent amongst these functions is that of dealing with anxiety. I hold that anxiety arises from the operation of the death instinct within the organism, is felt as fear of annihilation (death) and takes the form of fear of persecution. The fear of the destructive impulse seems to attach itself at once to an object—or rather it is experienced as the fear of an uncontrollable overpowering object. Other important sources of primary anxiety are the trauma of birth (separa-

[1] Cf. 'A Revised Psychopathology' (1941).

[2] Cf. D. W. Winnicott, 'Primitive Emotional Development' (1945). In this paper Winnicott also described the pathological outcome of states of unintegration, for instance the case of a woman patient who could not distinguish between her twin sister and herself.

[3] The greater or lesser cohesiveness of the ego at the beginning of postnatal life should be considered in connection with the greater or lesser capacity of the ego to tolerate anxiety which, as I have previously contended (*Psycho-Analysis of Children*, particularly p. 49), is a constitutional factor.

4

tion anxiety) and frustration of bodily needs; and these experiences too are from the beginning felt as being caused by objects. Even if these objects are felt to be external, they become through introjection internal persecutors and thus reinforce the fear of the destructive impulse within.

The vital need to deal with anxiety forces the early ego to develop fundamental mechanisms and defences. The destructive impulse is partly projected outwards (deflection of the death instinct) and, I think, attaches itself to the first external object, the mother's breast. As Freud has pointed out, the remaining portion of the destructive impulse is to some extent bound by the libido within the organism. However, neither of these processes entirely fulfils its purpose, and therefore the anxiety of being destroyed from within remains active. It seems to me in keeping with the lack of cohesiveness that under the pressure of this threat the ego tends to fall to pieces.[1] This falling to pieces appears to underlie states of disintegration in schizophrenics.

The question arises whether some active splitting processes within the ego may not occur even at a very early stage. As we assume, the early ego splits the object and the relation to it in an active way, and this may imply some active splitting of the ego itself. In any case, the result of splitting is a dispersal of the destructive impulse which is felt as the source of danger. I suggest that the primary anxiety of being annihilated by a destructive force within, with the ego's specific response of falling to pieces or splitting itself, may be extremely important in all schizophrenic processes.

## SPLITTING PROCESSES IN RELATION TO THE OBJECT

The destructive impulse projected outwards is first experienced as oral aggression. I believe that oral-sadistic impulses towards the mother's breast are active from the beginning of life, though with the onset of teething the cannibalistic impulses increase in strength —a factor stressed by Abraham.

In states of frustration and anxiety the oral-sadistic and cannibalistic desires are reinforced, and then the infant feels that he has taken in the nipple and the breast *in bits*. Therefore in addition to the divorce between a good and a bad breast in the young infant's phantasy, the frustrating breast—attacked in oral-sadistic phantasies—is felt to be in fragments; the gratifying breast, taken in

---

[1] Ferenczi in 'Notes and Fragments' (1930) suggests that most likely every living organism reacts to unpleasant stimuli by fragmentation, which might be an expression of the death instinct. Possibly, complicated mechanisms (living organisms) are only kept as an entity through the impact of external conditions. When these conditions become unfavourable the organism falls to pieces.

under the dominance of the sucking libido, is felt to be complete. This first internal good object acts as a focal point in the ego. It counteracts the processes of splitting and dispersal, makes for cohesiveness and integration, and is instrumental in building up the ego.[1] The infant's feeling of having inside a good and complete breast may, however, be shaken by frustration and anxiety. As a result, the divorce between the good and bad breast may be difficult to maintain, and the infant may feel that the good breast too is in pieces.

I believe that the ego is incapable of splitting the object—internal and external—without a corresponding splitting taking place within the ego. Therefore the phantasies and feelings about the state of the internal object vitally influence the structure of the ego. The more sadism prevails in the process of incorporating the object, and the more the object is felt to be in pieces, the more the ego is in danger of being split in relation to the internalized object fragments.

The processes I have described are, of course, bound up with the infant's phantasy-life; and the anxieties which stimulate the mechanism of splitting are also of a phantastic nature. It is in phantasy that the infant splits the object and the self, but the effect of this phantasy is a very real one, because it leads to feelings and relations (and later on, thought-processes) being in fact cut off from one another.[2]

## SPLITTING IN CONNECTION WITH PROJECTION AND INTROJECTION

So far, I have dealt particularly with the mechanism of splitting as one of the earliest ego-mechanisms and defences against anxiety. Introjection and projection are from the beginning of life also used in the service of this primary aim of the ego. Projection, as Freud described, originates from the deflection of the death instinct outwards and in my view it helps the ego to overcome anxiety by ridding it of danger and badness. Introjection of the good object is also used by the ego as a defence against anxiety.

Closely connected with projection and introjection are some other mechanisms. Here I am particularly concerned with the connection between splitting, idealization and denial. As regards splitting of

[1] D. W. Winnicott (*loc. cit.*) referred to the same process from another angle: he described how integration and adaptation to reality depend essentially on the infant's experience of the mother's love and care.

[2] In the discussion following the reading of this paper, Dr W. C. M. Scott referred to another aspect of splitting. He stressed the importance of the breaks in continuity of experiences, which imply a splitting in time rather than in space. He referred as an instance to the alternation between states of being asleep and states of being awake. I fully agree with his point of view.

the object, we have to remember that in states of gratification love-feelings turn towards the gratifying breast, while in states of frustration hatred and persecutory anxiety attach themselves to the frustrating breast.

Idealization is bound up with the splitting of the object, for the good aspects of the breast are exaggerated as a safeguard against the fear of the persecuting breast. While idealization is thus the corollary of persecutory fear, it also springs from the power of the instinctual desires which aim at unlimited gratification and therefore create the picture of an inexhaustible and always bountiful breast—an ideal breast.

We find an instance of such a cleavage in infantile hallucinatory gratification. The main processes which come into play in idealization are also operative in hallucinatory gratification, namely, splitting of the object and denial both of frustration and of persecution. The frustrating and persecuting object is kept widely apart from the idealized object. However, the bad object is not only kept apart from the good one but its very existence is denied, as is the whole situation of frustration and the bad feelings (pain) to which frustration gives rise. This is bound up with denial of psychic reality. The denial of psychic reality becomes possible only through strong feelings of omnipotence—an essential characteristic of early mentality. Omnipotent denial of the existence of the bad object and of the painful situation is in the unconscious equal to annihilation by the destructive impulse. It is, however, not only a situation and an object that are denied and annihilated—*it is an object-relation* which suffers this fate; and therefore a part of the ego, from which the feelings towards the object emanate, is denied and annihilated as well.

In hallucinatory gratification, therefore, two interrelated processes take place: the omnipotent conjuring up of the ideal object and situation, and the equally omnipotent annihilation of the bad persecutory object and the painful situation. These processes are based on splitting both the object and the ego.

In passing I would mention that in this early phase splitting, denial and omnipotence play a rôle similar to that of repression at a later stage of ego-development. In considering the importance of the processes of denial and omnipotence at a stage which is characterized by persecutory fear and schizoid mechanisms, we may remember the delusions of both grandeur and of persecution in schizophrenia.

So far, in dealing with persecutory fear, I have singled out the oral element. However, while the oral libido still has the lead, libidinal and aggressive impulses and phantasies from other sources come to the fore and lead to a confluence of oral, urethral and anal desires, both libidinal and aggressive. Also the attacks on the mother's breast develop into attacks of a similar nature on her body, which comes to be felt as it were as an extension of the breast, even before the mother is conceived of as a complete person. The phantasied onslaughts on the mother follow two main lines: one is the predominantly oral impulse to suck dry, bite up, scoop out and rob the mother's body of its good contents. (I shall discuss the bearing of these impulses on the development of object-relations in connection with introjection.) The other line of attack derives from the anal and urethral impulses and implies expelling dangerous substances (excrements) out of the self and into the mother. Together with these harmful excrements, expelled in hatred, split-off parts of the ego are also projected on to the mother or, as I would rather call it, *into* the mother.[1] These excrements and bad parts of the self are meant not only to injure but also to control and to take possession of the object. In so far as the mother comes to contain the bad parts of the self, she is not felt to be a separate individual but is felt to be *the* bad self.

Much of the hatred against parts of the self is now directed towards the mother. This leads to a particular form of identification which establishes the prototype of an aggressive object-relation. I suggest for these processes the term 'projective identification'. When projection is mainly derived from the infant's impulse to harm or to control the mother,[2] he feels her to be a persecutor. In psychotic disorders this identification of an object with the hated parts of the self contributes to the intensity of the hatred directed against other people. As far as the ego is concerned the excessive splitting off and expelling into the outer world of parts of itself considerably weaken it. For the aggressive component of feelings and of the personality is intimately bound up in the mind with power, potency, strength, knowledge and many other desired qualities.

It is, however, not only the bad parts of the self which are expelled and projected, but also good parts of the self. Excrements then have the significance of gifts; and parts of the ego which, together with

[1] The description of such primitive processes suffers from a great handicap, for these phantasies arise at a time when the infant has not yet begun to think in words. In this context, for instance, I am using the expression 'to project *into* another person' because this seems to me the only way of conveying the unconscious process I am trying to describe.

[2] M. G. Evans, in a short unpublished communication (read to the British Psycho-Analytical Society, January, 1946) gave some instances of patients in whom the following phenomena were marked: lack of sense of reality, a feeling of being divided and parts of the personality having entered the mother's body in order to rob and control her; as a consequence the mother and other people similarly attacked came to represent the patient. M. G. Evans related these processes to a very primitive stage of development.

excrements, are expelled and projected into the other person represent the good, *i.e.* the loving parts of the self. The identification based on this type of projection again vitally influences object-relations. The projection of good feelings and good parts of the self into the mother is essential for the infant's ability to develop good object-relations and to integrate his ego. However, if this projective process is carried out excessively, good parts of the personality are felt to be lost, and in this way the mother becomes the ego-ideal; this process too results in weakening and impoverishing the ego. Very soon such processes extend to other people,[1] and the result may be an over-strong dependence on these external representatives of one's own good parts. Another consequence is a fear that the capacity to love has been lost because the loved object is felt to be loved predominantly as a representative of the self.

The processes of splitting off parts of the self and projecting them into objects are thus of vital importance for normal development as well as for abnormal object-relations.

The effect of introjection on object-relations is equally important. The introjection of the good object, first of all the mother's breast, is a precondition for normal development. I have already described that it comes to form a focal point in the ego and makes for cohesiveness of the ego. One characteristic feature of the earliest relation to the good object—internal and external—is the tendency to idealize it. In states of frustration or increased anxiety, the infant is driven to take flight to his internal idealized object as a means of escaping from persecutors. From this mechanism various serious disturbances may result: when persecutory fear is too strong, the flight to the idealized object becomes excessive, and this severely hampers ego-development and disturbs object-relations. As a result the ego may be felt to be entirely subservient to and dependent on the internal object—only a shell for it. With an unassimilated idealized object there goes a feeling that the ego has no life and no value of its own.[2]

---

[1] W. C. M. Scott in an unpublished paper, read to the British Psycho-Analytical Society a few years ago, described three interconnected features which he came upon in a schizophrenic patient: a strong disturbance of her sense of reality, her feeling that the world round her was a cemetery, and the mechanism of putting all good parts of herself into another person—Greta Garbo—who came to stand for the patient.

[2] Cf. 'A Contribution to the Problem of Sublimation and its Relation to the Processes of Internalization' (1942) where Paula Heimann described a condition in which the internal objects act as foreign bodies embedded in the self. Whilst this is more obvious with regard to the bad objects, it is true even for the good ones, if the ego is compulsively subordinated to their preservation. When the ego serves its good internal objects excessively, they are felt as a source of danger to the self and come close to exerting a persecuting influence. Paula Heimann introduced the concept of the assimilation of the internal objects and applied it

I would suggest that the condition of flight to the unassimilated idealized object necessitates further splitting processes within the ego. For parts of the ego attempt to unite with the ideal object, while other parts strive to deal with the internal persecutors.

The various ways of splitting the ego and internal objects result in the feeling that the ego is in bits. This feeling amounts to a state of disintegration. In normal development, the states of disintegration which the infant experiences are transitory. Among other factors, gratification by the external good object[1] again and again helps to break through these schizoid states. The infant's capacity to overcome temporary schizoid states is in keeping with the strong elasticity and resilience of the infantile mind. If states of splitting and therefore of disintegration, which the ego is unable to overcome, occur too frequently and go on for too long, then in my view they must be regarded as a sign of schizophrenic illness in the infant, and some indications of such illness may already be seen in the first few months of life. In adult patients, states of depersonalization and of schizophrenic dissociation seem to be a regression to these infantile states of disintegration.[2]

In my experience, excessive persecutory fears and schizoid mechanisms in early infancy may have a detrimental effect on intellectual development in its initial stages. Certain forms of mental deficiency would therefore have to be regarded as belonging to the group of schizophrenias. Accordingly, in considering mental deficiency in children at any age one should keep in mind the possibility of schizophrenic illness in early infancy.

I have so far described some effects of excessive introjection and projection on object-relations. I am not attempting to investigate here in any detail the various factors which in some cases make for a predominance of introjective and in other cases for a predominance of projective processes. As regards normal personality, it may be

---

specifically to sublimation. As regards ego-development, she pointed out that such assimilation is essential for the successful exercise of ego-functions and for the achievement of independence.

[1] Looked at in this light, the mother's love and understanding of the infant can be seen as the infant's greatest stand-by in overcoming states of disintegration and anxieties of a psychotic nature.

[2] Herbert Rosenfeld, in 'Analysis of a Schizophrenic State with Depersonalization' (1947), has presented case-material to illustrate how the splitting mechanisms which are bound up with projective identification were responsible both for a schizophrenic state and depersonalization. In his paper 'A Note on the Psychopathology of Confusional States in Chronic Schizophrenias' (1950) he also pointed out that a confusional state comes about if the subject loses the capacity to differentiate between good and bad objects, between aggressive and libidinal impulses, and so on. He suggested that in such states of confusion splitting mechanisms are frequently reinforced for defensive purposes.

said that the course of ego-development and object-relations depends on the degree to which an optimal balance between introjection and projection in the early stages of development can be achieved. This in turn has a bearing on the integration of the ego and the assimilation of internal objects. Even if the balance is disturbed and one or the other of these processes is excessive, there is some interaction between introjection and projection. For instance the projection of a predominantly hostile inner world which is ruled by persecutory fears leads to the introjection—a taking-back—of a hostile external world; and *vice versa*, the introjection of a distorted and hostile external world reinforces the projection of a hostile inner world.

Another aspect of projective processes, as we have seen, concerns the forceful entry into the object and control of the object by parts of the self. As a consequence, introjection may then be felt as a forceful entry from the outside into the inside, in retribution for violent projection. This may lead to the fear that not only the body but also the mind is controlled by other people in a hostile way. As a result there may be a severe disturbance in introjecting good objects—a disturbance which would impede all ego-functions as well as sexual development and might lead to an excessive withdrawal to the inner world. This withdrawal is, however, caused not only by the fear of introjecting a dangerous external world but also by the fear of internal persecutors and an ensuing flight to the idealized internal object.

I have referred to the weakening and impoverishment of the ego resulting from excessive splitting and projective identification. This weakened ego, however, becomes also incapable of assimilating its internal objects, and this leads to the feeling that it is ruled by them. Again, such a weakened ego feels incapable of taking back into itself the parts which it projected into the external world. These various disturbances in the interplay between projection and introjection, which imply excessive splitting of the ego, have a detrimental effect on the relation to the inner and outer world and seem to be at the root of some forms of schizophrenia.

Projective identification is the basis of many anxiety-situations, of which I shall mention a few. The phantasy of forcefully entering the object gives rise to anxieties relating to the dangers threatening the subject from within the object. For instance, the impulses to control an object from within it stir up the fear of being controlled and persecuted inside it. By introjecting and re-introjecting the forcefully entered object, the subject's feelings of inner persecution are strongly reinforced; all the more since the re-introjected object is felt to contain the dangerous aspects of the self. The accumulation of anxieties of this nature, in which the ego is, as it were, caught between a variety of external and internal persecution-situations, is a basic element in paranoia.[1]

I have previously described[2] the infant's phantasies of attacking and sadistically entering the mother's body as giving rise to various anxiety-situations (particularly the fear of being imprisoned and persecuted within her) which are at the bottom of paranoia. I also showed that the fear of being imprisoned (and especially of the penis being attacked) inside the mother is an important factor in later disturbances of male potency (impotence) and also underlines claustrophobia.[3]

## SCHIZOID OBJECT-RELATIONS

To summarize now some of the disturbed object-relations which are found in schizoid personalities: the violent splitting of the self and excessive projection have the effect that the person towards whom this process is directed is felt as a persecutor. Since the destructive and hated part of the self which is split off and projected is felt as a danger to the loved object and therefore gives rise to guilt, this process of projection in some ways also implies a deflection of guilt from the self on to the other person. Guilt has, however, not been done away with, and the deflected guilt is felt as an unconscious responsibility for the people who have become representatives of the aggressive part of the self.

[1] Herbert Rosenfeld, in 'Analysis of a Schizophrenic State with Depersonalization' and 'Remarks on the Relation of Male Homosexuality to Paranoia' (1949), discussed the clinical importance of those paranoid anxieties which are connected with projective identification in psychotic patients. In the two schizophrenic cases he described, it became evident that the patients were dominated by the fear that the analyst was trying to force himself into the patient. When these fears were analysed in the transference-situation, improvement could take place. Rosenfeld has further connected projective identification (and the corresponding persecutory fears) with female sexual frigidity on the one hand and on the other with the frequent combination of homosexuality and paranoia in men.

[2] *Psycho-Analysis of Children*, Chapter 8, particularly p. 131, and Chapter 12, particularly p. 242.

[3] Joan Riviere, in an unpublished paper 'Paranoid Attitudes seen in Everyday Life and in Analysis' (read before the British Psycho-Analytical Society in 1948), reported a great deal of clinical material in which projective identification became apparent. Unconscious phantasies of forcing the whole self into the inside of the object (to obtain control and possession) led, through the fear of retaliation, to a variety of persecutory anxieties such as claustrophobia, or to such common phobias as of burglars, spiders, invasion in wartime. These fears are connected with the unconscious 'catastrophic' phantasies of being dismembered, disembowelled, torn to pieces and of total internal disruption of the body and personality and loss of identity—fears which are an elaboration of the fear of annihilation (death) and have the effect of reinforcing the mechanisms of splitting and the process of ego-disintegration as found in psychotics.

Another typical feature of schizoid object-relations is their narcissistic nature which derives from the infantile introjective and projective processes. For, as I suggested earlier, when the ego-ideal is projected into another person, this person becomes predominantly loved and admired because he contains the good parts of the self. Similarly, the relation to another person on the basis of projecting bad parts of the self into him is of a narcissistic nature, because in this case as well the object strongly represents one part of the self. Both these types of a narcissistic relation to an object often show strong obsessional features. The impulse to control other people is, as we know, an essential element in obsessional neurosis. The need to control others can to some extent be explained by a deflected drive to control parts of the self. When these parts have been projected excessively into another person, they can only be controlled by controlling the other person. One root of obsessional mechanisms may thus be found in the particular identification which results from infantile projective processes. This connection may also throw some light on the obsessional element which so often enters into the tendency for reparation. For it is not only an object about whom guilt is experienced but also parts of the self which the subject is driven to repair or restore.

All these factors may lead to a compulsive tie to certain objects or—another outcome—to a shrinking from people in order to prevent both a destructive intrusion into them and the danger of retaliation by them. The fear of such dangers may show itself in various negative attitudes in object-relations. For instance, one of my patients told me that he dislikes people who are too much influenced by him, for they seem to become too much like himself and therefore he gets tired of them.

Another characteristic of schizoid object-relations is a marked artificiality and lack of spontaneity. Side by side with this goes a severe disturbance of the feeling of the self or, as I would put it, of the relation to the self. This relation, too, appears to be artificial. In other words, psychic reality and the relation to external reality are equally disturbed.

The projection of split-off parts of the self into another person essentially influences object-relations, emotional life and the person-ality as a whole. To illustrate this contention I will select as an instance two universal phenomena which are interlinked: the feeling of loneliness and fear of parting. We know that one source of the depressive feelings accompanying parting from people can be found in the fear of the destruction of the object by the aggressive impulses directed against it. But it is more specifically the splitting and pro-jective processes which underlie this fear. If aggressive elements in relation to the object are predominant and strongly aroused by the frustration of parting, the individual feels that the split-off components of his self, projected into the object, control this object in an aggressive and destructive way. At the same time the internal object is felt to be in the same danger of destruction as the external one in whom one part of the self is felt to be left. The result is an excessive weakening of the ego, a feeling that there is nothing to sustain it, and a corresponding feeling of loneliness. While this description applies to neurotic individuals, I think that in some degree it is a general phenomenon.

One need hardly elaborate the fact that some other features of schizoid object-relations, which I described earlier, can also be found in minor degrees and in a less striking form in normal people —for instance shyness, lack of spontaneity or, on the other hand, a particularly intense interest in people.

In similar ways normal disturbances in thought-processes link up with the developmental paranoid-schizoid position. For all of us are liable at times to a momentary impairment of logical thinking which amounts to thoughts and associations being cut off from one another and situations being split off from one another; in fact, the ego is temporarily split.

## THE DEPRESSIVE POSITION IN RELATION TO THE PARANOID-SCHIZOID POSITION

I now wish to consider further steps in the infant's development. So far I have described the anxieties, mechanisms and defences which are characteristic of the first few months of life. With the introjection of the complete object in about the second quarter of the first year marked steps in integration are made. This implies important changes in the relation to objects. The loved and hated aspects of the mother are no longer felt to be so widely separated, and the result is an increased fear of loss, states akin to mourning and a strong feeling of guilt, because the aggressive impulses are felt to be directed against the loved object. The depressive position has come to the fore. The very experience of depressive feelings in turn has the effect of further integrating the ego, because it makes for an increased understanding of psychic reality and better perception of the external world, as well as for a greater synthesis between inner and external situations.

The drive to make reparation, which comes to the fore at this stage, can be regarded as a consequence of greater insight into psychic reality and of growing synthesis, for it shows a more realistic response to the feelings of grief, guilt and fear of loss resulting from the aggression against the loved object. Since the drive to repair or protect the injured object paves the way for more satisfactory object-relations and sublimations, it in turn increases synthesis and contributes to the integration of the ego.

During the second half of the first year the infant makes some fundamental steps towards working through the depressive position. However, schizoid mechanisms still remain in force, though in a modified form and to a lesser degree, and early anxiety-situations are again and again experienced in the process of modification. The working through of the persecutory and depressive positions extends over the first few years of childhood and plays an essential part in the infantile neurosis. In the course of this process, anxieties lose in strength; objects become both less idealized and less terrifying, and the ego becomes more unified. All this is interconnected with the growing perception of reality and adaptation to it.

If development during the paranoid-schizoid position has not proceeded normally and the infant cannot—for internal or external reasons—cope with the impact of depressive anxieties a vicious circle arises. For if persecutory fear, and correspondingly schizoid mechanisms, are too strong, the ego is not capable of working through the depressive position. This forces the ego to regress to the paranoid-schizoid position and reinforces the earlier persecutory fears and schizoid phenomena. Thus the basis is established for various forms of schizophrenia in later life; for when such a regression occurs, not only are the fixation-points in the schizoid position reinforced, but there is a danger of greater states of disintegration setting in. Another outcome may be the strengthening of depressive features.

External experiences are, of course, of great importance in these developments. For instance, in the case of a patient who showed depressive and schizoid features, the analysis brought up with great vividness his early experiences in babyhood, to such an extent that in some sessions physical sensations in the throat or digestive organs occurred. The patient had been weaned suddenly at four months of age because his mother fell ill. In addition, he did not see his mother for four weeks. When she returned, she found the child greatly changed. He had been a lively baby, interested in his surroundings, and he seemed to have lost this interest. He had become apathetic. He had accepted the substitute food fairly easily and in fact never refused food. But he did not thrive on it any more, lost weight and had a good deal of digestive trouble. It was only at the end of the first year, when other food was introduced, that he again made good physical progress.

Much light was thrown in the analysis on the influence these experiences had on his whole development. His outlook and attitudes in adult life were based on the patterns established in this early stage. For instance, we found again and again a tendency to be influenced by other people in an unselective way'—in fact to take in greedily whatever was offered—together with great distrust during the process of introjection. This process was constantly disturbed by anxieties from various sources, which also contributed to an increase of greed.

Taking the material of this analysis as a whole, I came to the conclusion that at the time when the sudden loss of the breast and of the mother occurred, the patient had already to some extent established a relation to a complete good object. He had no doubt already entered the depressive position but could not work through it successfully and the paranoid-schizoid position became regressively reinforced. This expressed itself in the 'apathy' which followed a period when the child had already shown a lively interest in his surroundings. The fact that he had reached the depressive position and had introjected a complete object showed in many ways in his personality. He had actually a strong capacity for love and a great longing for a good and complete object. A characteristic feature of his personality was the desire to love people and trust them, unconsciously to regain and build up again the good and complete breast which he had once possessed and lost.

## CONNECTION BETWEEN SCHIZOID AND MANIC-DEPRESSIVE PHENOMENA

Some fluctuations between the paranoid-schizoid and the depressive positions always occur and are part of normal development. No clear division between the two stages of development can therefore be drawn; moreover, modification is a gradual process and the phenomena of the two positions remain for some time to some extent intermingled and interacting. In abnormal development this interaction influences, I think, the clinical picture both of some forms of schizophrenia and of manic-depressive disorders.

To illustrate this connection I shall briefly refer to some case-material. I do not intend to present a case-history here and am therefore only selecting some parts of material relevant to my topic. The patient I have in mind was a pronounced manic-depressive case (diagnosed as such by more than one psychiatrist) with all the characteristics of that disorder: there was the alternation between depressive and manic states, strong suicidal tendencies leading repeatedly to suicidal attempts, and various other characteristic manic and depressive features. In the course of her analysis a stage was reached in which a real and great improvement was achieved. Not only did the cycle stop but there were fundamental changes in her personality and her object-relations. Productivity on various lines developed, as well as actual feelings of happiness (not of a manic type). Then, partly owing to external circumstances, another phase set in. During this last phase, which continued for several months, the patient co-operated in the analysis in a particular way. She came regularly to the analytic sessions, associated fairly freely, reported dreams and provided material for the analysis. There was, however, no emotional response to my interpretations and a good deal of contempt of them. There was very seldom any conscious confirmation of what I suggested. Yet the material by which she responded to the interpretations reflected their unconscious effect. The powerful resistance shown at this stage seemed to come from one part of the personality only, while at the same time another part responded to the analytic work. It was not only that parts of her personality did not co-operate with me; they did not seem to co-operate with each other, and at the time the analysis was unable to help the patient to achieve synthesis. During this stage she decided to bring the analysis to an end. External circumstances contributed strongly to this decision and she fixed a date for the last session.

On that particular date she reported the following dream: there was a blind man who was very worried about being blind; but he seemed to comfort himself by touching the patient's dress and finding out how it was fastened. The dress in the dream reminded her of one of her frocks which was buttoned high up to the throat. The patient gave two further associations to this dream. She said, with some resistance, that the blind man was herself; and when referring to the dress fastened up to the throat, she remarked that she had again gone into her 'hide'. I suggested to the patient that she unconsciously expressed in the dream that she was blind to her own difficulties, and that her decisions with regard to the analysis as well as to various circumstances in her life were not in accordance with her unconscious knowledge. This was also shown by her admitting that she had gone into her 'hide', meaning by it that she was shutting herself off, an attitude well known to her from previous stages in her analysis. Thus the unconscious insight, and even some co-operation on the conscious level (recognition that *she* was the blind man and that she had gone into her 'hide'), derived from isolated parts of her personality only. Actually, the interpretation of this dream did not produce any effect and did not alter the patient's decision to bring the analysis to an end in that particular hour.[1]

The nature of certain difficulties encountered in this analysis as well as in others had revealed itself more clearly in the last few months before the patient broke off the treatment. It was the mixture

[1] I may mention that the analysis was resumed after a break.

of schizoid and manic-depressive features which determined the nature of her illness. For at times throughout her analysis—even in the early stage when depressive and manic states were at their height —depressive and schizoid mechanisms sometimes appeared simultaneously. There were, for instance, hours when the patient was obviously deeply depressed, full of self-reproaches and feelings of unworthiness; tears were running down her cheeks and her gestures expressed despair; and yet she said, when I interpreted these emotions, that she did not feel them at all. Whereupon she reproached herself for having no feelings at all, for being completely empty. In such sessions there was also a flight of ideas, the thoughts seemed to be broken up, and their expression was disjointed.

Following the interpretation of the unconscious reasons underlying such states, there were sometimes sessions in which the emotions and depressive anxieties came out fully, and at such times thoughts and speech were much more coherent.

This close connection between depressive and schizoid phenomena appeared, though in different forms, throughout her analysis but became very pronounced during the last stage preceding the break just described.

I have already referred to the developmental connection between the paranoid-schizoid and depressive positions. The question now arises whether this developmental connection is the basis for the mixture of these features in manic-depressive disorders and, as I would suggest, in schizophrenic disorders as well. If this tentative hypothesis could be proved, the conclusion would be that the groups of schizophrenic and manic-depressive disorders are more closely connected developmentally with one another than has been assumed. This would also account for the cases in which, I believe, the differential diagnosis between melancholia and schizophrenia is exceedingly difficult. I should be grateful if further light could be thrown on my hypothesis by colleagues who have had ample material for psychiatric observation.

## SOME SCHIZOID DEFENCES

It is generally agreed that schizoid patients are more difficult to analyse than manic-depressive types. Their withdrawn, unemotional attitude, the narcissistic elements in their object-relations (to which I referred earlier), a kind of detached hostility which pervades the whole relation to the analyst create a very difficult type of resistance. I believe that it is largely the splitting processes which account for the patient's failure in contact with the analyst and for his lack of response to the analyst's interpretations. The patient himself feels estranged and far away, and this feeling corresponds to the analyst's impression that considerable parts of the patient's personality and of his emotions are not available. Patients with schizoid features may say: 'I hear what you are saying. You may be right, but it has no meaning for me.' Or again they say they feel they are not there. The expression 'no meaning' in such cases does not imply an active rejection of the interpretation but suggests that parts of the personality and of the emotions are split off. These patients can, therefore, not deal with the interpretation; they can neither accept it nor reject it.

I shall illustrate the processes underlying such states by a piece of material taken from the analysis of a man patient. The session I have in mind started with the patient's telling me that he felt anxiety and did not know why. He then made comparisons with people more successful and fortunate than himself. These remarks also had a reference to me. Very strong feelings of frustration, envy and grievance came to the fore. When I interpreted—to give here again only the gist of my interpretations—that these feelings were directed against the analyst and that he wanted to destroy me, his mood changed abruptly. The tone of his voice became flat, he spoke in a slow, expressionless way, and he said that he felt detached from the whole situation. He added that my interpretation seemed correct, but that it did not matter. In fact, he no longer had any wishes, and nothing was worth bothering about.

My next interpretations centred on the causes for this change of mood. I suggested that at the moment of my interpretation the danger of destroying me had become very real to him and the immediate consequence was the fear of losing me. Instead of feeling guilt and depression, which at certain stages of his analysis followed such interpretations, he now attempted to deal with these dangers by a particular method of splitting. As we know, under the pressure of ambivalence, conflict and guilt, the patient often splits the figure of the analyst; then the analyst may at certain moments be loved, at other moments hated. Or the relations to the analyst may be split in such a way that he remains the good (or bad) figure while somebody else becomes the opposite figure. But this was not the kind of splitting which occurred in this particular instance. The patient split off those parts of himself, *i.e.* of his ego which he felt to be dangerous and hostile towards the analyst. He turned his destructive impulses from his object *towards his ego*, with the result that parts of his ego temporarily went out of existence. In unconscious phantasy this amounted to annihilation of part of his personality. The particular mechanism of turning the destructive impulse against one part of his personality, and the ensuing dispersal of emotions, kept his anxiety in a latent state.

My interpretation of these processes had the effect of again altering the patient's mood. He became emotional, said he felt like crying, was depressed, but felt more integrated; then he also expressed a feeling of hunger.[1]

The violent splitting off and destroying of one part of the personality under the pressure of anxiety and guilt is in my experience an important schizoid mechanism. To refer briefly to another instance: a woman patient had dreamed that she had to deal with a wicked girl child who was determined to murder somebody. The patient tried to influence or control the child and to extort a confession from her which would have been to the child's benefit; but she was unsuccessful. I also entered into the dream and the patient felt that I might help her in dealing with the child. Then the patient strung up the child on a tree in order to frighten her and also prevent her from doing harm. When the patient was about to pull the rope and kill the child, she woke. During this part of the dream the analyst was also present but again remained inactive.

I shall give here only the essence of the conclusions I arrived at from the analysis of this dream. In the dream the patient's personality was split into two parts: the wicked and uncontrollable child on the one hand, and on the other hand the person who tried to influence and control her. The child, of course, stood also for various figures in the past, but in this context she mainly represented one part of the patient's self. Another conclusion was that the analyst was the person whom the child was going to murder; and my rôle in the dream was partly to prevent this murder from taking place. Killing the child—to which the patient had to resort—represented the annihilation of one part of her personality.

The question arises how the schizoid mechanism of annihilating part of the self connects with repression which, as we know, is directed against dangerous impulses. This, however, is a problem with which I cannot deal here.

Changes of mood, of course, do not always appear as dramatically within a session as in the first instance I have given in this section.

---

[1] The feeling of hunger indicated that the process of introjection had been set going again un .er the dominance of the libido. While to my first interpretation of his fear of destroying me by his aggression he had responded at once with the violent splitting off and annihilation of parts of his personality, he now experienced more fully the emotions of grief, guilt and fear of loss, as well as some relief of these depressive anxieties. The relief of anxiety resulted in the analyst again coming to stand for a good object which he could trust. Therefore the desire to introject me as a good object could come to the fore. If he could build up again the good breast inside himself, he would strengthen and integrate his ego, would be less afraid of his destructive impulses; in fact he could then preserve himself and the analyst.

But I have repeatedly found that advances in synthesis are brought about by interpretations of the specific causes for splitting. Such interpretations must deal in detail with the transference-situation at that moment, including of course the connection with the past, and must contain a reference to the details of the anxiety-situations which drive the ego to regress to schizoid mechanisms. The synthesis resulting from interpretations on these lines goes along with depression and anxieties of various kinds. Gradually such waves of depression —followed by greater integration—lead to a lessening of schizoid phenomena and also to fundamental changes in object-relations.

## LATENT ANXIETY IN SCHIZOID PATIENTS

I have already referred to the lack of emotion which makes schizoid patients unresponsive. This is accompanied by an absence of anxiety. An important support for the analytic work is therefore lacking. For with other types of patients who have strong manifest and latent anxiety. the relief of anxiety derived from analytic inter- pretation becomes an experience which furthers their capacity to co-operate in the analysis.

This lack of anxiety in schizoid patients is only apparent. For the schizoid mechanisms imply a dispersal of emotions including anxiety, but these dispersed elements still exist in the patient. Such patients have a certain form of latent anxiety; it is kept latent by the particular method of dispersal. The feeling of being disintegrated, of being unable to experience emotions, of losing one's objects, is in fact the equivalent of anxiety. This becomes clearer when advances in synthesis have been made. The great relief which a patient then experiences derives from a feeling that his inner and outer worlds have not only come more together but back to life again. At such moments it appears in retrospect that when emotions were lacking, relations were vague and uncertain and parts of the personality were felt to be lost, everything seemed to be dead. All this is the equivalent of anxiety of a very serious nature. This anxiety, kept latent by dispersal, is to some extent experienced all along, but its form differs from the latent anxiety which we can recognize in other types of cases.

Interpretations which tend towards synthesizing the split in the self, including the dispersal of emotions, make it possible for the anxiety gradually to be experienced as such, though for long stretches we may in fact only be able to bring the ideational contents together but not to elicit the emotions of anxiety.

I have also found that interpretations of schizoid states make particular demands on our capacity to put the interpretations in an intellectually clear form in which the links between the conscious, pre-conscious and unconscious are established. This is, of course, always one of our aims, but it is of special importance at times when the patient's emotions are not available and we seem to address ourselves only to his intellect, however much broken up.

It is possible that the few hints I have given may to some extent apply as well to the technique of analysing schizophrenic patients.

## SUMMARY OF CONCLUSIONS

I will now summarize some of the conclusions presented in this paper. One of my main points was the suggestion that in the first few months of life anxiety is predominantly experienced as fear of persecution and that this contributes to certain mechanisms and defences which are significant for the paranoid-schizoid position. Outstanding among these defences are the mechanisms of splitting internal and external objects, emotions and the ego. These mechanisms and defences are part of normal development and at the same time form the basis for later schizophrenic illness. I described the processes underlying identification by projection as a combination of splitting off parts of the self and projecting them on to another person, and some of the effects this identification has on normal and schizoid object-relations. The onset of the depressive position is the juncture at which by regression schizoid mechanisms may be reinforced. I also suggested a close connection between the manic-depressive and schizoid disorders, based on the interaction between the infantile paranoid-schizoid and depressive positions.

## APPENDIX

FREUD's analysis of the Schreber case[1] contains a wealth of material which is very relevant to my topic but from which I shall here draw only a few conclusions.

Schreber described vividly the splitting of the soul of his physician Flechsig (his loved and persecuting figure). The 'Flechsig soul' at one time introduced the system of 'soul divisions', splitting into as many as forty to sixty sub-divisions. These souls having multiplied till they became a 'nuisance', God made a raid on them and as a result the Flechsig soul survived in 'only one or two shapes'. Another point which Schreber mentions is that the fragments of the Flechsig soul slowly lost both their intelligence and their power.

One of the conclusions Freud arrived at in his analysis of this case was that the persecutor was split into God and Flechsig, and also that God and Flechsig represented the patient's father and brother.

---

[1] 'Psycho-Analytic Notes upon an Autobiographical Account of a Case of Paranoia (Dementia Paranoides)' (*S.E.* **12**).

In discussing the various forms of Schreber's delusion of the destruction of the world, Freud states: 'In any case the end of the world was the consequence of the conflict which had broken out between him, Schreber, and Flechsig, or, according to the aetiology adopted in the second phase of his delusion, of the indissoluble bond which had been formed between him and God. . . .' (*Loc. cit.*, p. 69).

I would suggest, in keeping with the hypotheses outlined in the present chapter, that the division of the Flechsig soul into many souls was not only a splitting of the object but also a projection of Schreber's feeling that his ego was split. I shall here only mention the connection of such splitting processes with processess of introjection. The conclusion suggests itself that God and Flechsig also represented parts of Schreber's self. The conflict between Schreber and Flechsig, to which Freud attributed a vital role in the world-destruction delusion, found expression in the raid by God on the Flechsig souls. In my view this raid represents the annihilation by one part of the self of the other parts—which, as I contend, is a schizoid mechanism. The anxieties and phantasies about inner destruction and ego-disintegration bound up with this mechanism are projected on to the external world and underlie the delusions of its destruction.

Regarding the processes which are at the bottom of the paranoic 'world catastrophe', Freud arrived at the following conclusions: 'The patient has withdrawn from the people in his environment and from the external world generally the libidinal cathexis which he has hitherto directed on to them. Thus everything has become indifferent and irrelevant to him, and has to be explained by means of a secondary rationalization as being "miracled up, cursorily improvised". The end of the world is the projection of this internal catastrophe; for his subjective world has come to an end since he has withdrawn his love from it.' (*Loc. cit.*, p. 70.) This explanation specifically concerns the disturbance in object-libido and the ensuing breakdown in relation to people and to the external world. But a little further on Freud considered another aspect of these disturbances. He said: 'We can no more dismiss the possibility that disturbances of the libido may react upon the egoistic cathexes than we can overlook the *converse possibility*—namely, that *a secondary or induced disturbance of the libidinal processes may result from abnormal changes in the ego. Indeed it is probable that processes of this kind constitute the distinctive characteristic of psychoses*' (my italics). It is particularly the possibility expressed in the last two sentences which provides the link between Freud's explanation of the 'world catastrophe' and my hypothesis. 'Abnormal changes in the ego' derive, as I have suggested in this chapter, from excessive splitting processes in the early ego. These processes are inextricably linked with instinctual development, and with the anxieties to which instinctual desires give rise. In the light of Freud's later theory of the life and death instincts, which replaced the concept of the egoistic and sexual instincts, disturbances in the distribution of the libido presuppose a defusion between the destructive impulse and the libido. The mechanism of one part of the ego annihilating other parts which, I suggest, underlies 'world catastrophe' phantasy (the raid by God on the Flechsig souls) implies a preponderance of the destructive impulse over the libido. Any disturbance in the distribution of the narcissistic libido is in turn bound up with the relation to introjected objects which (according to my work) from the beginning come to form part of the ego. The interaction between narcissistic libido and object-libido corresponds thus to the interaction between the relation to introjected and external objects. If the ego and the internalized objects are felt to be in bits, an internal catastrophe is experienced by the infant which both extends to the external world and is projected on to it. Such anxiety-states relating to an internal catastrophe arise, according to the hypothesis discussed in the present chapter, during the period of the infantile paranoid-schizoid position and form the basis for later schizophrenia. In Freud's view the dispositional fixation to dementia praecox is found in a very early stage of development. Referring to dementia praecox, which Freud distinguished from paranoia, he said: 'The dispositional point of fixation must therefore be situated further back than in paranoia, and must lie somewhere at the beginning of the course of development from auto-erotism to object-love.' (*Loc. cit.*, p. 77.)

I wish to draw one more conclusion from Freud's analysis of the Schreber case. I suggest that the raid, which ended in the Flechsig souls being reduced to one or two, was part of the attempt towards recovery. For the raid was to undo, or, one may say, heal the split in the ego by annihilating the split-off parts of the ego. As a result only one or two of the souls were left which, as we may assume, were meant to regain their intelligence and their power. This attempt towards recovery, however, was effected by very destructive means used by the ego against itself and its projected objects.

Freud's approach to the problems of schizophrenia and paranoia has proved of fundamental importance. His Schreber paper (and here we also have to remember Abraham's paper[1] quoted by Freud) opened up the possibility of understanding psychosis and the processes underlying it.

[1] 'The Psycho-Sexual Differences between Hysteria and Dementia Praecox' (1908).

24

# 2

# ON THE THEORY OF ANXIETY
# AND GUILT

## (1948)

MY conclusions regarding anxiety and guilt have evolved gradually over a number of years; it may be useful to retrace some of the steps by which I arrived at them.

### I

Concerning the origins of anxiety, Freud put forward to begin with the hypothesis that anxiety arises out of a direct transformation of libido. In *Inhibitions, Symptoms and Anxiety* he reviewed his various theories on the origin of anxiety. As he put it: 'I propose to assemble quite impartially, all the facts that we know about anxiety without expecting to arrive at a fresh synthesis' (*S.E.* **20**, p. 132). He stated again that anxiety arises from direct transformation of libido but now seemed to attribute less importance to this 'economic' aspect of the origin of anxiety. He qualified this view in the following statements: 'The whole matter can be clarified, I think, if we commit ourselves to the definite statement that as a result of repression the intended course of the excitatory process in the id does not occur at all; the ego succeeds in inhibiting or deflecting it. If this is so the problem of "transformation of affect" under repression disappears' (p. 91). And: 'The problem of how anxiety arises in connection with repression may be no simple one; but we may legitimately hold firmly to the idea that the ego is the actual seat of anxiety and give up our earlier view that the cathectic energy of the repressed impulse is automatically turned into anxiety' (p. 93).

Regarding the manifestations of anxiety in young children, Freud said that anxiety is caused by the child 'missing someone who is loved and longed for' (p. 136). In connection with the girl's most fundamental anxiety, he described the infantile fear of loss of love in terms which in some measure seem to apply to infants of both sexes: 'If a mother is absent or has withdrawn her love from her child, it is no longer sure of the satisfaction of its needs and is perhaps exposed to the most distressing feelings of tension' (*S.E.* **22**, p. 87).

In the *New Introductory Lectures*, referring to the theory that anxiety

25

arises from a transformation of unsatisfied libido, Freud said that it has 'found support in some quite regularly occurring phobias of small children. . . . Infantile phobias and the expectation of anxiety in anxiety neurosis offer us two examples of one way in which neurotic anxiety originates: by a direct transformation of libido' (*S.E.* **22**, pp. 82–83).

Two conclusions, to which I shall return later on, can be drawn from these and similar passages: (*a*) in young children it is unsatisfied libidinal excitation which turns into anxiety; (*b*) the earliest *content* of anxiety is the infant's feeling of danger lest his need should not be satisfied because the mother is 'absent'.

## II

As regards guilt, Freud held that it has its origin in the Oedipus complex and arises as a sequel to it. There are passages, however, in which Freud clearly referred to conflict and guilt arising at a much earlier stage of life. He wrote: '. . . the sense of guilt is an expression of the conflict due to ambivalence of the *eternal struggle between Eros and the instinct of destruction or death.*' (my italics) Also: '. . . as a result of the *inborn conflict arising from ambivalence* [my italics], of the eternal struggle between the trends of love and death—there is . . . an increase of the sense of guilt'.[1]

Furthermore, speaking of the view propounded by some authors that frustration heightens the sense of guilt, he said: 'For how are we to account, on dynamic and economic grounds, for an increase in the sense of guilt appearing in place of an unfulfilled *erotic* demand? This only seems possible in a round-about way—if we suppose, that is, that the prevention of an erotic satisfaction calls up a piece of aggressiveness against the person who has interfered with the satisfaction, and that this aggressiveness has itself to be suppressed in turn. But if this is so, it is *after all only the aggressiveness which is transformed into a sense of guilt*, by being suppressed and made over to the super-ego. I am convinced that many processes will admit of a simpler and clearer exposition if the findings of psycho-analysis with regard to the derivation of the sense of guilt are restricted to the aggressive instincts.' (my italics)[2].

Here Freud unequivocally stated that guilt derives from aggression and this, together with the sentences quoted above ('innate conflict of

[1] *Civilization and its Discontents*, S.E. **21**, pp. 132, 133.

[2] *Loc. cit.*, p. 138. In the same book (on p. 130) Freud accepted my hypothesis (expressed in my papers 'Early Stages of the Oedipus Conflict', 1928, and 'The Importance of Symbol-Formation in the Development of the Ego', 1930) that the severity of the super-ego to some extent results from the child's aggression which is projected on to the super-ego.

ambivalence') would point to guilt arising at a very early stage of development. Taking, however, Freud's views as a whole, as we find them summarized again in the *New Introductory Lectures on Psycho-Analysis*, it is clear that he maintained his hypothesis that guilt sets in as a sequel to the Oedipus complex.

Abraham, particularly in his study of the libidinal organization[1] threw much light on the earliest phases of development. His discoveries in the field of infantile sexuality were bound up with a new approach to the origin of anxiety and guilt. Abraham suggested that 'in the stage of narcissism with a cannibalistic sexual aim the first evidence of an instinctual inhibition appears in the shape of morbid anxiety. The process of overcoming the cannibalistic impulses is intimately associated with a sense of guilt which comes into the foreground as a typical inhibitory phenomenon belonging to the third (earlier anal-sadistic) stage.'[2]

Abraham thus contributed materially to our understanding of the origins of anxiety and guilt, since he was the first to point out the connection of anxiety and guilt with cannibalistic desires. He compared his brief survey of the psycho-sexual development to a 'time-table of express trains in which only the larger stations at which they stop are given'. He suggested that the 'halting-places that lie between cannot be marked in a summary of this kind'.[3]

### III

My own work not only corroborated Abraham's discoveries on anxiety and guilt and showed their importance in proper perspective, but also developed them further by bringing them together with a number of new facts discovered in the analyses of young children.

When I analysed infantile anxiety-situations, I recognized the fundamental importance of sadistic impulses and phantasies from all sources which converge and reach a climax in the earliest stages of development. I also came to see that the early processes of introjection and projection lead to establishing within the ego, side by side with extremely 'good' objects, extremely frightening and persecuting objects. These figures are conceived in the light of the infant's own aggressive impulses and phantasies, *i.e.* he projects his own aggression on to the internal figures which form part of his early super-ego. To anxiety from these sources is added the guilt

[1] 'A Short Study of the Development of the Libido, viewed in the Light of Mental Disorders.'
[2] *Loc. cit.*, p. 496.
[3] *Loc. cit.*, pp. 495–6.

derived from the infant's aggressive impulses against his first loved object, both external and internalized.[1]

In a later paper[2] I illustrated by an extreme case the pathological effects of the anxiety aroused in infants by their destructive impulses and concluded that the earliest defences of the ego (in normal as well as in abnormal development) are directed against the anxiety aroused by aggressive impulses and phantasies.[3]

Some years later, in my attempt to reach a fuller understanding of infantile sadistic phantasies and their origin, I was led to apply Freud's hypothesis of the struggle between the life and death instincts to the clinical material gained in the analysis of young children. We remember that Freud stated: 'The dangerous death instincts are dealt with in the individual in various ways: in part they are rendered harmless by being fused with erotic components, in part they are diverted towards the external world in the form of aggression, while to a large extent they undoubtedly continue their internal work unhindered.'[4]

Following this line of thought I put forward the hypothesis[5] that anxiety is aroused by the danger which threatens the organism from the death instinct; and I suggested that this is the primary cause of anxiety. Freud's description of the struggle between the life and death instincts (which leads to the deflection of one portion of the death instinct outwards and to the fusion of the two instincts) would point to the conclusion that anxiety has its origin in the fear of death.

In his paper on masochism[6] Freud drew some fundamental conclusions regarding the connections between masochism and the death instinct, and he considered in this light the various anxieties arising from the activity of the death instinct turned inwards.[7] Among these anxieties he does not, however, mention the fear of death.

In *Inhibitions, Symptoms and Anxiety* Freud discussed his reasons for not regarding the fear of death (or fear for life) as a primary anxiety. He based this view on his observation that 'the unconscious seems to

---

[1] Cf. my paper, 'Early Stages of the Oedipus Conflict' (1928).

[2] 'The Importance of Symbol-Formation in the Development of the Ego' (1930a).

[3] I have dealt with this problem more fully and from various angles in my book, *The Psycho-Analysis of Children*, Chapters 8 and 9.

[4] *The Ego and the Id* (1923), *S.E.* **19**, p. 54.

[5] Cf. *The Psycho-Analysis of Children*, pp. 126–27.

[6] 'The Economic Problem in Masochism' (1924). In this paper Freud first applied the new classification of instincts to clinical problems. 'Moral masochism thus becomes a classical piece of evidence for the existence of fusion of instincts' (*S.E.* **19**) p. 170.      [7] *Loc. cit.*, p. 164.

THE THEORY OF ANXIETY AND GUILT

contain nothing that could give any content to our concept of the annihilation of life' (*S.E.* **20,** p. 129). pointed out that nothing resembling death can ever have been experienced, except possibly fainting, and concluded that 'the fear of death should be regarded as analogous to the fear of castration'.

I do not share this view because my analytic observations show that there is in the unconscious a fear of annihilation of life. I would also think that if we assume the existence of a death instinct, we must also assume that in the deepest layers of the mind there is a response to this instinct in the form of fear of annihilation of life. Thus in my view the danger arising from the inner working of the death instinct is the first cause of anxiety.[1] Since the struggle between the life and death instincts persists throughout life, this source of anxiety is never eliminated and enters as a perpetual factor into all anxiety-situations.

My contention that anxiety originates in the fear of annihilation derives from experience accumulated in the analyses of young children. When in such analyses the earliest anxiety-situations of the infant are revived and repeated, the inherent power of an instinct ultimately directed against the self can be detected in such strength that its existence appears beyond doubt. This remains true even when we allow for the part which frustration, internal and external, plays in the vicissitudes of destructive impulses. This is not the place for detailed evidence in support of my argument, but I shall quote by way of illustration one instance mentioned in my *Psycho-Analysis of Children* (p. 127). A five-year-old boy used to pretend that he had all sorts of wild animals, such as elephants, leopards, hyenas and wolves, to help him against his enemies. They represented dangerous objects —persecutors—which he had tamed and could use as protection against his enemies. But it appeared in the analysis that they also stood for his own sadism, each animal representing a specfic source of sadism and the organs used in this connection. The elephants symbolized his muscular sadism, his impulses to trample and stamp. The tearing leopards represented his teeth and nails and their functions in his attacks. The wolves symbolized his excrements invested with destructive properties. He sometimes became very frightened that the wild animals he had tamed would turn against him and exterminate him. This fear expressed his sense of being threatened by his own destructiveness (as well as by internal persecutors).

As I have illustrated by this instance, the analysis of the anxieties arising in young children teaches us a good deal about the forms in

[1] See 'Notes on some Schizoid Mechanisms'. In 1946 I arrived at the conclusion that this primary anxiety-situation plays an important part in schizophrenic illness.

which the fear of death exists in the unconscious, that is to say, about the part this fear plays in various anxiety-situations. I have already mentioned Freud's paper on the 'Economic Problem in Masochism', which was based on his new discovery of the death instinct. To take the first anxiety-situation he enumerated:[1] 'the fear of being eaten up by the totem animal (father)'. This in my view is an undisguised expression of the fear of total annihilation of the self. The fear of being devoured by the father derives from the projection of the infant's impulses to devour his objects. In this way, first the mother's breast (and the mother) becomes in the infant's mind a devouring object[2] and these fears soon extend to the father's penis and to the father. At the same time, since devouring implies from the beginning the internalization of the devoured object, the ego is felt to contain devoured and devouring objects. Thus the super-ego is built up from the devouring breast (mother) to which is added the devouring penis (father). These cruel and dangerous internal figures become the representatives of the death instinct. Simultaneously the other aspect of the early super-ego is formed first by the internalized good breast (to which is added the good penis of the father), which is felt as a feeding and helpful internal object, and as the representative of the life instinct. The fear of being annihilated includes the anxiety lest the internal good breast be destroyed, for this object is felt to be indispensable for the preservation of life. The threat to the self from the death instinct working within is bound up with the dangers apprehended from the internalized devouring mother and father, and amounts to fear of death.

According to this view, the fear of death enters from the beginning into the fear of the super-ego and is not, as Freud remarked, a 'final transformation' of the fear of the super-ego.[3]

Turning to another essential danger-situation which Freud mentioned in his paper on Masochism, i.e. the fear of castration, I would suggest that the fear of death enters into and reinforces castration fear and is not 'analogous' to it.[4] Since the genital is not only the source of the most intense libidinal gratification, but also the representative of Eros, and since reproduction is the essential way of counteracting death, the loss of the genital would mean the end of the creative power which preserves and continues life.

[1] S.E. 19, p. 165.

[2] Cf. examples given in Isaacs's (1952) paper: the boy who said his mother's breast had bitten him and the girl who thought her mother's shoe would eat her up.

[3] Inhibitions, Symptoms and Anxiety (S.E. 20) p. 140.

[4] For a detailed discussion of the sources of anxiety which interact with the fear of castration, see my paper 'The Oedipus Complex in the Light of Early Anxieties', Writings, 1.

If we try to visualize in concrete form the primary anxiety, the fear of annihilation, we must remember the helplessness of the infant in face of internal and external dangers. I suggest that the primary danger-situation arising from the activity of the death instinct within is felt by him as an overwhelming attack, as persecution. Let us first consider in this connection some of the processes which ensue from the deflection of the death instinct outwards and the ways in which they influence anxieties relating to external and internal situations. We may assume that the struggle between life and death instincts already operates during birth and accentuates the persecutory anxiety aroused by this painful experience. It would seem that this experience has the effect of making the external world, including the first external object, the mother's breast, appear hostile. To this contributes the fact that the ego turns the destructive impulses against this primary object. The young infant feels that frustration by the breast, which in fact implies danger to life, is the retaliation for his destructive impulses towards it and that the frustrating breast is persecuting him. In addition he projects his destructive impulses on to the breast, that is to say, deflects the death instinct outwards; and in these ways the attacked breast becomes the external representative of the death instinct.[1] The 'bad' breast is also introjected, and this intensifies, as we may assume, the internal danger-situation, *i.e.* the fear of the activity of the death instinct within. For by the internalization of the 'bad' breast, the portion of the death instinct which had been deflected outwards, with all its associated dangers, is turned inwards again and the ego attaches its fear of its own destructive impulses to the internal bad object. These processes may well happen simultaneously and therefore my description of them is not to be taken as a chronological account. To summarize: the frustrating (bad) external breast becomes, owing to projection, the external representative of the death instinct; through introjection it reinforces the primary internal danger-situation; this leads to an increased urge on the part of the ego to deflect (project) internal dangers (primarily the activity of the death instinct) into the external world. There is therefore a constant fluctuation between the fear of internal and external bad objects, between the death instinct acting within

[1] In my *Psycho-Analysis of Children* (pp. 124 ff.) I suggested that the earliest feeding difficulties of infants are a manifestation of persecutory fears. (I was referring to those feeding difficulties which appear even though the mother's milk is plentiful and no external factors would seem to prevent a satisfactory feeding-situation.) I concluded that these persecutory fears, when excessive, lead to a far-reaching inhibition of libidinal desires. Cf. also my paper on 'The Emotional Life of the Infant'.

and deflected outwards. Here we see one important aspect of the interaction—from the beginning of life—between projection and introjection. External dangers are experienced in the light of internal dangers and are therefore intensified; on the other hand, any danger threatening from outside intensifies the perpetual inner danger-situation. This interaction exists in some measure throughout life. The very fact that the struggle has, to some extent, been externalized relieves anxiety. Externalization of internal danger-situations is one of the ego's earliest methods of defence against anxiety and remains fundamental in development.

The activity of the death instinct deflected outwards, as well as its working within, cannot be considered apart from the simultaneous activity of the life instinct. Side by side with the deflection of the death instinct outwards, the life instinct—by means of the libido—attaches itself to the external object, the gratifying (good) breast, which becomes the external representative of the life instinct. The introjection of this good object reinforces the power of the life instinct within. The good internalized breast, which is felt to be the source of life, forms a vital part of the ego and its preservation becomes an imperative need. The introjection of this first loved object is therefore inextricably linked with all the processes engendered by the life instinct. The good internalized breast and the bad devouring breast form the core of the super-ego in its good and bad aspects; they are the representatives within the ego of the struggle between the life and death instincts.

The second important part-object to be introjected is the penis of the father to which also both good and bad qualities are attributed. These two dangerous objects—the bad breast and the bad penis—are the prototypes of internal and external persecutors. Experiences of a painful nature, frustrations from internal and external sources, which are felt as persecution, are primarily attributed to the external and internal persecuting objects. In all such experiences, persecutory anxiety and aggression reinforce each other. For while the infant's aggressive impulse through projection play a fundamental part in his building up of persecutory figures, these very figures increase his persecutory anxiety and in turn reinforce his aggressive impulses and phantasies against the external and internal objects felt to be dangerous.

Paranoid disturbances in adults are, in my view, based on the persecutory anxiety experienced in the first few months of life. In the paranoid patient the essence of his fears of persecution is the feeling that there is a hostile agency which is bent on inflicting on him suffering, damage and ultimately annihilation. This persecutory agency may be represented by one or many people or even by the forces of nature. There are innumerable and in every case specific forms which the dreaded attack may take; but the root of persecutory fear in the paranoid individual is, I believe, the fear of annihilation of the ego—ultimately by the death instinct.

v

I shall now discuss more specifically the relation between guilt and anxiety and in this connection shall first reconsider some of Freud's and Abraham's views regarding anxiety and guilt. Freud approached the problem of guilt from two main angles. On the one hand he left no doubt that anxiety and guilt are closely connected with each other. On the other hand he came to the conclusion that the term 'guilt' is only applicable in regard to manifestations of conscience which are the result of super-ego development. The super-ego, as we know, in his view comes into being as a sequel to the Oedipus complex. Therefore with children under about four to five years of age, the terms 'conscience' and 'guilt' in his view do not yet apply and anxiety in the first few years of life is distinct from guilt.[1]

According to Abraham (1924) guilt arises in the overcoming of cannibalistic—*i.e.* aggressive—impulses during the earlier anal-sadistic stage (that is, at a much earlier age than Freud assumed); but he did not consider a differentiation between anxiety and guilt. Ferenczi, who was also not concerned with the distinction between anxiety and guilt, suggested that something in the nature of guilt arises during the anal stage. He concluded that there may be a kind of physiological precursor of the super-ego which he calls 'sphincter-morality'.[2]

Ernest Jones (1929) dealt with the interaction between hate, fear and guilt. He distinguished between two phases in the development of guilt and suggested for the first stage the term 'pre-nefarious'

---

[1] A significant reference to the connection between anxiety and guilt is contained in the following passage: 'Here perhaps we may be glad to have it pointed out that the sense of guilt is at bottom nothing else but a topographical variety of anxiety' (*Civilization and its Discontents*, S.E. **21**, p. 135). On the other hand, Freud definitely distinguishes between anxiety and guilt. In discussing the development of the sense of guilt, he says in reference to the use of the term 'guilt' in regard to early manifestations of 'bad conscience': 'This state of mind is called a "bad conscience"; but actually it does not deserve this name, for at this stage the sense of guilt is clearly only a fear of loss of love, "social" anxiety. In small children it can never be anything else, but in many adults, too, it has only changed to the extent that the place of the father or the two parents is taken by the larger human community . . . . A great change takes place only when the authority is internalized through the establishment of a super-ego. The phenomena of conscience then reach a higher stage. Actually, it is not until now that we should speak of conscience or a sense of guilt.' (*S.E.* **21**, pp. 124–5).

[2] Ferenczi, 'Psycho-Analysis of Sexual Habits' (1925), p. 267.

stage of guilt. This he connected with the sadistic pre-genital stages of super-ego development and stated that guilt is 'always and inevitably associated with the hate impulse'. The second stage is '. . . the stage of guilt proper, the function of which is to protect against the external dangers'.

In my paper 'A Contribution to the Psychogenesis of Manic-Depressive States' I differentiated between two main forms of anxiety—persecutory and depressive anxiety—but pointed out that the distinction between these two forms of anxiety is not by any means clear-cut. With this limitation in mind I think that a differentiation between the two forms of anxiety is valuable from both the theoretical and the practical point of view. In the paper referred to above I came to the conclusion that persecutory anxiety relates predominantly to the annihilation of the ego; depressive anxiety is predominantly related to the harm done to internal and external loved objects by the subject's destructive impulses. Depressive anxiety has manifold contents, such as: the good object is injured, it is suffering, it is in a state of deterioration; it changes into a bad object; it is annihilated, lost and will never be there any more. I also concluded that depressive anxiety is closely bound up with guilt and with the tendency to make reparation.

When I first introduced my concept of the depressive position in the paper referred to above, I suggested that depressive anxiety and guilt arise with the introjection of the object as a whole. My further work on the paranoid-schizoid position,[1] which precedes the depressive position, has led me to the conclusion that though in the first stage destructive impulses and persecutory anxiety predominate, depressive anxiety and guilt already play some part in the infant's earliest object-relation, i.e. in his relation to his mother's breast.

During the paranoid-schizoid position, that is, during the first three to four months of life, splitting processes, involving the splitting of the first object (the breast) as well as of the feelings towards it, are at their height. Hatred and persecutory anxiety become attached to the frustrating (bad) breast, and love and reassurance to the gratifying (good) breast. However, even at this stage such splitting processes are never fully effective; for from the beginning of life the ego tends towards integrating itself and towards synthesizing the different aspects of the object. (This tendency can be regarded as an expression of the life instinct.) There appear to be transitory states of integration even in very young infants—becoming more frequent and lasting as development goes on—in which the cleavage between the good and bad breast is less marked.

[1] 'Notes on some Schizoid Mechanisms'.

In such states of integration, a measure of synthesis between love and hatred in relation to part-objects comes about, which according to my present view gives rise to depressive anxiety, guilt and the desire to make reparation to the injured loved object—first of all to the good breast.[1] That is to say that I now link the onset of depressive anxiety with the relation to part-objects. This modification is the result of further work on the earliest stages of the ego and of a fuller recognition of the gradual nature of the infant's emotional development. There is no change in my view that the basis of depressive anxiety is the synthesis between destructive impulses and feelings of love towards *one* object.

Let us next consider how far this modification influences the concept of the depressive position. I would now describe this position as follows: during the period from three to six months considerable progress in the integration of the ego comes about. Important changes take place in the nature of the infant's object-relations and of his introjection-processes. The infant perceives and introjects the mother increasingly as a complete person. This implies a fuller identification and a more stable relation with her. Although these processes are still primarily focused on the mother, the infant's relation to the father (and other people in his environment) undergoes similar changes and the father too becomes established in his mind as a whole person. At the same time, splitting processes diminish in strength and are predominantly related to whole objects, while in the earlier stage they were mainly connected with part-objects.

The contrasting aspects of the objects and the conflicting feelings, impulses and phantasies towards it, come closer together in the infant's mind. Persecutory anxiety persists and plays its part in the depressive position, but it lessens in quantity and depressive anxiety gains the ascendancy over persecutory anxiety. Since it is a loved *person* (internalized and external) who is felt to be injured by aggressive impulses, the infant suffers from intensified depressive feelings, more lasting than the fleeting experiences of depressive anxiety and guilt in the earlier stage. The more integrated ego is now increasingly confronted with a very painful psychic reality—the complaints and reproaches emanating from the internalized injured mother and father who are now complete objects, persons—and feels compelled under the stress of greater suffering to deal with the painful psychic reality. This leads to an over-riding urge to preserve, repair or revive the loved objects: the tendency to make

[1] We must remember, though, that even during this stage the mother's face and hands, and her whole bodily presence, increasingly enter into the gradual building up of the child's relation to her as a person.

reparation. As an alternative method, very likely a simultaneous one, of dealing with these anxieties, the ego resorts strongly to the manic defence.[1]

The developments I have described imply not only important qualitative and quantitative changes in feelings of love, depressive anxiety and guilt but also a new combination of factors which constitute the depressive position.

It can be seen from the foregoing description that the modification of my views regarding the earlier onset of depressive anxiety and guilt have not in any essentials altered my concept of the depressive position.

At this point I wish to consider more specifically the processes by which depressive anxiety, guilt and the urge to make reparation come about. The basis of depressive anxiety is, as I described, the process by which the ego synthesizes destructive impulses and feelings of love towards one object. The feeling that the harm done to the loved object is caused by the subject's aggressive impulses I take to be the essence of guilt. (The infant's feeling of guilt may extend to every evil befalling the loved object—even the harm done by his persecutory objects.) The urge to undo or repair this harm results from the feeling that the subject has caused it, *i.e.* from guilt. The reparative tendency can, therefore, be considered as a consequence of the sense of guilt.

The question now arises: is guilt an element in depressive anxiety? Are they both aspects of the same process, or is one a result or a manifestation of the other? While I cannot at present give a definite answer to this question, I would suggest that depressive anxiety, guilt and the reparative urge are often experienced simultaneously.

It seems probable that depressive anxiety, guilt and the reparative tendency are only experienced when feelings of love for the object predominate over destructive impulses. In other words, we may assume that recurrent experiences of love surmounting hatred —ultimately of the life instinct surmounting the death instinct—are an essential condition for the ego's capacity to integrate itself and to synthesize the contrasting aspects of the object. In such states or moments the relation to the bad aspects of the object, including persecutory anxiety, has receded.

However, during the first three or four months of life, a stage at which (according to my present views) depressive anxiety and guilt arise, splitting processes and persecutory anxiety are at their

[1] The concept of the manic defence and its wider application to mental life has been dealt with in some detail in my papers 'A Contribution to the Psychogenesis of Manic-Depressive States' and 'Mourning and its Relation to Manic-Depressive States', both in *Writings*, **1**.

height. Therefore persecutory anxiety very quickly interferes with progress in integration, and experiences of depressive anxiety, guilt and reparation can only be of a transitory nature. As a result, the loved injured object may very swiftly change into a persecutor, and the urge to repair or revive the loved object may turn into the need to pacify and propitiate a persecutor. But even during the next stage, the depressive position, in which the more integrated ego introjects and establishes increasingly the whole person, persecutory anxiety persists. During this period, as I described it, the infant experiences not only grief, depression and guilt, but also persecutory anxiety relating to the bad aspect of the super-ego; and defences against persecutory anxiety exist side by side with defences against depressive anxiety.

I have repeatedly pointed out that the differentiation between depressive and persecutory anxieties is based on a limiting concept. However, in psycho-analytic practice it has been found by a number of workers that the differentiation between persecutory and depressive anxiety is helpful in the understanding and unravelling of emotional situations. To give one instance of a typical picture which may confront us in the analysis of depressive patients: during a particular session a patient may suffer from strong feelings of guilt and despair about his incapacity to restore the damage which he feels he has caused. Then a complete change occurs: the patient suddenly brings up material of a persecutory kind. The analyst and analysis are accused of doing nothing but harm, grievances which lead back to early frustrations are voiced. The processes which underlie this change can be summarized as follows: persecutory anxiety has become dominant, the feeling of guilt has receded, and with it the love for the object seems to have disappeared. In this altered emotional situation, the object has turned bad, cannot be loved, and therefore destructive impulses towards it seem justified. This means that persecutory anxiety and defences *have been reinforced* in order to escape from the overwhelming burden of guilt and despair. In many cases, of course, the patient may show a good deal of persecutory anxiety together with guilt, and the change to a predominance of persecutory anxiety does not always appear as dramatically as I have here described it. But in every such case the differentiation between persecutory and depressive anxiety helps our understanding of the processes we are trying to analyse.

The conceptual distinction between depressive anxiety, guilt and reparation on the one hand, and persecutory anxiety and the defences against it on the other, not only proves helpful in analytic work but also has wider implications. It throws light on many problems connected with the study of human emotions and behaviour.[1] One particular field in which I have found this concept illuminating is the observation and understanding of children.

I will here briefly summarize the theoretical conclusion regarding the relation between anxiety and guilt which I have put forward in this section. Guilt is inextricably bound up with anxiety (more exactly, with a specific form of it, depressive anxiety); it leads to the reparative tendency and arises during the first few months of life, in connection with the earliest stages of the super-ego.

## VI

The interrelation between the primary internal danger and the danger threatening from without throws light on the problem of 'objective' *versus* 'neurotic' anxiety. Freud defined the distinction between objective anxiety and neurotic anxiety as follows: 'Real danger is a danger that is known, and realistic anxiety is anxiety about a known danger of this sort. Neurotic anxiety is anxiety about an unknown danger. Neurotic danger is thus a danger that has still to be discovered. Analysis has shown that it is an instinctual danger.'[2] And, again: 'A real danger is a danger which threatens a person from an external object, and a neurotic danger is one which threatens him from an instinctual demand.'[3]

In some connections, however, Freud referred to an interaction between these two sources of anxiety,[4] and general analytic experience has shown that the distinction between objective and neurotic anxiety cannot be sharply drawn.

I shall here return to Freud's statement that anxiety is caused by the child 'missing someone who is loved and longed for'.[5] In describing the infant's fundamental fear of loss, Freud said: 'It cannot as yet distinguish between temporary absence and permanent loss. *As soon as it misses its mother it behaves as if it were never going to see her again;* and repeated consoling experiences to the contrary are necessary before it learns that her disappearance is usually followed by her re-appearance.'[6] (My italics.)

[1] In his paper, 'Towards a Common Aim—a Psycho-Analytical Contribution to Ethics', R. E. Money-Kyrle applied the distinction between persecutory and depressive anxieties to attitudes towards ethics in general and towards political beliefs in particular, and has since expanded these views in his book *Psycho-Analysis and Politics*.

[2] *Inhibitions, Symptoms and Anxiety*, S.E., **20**, p. 165.      [3] *Loc. cit.*, p. 167.

[4] This interaction between anxiety derived from external and internal causes is referred to by Freud with regard to some cases of neurotic anxiety. 'The danger is known but the anxiety in regard to it is over-great, greater than seems proper . . . analysis shows that to the known real danger an unknown instinctual one is attached' (*Loc. cit.*, pp. 165-6).

[5] *Loc. cit.*, p. 136.      [6] *Loc. cit.*, p. 163.

In another passage describing the fear of loss of love he said that it is 'evidently a later prolongation of the infant's anxiety if it finds its mother absent. You will realize how *real a situation of danger* is indicated by this anxiety. If a mother is absent or has withdrawn her love from her child, it is no longer sure of the satisfaction of its needs and is perhaps exposed to the most distressing feelings of tension.[1] (My italics).

However, a few pages earlier in the same book, Freud described this particular danger-situation from the point of view of neurotic anxiety, which seems to show that he approached this infantile-situation from both angles. In my view these two main sources of the infant's fear of loss can be described as follows: one is the child's complete dependence on the mother for the satisfaction of his needs and the relief of tension. The anxiety arising from this source could be called objective anxiety. The other main source of anxiety derives from the infant's apprehension that the loved mother has been destroyed by his sadistic impulses or is in danger of being destroyed, and this fear—which could be called 'neurotic anxiety'—relates to the mother as an indispensable external (and internal) good object and contributes to the infant's feeling that she will never return. There is from the beginning a constant interaction between these two sources of anxiety, that is to say, between objective and neurotic anxiety or in other words, anxiety from external and internal sources.

Furthermore, if external danger is from the beginning linked with internal danger from the death instinct, no danger-situation arising from external sources could ever be experienced by the young child as a purely external and known danger. But it is not only the infant who cannot make such a clear differentiation: to some extent the interaction between external and internal danger-situations persists throughout life.[2]

This was clearly shown in the analysis carried out in war-time. It appeared that even with normal adults anxiety stirred up by air-raids, bombs, fire, etc.—*i.e.* by an 'objective' danger-situation —could only be reduced by analysing, over and above the impact of the actual situation, the various early anxieties which were aroused by it. In many people excessive anxiety from these sources led to a powerful denial (manic defence) of the objective danger-situation,

[1] *New Introductory Lectures on Psycho-Analysis* (1932), *S.E.* **22**, p. 87.

[2] As I pointed out in my *Psycho-Analysis of Children*, p. 192: 'If a normal person is put under a severe internal or external strain, or if he falls ill or fails in some other way, we may observe in him the full and direct operation of his deepest anxiety-situations. Since, then, every healthy person *may* succumb to a neurotic illness, it follows that he can never have entirely given up his old anxiety-situations.'

which showed itself in an apparent lack of fear. This was a common observation with children and could not be explained only by their incomplete realization of the actual danger. Analysis revealed that the objective danger-situation had revived the child's early phantastic anxieties to such an extent that the objective danger-situation had to be denied. In other cases the relative stability of children in spite of war-time dangers was not determined so much by manic defences as by a more successful modification of early persecutory and depressive anxieties, resulting in a greater feeling of security regarding both the inner and the external world, and in a good relationship with their parents. With such children, even when the father was absent, the reassurance gained from the presence of the mother, and from home life, counteracted the fears stirred up by objective dangers.

These observations become understandable if we remember that the young child's perception of external reality and external objects is perpetually influenced and coloured by his phantasies, and that this in some measure continues throughout life. External experiences which rouse anxiety at once activate even in normal persons anxiety derived from intrapsychic sources. The interaction between objective anxiety and neurotic anxiety—or, to express it in other words, the interaction between anxiety arising from external and from internal sources—corresponds to the interaction between external reality and psychic reality.

In estimating whether anxiety is neurotic or not, we have to consider a point to which Freud repeatedly referred, the quantity of anxiety from inner sources. This factor is however linked with the ego's capacity of evolving adequate defences against anxiety, *i.e.* the proportion of the strength of anxiety to the strength of the ego.

## VII

It was implicit in this presentation of my views that they developed from an approach to aggression which differed substantially from the main trend in psycho-analytic thought. The fact that Freud discovered aggression first as an element in the child's sexuality —as it were as an adjunct to libido (sadism)—had the effect that for a long time psycho-analytical interest centred on the libido and that aggression was more or less considered as an auxiliary to libido.[1] In 1920 came Freud's discovery of the death instinct manifesting itself in destructive impulses and operating in fusion with the life instinct, and in 1924 followed Abraham's deeper

[1] Cf. Paula Heimann's (1952) paper in which she discusses this theoretical bias in favour of the libido and its influence on the development of theory.

exploration of sadism in the young child. But even after these discoveries, as can be seen from the bulk of psycho-analytical literature, psycho-analytical thought has remained predominantly concerned with the libido and with the defences against libidinal impulses and has correspondingly underrated the importance of aggression and its implications.

From the beginning of my psycho-analytic work, my interest was focused on anxiety and its causation, and this brought me nearer to the understanding of the relation between aggression and anxiety.[1] The analyses of young children, for which I evolved Play Technique, supported this angle of approach, for they revealed that anxiety in young children could only be alleviated by analysing their sadistic phantasies and impulses with a greater appreciation of the share aggression has in sadism and in the causation of anxiety. This fuller evaluation of the importance of aggression led me to certain theoretical conclusions which I presented in my paper 'The Early Stages of the Oedipus Conflict' (1927). There I put forward the hypothesis that—both in the normal and pathological development of the child—anxiety and guilt arising during the first year of life are closely connected with processes of introjection and projection, with the first stages of the super-ego development and of the Oedipus complex; and that in these anxieties aggression and the defences against it are of paramount importance.

Further work on these lines was carried out in the British Psycho-Analytical Society from about 1927 onwards. In this Society, a number of psycho-analysts, working in close co-operation, made numerous contributions[2] to the understanding of the cardinal rôle of aggression in mental life; while, taking psycho-analytic thought in general, a change of view in this direction has appeared only in sporadic contributions during the last ten to fifteen years; these have, however, increased of late.

One of the results of the new work on aggression was the recognition of the major function of the reparative tendency, which is an expression of the life instinct in its struggle against the death instinct. Not only were the destructive impulses thereby seen in better perspective, but a fuller light was thrown on the interaction of the life and death instincts, and therefore also on the rôle of the libido in all mental and emotional processes.

Throughout this paper I have made clear my contention that the death instinct (destructive impulses) is the primary factor in the causation of anxiety. It was, however, also implied, in my exposition of the processes leading to anxiety and guilt, that the primary object

[1] This strong emphasis on anxiety entered already into my first publications.
[2] Cf. the bibliography appended to Riviere's (1952) paper.

against which the destructive impulses are directed is the object of the libido, and that it is therefore the *interaction* between aggression and libido—ultimately the fusion as well as the polarity of the two instincts—which causes anxiety and guilt. Another aspect of this interaction is the mitigation of destructive impulses by libido. An optimum in the interaction between libido and aggression implies that the anxiety arising from the perpetual activity of the death instinct, though never eliminated, is counteracted and kept at bay by the power of the life instinct.

# 3

## ON THE CRITERIA
## FOR THE TERMINATION
## OF A PSYCHO-ANALYSIS

### (1950)

THE criteria for the ending of an analysis are an important problem in every psycho-analyst's mind. There are a number of criteria on which all of us would agree. Here I shall suggest a different approach to this problem.

It has often been observed that the termination of an analysis reactivates in the patient earlier situations of parting, and is in the nature of a weaning experience. This implies, as my work has shown me, that the emotions felt by the baby at weaning time, when early infantile conflicts come to a head, are strongly revived towards the end of an analysis. Accordingly, I arrived at the conclusion that before terminating an analysis I have to ask myself whether the conflicts and anxieties experienced during the first year of life have been sufficiently analysed and worked through in the course of the treatment.

My work on early development (Klein, 1935, 1940, 1946, 1948) has led me to distinguish between two forms of anxiety: persecutory anxiety, which is predominant during the first few months of life and gives rise to the 'paranoid-schizoid position', and depressive anxiety, which comes to a head at about the middle of the first year and gives rise to the depressive position'. I arrived at the further conclusion that at the beginning of his postnatal life the infant is experiencing persecutory anxiety both from external and internal sources: external, in so far as the experience of birth is felt as an attack inflicted on him; and internal, because the threat to the organism, which, according to Freud, arises from the death instinct, in my view stirs up the fear of annihilation—the fear of death. It is this fear which I take to be the primary cause of anxiety.

Persecutory anxiety relates mainly to dangers felt to threaten the ego; depressive anxiety relates to dangers felt to threaten the loved object, primarily through the subject's aggression. Depressive anxiety arises through synthetic processes in the ego; for as a result of growing integration, love and hatred and, accordingly, the good and bad

43

aspects of the objects, came closer together in the infant's mind. Some measure of integration is also one of the preconditions for the introjection of the mother as a complete person. Depressive feelings and anxiety come to a climax—the depressive position—at about the middle of the first year. By then persecutory anxiety has diminished, although still playing an important part.

Interlinked with depressive anxiety is the sense of guilt relating to harm done by cannibalistic and sadistic desires. Guilt gives rise to the urge to make reparation to the harmed loved object, to preserve or revive it—an urge which deepens feelings of love and promotes object relations.

At weaning time the infant feels that he has lost the first loved object—the mother's breast—both as an external and as an introjected object, and that his loss is due to his hatred, aggression and greed. Weaning thus accentuates his depressive feelings and amounts to a state of mourning. The suffering inherent in the depressive position is bound up with an increasing insight into psychic reality which in turn contributes to a better understanding of the external world. By means of the growing adaptation to reality and the expanding range of object relations, the infant becomes able to combat and diminish depressive anxieties and in some measure to establish securely his good internalized objects, that is to say the helpful and protective aspect of the super-ego.

Freud has described the testing of reality as an essential part of the work of mourning. In my view, it is in early infancy that the testing of reality is first applied in attempts to overcome the grief inherent in the depressive position; and whenever in later life mourning is experienced, these early processes are revived. I have found that in adults the success of the work of mourning depends not only on establishing within the ego the person who is mourned (as we learned from Freud and Abraham), but also on re-establishing the first loved objects, which in early infancy were felt to be endangered or destroyed by destructive impulses.

Although the fundamental steps in counteracting the depressive position are made during the first year of life, persecutory and depressive feelings recur throughout childhood. These anxieties are worked through and largely overcome in the course of the infantile neurosis, and normally by the onset of the latency period adequate defences have developed and some measure of stabilization has come about. This implies that genital primacy and satisfactory object relations have been achieved and that the Oedipus complex has been reduced in power.

I shall now draw a conclusion from the definition already given, namely that persecutory anxiety relates to dangers felt to threaten the ego and depressive anxiety to dangers felt to threaten the loved object. I wish to suggest that these two forms of anxiety comprise all anxiety situations the child goes through. Thus, the fear of being devoured, of being poisoned, of being castrated, the fear of attacks on the 'inside' of the body, come under the heading of persecutory anxiety, whereas all anxieties relating to loved objects are depressive in nature. However, persecutory and depressive anxieties, although conceptually distinct from one another, are clinically often mixed. For instance, I have defined castration fear, the leading anxiety in the male, as persecutory. This fear is mixed with depressive anxiety in so far as it gives rise to the feeling that he cannot fertilize a woman, at bottom that he cannot fertilize the loved mother and is therefore unable to make reparation for the harm done to her by his sadistic impulses. I need hardly remind you that impotence often leads to severe depression in men. To take now the leading anxiety in women. The girl's fear lest the dreaded mother will attack her body and the babies it contains, which is in my view the fundamental female anxiety situation, is by definition persecutory. Yet, as this fear implies the destruction of her loved objects—the babies she feels to be inside her—it contains a strong element of depressive anxiety.

In keeping with my thesis, it is a precondition for normal development that persecutory and depressive anxieties should have been largely reduced and modified. Therefore, as I hope has become clear in the foregoing exposition, my approach to the problem of terminating both child and adult analyses can be defined as follows: persecutory and depressive anxiety should be sufficiently reduced, and thus—in my view—presupposes the analysis of the first experiences of mourning.

In passing I should say that even if the analysis goes back to the earliest stages of development, which is the basis for my new criterion, the results will still vary according to the severity and structure of the case. In other words, notwithstanding progress made in our theory and technique, we have to keep in mind the limitations of psycho-analytic therapy.

The question arises how far the approach I am suggesting is related to some of the well-known criteria, such as an established potency and heterosexuality, capacity for love, object relations and work, and certain characteristics of the ego which make for mental stability and are bound up with adequate defences. All these aspects of development are inter-related with the modification of persecutory and depressive anxiety. Concerning the capacity for love and object relations, it can easily be seen that these develop freely only if persecutory and depressive anxiety are not excessive. The issue is more complex as regards the development of the ego. Two features are usually emphasized in this connection, growth in stability and in the sense of reality, but I hold that expansion in the depth of the ego is essential as well. An intrinsic element of a deep and full personality is wealth of phantasy life and the capacity for experiencing emotions freely. These characteristics, I think, presuppose that the infantile depressive position has been worked through, that is to say, that the whole gamut of love and hatred, anxiety, grief and guilt in relation to the primary objects has been experienced again and again. This emotional development is bound up with the nature of defences. Failure in working through the depressive position is inextricably linked with a predominance of defences which entail a stifling of emotions and of phantasy life, and hinder insight. Such defences, which I termed 'manic defences', although not incompatible with a measure of stability and strength of the ego, go with shallowness. If during analysis we succeed in reducing persecutory and depressive anxieties and, accordingly, in diminishing manic defences, one of the results will be an increase in *strength* as well as in *depth of the ego*.

Even if satisfactory results have been achieved, the termination of an analysis is bound to stir up painful feelings and revive early anxieties; it amounts to a state of mourning. When the loss represented by the end of the analysis has occurred, the patient still has to carry out by himself part of the work of mourning. This, I think, explains the fact that often after the termination of an analysis further progress is achieved; how far this is likely to happen can be foreseen more easily if we apply the criterion suggested by me. For only if persecutory and depressive anxieties have been largely modified, can the patient carry out by himself the final part of the work of mourning, which again implies a testing of reality. Moreover, when we decide that an analysis can be brought to an end, I think it is very helpful to let the patient know the date of the termination several months ahead. This helps him to work through and diminish the unavoidable pain of parting while he is still in analysis and prepares the way for him to finish the work of mourning successfully on his own.

I have made it clear throughout this paper that the criterion I suggest presupposes that the analysis has been carried back to the early stages of development and to deep layers of the mind and has included the working through of persecutory and depressive anxieties.

This leads me to a conclusion regarding technique. During an analysis the psycho-analyst often appears as an idealized figure. Idealization is used as a defence against persecutory anxiety and is its corollary. If the analyst allows excessive idealization to persist— that is to say, if he relies mostly on the positive transference—he may, it is true, be able to bring about some improvement. The same however, could be said of any successful psycho-therapy. It is only *by analysing the negative as well as the positive transference* that anxiety is reduced at the root. In the course of the treatment, the psycho-analyst comes to represent in the transference situation a variety of figures corresponding to those which were introjected in early development (Klein, 1929; Strachey, 1934). He is, therefore, at times introjected as a persecutor, at other times as an ideal figure, with all shades and degrees in between.

As persecutory and depressive anxieties are experienced and ultimately reduced during the analysis, a greater synthesis between the various aspects of the analyst comes about together with a greater synthesis between the various aspects of the super-ego. In other words, the earliest frightening figures undergo an essential alteration in the patient's mind—one might say that they basically improve. Good objects—as distinct from idealized ones—can be securely established in the mind only if the strong split between persecutory and ideal figures has diminished, if aggressive and libidinal impulses have come closer together and hatred has become mitigated by love. Such advance in the capacity to synthesize is proof that the splitting processes, which, in my view, originate in earliest infancy, have diminished and that integration of the ego in depth has come about. When these positive features are sufficiently established we are justified in thinking that the termination of an analysis is not premature, although it may revive even acute anxiety.

# 4

# THE ORIGINS OF TRANSFERENCE

## (1952)

IN his 'Fragment of an Analysis of a Case of Hysteria' Freud (1905) defines the transference situation in the following way:

'What are transferences? They are new editions or facsimiles of the impulses and phantasies which are aroused and made conscious during the progress of the analysis; but they have this peculiarity, which is characteristic for their species, that they replace some earlier person by the person of the physician. To put it another way: a whole series of psychological experiences are revived, not as belonging to the past, but as applying to the physician at the present moment.'

In some form or other transference operates throughout life and influences all human relations, but here I am only concerned with the manifestations of transference in psycho-analysis. It is characteristic of psycho-analytic procedure that, as it begins to open up roads into the patient's unconscious, his past (in its conscious and unconscious aspects) is gradually being revived. Thereby his urge to transfer his early experiences, object-relations and emotions, is reinforced and they come to focus on the psycho-analyst; this implies that the patient deals with the conflicts and anxieties which have been reactivated, by making use of the same mechanisms and defences as in earlier situations.

It follows that the deeper we are able to penetrate into the unconscious and the further back we can take the analysis, the greater will be our understanding of the transference. Therefore a brief summary of my conclusions about the earliest stages of development is relevant to my topic.

The first form of anxiety is of a persecutory nature. The working of the death instinct within—which according to Freud is directed against the organism—gives rise to the fear of annihilation, and this is the primordial cause of persecutory anxiety. Furthermore, from the beginning of post-natal life (I am not concerned here with pre-natal processes) destructive impulses against the object stir up fear of retaliation. These persecutory feelings from inner sources are intensified by painful external experiences for, from the earliest days onwards frustration and discomfort arouse in the infant the feeling

48

that he is being attacked by hostile forces. Therefore the sensations experienced by the infant at birth and the difficulties of adapting himself to entirely new conditions give rise to persecutory anxiety. The comfort and care given after birth, particularly the first feeding experiences, are felt to come from good forces. In speaking of 'forces' I am using a rather adult word for what the young infant dimly conceives of as objects, either good or bad. The infant directs his feelings of gratification and love towards the 'good' breast, and his destructive impulses and feelings of persecution towards what he feels to be frustrating, *i.e.* the 'bad' breast. At this stage splitting processes are at their height and love and hatred as well as the good and bad aspects of the breast are largely kept apart from one another. The infant's relative security is based on turning the good object into an ideal one as a protection against the dangerous and persecuting object. These processes—that is to say splitting, denial, omnipotence and idealization—are prevalent during the first three or four months of life (which I termed the 'paranoid-schizoid position' (1946)). In these ways at a very early stage persecutory anxiety and its corollary, idealization, fundamentally influence object relations.

The primal processes of projection and introjection, being inextricably linked with the infant's emotions and anxieties, initiate object-relations: by projecting, *i.e.* deflecting libido and aggression on to the mother's breast, the basis for object-relations is established: by introjecting the object, first of all the breast, relations to internal objects come into being. My use of the term 'object-relations' is based on my contention that the infant has from the beginning of post-natal life a relation to the mother (although focusing primarily on her breast) which is imbued with the fundamental elements of an object-relation, *i.e.* love, hatred, phantasies, anxieties, and defences.[1]

In my view—as I have explained in detail on other occasions —the introjection of the breast is the beginning of super-ego formation which extends over years. We have grounds for assuming that from the first feeding experience onwards the infant introjects the

[1] It is an essential feature of this earliest of all object-relations that it is the prototype of a relation between *two* people into which no other object enters. This is of vital importance for later object-relations, though in that exclusive form it possibly does not last longer than a very few months, for the phantasies relating to the father and his penis—phantasies which initiate the early stages of the Oedipus complex—introduce the relation to more than one object. In the analysis of adults and children the patient sometimes comes to experience feelings of blissful happiness through the revival of this early exclusive relation with the mother and her breast. Such experiences often follow the analysis of jealousy and rivalry situations in which a third object, ultimately the father, is involved.

49

breast in its various aspects. The core of the superego is thus the mother's breast, both good and bad. Owing to the simultaneous operation of introjection and projection, relations to external and internal objects interact. The father too, who soon plays a rôle in the child's life, early on becomes part of the infant's internal world. It is characteristic of the infant's emotional life that there are rapid fluctuations between love and hate; between external and internal situations; between perception of reality and the phantasies relating to it; and, accordingly, an interplay between persecutory anxiety and idealization—both referring to internal and external objects; the idealized object being a corollary of the persecutory, extremely bad one.

The ego's growing capacity for integration and synthesis leads more and more, even during these first few months, to states in which love and hatred, and correspondingly the good and bad aspects of objects, are being synthesized; and this gives rise to the second form of anxiety—depressive anxiety—for the infant's aggressive impulses and desires towards the bad breast (mother) are now felt to be a danger to the good breast (mother) as well. In the second quarter of the first year these emotions are reinforced, because at this stage the infant increasingly perceives and introjects the mother as a person. Depressive anxiety is intensified, for the infant feels he has destroyed or is destroying a whole object by his greed and uncontrollable aggression. Moreover, owing to the growing synthesis of his emotions, he now feels that these destructive impulses are directed against a *loved person*. Similar processes operate in relation to the father and other members of the family. These anxieties and corresponding defences constitute the 'depressive-position', which comes to a head about the middle of the first year and whose essence is the anxiety and guilt relating to the destruction and loss of the loved internal and external objects.

It is at this stage, and bound up with the depressive position, that the Oedipus complex sets in. Anxiety and guilt add a powerful impetus towards the beginning of the Oedipus complex. For anxiety and guilt increase the need to externalize (project) bad figures and to internalize (introject) good ones; to attach desires, love, feelings of guilt, and reparative tendencies to some objects, and hate and anxiety to others; to find representatives for internal figures in the external world. It is, however, not only the search for new objects which dominates the infant's needs, but also the drive towards the new aims: away from the breast towards the penis, *i.e.* from oral desires towards genital ones. Many factors contribute to these developments: the forward drive of the libido, the growing integration of the ego, physical and mental skills and progressive adaptation to the external world. These trends are bound up with the process of symbol formation, which enables the infant to transfer not only interest, but also emotions and phantasies, anxiety and guilt, from one object to another.

The processes I have described are linked with another fundamental phenomenon governing mental life. I believe that the pressure exerted by the earliest anxiety situations is one of the factors which brings about the repetition compulsion. I shall return to this hypothesis at a later point.

Some of my conclusions about the earliest stages of infancy are a continuation of Freud's discoveries; on certain points, however, divergencies have arisen, one of which is very relevant to my present topic. I am referring to my contention that object-relations are operative from the beginning of post-natal life.

For many years I have held the view that auto-erotism and narcissism are in the young infant contemporaneous with the first relation to objects—external and internalized. I shall briefly restate my hypothesis: auto-erotism and narcissism include the love for and relation with the internalized good object which in phantasy forms part of the loved body and self. It is to this internalized object that in auto-erotic gratification and narcissistic *states* a withdrawal takes place. Concurrently, from birth onwards, a relation to objects, primarily the mother (her breast) is present. This hypothesis contradicts Freud's concept of auto-erotic and narcissistic *stages* which preclude an object-relation. However, the difference between Freud's view and my own is less wide than appears at first sight, since Freud's statements on this issue are not unequivocal. In various contexts he explicitly and implicitly expressed opinions which suggested a relation to an object, the mother's breast, *preceding* auto-erotism and narcissism. One reference must suffice; in the first of two Encyclopaedia articles, Freud (1922) said;

'In the first instance the oral component instinct finds satisfaction by attaching itself to the sating of the desire for nourishment; and its object is the mother's breast. It then detaches itself, becomes independent and at the same time *auto-erotic*, that is, it finds an object in the child's own body' (p. 245).

Freud's use of the term object is here somewhat different from my use of this term, for he is referring to the object of an instinctual aim, while I mean in addition to this, an object-relation involving the infant's emotions, phantasies, anxieties, and defences. Nevertheless, in the sentence referred to, Freud clearly speaks of a libidinal attachment to an object, the mother's breast, which precedes auto-erotism and narcissism.

In this context I wish to remind you also of Freud's findings about early identifications. In *The Ego and the Id*,[1] speaking of abandoned object cathexes, he said; ' . . . the effects of the first identification in earliest childhood will be general and lasting. This leads us back to the origin of the ego-ideal; . . .' Freud then defines the first and most important identifications which lie hidden behind the ego-ideal as the identification with the father, or with the parents, and places them, as he expresses it, in the 'pre-history of every person'. These formulations come close to what I described as the first introjected objects, for by definition identifications are the result of introjection. From the statement I have just discussed and the passage quoted from the Encyclopaedia article it can be deduced that Freud, although he did not pursue this line of thought further, did assume that in earliest infancy both an object and introjective processes play a part.

That is to say, as regards auto-erotism and narcissism we meet with an inconsistency in Freud's views. Such inconsistencies which exist on a number of points of theory clearly show, I think, that on these particular issues Freud had not yet arrived at a final decision. In respect of the theory of anxiety he stated this explicitly in *Inhibitions, Symptoms and Anxiety* (1926, Chapter 8). His realization that much about the early stages of development was still unknown or obscure to him is also exemplified by his speaking of the first years of the girl's life as '. . . (Freud, 1931) grey with age and shadowy . . .'.

I do not know Anna Freud's view about this aspect of Freud's work. But, as regards the question of auto-erotism and narcissism, she seems only to have taken into account Freud's conclusion that an auto-erotic and a narcissistic stage precede object-relations, and not to have allowed for the other possibilities implied in some of Freud's statements such as the ones I referred to above. This is one of the reasons why the divergence between Anna Freud's conception and my conception of early infancy is far greater than that between Freud's views, taken as a whole, and my views. I am stating this because I believe it is essential to clarify the extent and nature of the differences between the two schools of psycho-analytic thought represented by Anna Freud and myself. Such clarification is required in the interests of psycho-analytic training and also because it could help to open up fruitful discussions between psycho-analysts and thereby contribute to a greater general understanding of the fundamental problems of early infancy.

The hypothesis that a stage extending over several months pre-

---

[1] p. 31. On the same page Freud suggests—still referring to these first identifications—that they are a direct and immediate identification which takes place earlier than any object cathexis. This suggestion seems to imply that introjection even precedes object-relations.

cedes object-relations implies that—except for the libido attached to the infant's own body—impulses, phantasies anxieties, and defences either are not present in him, or are not related to an object, that is to say, they would operate *in vacuo*. The analysis of very young children has taught me that there is no instinctual urge, no anxiety situation, no mental process which does not involve objects, external or internal; in other words, object-relations are at the *centre* of emotional life. Furthermore, love and hatred, phantasies, anxieties, and defences are also operative from the beginning and are *ab initio* indivisibly linked with object-relations. This insight showed me many phenomena in a new light.

I shall now draw the conclusion on which the present paper rests: I hold that transference originates in the same processes which in the earliest stages determine object-relations. Therefore we have to go back again and again in analysis to the fluctuations between objects, loved and hated, external and internal, which dominate early infancy. We can fully appreciate the interconnection between positive and negative transferences only if we explore the early interplay between love and hate, and the vicious circle of aggression, anxieties feelings of guilt and increased aggression, as well as the various aspects of objects towards whom these conflicting emotions and anxieties are directed. On the other hand, through exploring these early processes I became convinced that the analysis of the negative transference, which had received relatively little attention[1] in psycho-analytic technique, is a precondition for analysing the deeper layers of the mind. The analysis of the negative as well as of the positive transference and of their interconnection is, as I have held for many years, an indispensable principle for the treatment of all types of patients, children and adults alike. I have substantiated this view in most of my writings from 1927 onwards.

This approach, which in the past made possible the psycho-analysis of very young children, has in recent years proved extremely fruitful for the analysis of schizophrenic patients. Until about 1920 it was assumed that schizophrenic patients were incapable of forming a transference and therefore could not be psycho-analysed. Since then the psycho-analysis of schizophrenics has been attempted by various techniques. The most radical change of view in this respect. however, has occurred more recently and is closely connected with the greater knowledge of the mechanisms, anxieties, and defences operative in earliest infancy. Since some of these defences, evolved in primal object-relations against both love and hatred, have been discovered, the fact that schizophrenic patients are capable of developing both a positive and a negative transference has been fully

[1] This was largely due to the undervaluation of the importance of aggression.

understood; this finding is confirmed if we consistently apply in the treatment of schizophrenic patients[1] the principle that it is as necessary to analyse the negative as the positive transference—that in fact the one cannot be analysed without the other.

Retrospectively it can be seen that these considerable advances in technique are supported in psycho-analytic theory by Freud's discovery of the life and death instincts, which has fundamentally added to the understanding of the origin of ambivalence. Because the life and death instincts and therefore love and hatred, are at bottom in the closest interaction, negative and positive transference are basically inter-linked.

The understanding of earliest object-relations and the processes they imply has essentially influenced technique from various angles. It has long been known that the psycho-analyst in the transference situation may stand for mother, father, or other people, that he is also at times playing in the patient's mind the part of the superego, at other times that of the id or the ego. Our present knowledge enables us to penetrate to the specific details of the various rôles allotted by the patient to the analyst. There are in fact very few people in the young infant's life, but he feels them to be a multitude of objects because they appear to him in different aspects. Accordingly, the analyst may at a given moment represent a part of the self, of the superego or any one of a wide range of internalized figures. Similarly it does not carry us far enough if we realize that the analyst stands for the actual father or mother, unless we understand which aspect of the parents has been revived. The picture of the parents in the patient's mind has in varying degrees undergone distortion through the infantile processes of projection and idealization, and has often retained much of its phantastic nature. Altogether, in the young infant's mind every external experience is interwoven with his phantasies and on the other hand every phantasy contains elements of actual experience, and it is only by analysing the transference situation to its depth that we are able to discover the past both in its realistic and phantastic aspects. It is also the origin of these fluctuations in earliest infancy which accounts for their strength in the transference, and for the swift changes—sometimes even within one session—between father and mother, between omnipotently kind objects and dangerous persecutors, between internal and external figures. Sometimes the analyst appears simultaneously to represent

---

[1] This technique is illustrated by H. Segal's paper, 'Some Aspects of the Analysis of a Schizophrenic' (1950), and H. Rosenfeld's papers, 'Notes on the Psycho-Analysis of the Super-ego Conflict of an Acute Schizophrenic Patient' (1952a) and 'Transference Phenomena and Transference Analysis in an Acute Catatonic Schizophrenic Patient' (1952b).

both parents—in that case often in a hostile alliance against the patient, whereby the negative transference acquires great intensity. What has then been revived or has become manifest in the transference is the mixture in the patient's phantasy of the parents as one figure, the 'combined parent figure' as I described it elsewhere.[1] This is one of the phantasy formations characteristic of the earliest stages of the Oedipus complex and which, if maintained in strength is detrimental both to object-relations and sexual development. The phantasy of the combined parents draws its force from another element of early emotional life—*i.e.* from the powerful envy associated with frustrated oral desires. Through the analysis of such early situations we learn that in the baby's mind when he is frustrated (or dissatisfied from inner causes) his frustration is coupled with the feeling that another object (soon represented by the father) receives from the mother the coveted gratification and love denied to himself at that moment. Here is one root of the phantasy that the parents are combined in an everlasting mutual gratification of an oral, anal and genital nature. And this is in my view the prototype of situations of both envy and jealousy.

There is another aspect of the analysis of transference which needs mentioning. We are accustomed to speak of the transference *situation*. But do we always keep in mind the fundamental importance of this concept? It is my experience that in unravelling the details of the transference it is essential to think in terms of *total situations* transferred from the past into the present, as well as of emotions, defences, and object-relations.

For many years—and this is up to a point still true today—transference was understood in terms of direct references to the analyst in the patient's material. My conception of transference as rooted in the earliest stages of development and in deep layers of the unconscious is much wider and entails a technique by which from the whole material presented the *unconscious elements* of the transference are deduced. For instance, reports of patients about their everyday life, relations, and activities not only give an insight into the functioning of the ego, but also reveal—if we explore their unconscious content—the defences against the anxieties stirred up in the transference situation. For the patient is bound to deal with conflicts and anxieties re-experienced towards the analyst by the same methods he used in the past. That is to say, he turns away from the analyst as he attempted to turn away from his primal objects; he tries to split the relations to him, keeping him either as a good or as a bad figure: he deflects some of the feelings and attitudes experienced towards the

[1] See *The Psycho-Analysis of Children*, particularly Chapters 8 and 11.

analyst on to other people in his current life, and this is part of 'acting out'.[1]

In keeping with my subject matter, I have predominantly discussed here the earliest experiences, situations, and emotions from which transference springs. On these foundations, however, are built the later object-relations and the emotional and intellectual developments which necessitate the analyst's attention no less than the earliest ones; that is to say, our field of investigation covers *all* that lies between the current situation and the earliest experiences. In fact it is not possible to find access to earliest emotions and object-relations except by examining their vicissitudes in the light of later developments. It is only by linking again and again (and that means hard and patient work) later experiences with earlier ones and *vice versa*, it is only by consistently exploring their interplay, that present and past can come together in the patient's mind. This is one aspect of the process of integration which, as the analysis progresses, encompasses the whole of the patient's mental life. When anxiety and guilt diminish and love and hate can be better synthesized, splitting processes—a fundamental defence against anxiety—as well as repressions lessen while the ego gains in strength and coherence; the cleavage between idealized and persecutory objects diminishes; the phantastic aspects of objects lose in strength; all of which implies that unconscious phantasy life—less sharply divided off from the unconscious part of the mind—can be better utilized in ego activities, with a consequent general enrichment of the personality. I am touching here on the *differences*—as contrasted with the similarities—between transference and the first object-relations. These differences are a measure of the curative effect of the analytic procedure.

I suggested above that one of the factors which bring about the repetition compulsion is the pressure exerted by the earliest anxiety situations. When persecutory and depressive anxiety and guilt diminish, there is less urge to repeat fundamental experiences over and over again, and therefore early patterns and modes of feelings are maintained with less tenacity. These fundamental changes come about through the consistent analysis of the transference; they are bound up with a deep-reaching revision of the earliest object-relations and are reflected in the patient's current life as well as in the altered attitudes towards the analyst.

---

[1] The patient may at times try to escape from the present into the past rather than realize that his emotions, anxieties, and phantasies are at the time operative in full strength and focused on the analyst. At other times, as we know, the defences are mainly directed against re-experiencing the past in relation to the original objects.

# 5

## THE MUTUAL INFLUENCES IN
## THE DEVELOPMENT OF EGO AND ID

### (1952)

In 'Analysis Terminable and Interminable' (*S.E.* **23**) which contains Freud's latest conclusions about the ego, he assumed '. . . the existence and importance of original, innate distinguishing characteristics of the ego'. I have for many years held the view, and expressed it in my book, *The Psycho-Analysis of Children* (1932), that the ego functions from the beginning and that among its first activities are the defence against anxiety and the use of processes of introjection and projection. In that book I also suggested that the ego's initial capacity to tolerate anxiety depends on its innate strength, that is to say, on constitutional factors. I have also repeatedly expressed the view that the ego establishes object relations from the first contacts with the external world. More recently I defined the drive toward integration as another of the ego's primal functions.[1]

I shall now consider the part which the instincts—and particularly the struggle between life and death instincts—play in these functions of the ego. It is inherent in Freud's conception of the life and death instincts that the id as the reservoir of the instincts operates *ab initio*. With this conception I fully agree. I differ, however, from Freud in that I put forward the hypothesis that the primary cause of anxiety is the fear of annihilation, of death, arising from the working of the death instinct within. The struggle between life and death instincts emanates from the id and involves the ego. The primordial fear of being annihilated forces the ego into action and engenders the first defences. The ultimate source of these ego activities lies in the operation of the life instinct. The ego's urge toward integration and organization clearly reveals its derivation from the life instinct; as Freud put it '. . . . the main purpose of Eros—that of uniting and binding. . .'[2] Opposed to the drive toward integration and yet alternating with it, there are splitting processes which, together with introjection and projection, represent some of the most fundamental early mechanisms. All these, under the impetus of the life instinct, are from the beginning pressed into the service of defence.

[1] 'Notes on some Schizoid Mechanisms' (1946).
[2] (1923) *The Ego and the Id. S.E.* **19**, p. 45.

Another major contribution from instinctual drives to the primal functions of the ego needs consideration here. It is in keeping with my conception of early infancy that phantasy activity, being rooted in the instincts, is—to use an expression of Susan Isaacs—their mental corollary. I believe that phantasies operate from the outset, as do the instincts, and are the mental expression of the activity of both the life and death instincts. Phantasy activity underlies the mechanisms of introjection and projection, which enable the ego to perform one of the basic functions mentioned above, namely to establish object-relations. By projection, by turning outward libido and aggression and imbuing the object with them, the infant's first object-relation comes about. This is the process which, in my opinion, underlies the cathexis of objects. Owing to the process of introjection, this first object is simultaneously taken into the self. From the outset the relations to external and internal objects interact. The first of these 'internalized objects', as I termed them, is a part-object, the mother's breast; in my experience this applies even when the infant is bottle-fed, but it would take me too far if I were to discuss here the processes by which this symbolic equation comes about. The breast, to which are soon added other features of the mother, as an internalized object vitally influences ego development. As the relation to the whole object develops, the mother and the father, and other members of the family, are introjected as persons in good or bad aspects, according to the infant's experiences as well as according to his alternating feelings and fantasies. A world of good and bad objects is thus built up within, and here is the source of internal persecution as well as of internal riches and stability. During the first three or four months, persecutory anxiety is prevalent and exerts a pressure on the ego which severely tests its capacity to tolerate anxiety. This persecutory anxiety at times weakens the ego, at other times it acts as an impetus toward the growth of integration and intellect. In the second quarter of the first year the infant's need to preserve the loved internal object, which is felt to be endangered by his aggressive impulses, and the resulting depressive anxiety and guilt, again have a twofold effect on the ego: they may threaten to overcome it as well as spur it on toward reparation and sublimations. In these various ways at which I can only hint here, the ego is both assailed and enriched by its relation to internal objects.[1]

The specific system of phantasies centring on the infant's internal world is of supreme importance for the development of the ego. The internalized objects are felt by the young infant to have a life of their own, harmonizing or conflicting with each other and with the ego,

[1] The most up-to-date presentation of these early processes is contained in my papers.

according to the infant's emotions and experiences. When the infant feels he contains good objects, he experiences trust, confidence and security. When he feels he contains bad objects he experiences persecution and suspicion. The infant's good and bad relation to internal objects develops concurrently with that to external objects and perpetually influences its course. On the other hand, the relation to internal objects is from the outset influenced by the frustrations and gratifications which form part of the infant's everyday life. There is thus a constant interaction between the internal object world, which reflects in a phantastic way the impressions gained from without, and the external world which is decisively influenced by projection.

As I have often described, the internalized objects also form the core of the superego[1] which develops throughout the first years of childhood, reaching a climax at the stage when—according to classical theory—the super-ego as the heir of the Oedipus complex comes into being.

Since the development of ego and super-ego is bound up with processes of introjection and projection, they are inextricably linked from the outset, and since their development is vitally influenced by instinctual drives, all three regions of the mind are from the beginning of life in the closest interaction. I realize that in speaking here about the three regions of the mind I am not keeping within the topic suggested for discussion; but my conception of earliest infancy makes it impossible for me to consider exclusively the mutual influences of ego and id.

Because the perpetual interaction between the life and death instincts and the conflict arising from their antithesis (fusion and defusion) govern mental life there is in the unconscious an ever-changing flow of interacting events, of fluctuating emotions and anxieties. I have attempted to give an indication of the multitude of processes, focusing on the relation of internal and external objects which from the earliest stage onward exist in the unconscious, and I shall now draw some conclusions:

(1) The hypothesis which I have broadly outlined here represents a much wider view of early unconscious processes than was implied in Freud's concept of the structure of the mind.

(2) If we assume that the super-ego develops out of these early unconscious processes which also mould the ego, determine its functions, and shape its relation to the external world, the foundations

---

[1] The question arises: How far and under what conditions does the internalized object form part of the ego, how far of the super ego? This question, I think, raises problems which are still obscure and awaiting further elucidation. Paula Heimann (1952) has put forward some suggestions in this direction.

of ego development, as well as of super-ego formation, need to be re-examined.

(3) My hypothesis would thus lead to a reassessment of the nature and scope of the super-ego and of the ego, as well as of the inter-relation between the parts of the mind which make up the self.

I shall end by restating a well-known fact—one of which, however, we become more and more convinced the deeper we penetrate into the mind. It is the recognition that the unconscious is at the root of all mental processes, determines the whole of mental life, and therefore that only by exploring the unconscious in depth and width are we able to analyse the total personality.

# 6

## SOME THEORETICAL CONCLUSIONS REGARDING THE EMOTIONAL LIFE OF THE INFANT[1]

### (1952)

My study of the infant's mind has made me more and more aware of the bewildering complexity of the processes which operate, to a large extent simultaneously, in the early stages of development. In writing this chapter I have therefore attempted to elucidate some aspects only of the infant's emotional life during his first year, and have selected these with particular emphasis on anxieties, defences and object-relations.

### THE FIRST THREE OR FOUR MONTHS OF LIFE (THE PARANOID-SCHIZOID POSITION)[2]

#### I

At the beginning of post-natal life the infant experiences anxiety from internal and external sources. I have for many years held the view that the working of the death instinct within gives rise to the fear of annihilation and that this is the primary cause of persecutory anxiety. The first external source of anxiety can be found in the experience of birth. This experience, which, according to Freud, provides the pattern for all later anxiety-situations, is bound to influence the infant's first relations with the external world.[3] It would appear that the pain and discomfort he has suffered, as well as the loss of the intra-uterine state, are felt by him as an attack by

[1] have received valuable assistance in my contributions to this volume [*i.e. Developments in Psycho-Analysis*—see Explanatory Note to 'Anxiety and Guilt' p. 326 below.] from my friend, Lola Brook, who went carefully over my manuscripts and made a number of helpful suggestions, both as regards formulations and the arrangement of the material. I am much indebted to her for her unfailing interest in my work.

[2] In 'Notes on some Schizoid Mechanisms', which deals in more detail with this subject, I mention that I have adopted Fairbairn's term 'schizoid' in addition to my own term 'paranoid position'.

[3] In *Inhibitions, Symptoms and Anxiety*, Freud states that 'there is more continuity between intra-uterine life and earliest infancy than the impressive caesura of the act of birth would have us believe.' (*S.E.* **20**, p. 138).

hostile forces, *i.e.* as persecution.[1] Persecutory anxiety, therefore, enters from the beginning into his relation to objects in so far as he is exposed to privations.

The hypothesis that the infant's first experiences of feeding and of his mother's presence initiate an object-relation to her is one of the basic concepts put forward in this book.[2] This relation is at first a relation to a part-object, for both oral-libidinal and oral-destructive impulses from the beginning of life are directed towards the mother's breast in particular. We assume that there is always an interaction, although in varying proportions, between libidinal and aggressive impulses, corresponding to the fusion between life and death instincts. It could be conceived that in periods of freedom from hunger and tension there is an optimal balance between libidinal and aggressive impulses. This equilibrium is disturbed whenever, owing to privations from internal or external sources, aggressive impulses are reinforced. I suggest that such an alteration in the balance between libido and aggression gives rise to the emotion called greed, which is first and foremost of an oral nature. Any increase in greed strengthens feelings of frustration and in turn the aggressive impulses. In those children in whom the innate aggressive component is strong, persecutory anxiety, frustration and greed are easily aroused and this contributes to the infant's difficulty in tolerating privation and in dealing with anxiety. Accordingly, the strength of the destructive impulses in their interaction with libidinal impulses would provide the constitutional basis for the intensity of greed. However, while in some cases persecutory anxiety may increase greed, in others (as I suggested in *The Psycho-Analysis of Children*) it may become the cause of the earliest feeding inhibitions.

The recurrent experiences of gratification and frustration are powerful stimuli for libidinal and destructive impulses, for love and hatred. As a result, the breast, inasmuch as it is gratifying, is loved and felt to be 'good'; in so far as it is a source of frustration, it is hated and felt to be 'bad'. This strong antithesis between the good breast and the bad breast is largely due to lack of integration of the ego, as well as to splitting processes within the ego and in relation to the object. There are, however, grounds for assuming that even during the first three or four months of life the good and the bad object are not wholly distinct from one another in the infant's mind.

---

[1] I have suggested that the struggle between the life and death instincts already enters into the painful experience of birth and adds to the persecutory anxiety aroused by it. Cf. The 'Theory of Anxiety and Guilt'.

[2] [Melanie Klein is here referring to Isaacs (1952), Heimann (1952) and her own 'On Observing the Behaviour of Young Infants', which were published in the same volume, *Developments in Psycho-Analysis*.]

The mother's breast, both in its good and bad aspects, also seems to merge for him with her bodily presence; and the relation to her as a person is thus gradually built up from the earliest stage onwards.

In addition to the experiences of gratification and frustration derived from external factors, a variety of endopsychic processes—primarily introjection and projection—contribute to the twofold relation to the first object. The infant projects his love impulses and attributes them to the gratifying (good) breast, just as he projects his destructive impulses outwards and attributes them to the frustrating (bad) breast. Simultaneously, by introjection, a good breast and a bad breast are established inside.[1] Thus the picture of the object, external and internalized, is distorted in the infant's mind by his phantasies, which are bound up with the projection of his impulses on to the object. The good breast—external and internal—becomes the prototype of all helpful and gratifying objects, the bad breast the prototype of all external and internal persecutory objects. The various factors which enter into the infant's feelings of being gratified such as the alleviation of hunger, the pleasure of sucking, the freedom from discomfort and tension, i.e. from privations, and the experience of being loved—all these are attributed to the good breast. Conversely, every frustration and discomfort are attributed to the bad (persecuting) breast.

I shall first describe the ramifications of the infant's relation to the bad breast. If we consider the picture which exists in the infant's mind—as we can see it retrospectively in the analyses of children and adults—we find that the hated breast has acquired the oral-destructive qualities of the infant's own impulses when he is in states of frustration and hatred. In his destructive phantasies he bites and tears up the breast, devours it, annihilates it; and he feels that the breast will attack him in the same way. As urethral- and anal-sadistic impulses gain in strength, the infant in his mind attacks the breast with poisonous urine and explosive faeces, and therefore expects it to be posionous and explosive towards him. The details of his sadistic phantasies determine the content of his fear of internal and external persecutors, primarily of the retaliating (bad) breast.[2]

---

[1] These first introjected objects form the core of the super-ego. In my view the super-ego starts with the earliest introjection processes and builds itself up from the good and bad figures which are internalized in love and hatred in various stages of development and are gradually assimilated and integrated by the ego. Cf. Heimann (1952).

[2] The anxiety relating to attacks by internalized objects—first of all part-objects—is in my view the basis of hypochondria. I put forward this hypothesis in my book The Psycho-Analysis of Children, pp. 144, 264, 273, and also expounded there my view that the early infantile anxieties are psychotic in nature and the basis for later psychoses.

Since the phantasied attacks on the object are fundamentally influenced by greed, the fear of the object's greed, owing to projection, is an essential element in persecutory anxiety: the bad breast will devour him in the same greedy way as he desires to devour it.

Even during the earliest stage, however, persecutory anxiety is to some extent counteracted by the infant's relation to the good breast. I have indicated above that although his feelings focus on the feeding relationship with the mother, represented by her breast, other aspects of the mother enter already into the earliest relation to her; for even the very young infant responds to his mother's smile, her hands, her voice, her holding him and attending to his needs. The gratification and love which the infant experiences in these situations all help to counteract persecutory anxiety, even the feelings of loss and persecution aroused by the experience of birth. His physical nearness to his mother during feeding—essentially his relation to the good breast—recurrently helps him to overcome the longing for a former lost state, alleviates persecutory anxiety and increases the trust in the good object. (See note 1, p. 89.)

II

It is characteristic of the emotions of the very young infant that they are of an extreme and powerful nature. The frustrating (bad) object is felt to be a terrifying persecutor, the good breast tends to turn into the 'ideal' breast which should fulfil the greedy desire for unlimited, immediate and everlasting gratification. Thus feelings arise about a perfect and inexhaustible breast, always available, always gratifying. Another factor which makes for idealization of the good breast is the strength of the infant's persecutory fear, which creates the need to be protected from persecutors and therefore goes to increase the power of an all-gratifying object. The idealized breast forms the corollary of the persecuting breast; and in so far as idealization is derived from the need to be protected from persecuting objects, it is a method of defence against anxiety.

The instance of hallucinatory gratification may help us to understand the ways in which the process of idealization comes about. In this state, frustration and anxiety derived from various sources are done away with, the lost external breast is regained and the feeling of having the ideal breast inside (possessing it) is reactivated. We may also assume that the infant hallucinates the longed-for pre-natal state. Because the hallucinated breast is inexhaustible, greed is momentarily satisfied. (But sooner or later, the feeling of hunger turns the child back to the external world and then frustration, with all the emotions to which it gives rise, is again experienced.) In wish-fulfilling hallucination, a number of fundamental mechanisms and defences come into play. One of them is the omnipotent control of the internal and external object, for the ego assumes complete possession of both the external and internal breast. Furthermore, in hallucination the persecuting breast is kept widely apart from the ideal breast, and the experience of being frustrated from the experience of being gratified. It seems that such a cleavage, which amounts to a splitting of the object and of the feelings towards it, is linked with the process of denial. Denial in its most extreme form—as we find it in hallucinatory gratification—amounts to an annihilation of any frustrating object or situation, and is thus bound up with the strong feeling of omnipotence which obtains in the early stages of life. The situation of being frustrated, the object which causes it, the bad feelings to which frustration gives rise (as well as split-off parts of the ego) are felt to have gone out of existence, to have been annihilated, and by these means gratification and relief from persecutory anxiety are obtained. Annihilation of the persecutory object and of a persecutory situation is bound up with omnipotent control of the object in its most extreme form. I would suggest that in some measure these processes are operative in idealization as well.

It would appear that the early ego also employs the mechanism of annihilation of one split-off aspect of the object and situation in states other than wish-fulfilling hallucinations. For instance, in hallucinations of persecution, the *frightening* aspect of the object and situation seems to prevail to such an extent that the good aspect is felt to have been utterly destroyed—a process which I cannot discuss here. It seems that the extent to which the ego keeps the two aspects apart varies considerably in different states and on this may depend whether or not the aspect which is denied is felt to have gone completely out of existence.

Persecutory anxiety essentially influences these processes. We may assume that when persecutory anxiety is less strong, splitting is less far-reaching and the ego is therefore able to integrate itself and to synthesize in some measure the feelings towards the object. It might well be that any such step in integration can only come about if, at that moment, love towards the object predominates over the destructive impulses (ultimately the life instinct over the death instinct). The ego's tendency to integrate itself can, therefore, I think, be considered as an expression of the life instinct.

Synthesis between feelings of love and destructive impulses towards one and the same object—the breast—gives rise to depressive anxiety, guilt and the urge to make reparation to the injured loved object, the good breast. This implies that ambivalence is at times experienced in relation to a part-object—the mother's breast.[1] During the first few months of life, such states of integration are short-lived. At this stage the ego's capacity to achieve integration is naturally still very limited and to this contributes the strength of persecutory anxiety and of the splitting processes which are at their height. It seems that, as development proceeds, experiences of synthesis and, in consequence, of depressive anxiety, become more frequent and last longer; all this forms part of the growth of integration. With progress in integration and synthesis of the contrasting emotions towards the object, mitigation of destructive impulses by libido becomes possible.[2] This however leads to an *actual diminution* of anxiety which is a fundamental condition for normal development.

As I suggested, there are great variations in the strength, frequency and duration of splitting processes (not only between individuals but also in the same infant at different times). It is part of the complexity of early emotional life that a multitude of processes operate in swiftest alternation, or even, it seems, simultaneously. For instance, it appears that together with splitting the breast into two aspects, loved and hated (good and bad), splitting of a different nature exists which gives rise to the feeling that the ego, as well as its object, is in pieces; these processes underlie states of disintegration.[3] Such states, as I pointed out above, alternate with others in which a measure of integration of the ego and synthesis of the object increasingly comes about.

The early methods of splitting fundamentally influence the ways in which, at a somewhat later stage, repression is carried out and this in turn determines the degree of interaction between conscious and unconscious. In other words, the extent to which the various parts of the mind remain 'porous' in relation to one another is determined largely by the strength or weakness of the early schizoid mechanisms.[4] External factors play a vital part from the beginning;

[1] In my paper 'A Contribution to the Psychogenesis of Manic-Depressive States' (*Writings*, 1), I suggested that ambivalence is first experienced in relation to the complete object during the depressive position. In keeping with the modification of my view regarding the onset of depressive anxiety (cf. 'On the Theory of Anxiety and Guilt') I now consider that ambivalence, too, is already experienced in relation to part-objects.

[2] This form of interaction between libido and aggression would correspond to a particular state of fusion between the two instincts.

[3] Cf. 'Notes on some Schizoid Mechanisms'.

[4] I found that with patients of a schizoid type, the strength of their infantile schizoid mechanisms ultimately accounts for the difficulty of getting access to the unconscious. In such patients, the progress towards synthesis is hampered by the fact that under the pressure of anxiety they become again and again unable to maintain the links, which have been strengthened in the course of the analysis,

for we have reason to assume that every stimulus to persecutory fear reinforces the schizoid mechanisms, *i.e.* the tendency of the ego to split itself and the object; while every good experience strengthens the trust in the good object and makes for integration of the ego and synthesis of the object.

### III

Some of Freud's conclusions imply that the ego develops by introjecting objects. As regards the earliest phase, the good breast, introjected in situations of gratification and happiness, becomes in my view a vital part of the ego and strengthens its capacity for integration. For this internal good breast—forming also the helpful and benign aspect of the early super-ego—strengthens the infant's capacity to love and trust his objects, heightens the stimulus for introjection of good objects and situations, and is therefore an essential source of reassurance against anxiety; it becomes the representative of the life instinct within. The good object can, however, only fulfil these functions if it is felt to be in an undamaged state, which implies that it has been internalized predominantly with feelings of gratification and love. Such feelings presuppose that gratification by sucking has been relatively undisturbed by external or internal factors. The main source of internal disturbance lies in excessive aggressive impulses, which increase greed and diminish the capacity to bear frustration. In other terms, when, in the fusion of the two instincts, the life instinct predominates over the death instinct—and correspondingly libido over aggression— the good breast can be more securely established in the infant's mind.

However, the infant's oral-sadistic desires, which are active from the beginning of life and are easily stirred by frustration from external and internal sources, inevitably again and again give rise to a feeling that the breast is destroyed and in bits inside him, as a result of his greedy devouring attacks upon it. These two aspects of introjection exist side by side.

Whether feelings of frustration or gratification predominate in the infant's relation to the breast is no doubt largely influenced by external circumstances but there is little doubt that constitutional factors, influencing from the beginning the strength of the ego, have to be taken into account. I formerly made the suggestion that the

---

between different parts of the self. In patients of a depressive type, the division between unconscious and conscious is less pronounced and therefore such patients are much more capable of insight. In my view they have overcome more success-fully their schizoid mechanisms in early infancy.

ego's capacity to bear tension and anxiety, and therefore in some measure to tolerate frustration, is a constitutional factor.[1] This greater inborn capacity to bear anxiety seems ultimately to depend on the prevalence of libido over aggressive impulses, that is to say, on the part which the life instinct plays from the outset in the fusion of the two instincts.

My hypothesis that the oral libido expressed in the sucking function enables the infant to introject the breast (and nipple) as a relatively undestroyed object does not run counter to the assumption that destructive impulses are most powerful in the earliest stages. The factors which influence the fusion and defusion of the two instincts are still obscure, but there is little reason to doubt that in the relation to the first object—the breast—the ego is at times able, by means of splitting, to keep libido apart from aggression.[2]

I shall now turn to the part which projection plays in the vicissitudes of persecutory anxiety. I have described elsewhere[3] how the oral-sadistic impulses to devour and scoop out the mother's breast become elaborated into the phantasies of devouring and scooping out the mother's body. Attacks derived from all other sources of sadism soon become linked with these oral attacks and two main lines of sadistic phantasies develop. One form—mainly oral-sadistic and bound up with greed—is to empty the mother's body of everything good and desirable. The other form of phantasied attack —predominantly anal—is to fill her body with the bad substances and parts of the self which are split off and projected into her. These are mainly represented by excrements which become the means of damaging, destroying or controlling the attacked object. Or the whole self—felt to be the 'bad' self—enters the mother's body and takes control of it. In these various phantasies, the ego takes possession by projection of an external object—first of all the mother— and makes it into an extension of the self. The object becomes to some extent a representative of the ego, and these processes are in my view the basis for identification by projection or 'projective

[1] Cf. *The Psycho-Analysis of Children*, Chapter 3, p. 49 n.

[2] It is implicit in my argument (as presented here and in former writings) that I do not agree with Abraham's concept of a pre-ambivalent stage in so far as it implies that destructive (oral-sadistic) impulses first arise with the onset of teething. We have to remember, though, that Abraham has also pointed out the sadism inherent in 'vampire-like' sucking. There is no doubt that the onset of teething and the physiological processes which affect the gums are a strong stimulus for cannibalistic impulses and phantasies; but aggression forms part of the infant's earliest relation to the breast, though it is not usually expressed in biting at this stage.

[3] Cf. *The Psycho-Analysis of Children*, p. 128.

identification'.[1] Identification by introjection and identification by projection appear to be complementary processes. It seems that the processes underlying projective identification operate already in the earliest relation to the breast. The 'vampire-like' sucking, the scooping out of the breast, develop in the infant's phantasy into making his way into the breast and further into the mother's body. Accordingly, projective identification would start simultaneously with the greedy oral-sadistic introjection of the breast. This hypothesis is in keeping with the view often expressed by the writer that introjection and projection interact from the beginning of life. The introjection of a persecutory object is, as we have seen, to some extent determined by the projection of destructive impulses on to the object. The drive to project (expel) badness is increased by fear of internal persecutors. When projection is dominated by persecutory fear, the object into whom badness (the bad self) has been projected becomes the persecutor *par excellence*, because it has been endowed with all the bad qualities of the subject. The re-introjection of this object reinforces acutely the fear of internal and external persecutors. (The death instinct, or rather, the dangers attaching to it, has again been turned inwards.) There is thus a constant interaction between persecutory fear relating to the internal and external worlds, an interaction in which the processes involved in projective identification play a vital part.

The projection of love-feelings—underlying the process of attaching libido to the object—is, as I suggested, a precondition for finding a good object. The introjection of a good object stimulates the projection of good feelings outwards and this in turn by re-introjection strengthens the feeling of possessing a good internal object. To the projection of the bad self into the object and the external world corresponds the projection of good parts of the self, or of the whole good self. Re-introjection of the good object and of the good self reduces persecutory anxiety. Thus the relation to both the internal and external world improves simultaneously and the ego gains in strength and in integration.

Progress in integration which, as I suggested in an earlier section, depends on love-impulses predominating temporarily over destructive impulses, leads to transitory states in which the ego synthesizes feelings of love and destructive impulses towards one object (first the mother's breast). This synthetic process initiates further important steps in development (which may well occur simultaneously): the painful emotions of depressive anxiety and guilt arise; aggression is mitigated by libido; in consequence, persecutory anxiety is diminished; anxiety relating to the fate of the endangered external and

[1] 'Notes on some Schizoid Mechanisms'.

internal object leads to a stronger identification with it; the ego therefore strives to make reparation and also inhibits aggressive impulses felt to be dangerous to the loved object.[1]

With growing integration of the ego, experiences of depressive anxiety increase in frequency and duration. Simultaneously, as the range of perception increases, in the infant's mind the concept of the mother as a whole and unique person develops out of a relation to parts of her body and to various aspects of her personality (such as her smell, touch, voice, smile, the sound of her footsteps, etc.). Depressive anxiety and guilt gradually focus on the mother as a person and increase in intensity; the depressive position comes to the fore.

### IV

I have so far described some aspects of mental life during the first three or four months. (It must be kept in mind, though, that only a rough estimate can be given of the duration of stages of development, as there are great individual variations.) In the picture of this stage, as I presented it, certain features stand out as characteristic. The paranoid-schizoid position is dominant. The interaction between the processes of introjection and projection—re-introjection and re-projection—determines ego-development. The relation to the loved and hated—good and bad—breast is the infant's first object-relation. Destructive impulses and persecutory anxiety are at their height. The desire for unlimited gratification, as well as persecutory anxiety, contribute to the infant's feeling that both an ideal breast and a dangerous devouring breast exist, which are largely kept apart from each other in the infant's mind. These two aspects of the mother's breast are introjected and form the core of the super-ego. Splitting, omnipotence, idealization, denial and control of internal and external objects are dominant at that stage. These first methods of defence are of an extreme nature, in keeping with the intensity of early emotions and the limited capacity of the ego to bear acute anxiety. While in some ways these defences impede the path of integration, they are essential for the whole development of the ego, for they again and again relieve the young infant's anxieties. This relative and temporary security is achieved predominantly by the persecutory object being kept apart from the good one. The presence in the mind

---

[1] Abraham refers to instinctual inhibition appearing first at '. . . the stage of narcissism with a cannibalistic sexual aim' ('A Short Study of the Development of the Libido', p. 496). Since inhibition of aggressive impulses and of greed tends to involve libidinal desires as well, depressive anxiety becomes the cause of those difficulties in accepting food which occur in infants at a few months of age and increase at weaning time. As regards the earliest feeding difficulties, which arise with some infants from the first few days onwards, they are caused, in my view, by persecutory anxiety. (Cf. *The Psycho-Analysis of Children*, pp. 156–57.)

of the good (ideal) object enables the ego to maintain at times strong feelings of love and gratification. The good object also affords protection against the persecuting object because it is felt to have replaced it (as instanced by wish-fulfilling hallucination). These processes underlie, I think, the observable fact that young infants alternate so swiftly between states of complete gratification and of great distress. At this early stage the ego's ability to deal with anxiety by allowing the contrasting emotions towards the mother, and accordingly the two aspects of her, to come together is still very limited. This implies that a mitigation of the fear of the bad object by the trust in the good one and depressive anxiety only arise in fleeting experiences. Out of the alternating processes of disintegration and integration develops gradually a more integrated ego, with an increased capacity to deal with persecutory anxiety. The infant's relation to parts of his mother's body, focusing on her breast, gradually changes into a relation to her as a person.

These processes present in earliest infancy may be considered under a few headings:

(a) An ego which has some rudiments of integration and cohesion, and progresses increasingly in that direction. It also performs from the beginning of post-natal life some fundamental functions; thus it uses splitting processes and the inhibition of instinctual desires as some of the defences against persecutory anxiety, which is experienced by the ego from birth onwards.

(b) Object-relations, which are shaped by libido and aggression, by love and hatred, and permeated on the one hand by persecutory anxiety, on the other by its corollary, the omnipotent reassurance derived from the idealization of the object.

(c) Introjection and projection, bound up with the phantasy-life of the infant and all his emotions, and consequently internalized objects of a good and bad nature, which initiate super-ego development.

As the ego becomes increasingly able to sustain anxiety, the methods of defence alter correspondingly. To this contributes the growing sense of reality and the widening range of gratification, interests and object-relations. Destructive impulses and persecutory anxiety decrease in power; depressive anxiety gains in strength and comes to a climax at the period which I shall describe in the next section.

## THE INFANTILE DEPRESSIVE POSITION

I

During the second quarter of the first year certain changes in the infant's intellectual and emotional development become marked. His relation to the external world, to people as well as to things, grows more differentiated. The range of his gratifications and interests widens, and his power of expressing his emotions and communicating with people increases. These observable changes are evidence of the gradual development of the ego. Integration, consciousness, intellectual capacities, the relation to the external world and other functions of the ego are steadily developing. At the same time the infant's sexual organization is progressing; urethral, anal and genital trends increase in strength, though oral impulses and desires still predominate. There is thus a confluence of different sources of libido and aggression, which colours the infant's emotional life and brings into prominence various new anxiety-situations; the range of phantasies is widening, they become more elaborated and differentiated. Correspondingly there are important changes in the nature of defences.

All these developments are reflected in the infant's relation to his mother (and to some extent to his father and to other people). The relation to the mother as a person, which has been gradually developing while the breast still figured as the main object, becomes more fully established and the identification with her gains in strength when the infant can perceive and introject the mother as a person (or, in other words, as a 'complete object').

While some measure of integration is a precondition for the ego's capacity to introject the mother and the father as whole persons, further development on the line of integration and synthesis is initiated when the depressive position comes to the fore. The various aspects—loved and hated, good and bad—of the objects come closer together, and these objects are now whole persons. The processes of synthesis operate over the whole field of external and internal object-relations. They comprise the contrasting aspects of the internalized objects (the early super-ego) on the one hand and of the external objects on the other; but the ego is also driven to diminish the discrepancy between the external and internal world, or rather, the discrepancy between external and internal figures. Together with these synthetic processes go further steps in integration of the ego, which result in a greater coherence between the split-off parts of the ego. All these processes of integration and synthesis cause the conflict between love and hatred to come out in full force. The ensuing depressive anxiety and feeling of guilt alter not only in quantity but also in quality. Ambivalence is now experienced predominantly towards a complete object. Love and hatred have come much closer together and the 'good' and 'bad' breast, 'good' and 'bad' mother, cannot be kept as widely separated as in the earlier stage. Although the power of destructive impulses diminishes, these impulses are felt to be a great danger to the loved object, now perceived as a person. Greed and the defences against it play a significant part at this stage, for the anxiety of losing irretrievably the loved and indispensable object tends to increase greed. Greed, however, is felt to be uncontrollable and destructive and to endanger the loved external and internal objects. The ego therefore increasingly inhibits instinctual desires and this may lead to severe difficulties in the infant's enjoying or accepting food,[1] and later to serious inhibitions in establishing both affectionate and erotic relations.

The steps in integration and synthesis described above result in a greater capacity of the ego to acknowledge the increasingly poignant psychic reality. The anxiety relating to the internalized mother who is felt to be injured, suffering, in danger of being annihilated or already annihilated and lost for ever, leads to a stronger identification with the injured object. This identification reinforces both the drive to make reparation and the ego's attempts to inhibit aggressive impulses. The ego also again and again makes use of the manic defence. As we have seen already, denial, idealization, splitting and control of internal and external objects are used by the ego in order to counteract persecutory anxiety. These omnipotent methods are, in some measure, maintained when the depressive position arises but they are now predominantly used in order to counteract depressive anxiety. They also undergo changes, in keeping with the steps in integration and synthesis, that is to say they become less extreme and correspond more to the growing capacity of the ego to face psychic reality. With this altered form and aim, these early methods now constitute the manic defence.

Faced with a multitude of anxiety-situations, the ego tends to deny them and, when anxiety is paramount, the ego even denies the fact that it loves the object at all. The result may be a lasting stifling of love and turning away from the primary objects and an increase in persecutory anxiety, *i.e.* regression to the paranoid-schizoid position.[2]

[1] Such difficulties, which can be frequently observed in infants particularly at weaning (*i.e.* during the change-over from breast- to bottle-feeding or when new foods are added to bottle-feeding, etc.) can be regarded as a depressive symptom well known in the symptomatology of depressive states. This point is dealt with in some detail in 'On Observing the Behaviour of Young Infants Cf. also footnote on p. 70 above.

[2] This early regression may cause severe disturbances in early development, *e.g.* mental deficiency ('Notes on some Schizoid Mechanisms'); it may become the foundation for some form of schizophrenic illness. Another possible outcome of the failure in working through the infantile depressive position is manic-depressive illness; or a severe neurosis may ensue. I therefore hold that the infantile depressive position is of central importance in the development of the first year.

The ego's attempts to control external and internal objects—a method which, during the paranoid-schizoid position, is mainly directed against persecutory anxiety—also undergo changes. When depressive anxiety has the ascendancy, control of objects and impulses is mainly used by the ego to prevent frustration, to forestall aggression and the ensuing danger to the loved objects—that is to say, to keep depressive anxiety at bay.

There is also a difference in the use of splitting the object and the self. The ego, although earlier methods of splitting continue in some degree, now divides the complete object into an uninjured live object and an injured and endangered one (perhaps dying or dead); splitting thus becomes largely a defence against depressive anxiety.

At the same time, important steps in ego-development take place, which not only enable the ego to evolve more adequate defences against anxiety but also eventually result in an actual diminution of anxiety. The continued experience of facing psychic reality, implied in the working through of the depressive position, increases the infant's understanding of the external world. Accordingly the picture of his parents, which was at first distorted into idealized and terrifying figures, comes gradually nearer to reality.

As has been discussed earlier in this chapter, when the infant introjects a more reassuring external reality, his internal world improves; and this by projection in turn benefits his picture of the external world. Gradually, therefore, as the infant re-introjects again and again a more realistic and reassuring external world and also in some measure establishes within himself complete and uninjured objects, essential developments in the super-ego organization take place. As, however, good and bad internal objects come closer together—the bad aspects being mitigated by the good ones—the relation between the ego and super-ego alters, that is to say, a progressive assimilation of the super-ego by the ego takes place. (See note 2, p. 90.)

At this stage, the drive to make reparation to the injured object comes into full play. This tendency, as we have seen earlier, is inextricably linked with feelings of guilt. When the infant feels that his destructive impulses and phantasies are directed against the complete person of his loved object, guilt arises in full strength and, together with it, the over-riding urge to repair, preserve or revive the loved injured object. These emotions in my view amount to states of mourning, and the defences operating to attempts on the part of the ego to overcome mourning.

Since the tendency to make reparation ultimately derives from the life instinct, it draws on libidinal phantasies and desires. This tendency enters into all sublimations, and remains from that stage

74

onwards the great means by which depression is kept at bay and diminished.

It appears that there is no aspect of mental life which is not, in the early stages, used by the ego in defence against anxiety. The reparative tendency too, first employed in an omnipotent way, becomes an important defence. The infant's feelings (phantasy) might be described as follows: 'My mother is disappearing, she may never return, she is suffering, she is dead. No, this can't be, for I can revive her.'

Omnipotence decreases as the infant gradually gains a greater confidence both in his objects and in his reparative powers.[1] He feels that all steps in development, all new achievements are giving pleasure to the people around him and that in this way he expresses his love, counter-balances or undoes the harm done by his aggressive impulses and makes reparation to his injured loved objects.

Thus the foundations for normal development are laid: relations to people develop, persecutory anxiety relating to internal and external objects diminishes, the good internal objects become more firmly established, a feeling of greater security ensues, and all this strengthens and enriches the ego. The stronger and more coherent ego, although it makes much use of the manic defence, again and again brings together and synthesizes the split-off aspects of the object and of the self. Gradually the processes of splitting and synthesizing are applied to aspects kept apart less widely from one another; perception of reality increases and objects appear in a more realistic light. All these developments lead to a growing adaptation to external and internal reality.[2]

There is a corresponding change in the infant's attitude towards frustration. As we have seen, in the earliest stage the bad persecutory aspect of the mother (her breast) came to stand in the child's mind for everything frustrating and evil, internal as well as external. When the infant's sense of reality in relation to his objects and trust in them increases, he becomes more capable of distinguishing between frustration imposed from without and phantastic internal dangers. Accordingly hatred and aggression become more closely related to the actual frustration or harm derived from external factors. This is a step towards a more realistic and objective method of dealing with his own aggression, which rouses less guilt and ultimately enables the child to experience, as well as to sublimate, his aggression in a more ego-syntonic way.

[1] It can be observed in the analyses both of adults and children that, together with a full experience of depression, feelings of hope emerge. In early development, this is one of the factors which help the infant to overcome the depressive position.

[2] As we know, splitting under the stress of ambivalence to some extent persists throughout life and plays an important part in normal mental economy.

In addition, this more realistic attitude towards frustration—which implies that persecutory fear relating to internal and external objects has diminished—leads to a greater capacity in the infant to re-establish the good relation to his mother and to other people when the frustrating experience no longer operates. In other words, the growing adaptation to reality—bound up with changes in the working of introjection and projection—results in a more secure relation to the external and internal world. This leads to a lessening of ambivalence and aggression which makes it possible for the drive for reparation to play its full part. In these ways the process of mourning arising from the depressive position is gradually worked through.

When the infant reaches the crucial stage of about three to six months and is faced with the conflicts, guilt and sorrow inherent in the depressive position, his capacity for dealing with his anxiety is to some degree determined by his earlier development; that is to say by the extent to which during the first three or four months of life he has been able to take in and establish his good object which forms the core of his ego. If this process has been successful—and this implies that persecutory anxiety and splitting processes are not excessive and that a measure of integration has come about—persecutory anxiety and schizoid mechanisms gradually lose in strength, the ego is able to introject and establish the complete object and to go through the depressive position. If, however, the ego is unable to deal with the many severe anxiety-situations arising at this stage—a failure determined by fundamental internal factors as well as by external experiences—a strong regression from the depressive position to the earlier paranoid-schizoid position may take place. This would also impede the processes of introjection of the complete object and strongly affect the development during the first year of life and throughout childhood.

II

My hypothesis of the infantile depressive position is based on fundamental psycho-analytic concepts regarding the early stages of life; that is to say, primary introjection and the preponderance of oral libido and cannibalistic impulses in young infants. These discoveries by Freud and Abraham have materially contributed to the understanding of the etiology of mental illnesses. By developing these concepts and relating them to the understanding of infants, as it emerged from the analyses of young children, I came to realize the complexity of early processes and experiences and their effect on the infant's emotional life; and this in turn was bound to throw more light on the etiology of mental disturbances. One of my conclusions was that there exists a particularly close link between the infantile depressive position and the phenomena of mo irning and melancholia.[1]

Continuing Freud's work on melancholia, Abraham pointed out one of the fundamental differences between normal mourning on the one hand and abnormal mourning on the other. (See Note 3, p. 19.) In normal mourning the individual succeeds in establishing the lost loved person within his ego, whereas in melancholia and abnormal mourning this process is not successful. Abraham also described some of the fundamental factors upon which that success or failure depends. If cannibalistic impulses are excessive, the introjection of the lost loved object miscarries, and this leads to illness. In normal mourning, too, the subject is driven to reinstate the lost loved person within the ego; but this process succeeds. Not only are the cathexes attached to the lost loved object withdrawn and reinvested, as Freud put it, but during this process the lost object is established within.

In my paper on 'Mourning and its Relation to Manic-Depressive States', I expressed the following view: 'My experience leads me to conclude that, while it is true that the characteristic feature of normal mourning is the individual's setting up the lost loved object inside himself, he is not doing so for the first time but, through the work of mourning, is reinstating that object as well as all his loved *internal* objects which he feels he has lost.' Whenever grief arises, it undermines the feeling of secure possession of the loved internal objects, for it revives the early anxieties about injured and destroyed objects—about a shattered inner world. Feelings of guilt and persecutory anxieties—the infantile depressive position—are reactivated in full strength. A successful reinstating of the *external* love object which is being mourned, and whose introjection is intensified through the process of mourning, implies that the loved *internal* objects are restored and regained. Therefore the testing of reality characteristic of the process of mourning is not only the means of renewing the links to the external world but of *re-establishing the disrupted inner world*. Mourning thus involves the repetition of the emotional situation the infant experienced during the depressive position. For under the stress of fear of loss of the loved mother, the infant struggles with the task of establishing and integrating his inner world, of building up securely the good objects within himself.

One of the fundamental factors in determining whether or not the

[1] For the relation of the infantile depressive position to manic-depressive states on the one hand and to normal grief on the other, cf. my 'A Contribution to the Psychogenesis of Manic-Depressive States' and 'Mourning and its Relation to Manic-Depressive States' (both in *Writings*, 1).

loss of a loved object (through death or other causes) will lead to manic-depressive illness or will be normally overcome is, in my experience, the extent to which, in the first year of life, the depressive position has been successfully worked through and the loved introjected objects securely established within.

The depressive position is bound up with fundamental changes in the infant's libidinal organization, for during this period—about the middle of the first year—the infant enters upon the early stages of the direct and inverted Oedipus complex. I shall restrict myself here to the broadest outline only in giving an account of the early stages of the Oedipus complex.[1] These early stages are characterized by the important rôle which part-objects still play in the infant's mind while the relation to complete objects is being established. Also, though genital desires are coming strongly to the fore, the oral libido is still leading. Powerful oral desires, increased by the frustration experienced in relation to the mother, are transferred from the mother's breast to the father's penis.[2] Genital desires in the infant of either sex coalesce with oral desires and therefore an oral, as well as a genital, relation to the father's penis ensues. Genital desires are also directed towards the mother. The infant's desires for the father's penis are bound up with jealousy of the mother because he feels she receives this desired object. These manifold emotions and wishes in either sex underlie both the inverted and the direct Oedipus complex.

Another aspect of the early Oedipus stages is bound up with the essential part which the mother's 'inside', and his own 'inside', play in the young infant's mind. During the preceding period, when destructive impulses prevail (paranoid-schizoid position), the infant's urge to enter his mother's body, and take possession of its contents, is predominantly of an oral and anal nature. This urge is still active in the following stage (depressive position), but when genital desires increase it is directed more towards the father's penis (equated to babies and faeces) which, he feels, the mother's body contains. Simultaneously the oral desires for the father's penis lead to its internalization, and this internalized penis—both as a good and bad object—comes to play an important part in the infant's internal object world.

---

[1] See Heimann (1952), Part 2. I have given detailed accounts of the Oedipus development in my *Psycho-Analysis of Children* (particularly Chapter 8); also in my papers 'Early Stages of the Oedipus Conflict' and 'The Oedipus Complex in the Light of Early Anxieties' (*Writings*, 1).

[2] Abraham writes, in 'A Short Study of the Development of the Libido' (1924), p. 490: 'Another point to be noted in regard to the part of the body that has been introjected is that the penis is regularly assimilated to the female breast, and that other parts of the body, such as the finger, the foot, hair, faeces and buttocks, can be made to stand for those two organs in a secondary way. . . .'

The early stages of the Oedipus development are of the greatest complexity: desires from various sources converge; these desires are directed towards part-objects as well as towards whole objects; the father's penis, both desired and hated, exists not only as a part of the father's body, but is also simultaneously felt by the infant to be inside himself and inside the mother's body.

Envy appears to be inherent in oral greed. My analytic work has shown me that envy (alternating with feelings of love and gratification) is first directed towards the feeding breast. To this primary envy jealousy is added when the Oedipus situation arises. The infant's feelings in relation to both parents seem to run like this: when he is frustrated, father or mother enjoys the desired object of which he is deprived—mother's breast, father's penis—and enjoys it constantly. It is characteristic of the young infant's intense emotions and greed that he should attribute to the parents a constant state of mutual gratification of an oral, anal and genital nature.

These sexual theories are the foundation for combined parent figures such as: the mother containing the father's penis or the whole father; the father containing the mother's breast or the whole mother; the parents fused inseparably in sexual intercourse.[1] Phantasies of this nature also contribute to the notion of 'the woman with a penis'. Furthermore, owing to internalization, the infant establishes such combined parent figures within himself, and this proves fundamental for many anxiety-situations of a psychotic nature.

As, gradually, a more realistic relation to the parents develops, the infant comes to consider them as separate individuals, that is to say, the primitive combined parent figures lose in strength.[2]

These developments are interlinked with the depressive position. In both sexes, the fear of the loss of the mother, the primary loved object—that is to say, depressive anxiety—contributes to the need for substitutes; and the infant first turns to the father, who at this stage is also introjected as a complete person, to fulfil this need.

In these ways, libido and depressive anxiety are deflected to some extent from the mother, and this process of distribution stimulates

[1] Cf. the concept of the combined parent figure in *The Psycho-Analysis of Children*, particularly Chapter 8.

[2] The infant's capacity to enjoy at the same time the relation to *both* parents, which is an important feature in his mental life and conflicts with his desires, prompted by jealousy and anxiety, to separate them, depends on his feeling that they are separate individuals. This more integrated relation to the parents (which is distinct from the compulsive need to keep the parents apart from one another and to prevent their sexual intercourse) implies a greater understanding of their relation to one another and is a precondition for the infant's hope that he can bring them together and unite them in a happy way.

object-relations as well as diminishes the intensity of depressive feelings. The early stages of the direct and inverted Oedipus complex thus bring relief to the anxieties of the child and help him to overcome the depressive position. At the same time, however, new conflicts and anxieties arise, since the Oedipus wishes towards the parents imply that envy, rivalry and jealousy—at this stage still powerfully stirred by oral-sadistic impulses—are now experienced towards two people who are both hated and loved. The working through of these conflicts, first arising in the early stages of the Oedipus complex, is part of the process of modification of anxiety which extends beyond babyhood into the first years of childhood.

To sum up: the depressive position plays a vital part in the child's early development and, normally, when the infantile neurosis comes to an end at about five years of age, persecutory and depressive anxieties have undergone modification. The fundamental steps in working through the depressive position are, however, made when the infant is establishing the complete object—that is to say, during the second half of the first year—and one might contend that if these processes are successful, one of the preconditions for normal development is fulfilled. During this period persecutory and depressive anxiety are again and again activated, as for instance in the experiences of teething and weaning. This interaction between anxiety and physical factors is one aspect of the complex processes of development (involving all the infant's emotions and phantasies) during the first year; to some extent indeed this applies to the whole of life.

I have emphasized throughout this chapter that the changes in the emotional development and object-relations of the infant are of a gradual nature. The fact that the depressive position develops gradually explains why, usually, its effect on the infant does not appear in a sudden way.[1] Also we have to keep in mind that while depressive feelings are experienced, the ego simultaneously develops methods of counteracting them. This, is my view, is one of the fundamental differences between the infant who is experiencing anxieties of a psychotic nature and the psychotic adult; for, at the same time as the infant goes through these anxieties, the processes leading to their modification are already at work. (See Note 4, p. 92.)

[1] Nevertheless, signs of recurrent depressive feelings can, with close observation, be detected in normal infants. Severe symptoms of depression occur quite strikingly in young infants in certain circumstances, such as illness, sudden separation from the mother or nurse, or change of food.

## FURTHER DEVELOPMENT AND THE MODIFICATION OF ANXIETY

### I

The infantile neurosis can be regarded as a combination of processes by which anxieties of a psychotic nature are bound, worked through and modified. Fundamental steps in the modification of persecutory and depressive anxiety are part of the development during the first year. The infantile neurosis, as I see it, therefore begins within the first year of life and comes to an end when, with the onset of the latency period, modification of early anxieties has been achieved.

All aspects of development contribute towards the process of modifying anxiety and, therefore, the vicissitudes of anxiety can only be understood in their interaction with all developmental factors. For instance, acquiring physical skills; play activities; the development of speech and intellectual progress in general; habits of cleanliness; the growth of sublimations; the widening of the range of object-relations; the progress in the child's libidinal organization—all these achievements are inextricably interwoven with aspects of the infantile neurosis, ultimately with the vicissitudes of anxiety and the defences evolved against it. Here I can only single out a few of these interacting factors and indicate how they contribute to the modification of anxiety.

The first persecutory objects, external and internal, are—as discussed already—the mother's bad breast and the father's bad penis; and persecutory fears relating to internal and external objects interact. These anxieties, focusing first on the parents, find expression in the early phobias and greatly affect the relation of the child to his parents. Both persecutory and depressive anxiety contribute fundamentally to the conflicts arising in the Oedipus situation[1] and influence libidinal development.

The genital desires towards both parents, which initiate the early stages of the Oedipus complex (at about the middle of the first year), are at first interwoven with oral, anal and urethral desires and phantasies, both of a libidinal and aggressive nature. The anxieties of a psychotic nature, to which destructive impulses from all these sources give rise, tend to reinforce these impulses and, if excessive, make for strong fixations to the pre-genital stages.[2]

[1] The interrelation between persecutory and depressive anxieties on the one hand and castration fear on the other is discussed in detail in my paper 'The Oedipus Complex in the Light of Early Anxieties' (*Writings*, 1).

[2] Heimann and Isaacs (1952).

The libidinal development is thus at every step influenced by anxiety. For anxiety leads to fixation to pre-genital stages and again and again to regression to them. On the other hand, anxiety and guilt and the ensuing reparative tendency add impetus to libidinal desires and stimulate the forward trend of the libido; for giving and experiencing libidinal gratification alleviate anxiety and also satisfy the urge to make reparation. Anxiety and guilt, therefore, at times check, and at other times enhance the libidinal development. This varies not only between one individual and another but may vary in one and the same individual, according to the intricate inter-action between internal and external factors at any given time.

In the fluctuating positions of the direct and inverted Oedipus complex, all the early anxieties are experienced; for jealousy, rivalry and hatred in these positions again and again stir up persecutory and depressive anxiety. Anxieties focusing on the parents as internal objects, however, are gradually worked through and diminished as the infant derives an increasing feeling of security from the relation to the external parents.

In the interplay between progression and regression, which is strongly influenced by anxiety, genital trends gradually gain the ascendant. As a result, the capacity for reparation increases, its range widens and sublimations gain in strength and stability; for on the genital level they are bound up with the most creative urge of man. Genital sublimations in the feminine position are linked with fertility—the power to give life—and thus also with the re-creation of lost or injured objects. In the male position, the element of life-giving is reinforced by the phantasies of fertilizing and thus restoring or reviving the injured or destroyed mother. The genital, therefore, represents not only the organ of procreation but also the means of repairing and creating anew.

The ascendancy of genital trends implies a great progress in ego-integration, for these trends take over libidinal and reparative desires of a pre-genital nature and thus a synthesis between pre-genital and genital reparative tendencies comes about. For instance, the capacity to receive 'goodness', in the first place the desired food and love from the mother, and the urge to feed her in return, and thus to restore her—the basis for oral sublimations—are a precondition for a successful genital development.

The growing strength of the genital libido, which includes progress in the capacity to make reparation, goes side by side with a gradual lessening of the anxiety and guilt aroused by destructive tendencies, notwithstanding that in the oedipal situation genital desires are the cause of conflict and guilt. It follows that genital primacy implies a diminution of oral, urethral and anal trends and anxieties. In the process of working through the Oedipus conflicts and achieving genital primacy, the child becomes able to establish his good objects securely in his inner world and to develop a stable relation to his parents. All this means that he is gradually working through and modifying persecutory and depressive anxiety.

There are grounds to assume that as soon as the infant turns his interest towards objects other than the mother's breast—such as parts of her body, other objects around him, parts of his own body, etc.—a process starts which is fundamental for the growth of sublimations and object-relations. Love, desires (both aggressive and libidinal) and anxieties are transferred from the first and unique object, the mother, to other objects; and new interests develop which become substitutes for the relation to the primary object. This primary object is, however, not only the external but also the internalized good breast; and this deflection of the emotions and creative feelings, which become related to the external world, is bound up with projection. In all these processes, the function of symbol-formation and phantasy activity is of great significance.[1] When depressive anxiety arises, and particularly with the onset of the depressive position, the ego feels driven to project, deflect and distribute desires and emotions, as well as guilt and the urge to make reparation, on to new objects and interests. These processes, in my view, are a mainspring for sublimations throughout life. It is, however, a precondition for a successful development of sublimations (as well as of object-relations and of the libidinal organization), that love for the first objects can be maintained while desires and anxieties are deflected and distributed. For, if grievance and hatred towards the first objects predominate, they tend to endanger sublimations and the relation to substitute objects.

Another disturbance of the capacity for reparation and consequently for sublimations arises if, owing to a failure in overcoming the depressive position, the hope of making reparation is impeded or, to put it otherwise, if there is despair about the destruction wrought on loved objects.

## II

As suggested above, all aspects of development are bound up with infantile neurosis. A characteristic feature of the infantile neurosis is

[1] I have to refrain here from describing in detail the ways in which symbol-formation from the beginning is inextricably bound up with the phantasy-life of the child and with the vicissitudes of anxiety. I refer here to Isaacs (1952) and my 'On The Behaviour of Young Infants' (this volume); also to some of my former writings, 'Early Analysis' (1926) and 'The Importance of Symbol-Formation in the Development of the Ego' (1930).

the early phobias which begin during the first year of life and, changing in form and content, appear and reappear throughout the years of childhood. Both persecutory and depressive anxieties underlie the early phobias, which include difficulties with food, *pavor nocturnus*, anxiety relating to the mother's absence, fear of strangers, disturbances in relations with the parents and object-relations in general. The need to externalize persecutory objects is an intrinsic element in the mechanism of phobias.[1] This need derives from persecutory anxiety (relating to the ego) as well as from depressive anxiety (centring on the dangers threatening the good internal objects from internal persecutors). Fears of internal persecution also find expression in hypochrondriacal anxieties. They also contribute to a variety of physical illnesses, *e.g.* the frequent colds of young children.[2]

Oral, urethral and anal anxieties (which enter into both the acquiring and the inhibiting of habits of cleanliness) are basic features in the symptomatology of the infantile neurosis. It is also a characteristic feature of infantile neurosis that during the first years of life relapses of various kinds occur. As we have seen above, if anxiety of a persecutory and depressive nature is reinforced, a regression to the earlier stages and to the corresponding anxiety-situations takes place. Such regression manifests itself for instance in the breaking down of already established habits of cleanliness; or phobias apparently overcome may reappear in slightly changed forms.

During the second year, obsessional trends come to the fore; they both express and bind oral, urethral and anal anxieties. Obsessional features can be observed in bed-time rituals, rituals to do with cleanliness or food and so on, and in a general need for repetition (*e.g.* the desire to be told again and again the same stories, even with the same expressions, or to play the same games over and over again). These phenomena, though part of the child's normal development, can be described as neurotic symptoms. The lessening or overcoming of these symptoms amounts to a modification of oral, urethral and anal anxieties; this, in turn, implies a modification of persecutory and depressive anxieties.

The capacity of the ego step by step to evolve defences which enable it in some measure to work through anxieties is an essential

[1] Cf. *The Psycho-Analysis of Children*, pp. 125, 156-61.

[2] My experience has shown me that those anxieties which underlie hypochondriasis are also at the root of hysterical conversion symptoms. The fundamental factor common to both is the fear relating to persecution within the body (attacks by internalized persecutory objects, or to the harm done to internal objects by the subject's sadism, such as attacks by his dangerous excrements) — all of which is felt as physical damage inflicted on the ego. The elucidation of the processes underlying the transformation of these persecutory anxieties into physical symptoms might throw further light on the problems of hysteria.

part of the process of modification of anxiety. In the earliest stage (paranoid-schizoid), anxiety is counteracted by extreme and powerful defences, such as splitting, omnipotence and denial.[1] In the following stage (depressive position), the defences undergo, as we have seen, significant changes which are characterized by the ego's greater capacity to sustain anxiety. As in the second year further progress in ego-development takes place, the infant makes use of his growing adaptation to external reality and of his growing control of bodily functions in the testing of internal dangers by external reality.

All these changes are characteristic of the obsessional mechanisms which can also be regarded as a very important defence. For instance, by acquiring habits of cleanliness, the infant's anxieties about his dangerous faeces (i.e. his destructiveness), his bad internalized objects and internal chaos are again and again temporarily diminished. Control of the sphincter proves to him that he can control inner dangers and his internal objects. Furthermore, the actual excrements serve as evidence against his phantastic fears of their destructive quality. They can now be ejected in conformity with the demands of mother or nurse who, by showing approval of the conditions under which the excrements are produced, also seem to approve of the nature of the faeces, and this makes the faeces 'good'.[2] As a result, the infant might feel that the harm which, in his aggressive phantasies, was done by his excrements to his internal and external objects can be undone. The acquiring of habits of cleanliness, therefore, also diminishes guilt and satisfies the drive to make reparation.[3]

Obsessional mechanisms form an important part of ego-development. They enable the ego to keep anxiety temporarily at bay. This in turn helps the ego to achieve greater integration and strength;

[1] If these defences persist excessively beyond the early stage to which they are appropriate, development may suffer in various ways; integration is impeded, phantasy-life and libidinal desires are hampered; in consequence the reparative tendency, sublimations, object-relations and the relation to reality may be impaired.

[2] The recognition that there is a need in the child to acquire habits of cleanliness, a need which is bound up with anxiety and guilt and the defences against it, leads to the following conclusion. Training in cleanliness, if applied without pressure and at a stage when the urge for it becomes apparent (which is usually in the course of the second year) is helpful for the child's development. If imposed on the child at an earlier stage, it may be harmful. Furthermore, at any stage the child should only be encouraged but not forced to acquire habits of cleanliness. This is necessarily a very incomplete reference to an important problem of upbringing.

[3] Freud's view on reaction-formations and 'undoing' in the process of obsessional neurosis underlies my concept of reparation, which in addition embraces the various processes by which the ego feels it undoes harm done in phantasy, restores, preserves and revives the object.

thereby the gradual working through, diminishing and modifying of anxiety become possible. However, obsessional mechanisms are only one of the defences at this stage. If they are excessive and become the main defence, this can be taken as an indication that the ego cannot effectively deal with anxiety of a psychotic nature and that a severe obsessional neurosis is developing in the child.

Another fundamental change in defences characterizes the stage at which the genital libido gains in strength. When this happens, as we have seen, the ego is more integrated; the adaptation to external reality has improved; the function of consciousness has expanded; the super-ego is also more integrated; a fuller synthesis of unconscious processes, that is to say within the unconscious parts of the ego and super-ego, has come about; the demarcation between conscious and unconscious is more distinct. These developments make it possible for repression to take a leading part among the defences.[1] An essential factor in repression is the reprimanding and prohibiting aspect of the super-ego, an aspect which as a result of progress in the super-ego organization gains in strength. The demands of the super-ego to keep out of consciousness certain impulses and phantasies, both of an aggressive and libidinal nature, are more easily met by the ego because it has progressed both in integration and in assimilation of the super-ego.

I have described in a former section that even during the first months of life the ego inhibits instinctual desires, initially under pressure of persecutory and, somewhat later, of depressive anxieties. A further step in the development of instinctual inhibitions comes about when the ego can make use of repression.

We have seen the ways in which the ego uses splitting during the paranoid-schizoid phase.[2] The mechanism of splitting underlies repression (as is implied in Freud's concept); but in contrast to the earliest forms of splitting which lead to states of disintegration, repression does not normally result in a disintegration of the self. Since at this stage there is greater integration, within both the conscious and the unconscious parts of the mind, and since in repression the splitting predominantly effects a division between conscious and unconscious, neither part of the self is exposed to the degree of disintegration which may arise in previous stages. However, the extent to which splitting processes are resorted to in the first few months of

---

[1] Cf. Freud. '. . . we shall bear in mind for future consideration the possibility that repression is a process which has a special relation to the genital organization of the libido and that the ego resorts to other methods of defence when it has to secure itself against the libido on other levels of organization.' (*Inhibitions, Symptoms and Anxiety*, S.E. **20**, p. 125).

[2] Cf. 'Notes on some Schizoid Mechanisms'.

life vitally influences the use of repression at a later stage. For if early schizoid mechanisms and anxieties have not been sufficiently overcome, the result may be that instead of a fluid boundary between the conscious and unconscious, a rigid barrier between them arises; this indicates that repression is excessive and that, in consequence, development is disturbed. With moderate repression, on the other hand, the unconscious and conscious are more likely to remain 'porous' to one another and therefore impulses and their derivatives are, in some measure, allowed to come up again and again from the unconscious and are subjected by the ego to a procedure of selection and rejection. The choice of the impulses, phantasies and thoughts which are to be repressed depends on the increased capacity of the ego to accept the standards of the external objects. This capacity is linked with the greater synthesis within the super-ego and the growing assimilation of the super-ego by the ego.

The changes in the structure of the super-ego, which come about gradually, and are throughout linked with the oedipal development, contribute to the decline of the Oedipus complex at the onset of the latency period. In other words, the progress in the libidinal organization and the various adjustments of which the ego becomes capable at this stage are bound up with the modification of persecutory and depressive anxieties relating to the internalized parents, which implies greater security in the inner world.

Viewed in the light of the vicissitudes of anxiety, the changes characteristic of the onset of the latency period could be summarized as follows: the relation with the parents is more secure; the introjected parents approximate more closely to the picture of the real parents; their standards, their admonitions and prohibitions are accepted and internalized and therefore the repression of the Oedipus desires is more effective. All this represents a climax of the super-ego development which is the result of a process extending over the first years of life.

## CONCLUSION

I have discussed in detail the first steps in overcoming the depressive position which characterize the latter half of the first year of life. We have seen that in the earliest stages, when persecutory anxiety predominates, the infant's objects are of a primitive and persecutory nature; they devour, tear up, poison, flood, etc., that is to say, the variety of oral, urethral and anal desires and phantasies are projected on to the external as well as on to the internalized objects. The picture of these objects alters step by step in the infant's mind as the libidinal organization progresses and anxiety becomes modified.

His relations to both his internal and his external world improve simultaneously; the interdependence between these relations implies changes in the processes of introjection and projection which are an essential factor in diminishing persecutory and depressive anxieties. All this results in a greater capacity of the ego to assimilate the super-ego, and in this way the strength of the ego increases.

When stabilization is achieved, some fundamental factors have undergone alteration. I am not concerned at this point with the progress of the ego—which, as I have tried to show, is at every step bound up with the emotional development and the modification of anxiety—it is the *changes in unconscious* processes which I wish to underline. These changes become, I think, more understandable if we link them with the origin of anxiety. Here I refer back to my contention that destructive impulses (the death instinct) are the primary factor in the causation of anxiety.[1] Greed is increased by grievances and hatred, that is to say, by manifestations of the destructive instinct; but these manifestations are in turn reinforced by persecutory anxiety. When, in the course of development, anxiety both diminishes and is more securely kept at bay, grievances and hatred as well as greed diminish, and this ultimately leads to a lessening of ambivalence. To express this in terms of instincts: when the infantile neurosis has run its course, that is to say, when persecutory and depressive anxieties have been diminished and modified, the balance in the fusion of the life and death instincts (and thus between libido and aggression) has in some ways altered. This implies important changes in unconscious processes, that is to say, in the structure of the super-ego and in the structure and domain of the unconscious (as well as conscious) parts of the ego.

We have seen that the fluctuations between libidinal positions and between progression and regression which characterize the first years of childhood are inextricably linked with the vicissitudes of the persecutory and depressive anxieties arising in early infancy. These anxieties are thus not only an essential factor in fixation and regression but also perpetually influence the course of development.

It is a precondition for normal development that in the interplay between regression and progression fundamental aspects of the progress already achieved are maintained. In other words, that the process of integration and synthesis is not fundamentally and permanently disturbed. If anxiety is gradually modified, progression is bound to dominate over regression and, in the course of the infantile neurosis, the basis for mental stability is established.

[1] Cf. 'The Theory of Anxiety and Guilt' (this volume).

## NOTES

1 (*p.* 64)

Margaret A. Ribble has reported observations on 500 infants ('Infantile Experience in Relation to Personality Development', 1944), and expressed views, some of which are complementary to conclusions I reached through the analysis of young children.

Thus, regarding the relation to the mother from the beginning of life, she stresses the infant's need to be 'mothered' which goes beyond the gratification by sucking; *e.g.* on p. 631, she says:

'Much of the quality and the cohesiveness of a child's personality depends upon an emotional attachment to the mother. This attachment or, to use the psycho-analytic term, cathexis for the mother grows gradually out of the satisfaction it derives from her. We have studied the nature of this developing attachment which is so elusive yet so essential in considerable detail. Three types of sensory experience, namely, tactile, kinaesthetic, or the sense of body position, and sound, contribute primarily to its formation. The development of these sensory capacities has been mentioned by nearly all observers of infantile behaviour . . . but their particular importance for the personal relation between mother and child has not been emphasized.'

The importance of this personal relation for the physical development of the child is stressed by her in various places; *e.g.* on p. 630 she says:

'. . . the most trivial irregularities in the personal care and handling of any baby, such as too little contact with the mother, too little handling, or changes of nurses or in general routine, frequently result in such disturbances as pallor, irregular breathing, and feeding disturbances. In infants who are constitutionally sensitive or poorly organized, these disturbances, if they are too frequent, may permanently alter the organic and psychic development, and not infrequently they threaten life itself.'

In another passage the author summarizes these disturbances as follows (p. 630):

'The infant is, by its very incompleteness of brain and nervous system, continuously in potential danger of functional disorganization. Outwardly the danger is that of sudden separation from the mother who either intuitively or knowingly must sustain this functional balance. Actual neglect or lack of love may be equally disastrous. Inwardly the danger appears to be the mounting of tension from biological needs and the inability of the organism to maintain its inner energy or metabolic equilibrium and reflex excitability. The *need for oxygen* may become acute because the young infant's breathing mechanisms are not well enough developed to work adequately with the increasing inner demand caused by rapid forebrain development.'

These functional disturbances which, according to M. Ribble's observation, may amount to a danger to life, could be interpreted as an expression of the death instinct which, according to Freud, is primarily directed against the organism itself (*Beyond the Pleasure Principle*). I have contended that this danger which stirs up the fear of annihilation, of death, is the primary cause of anxiety. The fact that the biological, physiological and psychological factors are bound up from the beginning of post-natal life is illustrated by M. Ribble's observations. I would draw the further conclusion that the mother's consistent and loving care of the baby, which strengthens his libidinal relation to her (and which, with infants who are 'constitutionally sensitive or poorly organized', is even essential for keeping them alive), supports the life instinct in its struggle against the death instinct. In the present paper and in 'The Theory of Anxiety and Guilt' (this volume) I discuss this point more fully.

Another issue on which Dr Ribble's conclusions coincide with mine relates to the changes which she describes as occurring approximately by the third month. These changes can be regarded as the physiological counterpart to the features of emotional life which I describe as the onset of the depressive position. She says (p. 643):

'By this time, the organic activities of breathing, of digesting, and of circulating blood have begun to show considerable stability, indicating that the autonomic nervous system has taken over its specific functions. We know from anatomical studies that the foetal system of circulation is usually obliterated by this time. . . . At about this time, typical adult patterns of brain waves begin to appear in the electro-encephalogram . . . and they probably indicate a more mature form of cerebral activity. Outbursts of emotional reaction, not always well differentiated but obviously expressing positive or negative direction, are seen to involve the entire motor system. . . . The eyes focus well and can follow the mother about, the ears function well and can differentiate the sounds she makes. Sound or sight of her produces the positive emotional responses formerly obtained only from contact, and consist of appropriate smiling and even genuine outbursts of joy.'

These changes are, I think, bound up with the diminution of splitting processes and with progress in ego-integration and object-relations, particularly with the capacity of the infant to perceive and to introject the mother as a whole person—all of which I have described as happening in the second quarter of the first year with the onset of the depressive position.

## 2 (p. 74)

If these fundamental adjustments in the relation between the ego and the super-ego have not sufficiently come about in early development, it is one of the essential tasks of the psycho-analytic procedure to enable the patient to make them retrospectively. This is only possible by the analysis of the earliest stages of development (as well as of later ones), and by a thorough analysis of the negative as well as of the positive transference. In the fluctuating transference situation, the external and internal figures— good and bad — which primarily shape the super-ego development and object-relations, are transferred on to the psycho-analyst. Therefore at times he is bound to stand for frightening figures, and only in this way can the infantile persecutory anxieties be fully experienced, worked through and diminished. If the psycho-analyst is inclined to reinforce the positive transference, he avoids playing in the patient's mind the part of bad figures and is predominantly introjected as a good object. Then, in some cases, belief in good objects may be strengthened; but such a gain may be far from stable, for the patient has not been enabled to experience the hatred, anxiety and suspicion which in the early stages of life were related to the frightening and dangerous aspects of the parents. It is only by analysing the negative as well as the positive transference that the psychoanalyst appears alternately in the rôle of good and bad objects, is alternately loved and hated, admired and dreaded. The patient is thus enabled to work through, and therefore to modify, early anxiety-situations; the splitting between the good and bad figures decreases; they become more synthesized, that is to say, aggression becomes mitigated by libido. In other words, persecutory and depressive anxieties are diminished, as one might say, at the root.

## 3 (*p.* 91)

Abraham referred to the fixation of libido at the oral level as one of the fundamental etiological factors in melancholia. He described this fixation in a particular case as follows: 'In his depressive states he would be overcome by longing for his mother's breast, a longing that was indescribably powerful and different from anything else. If the libido still remains fixated on this point when the individual is grown up, then one of the most important conditions for the appearance of a melancholic depression is fulfilled.' (*Selected Papers*, p. 458.)

Abraham substantiated his conclusions, which threw new light on the connection between melancholia and normal mourning, by extracts from two case-histories. These were actually the first two cases of manic-depression to undergo a thorough analysis—a new venture in the development of psycho-analysis. Up to that time not much clinical material had been published in support of Freud's discovery regarding melancholia. As Abraham said (*loc. cit.*, pp. 433–4): 'Freud described in general outlines the psycho-sexual processes that take place in the melancholic. He was able to obtain an intuitive idea of them from the occasional treatment of depressive patients; but not very much clinical material has been published up till now in the literature of psycho-analysis in support of this theory.'

But even from these few cases Abraham had come to understand that already in childhood (at the age of five) there had been an actual state of melancholia. He said he would be inclined to speak of 'a "primal parathymia" ensuing from the boy's Oedipus complex' and concluded this description as follows: 'It is this state of mind that we call melancholia' (p. 469).

Sandor Radó, in his paper 'The Problem of Melancholia' (1928) went further and considered that the root of melancholia can be found in the hunger situation of the suckling baby. He said: 'The deepest fixation-point in the depressive disposition is to be found in the situation of threatened loss of love (Freud), more especially in the hunger situation of the suckling baby.' Referring to Freud's statement that in mania the ego is once more merged with the super-ego in unity, Radó inferred that 'this process is the faithful intra-psychic repetition of the experience of that fusing with the mother that takes place during drinking at her breast'. Nevertheless, Radó did not apply this conclusion to the emotional life of the infant; he referred only to the etiology of melancholia.

4 (p. 80)

The picture of the first six months of life which I have outlined in these two sections implies a modification of some concepts presented in my *Psycho-Analysis of Children*. I there described the confluence of aggressive impulses from all sources as the 'phase of maximal sadism'. I still believe that aggressive impulses are at their height during the stage in which persecutory anxiety predominates; or, in other words, that persecutory anxiety is stirred up by the destructive instinct and is constantly fed by the projection of destructive impulses on to objects. For it is inherent in the nature of persecutory anxiety that it increases hatred and attacks against the object who is felt to be persecutory, and this in turn reinforces the feeling of persecution.

Some time after *The Psycho-Analysis of Children* was published I worked out my concept of the depressive position. As I now see it, with the advance in object-relations between three to six months of age, both destructive impulses and persecutory anxiety diminish and the depressive position arises. While, therefore, my views have not altered regarding the close connection between persecutory anxiety and the predominance of sadism, I have to make an alteration as far as dating is concerned. Formerly I suggested that the phase when sadism is at its height is about the middle of the first year; now I would say that this phase extends over the first three months of life and corresponds to the paranoid-schizoid position described in the first section of this chapter. If we were to assume a certain individually varying sum-total of aggression in the young infant, this amount, I think, would be no less at the beginning of postnatal life than at the stage when cannibalistic, urethral and anal impulses and phantasies operate in full strength. Considered in terms of quantity only (a point of view which, however, does not take into account the various other factors determining the operation of the two instincts) it could be said that, as more sources of aggression are tapped and more manifestations of aggression become possible, a process of distribution takes place. It is inherent in development that an increasing number of aptitudes, both physical and mental, gradually come into play; and the fact that impulses and phantasies from various sources overlap, interact and reinforce one another can also be considered as expressing progress in integration and synthesis. Furthermore, to the confluence of aggressive impulses and phantasies corresponds the confluence of oral, urethral and anal phantasies of a libidinal nature. This means that the struggle between libido and aggression is carried out over a wider field. As I said in my *Psycho-Analysis of Children*, p. 150:

'The emergence of the stages of organization with which we are acquainted corresponds, I would say, not only to the positions which the libido has won and established in its struggle with the destructive instinct, but, since these two components are for ever united as well as opposed, to a growing adjustment between them.'

The infant's capacity to enter into the depressive position and to establish the complete object within himself implies that he is not as strongly ruled by destructive impulses and persecutory anxiety as at an earlier stage. Increasing integration brings about changes in the nature of his anxiety, for when love and hatred become more synthesized in relation to the object this gives rise, as we have seen, to great mental pain—to depressive feelings and guilt. Hatred becomes to some extent mitigated by love, whereas feelings of love are to some extent affected by hatred, the result being that the infant's emotions towards his objects change in quality. At the same time the progress in integration and in object-relations enables the ego to develop more effective ways of dealing with the destructive impulses and the anxiety to which they give rise. However, we must not lose sight of the fact that sadistic impulses, particularly since they are operative at various zones, are a most potent factor in the infant's conflicts arising at this stage; for the essence of the depressive position consists of the infant's anxiety lest his loved object be harmed or destroyed by his sadism.

The emotional and mental processes during the first year of life (and recurring throughout the first five or six years) could be defined in terms of success or failure in the struggle between aggression and libido; and the working through of the depressive position implies that in this struggle (which is renewed at every mental or physical crisis) the ego is able to develop adequate methods of dealing with and modifying persecutory and depressive anxieties—ultimately of diminishing and keeping at bay aggression directed against loved objects.

I chose the term 'position' in regard to the paranoid and depressive phases because these groupings of anxieties and defences, although arising first during the earliest stages, are not restricted to them but occur and recur during the first years of childhood and under certain circumstances in later life.

# 7

# ON OBSERVING THE BEHAVIOUR
# OF YOUNG INFANTS

## (1952)

I

THE theoretical conclusions presented in the previous chapter are derived from psycho-analytic work with young children.[1] We should expect such conclusions to be substantiated by observations of infants' behaviour during the first year of life. This corroborative evidence, however, has its limitations, for, as we know unconscious processes are only partly revealed in behaviour, whether of infants or adults. Keeping this reservation in mind, we are able to gain some confirmation of psycho-analytic findings in our study of babies.

Many details of infants' behaviour which formerly escaped attention or remained enigmatic, have become more understandable and significant through our increased knowledge of early unconscious processes; in other words, our faculty for observation in this particular field has been sharpened. We are, no doubt, hampered in our study of young infants by their inability to talk, but there are many details of early emotional development which we can gather by means other than language. If we are to understand the young infant, though, we need not only greater knowledge but also a full sympathy with him, based on our unconscious being in close touch with his unconscious.

I now propose to consider a few details of infant behaviour in the light of the theoretical conclusions put forward in various recent papers. Since I shall take little account here of the many variations which exist within the range of fundamental attitudes, my description is bound to be rather over-simplified. Also, all inferences which I shall draw as to further development must be qualified by the following consideration. From the beginning of postnatal life and at every stage of development, external factors affect the outcome. Even with adults, as we know, attitudes and character may be favourably or unfavourably influenced by environment and circum-

[1] The analysis of adults, too, if carried to deep layers of the mind, affords similar material and provides convincing proof regarding the earliest as well as later stages of development.

stances, and this applies to a far greater extent to children. Therefore, in relating conclusions drawn from my psycho-analytic experience to the study of young infants, I am only suggesting possible, or, one might say, probable lines of development.

The new-born infant suffers from persecutory anxiety aroused by the process of birth and by the loss of the intra-uterine situation. A prolonged or difficult delivery is bound to intensify this anxiety. Another aspect of this anxiety-situation is the necessity forced on the infant to adapt himself to entirely new conditions.

These feelings are in some degree relieved by the various measures taken to give him warmth, support and comfort, and particularly by the gratification he feels in receiving food and in sucking the breast. These experiences, culminating in the first experience of sucking, initiate, as we may assume, the relation to the 'good' mother. It appears that these gratifications in some way also go towards making up for the loss of the intra-uterine state. From the first feeding experience onwards, losing and regaining the loved object (the good breast) become an essential part of infantile emotional life.

The infant's relations to his first object, the mother, and towards food are bound up with each other from the beginning. Therefore the study of fundamental patterns of attitudes towards food seems the best approach to the understanding of young infants.[1]

The initial attitude towards food ranges from an apparent absence of greed to great avidity. At this point I shall, therefore, briefly recapitulate some of my conclusions regarding greed: I suggested in the previous paper that greed arises when, in the interaction between libidinal and aggressive impulses, the latter are reinforced; greed may be increased from the outset by persecutory anxiety. On the other hand, as I pointed out, the infant's earliest feeding inhibitions can also be attributed to persecutory anxiety; this means that persecutory anxiety in some cases increases greed and in others inhibits it. Since greed is inherent in the first desires directed towards the breast, it vitally influences the relation to the mother and object-relations in general.

II

Considerable differences in the attitude towards sucking are noticeable in babies even during the first few days of life,[2] and

[1] As regards the fundamental importance of oral traits for character-formation, cf. Abraham, 'Character-formation on the Genital Level of the Libido' (1925).

[2] Michael Balint (in 'Individual Differences in Early Infancy', pp. 57–79, 81–117) concluded from observations of 100 infants ranging in age from five days to eight months that the sucking rhythm varies from one infant to another, each infant having his individual rhythm or rhythms.

become more pronounced as time goes on. We have, of course, to take into full consideration every detail in the way the infant is fed and handled by his mother. It can be observed that an initially promising attitude towards food may be disrupted by adverse feeding conditions; whereas difficulties in sucking can sometimes be mitigated by the mother's love and patience.[1] Some children who, although good feeders, are not markedly greedy, show unmistakable signs of love and of a developing interest in the mother at a very early stage—an attitude which contains some of the essential elements of an object-relation. I have seen babies as young as three weeks interrupt their sucking for a short time to play with the mother's breast or to look towards her face. I have also observed that young infants—even as early as in the second month—would in wakeful periods after feeding lie on the mother's lap, look up at her, listen to her voice and respond to it by their facial expression; it was like a loving conversation between mother and baby. Such behaviour implies that gratification is as much related to the object which gives the food as to the food itself. Marked indications of an object-relation at an early stage, together with pleasure in food, augur well, I think, both for future relations with people and for emotional development as a whole. We might conclude that in these children anxiety is not excessive in proportion to the strength of the ego, *i.e.* that the ego is already in some measure able to sustain frustration and anxiety and to deal with them. At the same time we are bound to assume that the innate capacity for love which shows itself in an early object-relation can only develop freely because anxiety is not excessive.

It is interesting to consider from this angle the behaviour of some infants in their first few days of life, as described by Middlemore under the heading of 'sleepy satisfied sucklings'.[2] She accounts for their behaviour in the following terms: 'Because their sucking reflex was not immediately elicited, they were free to approach the breast in various ways.' These infants by the fourth day fed steadily and were very gentle in the approach to the breast. '. . . they seemed to like licking and mouthing the nipple as much as they liked sucking.

---

[1] We must keep in mind, though, that however important these first influences are, the impact of the environment is of major importance *at every stage* of the child's development. Even the good effect of the earliest upbringing can be to some extent undone through later harmful experiences, just as difficulties arising in early life may be diminished through subsequent beneficial influences. At the same time we have to remember that some children seem to bear unsatisfactory external conditions without severe harm to their character and mental stability, whereas with others, in spite of favourable surroundings, serious difficulties arise and persist.

[2] *The Nursing Couple*, pp. 49–50.

An interesting outcome of the forward distribution of pleasant feeling was the habit of play. One sleepy child began each feed by playing with the nipple in preference to sucking. During the third week, the mother contrived to shift the accustomed play to the end of the feed, and this persisted throughout ten months of breast-feeding, to the delight of mother and child' (*loc. cit.*). Since the 'sleepy satisfied sucklings' both developed into good feeders and continued the play at the breast, I would assume that with them the relation to the first object (the breast) was from the beginning as important as the gratification derived from sucking and from food. One could go still further. It may be due to somatic factors that in some babies the sucking reflex is not immediately elicited, but there is good reason to believe that mental processes are also involved. I would suggest that the gentle approach to the breast preceding the pleasure in sucking may also in some measure result from anxiety.

I have referred in the previous paper to my hypothesis that difficulties in sucking occurring at the beginning of life are bound up with persecutory anxiety. The infant's aggressive impulses towards the breast tend to turn it in his mind into a vampire-like or devouring object, and this anxiety could inhibit greed and in consequence the desire to suck. I would therefore suggest that the 'sleepy satisfied suckling' might deal with this anxiety by restraining the desire to suck until he has established a safe libidinal relation to the breast by licking and mouthing it. This would imply that from the beginning of post-natal life some infants attempt to counteract the persecutory anxiety about the 'bad' breast by establishing a 'good' relation to the breast. Those infants who are already able at such an early stage to turn markedly to the object appear to have, as suggested above, a strong capacity for love.

Let us consider from this angle another group Middlemore describes. She observed that four out of seven 'active satisfied sucklings' were biting the nipple and that these babies did not 'bite the nipple in trying to get a better hold on it; the two babies who bit most frequently had easy access to the breast'. Furthermore, 'the active babies who bit the nipple most often seemed somewhat to enjoy biting; their biting was leisurely and quite unlike the uneasy chewing and gnawing of unsatisfied babies. . . .'[1] This early expression of pleasure in biting might lead us to conclude that destructive impulses

[1] Middlemore suggests that impulses to bite enter into the infant's aggressive behaviour towards the nipple long before he has any teeth and even though he rarely grips the breast with his gums. In this connection (*loc. cit.*, pp. 58–9) she refers to Waller (section 'Breast Feeding' in *The Practitioner's Encyclopaedia of Midwifery and the Diseases of Women*), who 'speaks of excited babies biting angrily at the breast, and attacking it with painful vigour'.

were unrestrained in these children and therefore that greed and the libidinal desire to suck were unimpaired. However, even these babies were not as unrestrained as might appear, for three out of seven 'refused a few of their earlier feeds with struggles and screaming protests. Sometimes they screamed at the gentlest handling and contact with the nipple while evacuation occurred at the same time; but at the next feed they were sometimes intent upon sucking'.[1] This, I think, indicates that greed may be reinforced by anxiety in contrast to the 'sleepy satisfied sucklings' in whom anxiety causes greed to be restrained.

Middlemore mentioned that of the seven 'sleepy satisfied' infants she observed, six were handled very gently by their mothers, whereas with some 'unsatisfied sucklings' the mothers' anxiety was aroused and she became impatient. Such an attitude is bound to increase anxiety in the child and thus a vicious circle is established.

As regards the 'sleepy satisfied sucklings', if, as I suggested, the relation to the first object is used as a fundamental method of counteracting anxiety, any disturbance in the relation to the mother is bound to stir up anxiety and may lead to severe difficulties in taking food. The mother's attitude seems to matter less in the case of the 'active satisfied sucklings', but this may be misleading. As I see it, with these infants the danger does not lie so much in the disturbance in feeding (although even with very greedy children, feeding inhibitions occur) as in the impairment of the object-relation.

The conclusion is that with all children the mother's patient and understanding handling from the earliest days onwards is of the greatest moment. This is seen more clearly as a result of our increased knowledge of early emotional life. As I have pointed out, 'The fact that a good relation to its mother and to the external world helps the baby to overcome its early paranoid anxieties throws a new light on the importance of the earliest experiences. From its inception analysis has always laid stress on the importance of the child's early experiences, but it seems to me that only since we know more about the nature and contents of its early anxieties, and the continuous interplay between its actual experiences and its phantasy-life, are we able fully to understand *why* the external factor is so important.'[2]

At every step, persecutory and depressive anxieties may be reduced, or, for that matter, increased, by the mother's attitude; and the extent to which helpful or persecutory figures will prevail in the infant's unconscious is strongly influenced by his actual experiences, primarily with his mother, but also soon with the father and other members of the family.

[1] *Loc. cit.*, pp. 47–8.
[2] Cf. 'A Contribution to the Psychogenesis of Manic-Depressive States' (*Writings*, 1).

III

The close bond between a young infant and his mother centres on the relation to her breast. Although, from the earliest days onwards, the infant also responds to other features of the mother—her voice, her face, her hands—the fundamental experiences of happiness and love, of frustration and hatred, are inextricably linked with the mother's breast. This early bond with the mother, which is strengthened as the breast is being securely established in the inner world, basically influences all other relationships, in the first place with the father; it underlies the capacity to form any deep and strong attachment to one person.

With bottle-fed babies the bottle can take the place of the breast if it is given in a situation approximating to breast-feeding, *i.e.* if there is close physical nearness to the mother and the infant is handled and fed in a loving way. Under such conditions the infant may be able to establish within himself an object felt to be the primary source of goodness. In this sense he takes into himself the good breast, a process which underlies a secure relation to the mother. It would appear, however, that the introjection of the good breast (the good mother) differs in some ways between children who are breast-fed and those who are not. It is beyond the frame of the present chapter to elaborate on these differences and their effect on mental life. (See note 1, p. 117.)

In my description of very early object-relations I have referred to children who are good feeders but do not show excessive greed. Some very greedy infants also give early signs of a developing interest in people in which, however, a similarity to their greedy attitude towards food can be detected. For instance, an impetuous need for the presence of people often seems to relate less to the person than to the attention desired. Such children can hardly bear to be left alone and appear to require constantly either gratification by food or by attention. This would indicate that greed is reinforced by anxiety and that there is a failure both in establishing securely the good object in the inner world and in building up trust in the mother as a good external object. This failure may foreshadow future difficulties: for instance, a greedy and anxious need for company, which often goes with the fear of being alone, and may result in unstable and transitory object-relations which could be described as 'promiscuous'.

IV

To turn now to the bad feeders. A very slow taking of food often implies lack of enjoyment, *i.e.* of libidinal gratification; this, if coupled with an early and marked interest in the mother and in other people, suggests that object-relations are partly used as an escape from persecutory anxiety attaching to food. Although good relations to people may develop in such children, the excessive anxiety which manifests itself in this attitude to food remains a danger to emotional stability. One of the various difficulties which may arise later is an inhibition in taking in sublimated food, *i.e.* a disturbance in intellectual development.

A marked refusal of food (as compared with slow feeding) is clearly an indication of a severe disturbance, although with some children this difficulty diminishes when new foods are introduced, *e.g.* bottle instead of breast, or solid food instead of liquid.

A lack of enjoyment of food or complete refusal of it, if combined with a deficiency in developing object-relations, indicates that the paranoid and schizoid mechanisms, which are at their height during the first three to four months of life, are excessive or not being adequately dealt with by the ego. This in turn suggests that destructive impulses and persecutory anxiety are prevalent, ego-defences inadequate and modification of anxiety insufficient.

Another type of deficient object-relation is characteristic of some over-greedy children. With them food becomes almost the exclusive source of gratification and little interest in people develops. I would conclude that they too, do not successfully work through the paranoid-schizoid position.

v

The young infant's attitude towards frustration is revealing. Some infants—among them good feeders—may refuse food when a meal is delayed, or give other signs of a disturbance in the relation to the mother. Infants who show both pleasure in food and love for the mother bear frustration over food more easily, the ensuing disturbance in the relation to the mother is less severe and its effects do not last so long. This is an indication that trust in the mother and love for her are relatively well established.

These fundamental attitudes also influence the way bottle-feeding (supplementing breast-feeding or as a substitute for it) is accepted even by very young infants. Some babies experience a strong sense of grievance when the bottle is introduced; they feel it to be a loss of the primary good object and a deprivation imposed by the 'bad' mother. Such feelings do not necessarily manifest themselves in the repudiation of the new food; but the persecutory anxiety and distrust stirred up by this experience may disturb the relation to the mother and therefore increase phobic anxieties, such as fear of strangers (at this early stage new food is in a sense a stranger); or difficulties over food may appear later on, or the acceptance of food in sublimated forms, *e.g.* knowledge, may be impeded.

Other babies accept the new food with less resentment. This implies a greater actual tolerance of deprivation, which is different from an apparent submission to it and derives from a relatively secure relation to the mother, enabling the infant to turn to a new food (and object) while maintaining love for her.

The following instance illustrates the way in which a baby came to accept bottles supplementing breast-feeding. The infant girl *A* was a good feeder (but not excessively greedy) and soon gave those indications of a developing object-relation which I have described above. These good relations to food and to the mother were shown in the leisurely way in which she took her food, coupled with evident enjoyment of it; in her occasional interruption of her feed, when only a few weeks old, to look up at the mother's face or at her breast; a little later on, in even taking friendly notice of the family during her feed. In the sixth week a bottle had to be introduced following the evening feed, because the breast milk was insufficient. *A* took the bottle without difficulty. In the tenth week, however, she showed on two evenings signs of reluctance while drinking from the bottle, but finished it. On the third evening she refused it altogether. There seemed no physical nor mental disturbance at the time; sleep and appetite were normal. The mother, not wishing to force her, put her into the cot after the breast feed, thinking she might go to sleep. The child cried with hunger, so the mother, without picking her up, gave her the bottle which she now emptied eagerly. The same thing happened on the subsequent evenings: when on the mother's lap, the infant refused the bottle, but took it at once when she was put into her cot. After a few days the baby accepted the bottle while she was still in her mother's arms and sucked readily this time; there was no more difficulty when other bottles were introduced.

I would assume that depressive anxiety had been increasing and had, at this point, led to the baby's revulsion against the bottle given immediately after breast-feeding. This would suggest a relatively early onset of depressive anxiety[1] which, however, is in keeping with the fact that in this baby the relation to her mother developed very early and markedly; changes in this relation had been quite noticeable during the few weeks preceding the refusal of the bottle. I would conclude that because of the increase in depressive anxiety the nearness to the mother's breast and its smell heightened both the infant's desire to be fed by it and the frustration caused by the breast being empty. When she was lying in her cot *A* accepted the bottle because, as I would suggest, in this situation the new food was

[1] In my view, as stated in the preceding chapter, depressive anxiety already operates to some extent during the first three months of life and comes to a head during the second quarter of the first year.

kept apart from the desired breast which, at that moment, had turned into the frustrating and injured breast. In this way she may have found it easier to keep the relation to the mother unimpaired by the hatred stirred up by frustration, that is to say, to keep the good mother (the good breast) intact.

We have still to explain why after a few days the baby accepted the bottle on her mother's lap and subsequently had no more difficulties over bottles. I think that during these days she had succeeded in dealing with her anxiety sufficiently to accept with less resentment the substitute object together with the primary one; this would imply an early step towards a distinction between food and the mother, a distinction which in general proves of fundamental importance for development.

I shall now quote an instance in which a disturbance in the relation with the mother arose without being immediately connected with frustration over food. A mother told me that when her infant *B* was five months old she had been left crying longer than usual. When at last the mother came to pick up the child, she found her in a 'hysterical' state; the baby looked terrified, was evidently frightened of her, and did not seem to recognize her. Only after some time did she fully re-establish contact with her mother. It is significant that this happened in day-time, when the child was awake and not long after a meal. This child usually slept well, but from time to time woke up crying for no apparent reason. There are good grounds for the assumption that the same anxiety which was underlying the day-time crying was also the cause for the disturbed sleep. I would suggest that because the mother did not come when she was longed for, she turned in the child's mind into the bad (persecuting) mother, and that for this reason the child did not seem to recognize her and was frightened of her.

The following instance is also revealing. A twelve-week-old infant girl *C* was left sleeping in the garden. She woke and cried for her mother, but her crying was not heard because a strong wind was blowing. When the mother at last came to pick her up, the baby had obviously been crying for a long time, her face was bathed in tears, and her ordinarily plaintive cry had turned into uncontrollable screaming. She was carried indoors, still screaming, and her mother's attempts to soothe her came to nothing. Eventually, though it was nearly an hour before her next feed was due, the mother resorted to offering her the breast—a remedy which had never failed when the child had been upset on previous occasions (though she had never screamed so persistently and violently before). The baby took the breast and began sucking lustily, but after a few sucks she rejected the breast and resumed her screaming. This continued until she put her fingers into her mouth and began sucking them. She often sucked her fingers, and on many occasions put them into her mouth when offered the breast. As a rule, the mother had only gently to remove the fingers and substitute the nipple and the baby would begin feeding. This time, however, she refused the breast and again screamed loudly. It took a few moments before she sucked her fingers again; her mother allowed her to suck them for some minutes, rocking and soothing her at the same time, till the baby was sufficiently calm to take the breast and sucked herself to sleep. It would appear that with this baby, for the same reasons as in the previous instance, the mother (and her breast) had turned bad and persecuting, and therefore the breast could not be accepted. After an attempt to suck, she found that she could not re-establish the relation to the good breast. She resorted to sucking her fingers, that is to say to an auto-erotic pleasure (Freud). I would, however, add that in this instance the narcissistic withdrawal was caused by the disturbance in the relation to the mother, and that the infant refused to give up sucking her fingers because they were more trustworthy than the breast. By sucking them she re-established the relation to the internal breast and thus regained enough security to renew the good relation to the external breast and mother.[1] Both these instances also add, I think, to our understanding of the mechanism of early phobias, *e.g.* the fear stirred by the mother's absence (Freud).[2] I would suggest that the phobias which arise during the first months of life are caused by persecutory anxiety which disturbs the relation to the internalized and the external mother.[3]

The division between the good and bad mother and the strong (phobic) anxiety relating to the bad one are also illustrated by the following instance. A ten-month-old boy *D* was held up to the window by his grandmother and watched the street with great interest. When he looked round, he suddenly saw very close to him the unfamiliar face of a visitor, an elderly woman, who had just come in and was standing beside the grandmother. He had an anxiety-attack which only subsided when the grandmother took him out of the room. My conclusion is that at this moment the child felt that the 'good' grandmother had disappeared and that the stranger represented the 'bad' grandmother (a division based on the splitting of the mother into a good and bad object). I shall return to this instance later on.

[1] See Heimann (1952), Part 2, section (*b*), 'Auto-Erotism, Narcissism and the Earliest Relations to Objects'.

[2] *Inhibitions, Symptoms and Anxiety*, pp. 169, 170.

[3] See 'The Emotional life of the Infant' and 'The Theory of Anxiety and Guilt' (this volume).

This explanation of early anxieties also throws a new light on the phobia of strangers (Freud). In my view the persecutory aspect of the mother (or the father), which largely derives from destructive impulses towards them, is transferred on to strangers.

## VI

Disturbances of the kind I have described in the young infant's relation to his mother are already observable during the first three or four months of life. If these disturbances are very frequent and last long they can be taken as an indication that the paranoid-schizoid position is not being dealt with effectively.

A persistent lack of interest in the mother even at this early stage, to which a little later on is added an indifference towards people in general and towards toys, suggests a more severe disturbance of the same order. This attitude can also be observed in young infants who are not bad feeders. To the superficial observer these children, who do not cry much, may appear as contented and 'good'. From the analysis of adults and children, whose severe difficulties I could trace back to babyhood, I concluded that many such infants are in fact mentally ill and withdrawn from the external world owing to strong persecutory anxiety and excessive use of schizoid mechanisms. In consequence depressive anxiety cannot be successfully overcome; the capacity for love and object-relations, as well as phantasy-life, is inhibited; the process of symbol-formation is impeded, resulting in an inhibition of interests and sublimations.

Such an attitude which could be described as apathetic is distinct from the behaviour of a really contented infant who at times demands attention, cries when he feels frustrated, gives various signs of his interest in people and pleasure in their company, and is yet at other times quite happy by himself. This indicates a feeling of security about his internal and external objects; he can bear the temporary absence of the mother without anxiety because the good mother is relatively secure in his mind.

## VII

In other sections I have described the depressive position from various angles. To consider here the effect of depressive anxiety first of all in connection with phobias: so far I have related them to persecutory anxiety only and illustrated this point of view by some instances. Thus I assumed that the five-month-old baby girl B was frightened of her mother who in her mind had changed from the good into the bad mother, and that this persecutory anxiety also disturbed her sleep. I would now suggest that the disturbance in the relation to the mother was caused by depressive anxiety as well.

When the mother did not return, the anxiety lest the good mother was lost because greed and aggressive impulses had destroyed her came to the fore; this depressive anxiety was bound up with the persecutory fear that the good mother had changed into the bad one.

In the following instance depressive anxiety was also stirred up by the infant missing the mother. From the age of six or seven weeks, the infant girl C had been accustomed to play on her mother's lap during the hour preceding her evening feed. One day, when the baby was five months and one week old, the mother had visitors and was too busy to play with the baby who, however, received a good deal of attention from the family and the visitors. Her mother gave her the evening feed, put her to bed as usual, and the infant soon dropped off to sleep. Two hours later she woke and cried persistently; she refused milk (which at this stage was already occasionally given by spoon as a supplement and was usually accepted) and went on crying. Her mother gave up the attempt to feed her, and the baby settled down contentedly on her lap for an hour, playing with the mother's fingers, was then given her night feed at the usual time and quickly fell asleep. This disturbance was most unusual; she may have woken up on other occasions after the evening feed, but it was only once when she was ill (about two months previously) that she had woken up and cried. Except for the omission of the play with the mother there had been no break in the normal routine to account for the baby waking up and crying. There was no sign of hunger or physical discomfort; she had been happy all day and slept well during the night following the incident.

I would suggest that the baby's crying was caused by her having missed the playtime with her mother. C had a very strong personal relation with her and always thoroughly enjoyed this particular hour. While at other waking periods she was quite content by herself, at this time of the day she would get restless and obviously expected her mother to play with her until the evening feed. If having missed this gratification caused the disturbance in her sleep, we are led to further conclusions. We should have to assume that the baby had a memory of the experience of this particular enjoyment at this particular time of the day; that the playtime was for the baby not only a strong satisfaction of libidinal desires but was also felt to be a proof of the loving relationship with the mother—ultimately of the secure possession of the good mother; and that this gave her a feeling of security before falling asleep, bound up with the memory of the playtime. Her sleep was disturbed not only because she missed this libidinal gratification but also because this frustration stirred up in the infant both forms of anxiety: depressive anxiety lest she should have lost the good mother through her aggressive impulses and, consequently, feelings of guilt[1]; also persecutory anxiety lest the mother should have turned bad and destructive. My general conclusion is that from about three or four months onwards both forms of anxiety underlie phobias.

The depressive position is bound up with some of the important changes which can be observed in young infants towards the middle of the first year (although they begin somewhat earlier and develop gradually). Persecutory and depressive anxieties at this stage express themselves in various ways, e.g. an increased fretfulness, a greater need for attention, or temporary turning away from the mother, sudden attacks of temper, and a greater fear of strangers; also children who normally sleep well sometimes sob in their sleep or suddenly wake up crying with distinct signs of fear or sadness. At this stage the facial expression changes considerably; the greater capacity for perception, the greater interest in people and things and the ready response to human contacts are all reflected in the child's appearance. On the other hand, there are signs of sadness and suffering which, although transient, contribute to the face becoming more expressive of emotions, both of a deeper nature and a wider range.

## VIII

The depressive position comes to a head at the time of weaning. While, as described in earlier passages, progress in integration and the corresponding synthetic processes in relation to the object give rise to depressive feelings, these feelings are further intensified by the experience of weaning.[2] At this stage the infant has already under-

---

[1] With somewhat older infants it can easily be observed that if they are not given the particular signs of affection expected by them at bedtime their sleep is likely to be disturbed; and that this intensification of the need for love at the moment of parting is bound up with feelings of guilt and the wish to be forgiven and to be reconciled with the mother.

[2] S. Bernfeld in his *Psychology of the Infant* (1929) came to the important conclusion that weaning is bound up with depressive feelings. He describes the varied behaviour of infants at the time of weaning, ranging from hardly noticeable longing and sorrow to actual apathy and complete refusal of nourishment, and compares the states of anxiety and restlessness, irritability and a certain apathy which may take possession of an adult with a similar condition in the infant. Among the methods of overcoming the frustration of weaning he mentions the withdrawal of the libido from the disappointing object through projection and repression. He qualifies the use of the term 'repression' as borrowed from the developed state of the adult'. But he nevertheless concludes that '. . . its essential properties exist in these processes' (in the infant) (p. 296). Bernfeld suggests that weaning is the first obvious cause from which pathological mental development branches off and that the nutritional neuroses of infants are contributory factors to the predisposition to neurosis. One of his conclusions is that, since some of the processes by which the infant overcomes his sorrow and feeling of loss at weaning

gone earlier experiences of loss, *e.g.* when the intensely desired breast
(or bottle) does not immediately reappear and the infant feels that
it will never come back. The loss of the breast (or bottle), however,
occurring at weaning is of a different order. This loss of the first
loved object is felt to confirm all the infant's anxieties of a persecutory and depressive nature. See note 2, p. 118.)

The following instance will serve as an illustration. The infant
*E*, weaned from his last breast feed at nine months, showed no particular disturbance in his attitude to food. He had by that time
already accepted other foods and throve on them. But he showed an
increased need for the mother's presence and in general for attention
and company. One week after the last breast feed, he sobbed in his
sleep, woke up with signs of anxiety and unhappiness and could not
be comforted. The mother resorted to letting him suck the breast
once more. He sucked both breasts for about the usual time, and
although there was obviously little milk he seemed completely satisfied, went happily to sleep and the symptoms described above were
much reduced after this experience. This would go to show that
depressive anxiety relating to the loss of the good object, the breast,
had been allayed by the very fact that it reappeared.

At the time of weaning some infants show less appetite, some an
increased greed, while others oscillate between these two responses.
Such changes occur at every step in weaning. There are babies who
enjoy the bottle much more than being suckled even though some
of them have been satisfactorily breast-fed; with others appetite
much improves when solid foods are introduced, and again there are
infants who at this point develop difficulties over eating which persist in some form or other throughout the early years of childhood.[1]
Many infants find only certain tastes, certain textures of solid food
acceptable and repudiate others. When we analyse children we learn
a good deal about the motives of such 'fads' and come to recognize
as their deepest root the earliest anxieties in relation to the mother. I
shall illustrate this conclusion by an instance of the behaviour of a
five-month-old baby girl *F* who had been breast-fed but who had
also had bottles from the beginning. She refused with violent anger
solid food such as vegetables when given them by her mother, and

---

work noiselessly, a conclusion about 'the effects of weaning will have to be drawn
from an intimate knowledge of the child's reaction to its world and its activities,
*which are the expression of its phantasy-life, or at least are the nucleus of it*'. (*Loc. cit.*,
p. 259, my italics.)

[1] In her *Social Development in Young Children*, particularly Chapter 3, Section
II.A.i., Susan Isaacs gave instances of feeding difficulties and discussed them in
connection with anxieties arising from oral sadism. There are also some interesting
observations in D. W. Winnicott's *Disorders of Childhood*, particularly pp. 16 and 17.

accepted them quite calmly when her father fed her. After a fortnight she accepted the new foods from her mother. According to a reliable report, the child, who is now six years old, has a good relation with both parents as well as with her brother, but shows consistently little appetite.

We are reminded here of the baby girl *A* and the way she accepted supplementary bottles. With baby *F*, too, some time elapsed before she could adapt herself sufficiently to the new food to take it from her mother.

Throughout this paper I have attempted to show that the attitude towards food is fundamentally bound up with the relation to the mother and involves the whole of the infant's emotional life. The experience of weaning stirs up the infant's deepest emotions and anxieties, and the more integrated ego develops strong defences against them; both anxieties and defences enter into the infant's attitudes towards food. Here I must confine myself to a few generalizations about changes in attitudes towards food at the time of weaning. At the root of many difficulties over new food is the persecutory fear of being devoured and poisoned by the mother's bad breast, a fear which derives from the infant's phantasies of devouring and poisoning the breast.[1] To persecutory anxiety, at a somewhat later stage, is added (though in varying degrees) the depressive anxiety lest greed and aggressive impulses should destroy the loved object. During and after the process of being weaned this anxiety may have the effect of increasing or inhibiting the desire for new

---

[1] I suggested formerly that the young infant's phantasies of attacking the mother's body with poisonous (explosive and burning) excrements are a fundamental cause of his fear of being poisoned by her and lie at the root of paranoia; similarly, that the impulses to devour the mother (and her breast) turn her in the young infant's mind into a devouring and dangerous object. ('Early Stages of the Oedipus Conflict'; 'The Importance of Symbol-Formation in the Development of the Ego'; also *The Psycho-Analysis of Children*, particularly Chapter 8.)

Freud, too, refers to the little girl's fear of being murdered or poisoned by her mother; a fear of which he says 'may later form the core of a paranoic illness' (*New Introductory Lectures*, S.E. **22**, p. 120). Further: 'The fear of being poisoned is also probably connected with the withdrawal of the breast. Poison is nourishment that makes one ill' (*ibid.*, p. 122). In his earlier paper, 'Female Sexuality', Freud also refers to the girl's dread in the pre-oedipal stage 'of being killed (devoured?) by the mother'. He suggests that 'this fear corresponds to a hostility which develops in the child towards her mother in consequence of the manifold restrictions imposed by the latter in the course of training and bodily care and that the mechanism of projection is favoured by the early age of the child's psychical organization.' He also concludes 'that in this dependence on the mother we have the germ of later paranoia in women.' In this context he refers to the case reported in 1928 by Ruth Mack Brunswick ('The Analysis of a Case of Paranoia'), in which the direct source of the disorder was the patient's Oedipus fixation to her sister' (*S.E.* **21**, p. 227).

food.[1] As we have seen earlier, anxiety may have varying effects on greed: it may reinforce it or may lead to strong inhibitions of greed and of the pleasure in taking nourishment.

An increase in appetite at the time of weaning would in some cases suggest that during the period of being suckled the bad (persecutory) aspect of the breast had predominated over the good one; furthermore, depressive anxiety about the apprehended danger to the loved breast would contribute to inhibiting the desire for food (that is to say, that both persecutory and depressive anxieties are operative in varying proportions). Therefore the bottle, which is in some measure removed in the infant's mind from the first object, the breast—while also symbolizing it—can be taken with less anxiety and more pleasure than the mother's breast. Some infants, however, do not succeed in the symbolic substitution of the bottle for the breast, and if they enjoy their meals at all it is when they are given solid foods.

A decrease in appetite when breast- or bottle-feeding is first withdrawn is a frequent occurrence and clearly indicates depressive anxiety relating to the loss of the primary loved object. But persecutory anxiety, I think, always contributes to the dislike of the new food. The bad (devouring and poisonous) aspect of the breast which, while the infant was being suckled, was counteracted by the relation to the good breast, is reinforced by the deprivation of being weaned, and is transferred on to the new food.

As I indicated above, during the process of being weaned both persecutory and depressive anxieties strongly affect the relation to the mother and food. It is, however, the intricate interaction of a variety of factors (internal and external) which at this stage determines the issue; by which I mean, not only the individual variations in the attitudes towards objects and food, but over and above this, the success or failure in working through and in some measure overcoming the depressive position. Much depends on how far in the earlier stage the breast has been securely established within, and consequently how far love for the mother can be maintained in spite of deprivations—all of which partly depends on the relation between mother and child. As I suggested, even very young infants can accept a new food (the bottle) with comparatively little grievance (instance A). This better inner adaptation towards frustration, which develops from the first days of life onwards, is bound up with steps towards the distinction between mother and food. These funda-

[1] We may draw a comparison here with the attitude of manic-depressive patients towards food. As we know, some patients refuse food; others show temporarily an increase of greed; again others oscillate between these two responses.

mental attitudes largely determine, particularly during the process of being weaned, the infant's capacity to accept, in the full sense of the word, substitutes for the primary object. Here again the mother's behaviour and feelings towards the child are of major importance; the loving attention and the time she devotes to him help him with his depressive feelings. The good relationship with the mother may in some measure counteract the loss of his primary loved object, the breast, and thus favourably influence the working through of the depressive position.

The anxiety about the loss of the good object, coming to a head at weaning time, is also stirred up by other experiences such as physical discomfort, illnesses and in particular teething. These experiences are bound to reinforce persecutory and depressive anxieties in the infant. In other words, the physical factor can never solely account for the emotional disturbance to which illnesses or teething give rise at this stage.

IX

Among the important developments we find towards the middle of the first year is the widening of the range of object-relations and in particular the increasing importance of the father for the young infant. I have shown in other contexts that depressive feelings and the fear of losing the mother, in addition to other developmental factors, add impetus to the infant's turning to the father. The early stages of the Oedipus complex and the depressive position are closely linked and develop simultaneously. I shall mention only one instance, the little girl *B* already referred to.

From the age of about four months onwards, the relation with her brother, several years her senior, played a prominent and noticeable part in her life; it differed, as could easily be seen, in various ways from her relation with the mother. She admired everything her brother said and did, and persistently wooed him. She used all her little tricks to ingratiate herself, to win his attention and displayed a conspicuously feminine attitude towards him. At that time the father was absent, except for very short periods, and it was not until she was ten months old that she saw him more often, and from that time onwards developed a very close and loving relation with him, which in some essentials paralleled the relation with her brother. At the beginning of her second year she often called her brother 'Daddy'; by then father had become the favourite. The delight in seeing him, the rapture when she heard his steps or his voice, the ways in which she mentioned him again and again in his absence, and many other expressions of her feelings towards him can only be described as being in love. The mother clearly recognized that at this stage the little girl was in some ways more fond of the father than of her. Here we have an instance of the early Oedipus situation which, in this case, was experienced first with the brother and then transferred to the father.

X

The depressive position, as I have argued in various connections, is an important part of normal emotional development, but the ways in which the child deals with these emotions and anxieties, and the defences he uses, are an indication of whether or not development is proceeding satisfactorily. (See note 3, p. 119.)

The fear of losing the mother makes parting from her, even for short periods, painful; and various forms of play both give expression to this anxiety and are a means of overcoming it. Freud's observation of the eighteen-month-old boy with his cotton-reel pointed in this direction.[1] As I see it, by means of this play the child was overcoming not only his feelings of loss but also his depressive anxiety.[2] There are various typical forms of play similar to that with the cotton-reel. Susan Isaacs (1952) has mentioned a few instances and I shall now add some observations of this nature. Children, sometimes even before the second half of the first year, enjoy throwing things out of the pram again and again, and expect them back. I observed a further development of such play in G, an infant of ten months, who had recently begun to crawl. He never tired of throwing a toy away from himself and then getting hold of it by crawling towards it. I was told that he started his play about two months earlier when he made his first attempts to move himself forward. The infant E between six and seven months once noticed, while lying in his pram, that when he lifted his legs a toy which he had thrown aside rolled back to him, and he developed this into a game.

Already in the fifth or sixth month many infants respond with pleasure to 'peep-bo' (see note 4, p. 120); and I have seen babies playing this actively by pulling the blanket over the head and off again as early as seven months. The mother of the infant B made a bed-time habit of this game, thus leaving the child to go to sleep in a happy mood. It seems that the *repetition* of such experiences is an important factor in helping the infant to overcome his feelings of loss and grief. Another typical game which I found to be of great help and comfort to young children is to part from the child at

[1] *Beyond the Pleasure Principle* (1920). Cf. Chapter III where a description of this game is given.

[2] In 'The Observation of Infants in a Set Situation', D. W. Winnicott discussed in detail the game with the cotton-reel.

bed-time saying 'bye-bye' and waving, leaving the room slowly, as it were disappearing gradually. The use of 'bye-bye' and waving, and later on saying 'back again', 'back soon' or similar words when the mother leaves the room, proves generally helpful or comforting. I know of some infants among whose first words were 'back' or 'again'.

To return to the infant girl B, with whom 'bye-bye' was one of the first words, I often noticed that when her mother was about to leave the room, a fleeting expression of sadness came into the child's eyes, or she seemed near crying. But when the mother waved to her and said 'bye-bye', she appeared comforted and went on with her play activities. I saw her when she was between ten and eleven months practise the gesture of waving and I gained the impression that this had become a source not only of interest but of comfort.

The infant's growing capacity to perceive and understand the things around him increases his confidence in his own ability to deal with and even to control them, as well as his trust in the external world. His repeated experiences of the external reality become the most important means of overcoming his persecutory and depressive anxieties. This, in my view, is reality-testing and underlies the process in adults which Freud has described as part of the work of mourning.[1]

When an infant is able to sit up or to stand in his cot, he can look at people, and in some sense comes nearer to them; this happens to an even greater extent when he can crawl and walk. Such achievements imply not only a greater ability to come close to his object of his own will but also a greater independence from the object. For instance, the infant girl B (at about eleven months) thoroughly enjoyed crawling up and down a passage for hours on end and was quite contented by herself; but from time to time she crawled into the room where her mother was (the door had been left open), had a look at her or attempted to talk to her and returned to the passage.

The great psychological importance of standing, crawling and walking has been described by some psycho-analytic writers. My point here is that all these achievements are used by the infant as a means of regaining his lost objects as well as of finding new objects in their stead; all this helps the infant to overcome his depressive position. Speech development, beginning with the imitation of sounds, is another of those great achievements which bring the child nearer to the people he loves and also enables him to find new objects. In gaining gratifications of a new kind, the frustration and grievance relating to the earlier situations are lessened, which again makes for greater security. Another element in the progress achieved derives from the infant's attempts to control his objects, his external as well

[1] 'Mourning and Melancholia' (1917).

as his internal world. Every step in development is also used by the ego as a defence against anxiety, at this stage predominantly against depressive anxiety. This would contribute to the fact, which can often be observed, that, together with advances in development, such as walking or talking, children become happier and more lively. To put it from another angle, the ego's striving to overcome the depressive position furthers interests and activities, not only during the first year of life but throughout the early years of childhood.[1]

The following instance illustrates some of my conclusions regarding early emotional life. The infant boy *D* showed at the age of three months a very strong and personal relation to his toys, *i.e.* beads, wooden rings and rattle. He looked at them intently, touched them again and again, took them into his mouth and listened to the noise they made; he was angry with these toys and screamed when they were not in the position he wanted; he was pleased and liked them once more when they were fixed for him in the right position. His mother remarked, when he was four months old, that he worked off a good deal of anger on his toys; on the other hand, they were also a consolation to him in feelings of distress. At times he stopped crying when they were shown to him, and they also comforted him before going to sleep.

In the fifth month he clearly distinguished between father, mother and the maid; he showed this unmistakably in his look of recognition and in his expecting certain types of play from each of them. His personal relations were already very marked at that stage; he had also developed a particular attitude towards his bottle. For instance, when it was standing empty beside him on a table, he turned to it, making sounds, caressing it and from time to time sucking the teat. From his facial expression it could be gathered that he was behaving towards the bottle in the same way as towards a loved person. At the age of nine months he was observed looking at the bottle lovingly and talking to it, and apparently waiting for a reply. This relation to the bottle is all the more interesting since the little boy was never a good feeder, and showed no greed, in fact no particular pleasure in taking food. There had been difficulties in breast-feeding almost from the beginning, since the mother's milk gave out, and when a few weeks old he was entirely changed over to bottle-feeding. His appetite only began to develop in the second year, and even then

---

[1] As I have pointed out in the previous paper, although the crucial experiences of depressive feelings and the defences against them arise during the first year of life, it takes years for the child to overcome his persecutory and depressive anxieties. They are again and again activated and overcome in the course of the infantile neurosis. But these anxieties are never eradicated, and therefore are liable to be revived, though to a lesser extent, throughout life.

largely depended on the pleasure of sharing his meal with his parents. We are reminded here of the fact that at nine months his main interest in the bottle seemed to be of an almost personal nature and did not relate only to the food it contained.

At ten months he became very fond of a humming top, being first attracted by its red knob, which he immediately sucked; this led to a great interest in the way it could be set to spin and the noise it made. He soon gave up his attempts to suck it, but his absorption in the top remained. When he was fifteen months old it happened that another humming top, of which he was also very fond, dropped on the floor while he was playing with it and the two halves came apart. The child's reaction to this incident was striking. He cried, was inconsolable and would not go back into the room where the incident had happened. When at last his mother succeeded in taking him there to show him that the top had been put together again, he refused to look at it and ran out of the room (even on the next day he did not want to go near the toy cupboard where the humming top was kept). Moreover, several hours after the incident, he refused to eat his tea. A little later on, however, it happened that his mother took up his toy dog and said: 'What a nice little doggie.' The boy brightened up, picked up the dog and kept on walking with it from one person to another expecting them to say, 'Nice little doggie'. It was clear that he identified himself with the toy dog, and therefore that the affection shown to it reassured him about the harm which he felt he had inflicted on the humming top.

It is significant that already at an earlier stage the child had shown outspoken anxiety about broken things. At about eight months, for instance, he cried when he dropped a glass—and another time a cup—and it broke. Soon he was so disturbed by the sight of broken things, irrespective of who had caused the damage, that his mother at once put them out of his sight.

His distress on such occasions was an indication of both persecutory and depressive anxiety. This becomes clear if we link his behaviour at about eight months with the later incident of the humming top. My conclusion is that both bottle and humming top symbolically represented the mother's breast (we shall remember that at ten months he behaved towards the humming top as he did at nine months towards his bottle), and that when the humming top came apart this meant to him the destruction of the mother's breast and body. This would explain his emotions of anxiety, guilt and grief with regard to the broken humming top.

I have already linked the broken top with the broken cup and the bottle, but there is an earlier connection to be made. As we have seen, the child showed at times great anger towards his toys, which he treated in a very personal way. I would suggest that his anxiety and guilt observed at a later stage could be traced back to the aggression expressed towards the toys, particularly when they were not accessible. There is a still earlier link with the relation to his mother's breast which had not satisfied him and had been withdrawn. Accordingly, the anxiety over the broken cup or glass would be an expression of guilt about his anger and destructive impulses, primarily directed against his mother's breast. By symbol-formation, therefore, the child had displaced his interest on to a series of objects,[1] from the breast to the toys: bottle—glass—cup—humming top, and transferred personal relations and emotions such as anger, hatred, persecutory and depressive anxieties and guilt on to these objects.

Earlier in this paper I described this child's anxiety relating to a stranger, and illustrated by the instance the splitting of the mother figure (here the grandmother figure) into a good and bad mother. The fear of the bad mother as well as love for the good one, which showed strongly in his personal relations, were marked. I suggest that both these aspects of personal relations entered into his attitude towards broken things.

The mixture of persecutory and depressive anxieties which he manifested in the incident of the broken humming top, refusing to go into the room, and later even near the toy-cupboard, shows the fear of the object having turned into a dangerous object (persecutory anxiety) because it has been injured. There was no doubt, however, about the strong depressive feelings which were also operative on this occasion. All these anxieties were relieved when he became reassured by the fact that the little dog (standing for himself) was 'nice', i.e. good, and was still loved by his parents.

## CONCLUSION

Our knowledge of constitutional factors and their interaction is still incomplete. In the chapters which I have contributed to this book I have touched upon some factors, which I shall now summarize. The innate capacity of the ego to tolerate anxiety may depend on a greater or lesser cohesiveness of the ego at birth; this in turn makes for a greater or lesser activity of schizoid mechanisms, and correspondingly for a greater or lesser capacity for integration. Other factors present from the beginning of post-natal life are the capacity for love, the strength of greed and the defences against greed.

I suggest that these interrelated factors are the expression of certain states of fusion between the life and death instincts. These

[1] As regards the importance of symbol-formation for mental life cf. Isaacs (1952), also my papers 'Early Analysis' and 'The Importance of Symbol-Formation in the Development of the Ego'.

states basically influence the dynamic processes by which destructive impulses are counteracted and mitigated by the libido, processes of great moment in moulding the infant's unconscious life. From the beginning of post-natal life constitutional factors are bound up with external ones, starting with the experience of birth and the earliest situations of being handled and fed.[1] Furthermore, as we have good grounds to assume, from early days onwards the mother's unconscious attitude strongly affects the infant's unconscious processes.

We are, therefore, bound to conclude that constitutional factors cannot be considered apart from environmental ones and *vice versa*. They all go to form the earliest phantasies, anxieties and defences which, while falling into certain typical patterns, are infinitely variable. This is the soil from which springs the individual mind and personality.

I have endeavoured to show that by carefully observing young infants, we can gain some insight into their emotional life as well as indications for their future mental development. Such observations, within the limits mentioned above, to some extent support my findings about the earliest stages of development. These findings were arrived at in the psycho-analysis of children and adults, as I was able to trace their anxieties and defences back to babyhood. We may recall that Freud's discovery of the Oedipus complex in the unconscious of his adult patients led to a more enlightened observation of children, which in turn fully confirmed his theoretical conclusions. During the last few decades the conflicts inherent in the Oeidpus complex have been more widely recognized and as a result the understanding of the child's emotional difficulties has increased; but this applies mainly to children in a more advanced stage of development. The very young infant's mental life is still a mystery to most adults. I venture to suggest that a closer observation of babies, stimulated by the increased knowledge of early mental processes which was derived from the psycho-analysis of young children, should in time to come lead to a better insight into the baby's emotional life.

It is my contention—put forward in some chapters of this book and in previous writings—that excessive persecutory and depressive anxieties in young infants are of crucial significance in the psychogenesis of mental disorders. In the present paper I have repeatedly pointed out that an understanding mother may by her attitude

---

[1] Recent studies of pre-natal modes of behaviour, particularly as described and summarized by A. Gesell (*The Embryology of Behaviour*) provide food for thought about a rudimentary ego and the extent to which constitutional factors are already at work in the foetus. It is also an open question whether or not the mother's mental and physical state influences the foetus as regards the constitutional factors mentioned above.

diminish her baby's conflicts and thus in some measure help him to cope more effectively with his anxieties. A fuller and more general realization of the young infant's anxieties and emotional needs will therefore lessen suffering in infancy and so prepare the ground for greater happiness and stability in later life.

## NOTES

1 (*p.* 99)

There is one fundamental aspect of this problem which I wish to mention. My psycho-analytic work has led me to conclude that the new-born infant unconsciously feels that an object of unique goodness exists, from which a maximal gratification could be obtained, and that this object is the mother's breast. I furthermore believe that this unconscious knowledge implies that the relation to the mother's breast and a feeling of possessing the breast develop even in children who are not being breast-fed. This would explain the fact referred to above that bottle-fed children, too, introject the mother's breast in both its good and bad aspects. How strong the capacity of a bottle-fed infant is to establish securely the good breast in his inner world depends on a variety of internal and external factors, among which the inherent capacity for love plays a vital part.

The fact that at the beginning of post-natal life an unconscious knowledge of the breast exists and that feelings towards the breast are experienced can only be conceived of as a phylogenetic inheritance.

To consider now the part ontogenetic factors play in these processes. We have good reason to assume that the infant's impulses bound up with the sensations of the mouth direct him towards the mother's breast, for the object of his first instinctual desires is the nipple and their aim is to suck the nipple. This would imply that the teat of the bottle cannot fully replace the desired nipple, nor the bottle the desired smell, warmth and softness of the mother's breast. Therefore, notwithstanding the fact that the infant may readily accept and enjoy bottle-feeding (particularly if a situation approximating to breast-feeding is established) he may still feel that he is not receiving the maximal gratification, and consequently experiences a deep longing for the unique object which could provide it.

The desire for unobtainable, ideal objects is a general feature in mental life, for it derives from the various frustrations the child undergoes in the course of his development, culminating in the necessity to renounce the Oedipus object. Feelings of frustration and grievance lead to phantasying backwards and often focus in retrospect on the privations suffered in relation to the mother's breast, even in people who have been satisfactorily breast-fed. I found, however, in a number of analyses that, in people who have not been breast-fed, the nature of the longing for an unobtainable object shows a particular intensity and quality, something so deep-rooted that its origin in the first feeding experience and first object-relation of the infant becomes apparent. Such emotions vary in strength between one individual and another, and have different effects on mental development. For instance, in some people the feeling of having been deprived of the breast may contribute to a strong sense of grievance and insecurity, with various implications for object-relations and the development of the personality. In other people the longing for a unique object which, although it has eluded them, is yet felt to exist somewhere may strongly stimulate certain lines of sublimations, such as the search for an ideal, or high standards for one's own attainments.

I will now compare these observations with a statement by Freud. Speaking of the fundamental importance of the infant's relation to the mother's breast and to the mother, Freud says:

'The phylogenetic foundation has so much the upper hand in all this over accidental personal experience that it makes no difference whether a child has really sucked at the breast or has been brought up on the bottle and never enjoyed the tenderness of a mother's care. His development takes the same path in both cases; *it may be that in the latter event his later longing is all the greater.*' (*An Outline of Psycho-Analysis*, p. 56.) (My italics.)

Here Freud attributes to the phylogenetic factor such over-riding importance that the actual feeding experience of the infant becomes relatively insignificant. This goes further than the conclusions to which my experience has led me. However, in the passage italicized by me, Freud seems to consider the possibility that having missed the experience of breast-feeding is felt as a deprivation, for otherwise we could not account for the longing for the mother's breast being 'all the greater'.

2 (*p.* 107)

I have made it clear that the processes of integration, which express themselves in the infant's synthesizing his contrasting emotions towards the mother—and consequently the bringing together of the good and bad aspects of the object—underlie depressive anxiety and the depressive position. It is implied that these processes are from the outset related to the object. In the weaning experience it is the primary loved object which is felt to be lost and therefore the persecutory and depressive anxieties relating to it are reinforced. The beginning of weaning thus constitutes a major crisis in the infant's life and his conflicts come to another climax during the final stage of weaning Every detail in the way weaning is carried out has a bearing on the intensity of the infant's depressive anxiety and may increase or diminish his capacity to work through the depressive position. Thus a careful and slow weaning is favourable while an abrupt weaning, by suddenly reinforcing his anxiety, may impair his emotional development. A number of pertinent questions arise here. For instance, what is the effect of a substitution of bottle-feeding for breast-feeding in the first weeks, or even months, of life? We have reason to assume that this situation differs from normal weaning, starting at about five months. Would this imply that, since in the first three months persecutory anxiety predominates, this form of anxiety is increased by early weaning, or does this experience produce an earlier onset of depressive anxiety in the infant? Which of these two outcomes will prevail may depend partly on external factors, such as the actual moment when weaning is begun and the way the mother handles the situation; partly on internal factors which could be broadly summarized as the strength of the inherent capacity for love and integration—which in turn implies also an inherent strength of the ego at the beginning of life. These factors, as I have repeatedly contended, underlie the infant's capacity to establish his good object securely, to some degree even when he has never had the experience of being fed by the breast.

Another question applies to the effect of late weaning, as is customary with primitive peoples and also in certain sections of civilized communities. I have not enough data on which to base an answer to this problem. I can, however, say that as far as I can judge from observation as well as from psycho-analytic experience, there is an optimum period for starting weaning at about the middle of the first year. For at this stage the infant is going through the depressive position, and weaning in some ways helps him to work through the inescapable depressive feelings. In this process he is supported by the increasing range of object-relations, interests, sublimations and defences which he develops at this stage.

As regards the completion of weaning—that is, the final changeover from sucking to drinking from a cup—it is more difficult to make a general suggestion as regards an optimum time. Here the needs of the individual child, which at this stage can be more easily gauged by observation, should be taken as the decisive criterion.

With some infants there is even a further stage in the process of weaning to be considered, and this is the giving up of thumb- or finger-sucking. Some infants give it up under pressure from the mother or nurse, but, according to my observation, even if infants seem to renounce finger-sucking of their own accord (and here, too, external influences cannot altogether be discounted) this entails conflict, anxiety and depressive feelings characteristic of weaning, in some cases with loss of appetite.

The question of weaning links up with the more general problem of frustration. Frustration, if not excessive (and we shall remember here that up to a point frustrations are inevitable), may even help the child to deal with his depressive feelings. For the very experience that frustration can be overcome tends to strengthen the ego and is part of the work of mourning which supports the infant in dealing with depression. More specifically, the mother's reappearance proves again and again that she has not been destroyed and has not been turned into the bad mother, which implies that the infant's aggression has not had the dreaded consequences. There is thus a delicate and individually variable balance between the harmful and helpful effects of frustration, a balance which is determined by a variety of internal and external factors.

3 (p. 111)

It is my contention that both the paranoid-schizoid and the depressive position are part of normal development. My experience has led me to conclude that if persecutory and depressive anxieties in early infancy are excessive in proportion to the capacity of the ego to deal step by step with anxiety, this may result in the pathological development of the child. I have described in the previous chapter the division in the relation to the mother (the 'good' and the 'bad' mother), which is characteristic of an ego not yet sufficiently integrated, as well as of the splitting mechanisms which are at their height during the first three or four months of life. Normally, the fluctuations in the relation to the mother, and temporary states of withdrawal—influenced by splitting processes—cannot be easily gauged, since at that stage they are closely linked with the immature state of the ego. However, when development is not proceeding satisfactorily, we can get certain indications of this failure. In the present chapter I have referred to some typical difficulties which indicate that the paranoid-schizoid position is not being satisfactorily worked through. Though the picture differed in some points, all these instances had one important feature in common: a disturbance in the development of object-relations which can already be observed during the first three or four months of life.

Again, certain difficulties are part of the normal process of going through the depressive position, such as fretfulness, irritability, disturbed sleep, greater need for attention, and changes in the attitude towards the mother and food. If such disturbances are excessive and persist unduly, they may indicate a failure to work through the depressive position and may become the basis for manic-depressive illness in later life. The failure to work through the depressive position may, however, lead to a different outcome: certain symptoms, such as withdrawal from the mother and other people, may become stabilized instead of being transitory and partial. If together with this the infant becomes more apathetic, failing to develop the widening of interests and acceptance of substitutes which is normally present simultaneously with depressive symptoms, and is partly a way of overcoming them, we may surmise that the depressive position is not being successfully worked through; that a regression to the former position, the paranoid-schizoid position, has taken place—a regression to which we have to attribute great importance.

To repeat my conclusion expressed in earlier writings: persecutory and depressive anxieties, if excessive, may lead to severe mental illnesses and mental deficiency in childhood. These two forms of anxiety also provide the fixation-points for paranoic, schizophrenic and manic-depressive illnesses in adult life.

4 (*p.* 111)

Freud mentions the infant's pleasure in the game played with his mother when she hides her face and then reappears. (Freud does not say what stage of infancy he is referring to; but from the nature of the game one might assume that he is referring to infants in the middle or later months of the first year, as well as perhaps to older ones.) In this connection he states that the infant 'cannot as yet distinguish between temporary absence and permanent loss. As soon as it loses sight of its mother it behaves as if it were never going to see her again; and repeated consoling experiences to the contrary are necessary before it learns that her disappearance is usually followed by her reappearance.' (*S.E.* **20,** p. 169).

As regards further conclusions, the same difference of view exists on this point as in the interpretation of the cotton-reel game mentioned earlier. According to Freud, the anxiety which a young infant experiences when he misses his mother produces '. . . a traumatic situation if the infant happens at the time to be feeling a need which its mother should be the one to satisfy. It turns into a danger-situation if this need is not present at the moment. Thus, the first determinant of anxiety, which the ego itself introduces, is loss of perception of the object (which is equated with loss of the object itself). There is as yet no question of loss of love. Later on, experience teaches the child that the object can be present but angry with it; and then the loss of love from the object becomes a new and much more enduring danger and determinant of anxiety' (*ibid.* p. 170). In my view, which I have stated in various connections and am briefly recapitulating here, the young infant experiences love as well as hatred towards his mother, and when he misses her and his needs are not satisfied her absence is felt to be the result of his destructive impulses; hence persecutory anxiety results (lest the good mother may have turned into the angry persecuting mother) and mourning, guilt and anxiety (lest the loved mother be destroyed by his aggression). These anxieties, constituting the depressive position, are again and again overcome, *e.g.* by play of a consolatory nature.

After having considered some differences of opinion as regards the emotional life and anxieties of the young infant, I would draw attention to a passage in the same context as the above quotation, where Freud seems to qualify his conclusions about the subject of mourning. He says, '. . . when does separation from an object produce anxiety, when does it produce mourning and when does it produce, it may be, only pain? Let me say at once that there is no prospect in sight of answering these questions. We must content ourselves with drawing certain distinctions and adumbrating certain possibilities.' (*ibid.* p. 169).

# 8

## THE PSYCHO-ANALYTIC PLAY
## TECHNIQUE: ITS HISTORY
## AND SIGNIFICANCE

### (1955)

In offering a paper mainly concerned with play technique as an introduction to this book,[1] I have been prompted by the consideration that my work with both children and adults, and my contributions to psycho-analytic theory as a whole, derive ultimately from the play technique evolved with young children. I do not mean by this that my later work was a direct application of the play technique; but the insight I gained into early development, into unconscious processes, and into the nature of the interpretations by which the unconscious can be approached, has been of far-reaching influence on the work I have done with older children and adults.

I shall, therefore, briefly outline the steps by which my work developed out of the psycho-analytic play technique, but I shall not attempt to give a complete summary of my findings. In 1919, when I started my first case, some psycho-analytic work with children had already been done, particularly by Dr Hug-Hellmuth (1921). However, she did not undertake the psycho-analysis of children under six and, although she used drawings and occasionally play as material, she did not develop this into a specific technique.

At the time I began to work it was an established principle that interpretations should be given very sparingly. With few exceptions psycho-analysts had not explored the deeper layers of the unconscious—in children such exploration being considered potentially dangerous. This cautious outlook was reflected in the fact that then, and for years to come, psycho-analysis was held to be suitable only for children from the latency period onwards.[2]

My first patient was a five-year-old boy. I referred to him under the name 'Fritz' in my earliest published papers.[3] To begin with I

---

[1] *New Directions in Psycho-Analysis.*

[2] A description of this early approach is given in Anna Freud's book *The Psycho-Analytical Treatment of Children* (1927).

[3] 'The Development of a Child', (1923); 'The Rôle of the School in the Libidinal Development of the Child', (1924); and 'Early Analysis', (1926).

thought it would be sufficient to influence the mother's attitude. I suggested that she should encourage the child to discuss freely with her the many unspoken questions which were obviously at the back of his mind and were impeding his intellectual development. This had a good effect, but his neurotic difficulties were not sufficiently alleviated and it was soon decided that I should psycho-analyse him. In doing so, I deviated from some of the rules so far established, for I interpreted what I thought to be most urgent in the material the child presented to me and found my interest focusing on his anxieties and the defences against them. This new approach soon confronted me with serious problems. The anxieties I encountered when analysing this first case were very acute, and although I was strengthened in the belief that I was working on the right lines by observing the alleviation of anxiety again and again produced by my interpretations, I was at times perturbed by the intensity of the fresh anxieties which were being brought into the open. On one such occasion I sought advice from Dr Karl Abraham. He replied that since my interpretations up to then had often produced relief and the analysis was obviously progressing, he saw no ground for changing the method of approach. I felt encouraged by his support and, as it happened, in the next few days the child's anxiety, which had come to a head, greatly diminished, leading to further improvement. The conviction gained in this analysis strongly influenced the whole course of my analytic work.

The treatment was carried out in the child's home with his own toys. This analysis was the beginning of the psycho-analytic play technique, because from the start the child expressed his phantasies and anxieties mainly in play, and I consistently interpreted its meaning to him, with the result that additional material came up in his play. That is to say, I already used with this patient, in essence, the method of interpretation which became characteristic of my technique. This approach corresponds to a fundamental principle of psycho-analysis—free association. In interpreting not only the child's words but also his activities with his toys, I applied this basic principle to the mind of the child, whose play and varied activities—in fact his whole behaviour—are means of expressing what the adult expresses predominantly by words. I was also guided throughout by two other tenets of psycho-analysis established by Freud, which I have from the beginning regarded as fundamental: that the exploration of the unconscious is the main task of psycho-analytic procedure, and that the analysis of the transference is the means of achieving this aim.

Between 1920 and 1923 I gained further experience with other child cases, but a definite step in the development of play technique was the treatment of a child of two years and nine months whom I psycho-analysed in 1923. I have given some details of this child's case under the name 'Rita' in my book, *The Psycho-Analysis of Children*.[1] Rita suffered from night terrors and animal phobias, was very ambivalent towards her mother, at the same time clinging to her to such an extent that she could hardly be left alone. She had a marked obsessional neurosis and was at times very depressed. Her play was inhibited and her inability to tolerate frustrations made her upbringing increasingly difficult. I was very doubtful about how to tackle this case since the analysis of so young a child was an entirely new experiment. The first session seemed to confirm my misgivings. Rita, when left alone with me in her nursery, at once showed signs of what I took to be a negative transference: she was anxious and silent and very soon asked to go out into the garden. I agreed and went with her—I may add, under the watchful eyes of her mother and aunt, who took this as a sign of failure. They were very surprised to see that Rita was quite friendly towards me when we returned to the nursery some ten to fifteen minutes later. The explanation of this change was that while we were outside I had been interpreting her negative transference (this again being against the usual practice). From a few things she said, and the fact that she was less frightened when we were in the open, I concluded that she was particularly afraid of something which I might do to her when she was alone with me in the room. I interpreted this and, referring to her night terrors, I linked her suspicion of me as a hostile stranger with her fear that a bad woman would attack her when she was by herself at night. When, a few minutes after this interpretation, I suggested that we should return to the nursery, she readily agreed. As I mentioned, Rita's inhibition in playing was marked, and to begin with she did hardly anything but obsessionally dress and undress her doll. But soon I came to understand the anxieties underlying her obsessions, and interpreted them. This case strengthened my growing conviction that a precondition for the psycho-analysis of a child is to understand and to interpret the phantasies, feelings, anxieties, and experiences expressed by play or, if play activities are inhibited, the causes of the inhibition.

As with Fritz, I undertook this analysis in the child's home and with her own toys; but during this treatment, which lasted only a few months, I came to the conclusion that psycho-analysis should not be carried out in the child's home. For I found that, although she was in great need of help and her parents had decided that I should try psycho-analysis, her mother's attitude towards me was very

[1] See also *On the Bringing up of Children* ed. Rickman (1936), and 'The Oedipus Complex in the Light of Early Anxieties' (1945).

ambivalent and the atmosphere was on the whole hostile to the treatment. More important still, I found that the transference situation—the backbone of the psycho-analytic procedure—can only be established and maintained if the patient is able to feel that the consulting-room or the play-room, indeed the whole analysis, is something separate from his ordinary home life. For only under such conditions can he overcome his resistances against experiencing and expressing thoughts, feelings, and desires, which are incompatible with convention, and in the case of children, felt to be in contrast to much of what they have been taught.

I made further significant observations in the psycho-analysis of a girl of seven, also in 1923. Her neurotic difficulties were apparently not serious, but her parents had for some time been concerned about her intellectual development. Although quite intelligent she did not keep up with her age group, she disliked school, and sometimes played truant. Her relation to her mother, which had been affectionate and trusting, had changed since she had started school: she had become reserved and silent. I spent a few sessions with her without achieving much contact. It had become clear that she disliked school, and from what she diffidently said about it, as well as from other remarks, I had been able to make a few interpretations which produced some material. But my impression was that I should not get much further in that way. In a session in which I again found the child unresponsive and withdrawn I left her, saying that I would return in a moment. I went into my own children's nursery, collected a few toys, cars, little figures, a few bricks, and a train, put them into a box and returned to the patient. The child, who had not taken to drawing or other activities, was interested in the small toys and at once began to play. From this play I gathered that two of the toy figures represented herself and a little boy, a school-mate about whom I had heard before. It appeared that there was something secret about the behaviour of these two figures and that other toy people were resented as interfering or watching and were put aside. The activities of the two toys led to catastrophies, such as their falling down or colliding with cars. This was repeated with signs of mounting anxiety. At this point I interpreted, with reference to the details of her play, that some sexual activity seemed to have occurred between herself and her friend, and that this had made her very frightened of being found out and therefore distrustful of other people. I pointed out that while playing she had become anxious and seemed on the point of stopping her play. I reminded her that she disliked school, and that this might be connected with the fear that the teacher would find out about her relation with her school-mate and punish her. Above all she was frightened and therefore distrustful of her mother, and now she might feel the same way about me. The effect of this interpretation on the child was striking: her anxiety and distrust first increased, but very soon gave way to obvious relief. Her facial expression changed, and although she neither admitted nor denied what I had interpreted, she subsequently showed her agreement by producing new material and by becoming much freer in her play and speech; also her attitude towards me became much more friendly and less suspicious. Of course the negative transference, alternating with the positive one, came up again and again; but, from this session onwards, the analysis progressed well. Concurrently there were favourable changes, as I was informed, in her relation to her family—in particular to her mother. Her dislike of school diminished and she became more interested in her lessons, but her inhibition in learning, which was rooted in deep anxieties, was only gradually resolved in the course of her treatment.

## II

I have described how the use of the toys I kept especially for the child patient in the box in which I first brought them proved essential for her analysis. This experience, as well as others, helped me to decide which toys are most suitable for the psycho-analytic play technique.[1] I found it essential to have *small* toys because their number and variety enable the child to express a wide range of phantasies and experiences. It is important for this purpose that these toys should be non-mechanical and that the human figures, varying only in colour and size, should not indicate any particular occupation. Their very simplicity enables the child to use them in many different situations, according to the material coming up in his play. The fact that he can thus present simultaneously a variety of experiences and phantasies or actual situations also makes it possible for us to arrive at a more coherent picture of the workings of his mind.

In keeping with the simplicity of the toys, the equipment of the play-room is also simple. It does not contain anything except what is needed for the psycho-analysis.[2] Each child's playthings are kept locked in one particular drawer, and he therefore knows that his toys and his play with them, which is the equivalent of the adult's associations, are only known to the analyst and to himself. The box in which I first introduced the toys to the little girl mentioned above

[1] They are mainly: little wooden men and women, usually in two sizes, cars, wheelbarrows, swings, trains, aeroplanes, animals, trees, bricks, houses, fences, paper, scissors, a knife, pencils, chalks or paints, glue, balls and marbles, plasticine and string.

[2] It has a washable floor, running water, a table, a few chairs, a little sofa, some cushions and a chest of drawers.

turned out to be the prototype of the individual drawer, which is part of the private and intimate relation between analyst and patient, characteristic of the psycho-analytic transference situation.

I do not suggest that the psycho-analytic play technique depends entirely on my particular selection of play-material. In any case, children often spontaneously bring their own things and the play with them enters as a matter of course into the analytic work. But I believe that the toys provided by the analyst should on the whole be of the type I have described, that is to say, simple, small, and non-mechanical.

Toys, however, are not the only requisites for a play analysis. Many of the child's activities are at times carried out round the wash-hand basin, which is equipped with one or two small bowls, tumblers, and spoons. Often he draws, writes, paints, cuts out, repairs toys, and so on. At times he plays games in which he allots rôles to the analyst and himself such as playing shop, doctor and patient, school, mother and child. In such games the child frequently takes the part of the adult, thereby not only expressing his wish to reverse the rôles but also demonstrating how he feels that his parents or other people in authority behave towards him—or *should* behave. Sometimes he gives vent to his aggressiveness and resentment by being, in the rôle of parent, sadistic towards the child, represented by the analyst. The principle of interpretation remains the same whether the phantasies are presented by toys or by dramatization. For, whatever material is used, it is essential that the analytic principles underlying the technique should be applied.[1]

Aggressiveness is expressed in various ways in the child's play, either directly or indirectly. Often a toy is broken or, when the child is more aggressive, attacks are made with knife or scissors on the table or on pieces of wood; water or paint is splashed about and the room generally becomes a battlefield. It is essential to enable the child to bring out his aggressiveness; but what counts most is to understand why at this particular moment in the transference situation destructive impulses come up and to observe their consequences in the child's mind. Feelings of guilt may very soon follow after the child has broken, for instance, a little figure. Such guilt refers not only to the actual damage done but to what the toy stands for in the child's unconscious, *e.g.* a little brother or sister, or a parent; the interpretation has therefore to deal with these deeper levels as well. Sometimes we can gather from the child's behaviour towards the analyst that not only guilt but also persecutory anxiety

---

[1] Instances both of play with toys and of the games described above can be found in *The Psycho-Analysis of Children* (particularly in Chapters II, III and IV). See also 'Personification in the Play of Children' (1929).

has been the sequel to his destructive impulses and that he is afraid of retaliation.

I have usually been able to convey to the child that I would not tolerate physical attacks on myself. This attitude not only protects the psycho-analyst but is of importance for the analysis as well. For such assaults, if not kept within bounds, are apt to stir up excessive guilt and persecutory anxiety in the child and therefore add to the difficulties of the treatment. I have sometimes been asked by what method I prevented physical attacks, and I think the answer is that I was very careful not to inhibit the child's aggressive *phantasies*; in fact he was given opportunity to act them out in other ways, including verbal attacks on myself. The more I was able to interpret in time the motives of the child's aggressiveness the more the situation could be kept under control. But with some psychotic children it has occasionally been difficult to protect myself against their aggressiveness.

### III

I have found that the child's attitude towards a toy he has damaged is very revealing. He often puts aside such a toy, representing for instance a sibling or a parent, and ignores it for a time. This indicates dislike of the damaged object, due to the persecutory fear that the attacked person (represented by the toy) has become retaliatory and dangerous. The sense of persecution may be so strong that it covers up feelings of guilt and depression which are also aroused by the damage done. Or guilt and depression may be so strong that they lead to a reinforcing of persecutory feelings. However, one day the child may search in his drawer for the damaged toy. This suggests that by then we have been able to analyse some important defences, thus diminishing persecutory feelings and making it possible for the sense of guilt and the urge to make reparation to be experienced. When this happens we can also notice that a change in the child's relation to the particular sibling for whom the toy stood, or in his relations in general, has occurred. This change confirms our impression that persecutory anxiety has diminished and that, together with the sense of guilt and the wish to make reparation, feelings of love which had been impaired by excessive anxiety have come to the fore. With another child, or with the same child at a later stage of the analysis, guilt and the wish to repair may follow very soon after the act of aggression, and tenderness towards the brother or sister who may have been damaged in phantasy becomes apparent. The importance of such changes for character formation and object relations, as well as for mental stability, cannot be overrated.

It is an essential part of the interpretative work that it should keep in step with fluctuations between love and hatred; between happiness and satisfaction on the one hand and persecutory anxiety and depression on the other. This implies that the analyst should not show disapproval of the child having broken a toy; he should not, however, encourage the child to express his aggressiveness, or suggest to him that the toy could be mended. In other words, he should enable the child to experience his emotions and phantasies as they come up. It was always part of my technique not to use educative or moral influence, but to keep to the psycho-analytic procedure only, which, to put it in a nutshell, consists in understanding the patient's mind and in conveying to him what goes on in it.

The variety of emotional situations which can be expressed by play activities is unlimited: for instance, feelings of frustration and of being rejected; jealousy of both father and mother, or of brothers and sisters; aggressiveness accompanying such jealousy; pleasure in having a playmate and ally against the parents; feelings of love and hatred towards a newborn baby or one who is expected, as well as the ensuing anxiety, guilt, and urge to make reparation. We also find in the child's play the repetition of actual experiences and details of everyday life, often interwoven with his phantasies. It is revealing that sometimes very important actual events in his life fail to enter either into his play or into his associations, and that the whole emphasis at times lies on apparently minor happenings. But these minor happenings are of great importance to him because they have stirred up his emotions and phantasies.

## IV

There are many children who are inhibited in play. Such inhibition does not always completely prevent them from playing, but may soon interrupt their activities. For instance, a little boy was brought to me for one interview only (there was a prospect of an analysis in the future; but at the time the parents were going abroad with him). I had some toys on the table and he sat down and began to play, which soon led to accidents, collisions, and toy people falling down whom he tried to stand up again. In all this he showed a good deal of anxiety, but since no treatment was yet intended, I refrained from interpreting. After a few minutes he quietly slipped out of his chair and saying: 'Enough of playing', went out. I believe from my experience that if this had been the beginning of a treatment and I had interpreted the anxiety shown in his actions with the toys and the corresponding negative transference towards me, I should have been able to resolve his anxiety sufficiently for him to continue playing.

The next instance may help me to show some of the causes of a play inhibition. The boy, aged three years nine months, whom I described under the name 'Peter' in *The Psycho-Analysis of Children*, was very neurotic.[1] To mention some of his difficulties: he was unable to play, could not tolerate any frustration, was timid, plaintive, and unboyish, yet at times aggressive and overbearing, very ambivalent towards his family, and strongly fixated on his mother. She told me that Peter had greatly changed for the worse after a summer holiday during which at the age of eighteen months he shared his parents' bedroom and had opportunity of observing their sexual intercourse. On that holiday he became very difficult to manage, slept badly, and relapsed into soiling his bed at night, which he had not done for some months. He had been playing freely until then, but from that summer onwards he stopped playing and became very destructive towards his toys; he would no nothing with them but break them. Shortly afterwards his brother was born, and this increased all his difficulties.

In the first session Peter started to play; he soon made two horses bump into each other, and repeated the same action with different toys. He also mentioned that he had a little brother. I interpreted to him that the horses and the other things which had been bumping together represented people, an interpretation which he first rejected and then accepted. He again bumped the horses together, saying that they were going to sleep, covered them up with bricks, and added: 'Now they're quite dead; I've buried them.' He put the motor-cars front to rear in a row which, as became clear later in the analysis, symbolized his father's penis, and made them run along, then suddenly lost his temper and threw them about the room, saying: 'We always smash our Christmas presents straight away; we don't want any.' Smashing his toys thus stood in his unconscious for smashing his father's genital. During this first hour he did in fact break several toys.

In the second session Peter repeated some of the material of the first hour, in particular the bumping together of cars, horses, etc., and speaking again of his little brother, whereupon I interpreted that he was showing me how his Mummy and Daddy bumped their genitals (of course using his own word for genitals) and that he thought that their doing so caused his brother to be born. This interpretation produced more material, throwing light on his very ambivalent relation towards his little brother and towards his father. He laid a toy man on a brick which he called a 'bed', threw him down and said he was 'dead and done for'. He next re-enacted the same thing with two toy men, choosing figures he had already damaged. I interpreted that the first toy man stood for his father

---

[1] This child, whose analysis was begun in 1924, was another of the cases that helped to develop my play technique.

whom he wanted to throw out of his mother's bed and kill, and that one of the two toy men was again the father and the other represented himself to whom his father would do the same. The reason why he had chosen two damaged figures was that he felt that both his father and himself would be damaged if he attacked his father.

This material illustrates a number of points, of which I shall only mention one or two. Because Peter's experience of witnessing the sexual intercourse of his parents had made a great impact on his mind, and had aroused strong emotions such as jealousy, aggressiveness and anxiety, this was the first thing which he expressed in his play. There is no doubt that he had no longer any conscious knowledge of this experience, that it was repressed, and that only the symbolical expression of it was possible for him. I have reason to believe that if I had not interpreted that the toys bumping together were people, he might not have produced the material which came up in the second hour. Furthermore, had I not, in the second hour, been able to show him some of the reasons for his inhibition in play, by interpreting the damage done to the toys, he would very likely—as he did in ordinary life—have stopped playing after breaking the toys.

There are children who at the beginning of treatment may not even play in the same way as Peter, or the little boy who came for one interview only. But it is very rare for a child completely to ignore the toys laid out on the table. Even if he turns away from them, he often gives the analyst some insight into his motives for not wishing to play. In other ways, too, the child analyst can gather material for interpretation. Any activity, such as using paper to scribble on or to cut out, and every detail of behaviour, such as changes in posture or in facial expression, can give a clue to what is going on in the child's mind, possibly in connection with what the analyst has heard from the parents about his difficulties.

I have said much about the importance of interpretations for play technique and have given some instances to illustrate their content. This brings me to a question which I have often been asked: 'Are young children intellectually able to understand such interpretations?' My own experience and that of my colleagues has been that if the interpretations relate to the salient points in the material, they are fully understood. Of course the child analyst must give his interpretations as succinctly and as clearly as possible, and should also use the child's expressions in doing so. But if he translates into simple words the essential points of the material presented to him, he gets into touch with those emotions and anxieties which are most operative at the moment; the child's conscious and intellectual understanding is often a subsequent process. One of the many interesting and surprising experiences of the beginner in child analysis is to find in even very young children a capacity for insight which is often far greater than that of adults. To some extent this is explained by the fact that the connections between conscious and unconscious are closer in young children than in adults, and that infantile repressions are less powerful. I also believe that the infant's intellectual capacities are often underrated and that in fact he understands more than he is credited with.

I shall now illustrate what I have said by a young child's response to interpretations. Peter, of whose analysis I have given a few details, had strongly objected to my interpretation that the toy man he had thrown down from the 'bed' and who was 'dead and done for' represented his father. (The interpretation of death-wishes against a loved person usually arouses great resistance in children as well as in adults.) In the third hour Peter again brought similar material, but now accepted my interpretation and said thoughtfully: 'And if I were a Daddy and someone wanted to throw me down behind the bed and make me dead and done for, what would I think of it?' This shows that he had not only worked through, understood and accepted my interpretation, but that he had also recognized a good deal more. He understood that his own aggressive feelings towards his father contributed to his fear of him, and also that he had projected his own impulses on to his father.

One of the important points in play technique has always been the analysis of the transference. As we know, in the transference on the analyst the patient repeats earlier emotions and conflicts. It is my experience that we are able to help the patient fundamentally by taking his phantasies and anxieties back in our transference inter-pretations to where they originated—namely, in infancy and in rela-tion to his first objects. For by re-experiencing early emotions and phantasies and understanding them in relation to his primal objects, he can, as it were, revise these relations at their root, and thus effectively diminish his anxieties.

V

In looking back over the first few years of my work, I would single out a few facts. I mentioned at the beginning of this paper that in analysing my earliest child case I found my interest focusing on his anxieties and defences against them. My emphasis on anxiety led me deeper and deeper into the unconscious and into the phantasy life of the child. This particular emphasis ran counter to the psycho-analytical point of view that interpretations should not go very deep and should not be given frequently. I persisted in my approach, in spite of the fact that it involved a radical change in technique. This approach took me into new territory, for it opened up the understanding of the early infantile phantasies, anxieties and defences, which were at that time still largely unexplored. This became clear to me when I began the theoretical formulation of my clinical findings.

One of the various phenomena which struck me in the analysis of Rita was the harshness of her super-ego. I have described in *The Psycho-Analysis of Children* how Rita used to play the rôle of a severe and punishing mother who treated the child (represented by the doll or by myself) very cruelly. Furthermore, her ambivalence towards her mother, her extreme need to be punished, her feelings of guilt and her night terrors led me to recognize that in this child aged two years and nine months—and quite clearly going back to a much earlier age—a harsh and relentless super-ego operated. I found this discovery confirmed in the analyses of other young children and came to the conclusion that the super-ego arises at a much earlier stage than Freud assumed. In other words, it became clear to me that the super-ego, as conceived by him, is the end-product of a development which extends over years. As a result of further observations, I recognized that the super-ego is something which is felt by the child to operate internally in a concrete way; that it consists of a variety of figures built up from his experiences and phantasies and that it is derived from the stages in which he had internalized (introjected) his parents.

These observations in turn led, in the analyses of little girls, to discovery of the leading female anxiety situation: the mother is felt to be the primal persecutor who, as an external and internalized object, attacks the child's body and takes from it her imaginary children. These anxieties arise from the girl's phantasied attacks on the mother's body, which aim at robbing her of its contents, *i.e.* of faeces, of the father's penis, and of children, and result in the fear of retaliation by similar attacks. Such persecutory anxieties I found combined or alternating with deep feelings of depression and guilt, and these observations then led to my discovery of the vital part which the tendency to *make reparation* plays in mental life. Reparation in this sense is a wider concept than Freud's concepts of 'undoing in the obsessional neurosis' and of 'reaction-formation'. For it includes the variety of processes by which the ego feels it undoes harm done in phantasy, restores, preserves and revives objects. The importance of this tendency, bound up as it is with feelings of guilt, also lies in the major contribution it makes to all sublimations, and in this way to mental health.

In studying the phantasied attacks on the mother's body, I soon came upon anal- and urethral-sadistic impulses. I have mentioned above that I recognized the harshness of the super-ego in Rita

(1923) and that her analysis greatly helped me to understand the way in which destructive impulses towards the mother become the cause of feelings of guilt and persecution. One of the cases through which the anal- and urethral-sadistic nature of these destructive impulses became clear to me was that of 'Trude', aged three years and three months, whom I analysed in 1924.[1] When she came to me for treatment, she suffered from various symptoms, such as night terrors and incontinence of urine and faeces. Early on in her analysis she asked me to pretend that I was in bed and asleep. She would then say that she was going to attack me and look into my buttocks for faeces (which I found also represented children) and that she was going to take them out. Such attacks were followed by her crouching in a corner, playing that she was in bed, covering herself with cushions (which were to protect her body and which also stood for children); at the same time she actually wetted herself and showed clearly that she was very much afraid of being attacked by me. Her anxieties about the dangerous internalized mother confirmed the conclusions I first formed in Rita's analysis. Both these analyses had been of short duration, partly because the parents thought that enough improvement had been achieved.[2]

Soon afterwards I became convinced that such destructive impulses and phantasies could always be traced back to oral-sadistic ones. In fact Rita had already shown this quite clearly. On one occasion she blackened a piece of paper, tore it up, threw the scraps into a glass of water which she put to her mouth as if to drink from it, and said under her breath 'dead woman'.[3] This tearing up and soiling of paper I had at the time understood to express phantasies of attacking and killing her mother which gave rise to fears of retaliation. I have already mentioned that it was with Trude that I became aware of the specific anal- and urethral-sadistic nature of such attacks. But in other analyses, carried out in 1924 and 1925 (Ruth and Peter, both described in *The Psycho-Analysis of Children*), I also became aware of the fundamental part which oral-sadistic impulses play in destructive phantasies and corresponding anxieties, thus finding in the analysis of young children full confirmation of Abraham's discoveries.[4] These analyses, which gave me further scope for observation, since they lasted longer than Rita's and Trude's,[5] led me towards a fuller insight into the fundamental rôle of oral

[1] Cf. The *Psycho-Analysis of Children*.

[2] Rita had eighty-three sessions, Trude eighty-two sessions.

[3] See 'The Oedipus Complex in the Light of Early Anxieties' (1945), *Writings*, **I**, p. 404.

[4] Cf. 'A Short History of the Development of the Libido, Viewed in the Light of Mental Disorders' (1924).

[5] Ruth had 190 sessions, Peter 278 sessions.

desires and anxieties in mental development, normal and abnormal.[1]

As I have mentioned, I had already recognized in Rita and Trude the internalization of an attacked and therefore frightening mother —the harsh super-ego. Between 1924 and 1926 I analysed a child who was very ill indeed.[2] Through her analysis I learned a good deal about the specific details of such internalization and about the phantasies and impulses underlying paranoid and manic-depressive anxieties. For I came to understand the oral and anal nature of her introjection processes and the situations of internal persecution they engendered. I also became more aware of the ways in which internal persecutions influence, by means of projection, the relation to external objects. The intensity of her envy and hatred unmistakably showed its derivation from the oral-sadistic relation to her mother's breast, and was interwoven with the beginnings of her Oedipus complex. Erna's case much helped to prepare the ground for a number of conclusions which I presented to the Tenth International Psycho-Analytical Congress in 1927,[3] in particular the view that the early super-ego, built up when oral-sadistic impulses and phantasies are at their height, underlies psychosis—a view which two years later I developed by stressing the importance of oral-sadism for schizophrenia.[4]

Concurrently with the analyses so far described I was able to make some interesting observations regarding anxiety situations in boys. The analyses of boys and men fully confirmed Freud's view that castration fear is the leading anxiety of the male, but I recognized that owing to the early identification with the mother (the feminine position which ushers in the early stages of the Oedipus complex) the anxiety about attacks on the inside of the body is of great importance in men as well as women, and in various ways influences and moulds their castration fears.

The anxieties derived from phantasied attacks on the mother's body and on the father she is supposed to contain, proved in both sexes to underlie claustrophobia (which includes the fear of being imprisoned or entombed in the mother's body). The connection of these anxieties with castration fear can be seen for instance in the phantasy of losing the penis or having it destroyed inside the mother —phantasies which may result in impotence.

[1] This growing conviction about the fundamental importance of Abraham's discoveries was also the result of my analysis with him, which began in 1924 and was cut short fourteen months later through his illness and death.

[2] Described under the name 'Erna' in *The Psycho-Analysis of Children*, Chapter III.

[3] Cf. 'Early Stages of the Oedipus Conflict' (1928).

[4] Cf. 'The Importance of Symbol-Formation in the Development of the Ego' (1930).

I came to see that the fears connected with attacks on the mother's body and of being attacked by external and internal objects had a particular quality and intensity which suggested their psychotic nature. In exploring the child's relation to internalized objects, various situations of internal persecution and their psychotic contents became clear. Furthermore, the recognition that fear of retaliation derives from the individual's own aggressiveness led me to suggest that the initial defences of the ego are directed against the anxiety aroused by destructive impulses and phantasies. Again and again, when these psychotic anxieties were traced to their origin, they were found to stem from oral-sadism. I recognized also that the oral-sadistic relation to the mother and the internalization of a devoured, and therefore devouring, breast create the prototype of all internal persecutors; and furthermore that the internalization of an injured and therefore dreaded breast on the one hand, and of a satisfying and helpful breast on the other, is the core of the super-ego. Another conclusion was that, although oral anxieties come first, sadistic phantasies and desires from all sources are operative at a very early stage of development and overlap the oral anxieties.[1]

The importance of the infantile anxieties I have described above was also shown in the analysis of very ill adults, some of whom were border-line psychotic cases.[2]

[1] These and other conclusions are contained in the two papers I have already mentioned, 'Early Stages of the Oedipus Conflict' and 'The Importance of Symbol-Formation in the Development of the Ego'. See also 'Personification in the Play of Children' (1929).

[2] It is possible that the understanding of the contents of psychotic anxieties and of the urgency to interpret them was brought home to me in the analysis of a paranoic schizophrenic man who came to me for one month only. In 1922 a colleague who was going on holiday asked me to take over for a month a schizophrenic patient of his. I found from the first hour onwards that I must not allow the patient to remain silent for any length of time. I felt that his silence implied danger, and in every such instance I interpreted his suspicions of me, e.g. that I was plotting with his uncle and would have him certified again (he had recently been de-certified)—material which on other occasions he verbally expressed. Once when I had interpreted his silence in this way, connecting it with former material, the patient, sitting up, asked me in a threatening tone: 'Are you going to send me back to the asylum?' But he soon became quieter and began to speak more freely. That showed me that I had been on the right lines and should continue to interpret his suspicions and feelings of persecution. To some extent a positive as well as a negative transference to me came about; but at one point, when his fear of women came up very strongly, he demanded from me the name of a male analyst to whom he could turn. I gave him a name, but he never approached this colleague. During that month I saw the patient every day. The analyst who had asked me to take over found some progress on his return and wished me to continue the analysis. I refused, having become fully aware of the danger of treating a paranoic without any protection or other suitable management. During the time when I analysed him, he often stood for hours opposite my

There were other experiences which helped me to reach yet a further conclusion. The comparison between the undoubtedly paranoic Erna and the phantasies and anxieties that I had found in less ill children, who could only be called neurotic, convinced me that psychotic (paranoid and depressive) anxieties underlie infantile neurosis. I also made similar observations in the analyses of adult neurotics. All these different lines of exploration resulted in the hypothesis that anxieties of a psychotic nature are in some measure part of normal infantile development and are expressed and worked through in the course of the infantile neurosis.[1] To uncover these infantile anxieties the analysis has, however, to be carried into deep layers of the unconscious, and this applies both to adults and to children.[2]

It has already been pointed out in the introduction to this paper that my attention from the beginning focused on the child's anxieties and that it was by means of interpreting their contents that I found myself able to diminish anxiety. In order to do this, full use had to be made of the symbolic language of play which I recognized to be an essential part of the child's mode of expression. As we have seen, the brick, the little figure, the car, not only represent things which interest the child in themselves, but in his play with them they always have a variety of symbolical meanings as well which are bound up with his phantasies, wishes, and experiences. This archaic mode of expression is also the language with which we are familiar in dreams, and it was by approaching the play of the child in a way similar to Freud's interpretation of dreams that I found I could get access to the child's unconscious. But we have to consider each child's use of symbols in connection with his particular emotions and anxieties and in relation to the whole situation which is presented in the analysis; mere generalized translations of symbols are meaningless.

The importance I attributed to symbolism led me—as time went

---

house, looking up at my window, though it was only on a few occasions that he rang the bell and asked to see me. I may mention that after a short time he was again certified. Although I did not at the time draw any theoretical conclusions from this experience, I believe that this fragment of an analysis may have contributed to my later insight into the psychotic nature of infantile anxieties and to the development of my technique.

[1] As we know, Freud found that there is no structural difference between the normal and the neurotic, and this discovery has been of the greatest importance in the understanding of mental processes in general. My hypothesis that anxieties of a psychotic nature are ubiquitous in infancy, and underlie the infantile neurosis, is an extension of Freud's discovery.

[2] The conclusions I have presented in the last paragraph can be found fully dealt with in *The Psycho-Analysis of Children*.

on—to theoretical conclusions about the process of symbol formation. Play analysis had shown that symbolism enabled the child to
transfer not only interests, but also phantasies, anxieties, and guilt
to objects other than people.[1] Thus a great deal of relief is experienced in play and this is one of the factors which make it so
essential for the child. For instance, Peter to whom I have referred
earlier, pointed out to me, when I interpreted his damaging a toy
figure as representing attacks on his brother, that he would not do
this to his *real* brother, he would only do it to the *toy* brother. My
interpretation of course made it clear to him that it was really his
brother whom he wished to attack; but the instance shows that only
by symbolic means was he able to express his destructive tendencies
in the analysis.

I have also arrived at the view that, in children, a severe inhibition
of the capacity to form and use symbols, and so to develop phantasy
life, is a sign of serious disturbance.[2] I suggested that such inhibitions,
and the resulting disturbance in the relation to the external world
and to reality, are characteristic of schizophrenia.[3]

In passing I may say that I found it of great value from the clinical
and theoretical point of view that I was analysing both adults and
children. I was thereby able to observe the infant's phantasies and
anxieties still operative in the adult and to assess in the young child
what his future development might be. It was by comparing the
severely ill, the neurotic, and the normal child, and by recognizing
infantile anxieties of a psychotic nature as the cause of illness in
adult neurotics, that I had arrived at the conclusions I have described above.[4]

VI

In tracing, in the analyses of adults and children, the development
of impulses, phantasies, and anxieties back to their origin, *i.e.* to the
feelings towards the mother's breast (even with children who have
not been breast-fed), I found that object relations start almost at
birth and arise with the first feeding experience; furthermore, that
all aspects of mental life are bound up with object relations. It also
emerged that the child's experience of the external world, which very
soon includes his ambivalent relation to his father and to other
members of his family, is constantly influenced by—and in turn

[1] In this connection, cf. Dr Ernest Jones's important paper 'The Theory of
Symbolism', (1916).

[2] 'The Importance of Symbol-Formation in the Development of the Ego' (1930).

[3] This conclusion has since influenced the understanding of the schizophrenic
mode of communication and has found its place in the treatment of schizophrenia.

[4] I cannot deal here with the fundamental difference which, besides common
features, exist between the normal, the neurotic and the psychotic.

influences—the internal world he is building up, and that external and internal situations are always interdependent, since introjection and projection operate side by side from the beginning of life.

The observations that in the infant's mind the mother primarily appears as good and bad breast split off from each other, and that within a few months, with growing ego integration the contrasting aspects are beginning to be synthesized, helped me to understand the importance of the processes of splitting and keeping apart good and bad figures,[1] as well as the effect of such processes on ego development. The conclusion to be drawn from the experience that depressive anxiety arises as a result of the ego synthesizing the good and bad (loved and hated) aspects of the object led me in turn to the concept of the depressive position which reaches its climax towards the middle of the first year. It is preceded by the paranoid position, which extends over the first three or four months of life and is characterized by persecutory anxiety and splitting processes.[2] Later on, in 1946[3], when I reformulated my views on the first three or four months of life, I called this stage (making use of a suggestion of Fairbairn's)[4] the paranoid-schizoid position, and, in working out its significance, sought to co-ordinate my findings about splitting, projection, persecution and idealization.

My work with children and the theoretical conclusions I drew from it increasingly influenced my technique with adults. It has always been a tenet of psycho-analysis that the unconscious, which originates in the infantile mind, has to be explored in the adult. My experience with children had taken me much deeper in that direction than was formerly the case, and this led to a technique which made access to those layers possible. In particular, my play technique had helped me to see which material was most in need of interpretation at the moment and the way in which it would be most easily conveyed to the patient; and some of this knowledge I could apply to the analysis of adults.[5] As has been pointed out earlier, this does not

[1] 'Personification in the Play of Children' (1929).
[2] 'A Contribution to the Psychogenesis of Manic-Depressive States' (1935).
[3] 'Notes on Some Schizoid Mechanisms' (1946).
[4] Fairbairn, W. R. D., 'A Revised Psychopathology of the Psychoses and Neuroses' (1941).
[5] The play technique has also influenced work with children in other fields, as for example in child guidance work and in education. The development of educational methods in England has been given fresh impetus by Susan Isaacs' research at the Malting House School. Her books about that work have been widely read and have had a lasting effect on educational techniques in this country, especially where young children are concerned. Her approach was strongly influenced by her great appreciation of child analysis, in particular of play technique; and it is largely due to her that in England the psycho-analytic understanding of children has contributed to developments in education.

mean that the technique used with children is identical with the approach to adults. Though we find our way back to the earliest stages, it is of great importance in analysing adults to take account of the adult ego, just as with children we keep in mind the infantile ego according to the stage of its development.

The fuller understanding of the earliest stages of development, of the rôle of phantasies, anxieties, and defences in the emotional life of the infant has also thrown light on the fixation points of adult psychosis. As a result there has opened up a new way of treating psychotic patients by psycho-analysis. This field, in particular the psycho-analysis of schizophrenic patients, needs much further exploration; but the work done in this direction by some psycho-analysts, who are represented in this book, seems to justify hopes for the future.

# 9

# ON IDENTIFICATION

## (1955)

### INTRODUCTION

In 'Mourning and Melancholia'[1] Freud (1917) showed the intrinsic connection between identification and introjection. His later discovery of the super-ego,[2] which he ascribed to the introjection of the father and identification with him, has led to the recognition that identification as a sequel to introjection is part of normal development. Since this discovery, introjection and identification have played a central rôle in psycho-analytic thought and research.

Before starting on the actual topic of this paper, I think it would be helpful to recapitulate my main conclusions on this theme. Super-ego development can be traced back to introjection in the earliest stages of infancy; the primal internalized objects form the basis of complex processes of identification; persecutory anxiety, arising from the experience of birth, is the first form of anxiety, very soon followed by depressive anxiety; introjection and projection operate from the beginning of post-natal life and constantly interact. This interaction both builds up the internal world and shapes the picture of external reality. The inner world consists of objects, first of all the mother, internalized in various aspects and emotional situations. The relationships between these internalized figures, and between them and the ego, tend to be experienced'—when persecutory anxiety is dominant—as mainly hostile and dangerous; they are felt to be loving and good when the infant is gratified and happy feelings prevail. This inner world, which can be described in terms of internal relations and happenings, is the product of the infant's own impulses, emotions, and phantasies. It is of course profoundly influenced by his good and bad experiences from external sources.[3] But at the same

---

[1] Abraham's work on melancholia, as early as 1911 ('Notes on the Psycho-Analytical investigation and Treatment of Manic-Depressive Insanity and Allied Conditions') and 1924 ('A Short History of the Development of the Libido, viewed in the Light of Mental Disorders') was also of great importance in this connection.

[2] *The Ego and the Id* (1923).

[3] Among them from the beginning of life the mother's attitude is of vital importance and remains a major factor in the development of the child. Cf., for instance, *Developments in Psycho-Analysis* (Klein *et al.*, 1952).

time the inner world influences his perception of the external world in a way that is no less decisive for his development. The mother, first of all her breast, is the primal object for both the infant's introjective and projective processes. Love and hatred are from the beginning projected on to her, and concurrently she is internalized with both these contrasting primordial emotions, which underlie the infant's feeling that a good and a bad mother (breast) exist. The more the mother and her breast are cathected—and the extent of the cathexis depends on a combination of internal and external factors, among which the inherent capacity for love is of utmost importance —the more securely will the internalized good breast, the prototype of good internal objects, be established in the infant's mind. This in turn influences both the strength and the nature of projections; in particular it determines whether feelings of love or destructive impulses predominate in them.[1]

I have in various connections described the infant's sadistic phantasies directed against the mother. I found that aggressive impulses and phantasies arising in the earliest relation to the mother's breast, such as sucking the breast dry and scooping it out, soon lead to further phantasies of entering the mother and robbing her of the contents of her body. Concurrently, the infant experiences impulses and phantasies of attacking the mother by putting excrements into her. In such phantasies, products of the body and parts of the self are felt to have been split off, projected into the mother, and to be continuing their existence within her. These phantasies soon extend to the father and to other people. I also contended that the persecutory anxiety and the fear of retaliation, which result from oral-, urethal- and anal-sadistic impulses, underlie the development of paranoia and schizophrenia.

It is not only what are felt to be destructive and 'bad' parts of the self which are split off and projected into another person, but also parts which are felt to be good and valuable. I have pointed out earlier that from the beginning of life the infant's first object, the mother's breast (and the mother), is invested with libido and that this vitally influences the way in which the mother is internalized. This in turn is of great importance for the relation with her as an external and internal object. The process by which the mother is invested with libido is bound up with the mechanism of projecting good feelings and good parts of the self into her.

In the course of further work, I also came to recognize the major importance for identification of certain projective mechanisms which are complementary to the introjective ones. The process which

[1] To put it in terms of the two instincts, it is a question whether in the struggle between the life and death instincts the life instinct prevails.

underlies the feeling of identification with other people, because one has attributed qualities or attitudes of one's owr to them, was generally taken for granted even before the corresponding concept was incorporated in psycho-analytic theory. For instance, the projective mechanism underlying empathy is familiar in everday life. Phenomena well known in psychiatry, *e.g.* a patient's feeling that he *actually is* Christ, God, a king, a famous person, are bound up with projection. The mechanisms underlying such phenomena, however, had not been investigated in much detail when, in my 'Notes on Some Schizoid Mechanisms' (1946), I suggested the term 'projective identification'[1] for those processes that form part of the paranoid-schizoid position. The conclusions I arrived at in that paper were, however, based on some of my earlier findings,[2] in particular on that of the infantile oral-, urethral- and anal-sadistic phantasies and impulses to attack the mother's body in many ways, including the projection of excrements and parts of the self into her.

Projective identification is bound up with developmental processes arising during the first three or four months of life (the paranoid-schizoid position) when splitting is at its height and persecutory anxiety predominates. The ego is still largely unintegrated and is therefore liable to split itself, its emotions and its internal and external objects, but splitting is also one of the fundamental defences against persecutory anxiety. Other defences arising at this stage are idealization, denial, and omnipotent control of internal and external objects. Identification by projection implies a combination of splitting off parts of the self and projecting them on to (or rather into) another person. These processes have many ramifications and fundamentally influence object relations.

In normal development, in the second quarter of the first year, persecutory anxiety diminishes and depressive anxiety comes to the fore, as a result of the ego's greater capacity to integrate itself and to synthesize its objects. This entails sorrow and guilt about the harm done (in omnipotent phantasies) to an object which is now felt to be both loved and hated; these anxieties and the defences against them represent the depressive position. At this juncture a regression to the paranoid-schizoid position may occur in the attempt to escape from depression.

I also suggested that internalization is of great importance for

---

[1] In this connection I refer to the papers by Herbert Rosenfeld, 'Analysis of a Schizophrenic State with Depersonalization' (1947) 'Remarks on the Relation of Male Homosexuality to Paranoia, Paranoid Anxiety, and Narcissism' (1949); and 'Notes on the Psychopathology of Confusional States in Chronic Schizophrenias' (1950), which are relevant to these problems.

[2] Cf. my *Psycho-Analysis of Children;* for instance, pp. 128 ff.

projective processes, in particular that the good internalized breast acts as a focal point in the ego, from which good feelings can be projected on to external objects. It strengthens the ego, counteracts the processes of splitting and dispersal and enhances the capacity for integration and synthesis. The good internalized object is thus one of the preconditions for an integrated and stable ego and for good object relations. The tendency towards integration, which is concurrent with splitting, I assume to be, from earliest infancy, a dominant feature of mental life. One of the main factors underlying the need for integration is the individual's feeling that integration implies being alive, loving, and being loved by the internal and external good object; that is to say, there exists a close link between integration and object relations. Conversely, the feeling of chaos, of disintegration, of lacking emotions as a result of splitting, I take to be closely related to the fear of death. I have maintained (in 'Schizoid Mechanisms') that the fear of annihilation by the destructive forces within is the deepest fear of all. Splitting as a primal defence against this fear is effective to the extent that it brings about a dispersal of anxiety and a cutting off of emotions. But it fails in another sense because it results in a feeling akin to death—that is what the accompanying disintegration and feeling of chaos amount to. The sufferings of the schizophrenic are, I think, not fully appreciated, because he appears to be devoid of emotions.

Here I wish to go somewhat beyond my paper on 'Schizoid Mechanisms'. I would suggest that a securely established good object, implying a securely established love for it, gives the ego a feeling of riches and abundance which allows for an outpouring of libido and projection of good parts of the self into the external world without a sense of depletion arising. The ego can then also feel that it is able to re-introject the love it has given out, as well as take in goodness from other sources, and thus be enriched by the whole process. In other words, in such cases there is a balance between giving out and taking in, between projection and introjection.

Furthermore, whenever an unharmed breast is taken in, in states of gratification and love, this affects the ways in which the ego splits and projects. As I suggested, there are a variety of splitting processes (about which we have still a good deal to discover) and their nature is of great importance for the development of the ego. The feeling of containing an unharmed nipple and breast—although co-existing with phantasies of a breast devoured and therefore in bits—has the effect that splitting and projecting are not *predominantly* related to fragmented parts of the personality but to more coherent parts of the self. This implies that the ego is not exposed to a fatal weakening by dispersal and for this reason is more capable of repeatedly undoing splitting and achieving integration and synthesis in its relation to objects.

Conversely, the breast taken in with hatred, and therefore felt to be destructive, becomes the prototype of all bad internal objects, drives the ego to further splitting and becomes the representative of the death-instinct within.

I have already mentioned that concurrently with the internalization of the good breast, the external mother too is cathected with libido. In various connections Freud has described this process and some of its implications: for instance, referring to idealization in a love relation, he states[1] that 'the object is being treated in the same way as our own ego, so that when we are in love, a considerable amount of narcissistic libido overflows on to the object. . . . We love it on account of the perfections which we have striven to reach for our own ego. . . .'[2]

In my view, the process which Freud describes imply that this loved object is felt to contain the split-off, loved, and valued part of the self, which in this way continues its existence inside the object. It thereby becomes an extension of the self.[3]

The above is a brief summary of my findings presented in 'Notes on some Schizoid Mechanisms'.[4] I have not confined myself, however, to the points discussed there but have added a few further suggestions and amplified some which were implied but not explicitly stated in that paper. I now propose to exemplify some of these findings by an analysis of a story by the French novelist Julian Green.[5]

## A NOVEL ILLUSTRATING PROJECTIVE IDENTIFICATION

The hero, a young clerk called Fabian Especel, is unhappy and dissatisfied with himself, in particular with his appearance, his lack of success with women, his poverty, and the inferior work to which he feels condemned. He finds his religious beliefs, which he attributes

[1] (1921) *Group Psychology and the Analysis of the Ego* (*S.E.* **18**), p. 112.

[2] Anna Freud has described another aspect of the projection on to a loved object and identification with it in her concept of 'altruistic surrender'. *The Ego and the Mechanisms of Defence* (1937), Ch. X.

[3] On re-reading recently Freud's *Group Psychology and the Analysis of the Ego*, it appeared to me that he was aware of the process of identification by projection, although he did not differentiate it by means of a special term from the process of identification by introjection with which he was mainly concerned. Elliott Jaques (1955) quotes some passages from *Group Psychology* as implicitly referring to identification by projection.

[4] Cf. also 'Some Theoretical Conclusions Regarding the Emotional Life of the Infant' (1952).

[5] *If I Were You* (Translated from the French by J. H. F. McEwen) (London, 1950).

to his mother's demands, very burdensome, yet cannot free himself from them. His father, who died when Fabian was still at school, had squandered all his money on gambling, had led a 'gay' life with women, and died of heart failure, thought to be a result of his dissolute life. Fabian's pronounced grievance and rebellion against fate are bound up with his resentment against his father, whose irresponsibility had deprived him of his further education and prospects. These feelings, it appears, contribute to Fabian's insatiable desire for wealth and success, and to his intense envy and hatred of those who possess more.

The essence of the story is the magic power to change himself into other people which is conferred on Fabian by a compact with the Devil, who seduces him by false promises of happiness into accepting this sinister gift; he teaches Fabian a secret formula by which the change into another person can be effected. This formula includes his own name, Fabian, and it is of great importance that he should—whatever happens—remember the formula and his name.

Fabian's first choice is the waiter who brings him a cup of coffee which is all that he can afford for his breakfast. This attempt at projection comes to nothing because at this point he still considers the feelings of his prospective victims, and the waiter, on being asked by Fabian whether he would like to change places with him, refuses. Fabian's next choice is his employer Poujars. He greatly envies this man who is wealthy, can—as Fabian thinks—enjoy life to the full, and has power over other people, in particular over Fabian. The author describes Fabian's envy of Poujars in these words: 'Ah! the sun. It often seemed to him that M. Poujars kept it hidden in his pocket.' Fabian is also very resentful of his employer because he feels humiliated by him and imprisoned in his office.

Before he whispers the formula into Poujars' ear, Fabian speaks to Poujars in the same contemptuous and humiliating way as Poujars used to speak to him. The transformation has the effect of making his victim enter Fabian's body and collapse; Fabian (now in the body of Poujars) writes out a large cheque in Fabian's favour. He finds in Fabian's pocket his address which he carefully writes down. (This slip of paper with Fabian's name and address he carries with him into his next two transformations.) He also arranges that Fabian, into whose pocket he has put the cheque, should be taken home, where he would be looked after by his mother. The fate of Fabian's body is very much in Fabian-Poujars' mind, for he feels that he might one day wish to return to his old self; he therefore does not want to see Fabian recover consciousness because he dreads the frightened eyes of Poujars (with whom he has changed places) looking out of his

own former face. He wonders, looking at Fabian who is still unconscious, whether anybody ever loved him, and is glad that he got rid
of that unprepossessing appearance and those miserable clothes.

Fabian–Poujars very soon finds out some drawbacks to this transformation. He feels oppressed by his new corpulence; he has lost his
appetite and becomes aware of the kidney trouble from which
Poujars suffers. He discovers with dislike that he has not only taken
on Poujars' looks but also his personality. He has already become
estranged from his old self and remembers little about Fabian's life
and circumstances. He decides that he is not going to stay a minute
longer than necessary in Poujars' skin.

On leaving the office with Poujars' pocket-book in his possession
he gradually realizes that he has put himself into an extremely
serious situation. For not only does he dislike the personality, outlook, and unpleasant memories which he has acquired, but he is also
very worried about the lack of will-power and initiative which are in
keeping with Poujars' age. The thought that he might not be able
to muster the energy to transform himself into somebody else fill him
with horror. He decides that for his next object he must choose somebody who is young and healthy. When he sees in a café an athletic
young man with an ugly face, looking arrogant and quarrelsome but
whose whole bearing shows self-assurance, vigour, and health,
Fabian-Poujars—feeling increasingly worried that he might never
get rid of Poujars—decides to approach the young man although he is
very afraid of him. He offers him a packet of banknotes which Fabian-
Poujars wants to have after the transformation, and while thus dis-
tracting the man's attention he manages to whisper the formula into
his ear and to put the slip with Fabian's name and address into his
pocket. Within a few moments Poujars, whose person Fabian has
just left, has collapsed and Fabian has turned into the young man,
Paul Esménard. He is filled with the great joy of feeling young,
healthy, and strong. He has much more than in the first transformation lost his original self and turned into the new personality; he is
amazed to find a packet of banknotes in his hand and in his pocket
a slip of paper, with Fabian's name and address. Soon he thinks of
Berthe, the girl whose favour Paul Esménard has been trying to win,
so far without success. Among other unpleasant things Berthe told
him that he has the face of a murderer and that she is afraid of him.
The money in his pocket gives him confidence and he goes straight
to her house, determined to make her comply with his desires.

Although Fabian has become submerged in Paul Esménard, he
feels increasingly bewildered about the name Fabian which he has
read on the slip of paper. 'That name remained in some way at the
very core of his being.' A feeling of being imprisoned in an unknown

body and burdened with huge hands and a slow-working brain takes possession of him. He cannot puzzle it out, struggling unavailingly with his own stupidity; he wonders what he could mean by wishing to be free. All this goes through his mind as he goes to Berthe. He forces his way into her room although she tries to lock the door against him. Berthe screams, he silences her by clapping his hand over her mouth, and in the ensuing struggle strangles her. Only gradually does he realize what he has done; he is terrified and does not dare to leave Berthe's flat since he hears people moving about in the house. Suddenly he hears a knock at the door, opens it and finds the Devil whom he does not recognize. The Devil leads him away, teaches him again the formula which Fabian-Esménard has forgotten, and helps him to remember something about his original self. He also warns him that in future he must not enter a person too stupid to use the formula and therefore incapable of effecting further transformations.

The Devil takes him into a reading-room in search of a person into whom Fabian-Esménard could change himself and picks out Emmanuel Fruges; Fruges and the Devil recognize each other immediately, for Fruges has all the time been struggling against the Devil, who has 'so often and so patiently hung about that unquiet soul'. The Devil directs Fabian-Esménard to whisper the formula into Fruges' ear and the transformation is effected. As soon as Fabian has entered into Fruges' body and personality, he recovers his capacity to think. He wonders about the fate of his last victim and is somewhat concerned about Fruges (now in the body of Esménard) who will be condemned for Fabian-Esménard's crime. He feels partly responsible for the crime because, as the Devil points out to him, the hands which committed the murder belonged to him only a few minutes ago. Before parting from the Devil he also inquires after the original Fabian and after Poujars. While recovering some memories of his former selves, he notices that he is more and more turning into Fruges and acquiring his personality. At the same time he becomes aware that his experiences have increased his comprehension of other people, for he can now understand better what went on in the minds of Poujars, Paul Esménard, and Fruges. He also feels sympathy, an emotion he has never known before, and goes back once more to see what Fruges—in the body of Paul Esménard—is doing. Yet he relishes the thought not only of his own escape but also of what his victim will suffer in his place.

The author tells us that some elements of Fabian's original nature enter more into this transformation than into either of the previous ones. In particular the inquiring side of Fabian's character influences Fabian-Fruges to discover more and more about Fruges' personality.

Among other things he finds that he is drawn to obscene postcards which he buys from an old woman in a little stationer's shop, where the cards are hidden behind other articles. Fabian is disgusted with this side of his new nature; he hates the noise made by the revolving stand on which the cards are arranged, and feels that this noise will haunt him for ever. He decides to get rid of Fruges whom he is now able to judge to some extent with the eyes of Fabian.

Soon a little boy of about six comes into the shop. George is the picture of 'apple-cheeked innocence' and Fabian-Fruges is at once very much attracted to him. George reminds him of himself at that age and he feels very tender towards the child. Fabian-Fruges follows George out of the shop and observes him with great interest. Suddenly he is tempted to transform himself into the boy. He fights this temptation as he has never, he thinks, fought temptation before, for he knows that it would be criminal to steal this child's personality and life. Nevertheless he decides to turn himself into George, kneels down beside him and whispers the formula in his ear, in a state of great emotion and remorse. But nothing happens, and Fabian-Fruges realizes that the magic does not work with the child because the Devil has no power over him.

Fabian-Fruges is horrified at the thought that he might not be able to get away from Fruges whom he dislikes more and more. He feels he is the prisoner of Fruges and struggles to keep the Fabian aspect of himself alive, for he realizes that Fruges lacks the initiative which would help him to escape. He makes several attempts to approach people but fails and is soon in despair, being afraid that Fruges' body will be his tomb, that he will have to remain there until his death. 'All the time he got the impression that he was being slowly but surely shut in; that a door which had stood open was now gradually closing on him.' Eventually he succeeds in changing himself into a handsome and healthy young man of twenty, called Camille. At this point the author introduces us for the first time to a family circle, consisting of Camille's wife Stéphanie, her cousin Elise, Camille himself, his young brother, and the old uncle who had adopted them all when they were children.

When he enters the house Fabian-Camille seems to be searching for something. He goes upstairs looking into different rooms until he comes into Elise's room. When he sees there his reflection in a mirror he is overjoyed to find that he is handsome and strong but a moment later he discovers that he has actually turned himself into an unhappy, weak, and useless person, and decides to get rid of Camille. At the same time he has become aware of Elise's passionate and unrequited love for Camille. Elise comes in, and he tells her that he loves her and should have married her instead of her cousin Stéphanie.

Elise, amazed and frightened since Camille has never given her a sign of returning her love, runs away. Left alone in Elise's room Fabian-Camille thinks with sympathy of the girl's sufferings and that he could make her happy by loving her. Then he suddenly thinks that if this were so he could become happy by turning himself into Elise. However, he dismisses this possibility because he cannot be sure that Camille, if Fabian were to turn himself into Elise, would love her. He is not even sure whether he himself—Fabian—loves Elise. While he wonders about this, it occurs to him that what he loves in Elise are her eyes which are somehow familiar to him.

Before leaving the house, Fabian-Camille takes revenge on the uncle, who is a hypocritical and tyrannical man, for all the harm he has done to the family. He also particularly avenges Elise by punishing and humiliating her rival Stéphanie. Fabian-Camille, having insulted the old man, leaves him in a state of impotent rage and goes away knowing that he has made it impossible for himself ever to return to this house in the shape of Camille. But before leaving he insists that Elise, who is still frightened of him, should listen to him once more. He tells her that he does not really love her and that she must give up her unfortunate passion for Camille or she will always be unhappy.

As before, Fabian feels resentment against the person into whom he has turned himself, because he has found him to be worthless; he therefore pictures with glee how Camille, when Fabian has left him, will be received at home by his uncle and his wife. The one person he regrets leaving is Elise; and suddenly it occurs to him whom she resembles. Her eyes have 'in them all the tragedy of a longing which can never be satisfied'; and all at once he knows that they are Fabian's eyes. When this name, which he has completely forgotten, comes back to him and he says it aloud, its sound reminds him dimly of 'a far country' known only in the past from dreams. For his actual memory of Fabian has completely disappeared, and in his hurry to escape from Fruges and transform himself into Camille he has not taken with him either Fabian's name and address or the money. From this moment onwards the longing for Fabian gets hold of him and he struggles to recover his old memories. It is a child who helps him to recognize that he himself is Fabian, for when the child asks what his name is, he straightway answers 'Fabian'. Now Fabian-Camille physically and mentally moves more and more in the direction where Fabian can be found, for, as he puts it, 'I want to be myself again'. Walking through the streets he calls out this name, which embodies his greatest longing, and waits to get a reply. The formula which he has forgotten occurs to him and he hopes that he will also remember Fabian's surname. On his way home every building, stone and tree takes on a particular meaning; he feels that they are 'charged with some message for him' and walks on, driven by an impulse. This is how he comes to enter the old woman's shop which had been so familiar to Fruges. He feels that in looking round in this dark shop he is also 'exploring a secret corner of his own memory, looking around his own mind, as it were' and he is filled with 'abysmal depression'. When he pushes the revolving stand with the postcards on it the squeaking noise affects him strangely. He leaves the shop hurriedly. The next landmark is the reading-room in which, with the Devil's help, Fabian-Esménard was turned into Fruges. He calls out 'Fabian' but gets no answer. Next he passes the house where Fabian-Esménard killed Berthe and feels impelled to go in and find out what happened behind that window at which some people are pointing; he wonders whether this is perhaps the room in which Fabian lives, but he is filled with fear and slinks away when he hears the people talking about the murder which was committed three days before; the murderer has not yet been found. As he walks on, the houses and shops become even more familiar to him, and he is deeply moved when he reaches the place where the Devil first tried to win Fabian over. At last he comes to the house in which Fabian lives and the concierge lets Fabian-Camille in. When he begins to climb the stairs a sudden pain grips his heart.

During the three days when all these events took place Fabian had been lying unconscious in his bed, looked after by his mother. He begins to come to and grows restless when Fabian-Camille approaches the house and comes up the stairs. Fabian hears Fabian-Camille call out his name from behind the door, gets out of bed and goes to the door, but is unable to open it. Through the keyhole Fabian-Camille speaks the formula and then goes away. Fabian is found by his mother lying unconscious by the door, but he soon comes to and regains some strength. He desperately wants to find out what happened during the days when he was unconscious and in particular about the encounter with Fabian-Camille, but is told that nobody has come and that he has been lying in a coma for three days ever since he collapsed in the office. With his mother sitting by his bedside he is overcome by the longing to be loved by her and to be able to express his love to her. He wishes to touch her hand, to throw himself into her arms, but feels that she would not respond. In spite of this he realizes that if his love for her had been stronger she would have loved him more. The intense affection which he experiences towards her extends suddenly to the whole of humanity and he feels overflowing with an unaccountable happiness. His mother suggests that he should pray, but he can only recall the words 'Our Father'. Then he is again overcome by this mysterious happiness, and dies.

## INTERPRETATIONS

### I

The author of this story has deep insight into the unconscious mind; this is seen both in the way he depicts the events and characters and—what is of particular interest here—in his choice of the people into whom Fabian projects himself. My interest in Fabian's personality and adventures, illustrating, as they do, some of the complex and still obscure problems of projective identification, led me to attempt an analysis of this rich material almost as if he were a patient.

Before discussing projective identification, which to me is the main theme of this book, I shall consider the interaction between introjective and projective processes which is, I think, also illustrated in the novel. For instance, the author describes the unhappy Fabian's urge to gaze at the stars. 'Whenever he stared like this into the all-enveloping night he had a sensation of being lifted gently above the world. . . . It was almost as if by the very effort of gazing into space a sort of gulf in himself, corresponding to the giddy depths into which his imagination peered, was being opened.' This, I think, means that Fabian is simultaneously looking into distance and into himself; taking in the sky and the stars as well as projecting into the sky and stars his loved internal objects and the good parts of himself. I would also interpret his intent gazing at the stars as an attempt to regain his good objects which he feels are lost or far away.

Other aspects of Fabian's introjective identifications throw light on his projective processes. On one occasion, when he is lonely in his room at night, he feels, as so often, that he longs 'to hear some signs of life coming from the other inhabitants of the building around him'. Fabian lays his father's gold watch on the table; he has a great affection for it and particularly likes it because of 'its opulence and glossiness and the clearly marked figures on its face'. In a vague way this watch also gives him a feeling of confidence. As it lies on the table among his papers he feels that the whole room acquires an air of greater order and seriousness, perhaps owing to 'the fussy and yet soothing sound of its ticking, comforting amid the pervading stillness'. Looking at the watch and listening to its ticking, he muses upon the hours of joy and misery in his father's life which it has ticked away, and it seems to him alive and independent of its dead former owner. In an earlier passage the author says that ever since childhood Fabian 'had been haunted by a feeling of some inner presence which, in some way which he could not have described, was ever beyond the reach of his own consciousness. . . .' I would conclude that the watch has some qualities of a fatherly nature, such as order and seriousness, which it imparts to his room and in a deeper sense to Fabian himself; in other words, the watch stands for the good internalized father whom he wishes to feel ever present. This aspect of the super-ego, which links with the highly moral and orderly attitude of his mother, is in contrast to his father's passions and his 'gay' life, of which the ticking of the watch also reminds Fabian. He identifies himself with this frivolous side too, as is shown in his setting so much store on his conquests of women—although such successes do not afford him much satisfaction.

Yet another aspect of the internalized father appears in the shape of the Devil. For we read that when the Devil is on his way to him, Fabian hears footsteps resounding on the stairs: 'He began to feel those thudding footsteps as a pulse beating in his own temples.' A little later, when face to face with the Devil, it seems to him that 'the figure in front of him would go on rising and rising until it spread like a darkness through the whole room'. This, I think, expresses the internalization of the Devil (the bad father), the darkness indicating also the terror he feels at having taken in such a sinister object. At a later point, when Fabian is travelling in a carriage with the Devil, he falls asleep and dreams 'that his companion edged along the seat towards him' and that his voice 'seemed to wrap itself about him, tying his arms, choking him with its oily flow'. I see in that Fabian's fear of the bad object intruding into him. In my 'Notes on Some Schizoid Mechanisms' I described these fears as a consequence of the impulse to intrude into another person, *i.e.* of projective identification. The external object intruding into the self and the bad object which has been introjected have much in common; these two anxieties are closely linked and apt to reinforce each other. This relation with the Devil repeats, I think, Fabian's early feelings about one aspect of his father—the seductive father felt to be bad. On the other hand, the moral component of his internalized objects can be seen in the Devil's ascetic contempt of the 'lusts of the flesh'.[1] This aspect was influenced by Fabian's identification with the moral and ascetic mother, the Devil thus representing simultaneously both parents.

I have indicated some aspects of his father which Fabian had internalized. Their incompatibility was a source of never-ending conflict in him, which was increased by the actual conflict between his parents and had been perpetuated by his internalizing the parents

[1] The various and contradictory characteristics—both ideal and bad—with which the father, as well as the mother, are endowed are a familiar feature in the development of the child's object relations. Similarly, such conflicting attitudes are also attributed to the internalized figures some of which form the super-ego.

in their unhappy relation with each other. The various ways in which he identified himself with his mother were no less complex, as I hope to show. The persecution and depression arising from these inner relations contributed much to Fabian's loneliness, his restless moods and his urge to escape from his hated self.[1] The author quotes in his preface Milton's lines 'Thou art become (O worst imprisonment) the Dungeon of thyself.'

One evening, when Fabian has been wandering aimlessly through the streets, the idea of returning to his own lodgings fills him with horror. He knows that all he will find there is himself; nor can he escape into a new love affair, for he realizes that he would again, as usual, grow tired of it very quickly. He wonders why he should be so hard to please and remembers that somebody had told him that what he wanted was a 'statue of ivory and gold'; he thinks that this over-fastidiousness might be an inheritance from his father (the Don Juan theme). He longs to escape from himself, if only for an hour, to get away from the 'never ending arguments' which go on within him. It would appear that his internalized objects were making incompatible demands on him and that these were the 'never ending arguments' by which he felt so persecuted.[2] He not only hates his internal persecutors but also feels worthless because he contains such bad objects. This is a corollary of the sense of guilt; for he feels that his aggressive impulses and phantasies have changed the parents into retaliatory persecutors or have destroyed them. Thus self-hatred, although directed against the bad internalized objects, ultimately focuses on the individual's own impulses which are felt to have been and to be destructive and dangerous to the ego and its good objects.

Greed, envy and hatred, the prime movers of aggressive phantasies, are dominant features in Fabian's character, and the author

---

[1] I have suggested ('Notes on some Schizoid Mechanisms') that projective identification arises during the paranoid-schizoid position which is characterized by splitting processes. I have pointed out above that Fabian's depression and his feeling of worthlessness gave additional impetus to his need to escape from his self. The heightened greed and denial which characterize manic defences against depression are, together with envy, also an important factor in projective identifications.

[2] In *The Ego and the Id* Freud writes (*S.E.* **19,** pp. 30-1): 'If they [the object-identifications] obtain the upper hand and become too numerous, unduly powerful and incompatible with one another, a pathological outcome will not be far off. It may come to a disruption of the ego in consequence of the different identifications becoming cut off from one another by resistances; perhaps the secret of the cases of what is described as 'multiple personality' is that the different identifications seize hold of consciousness in turn. Even when things do not go so far as this, there remains the question of conflicts between the various identifications into which the ego comes apart, conflicts which cannot after all be described as entirely pathological.'

shows us that these emotions urge Fabian to get hold of other people's possessions, both material and spiritual; they drive him irresistibly towards what I described as projective identifications. At one point, when Fabian has already made his pact with the Devil and is about to try out his new power, he cries out: 'Humanity, the great cup from which I shall shortly drink!' This suggests the greedy wish to drink from an inexhaustible breast. We may assume that these emotions and the greedy identifications by introjection and projection were first experienced in Fabian's relations to his primal objects, mother and father. My analytic experience has shown me that processes of introjection and projection in later life repeat in some measure the pattern of the earliest introjections and projections; the external world is again and again taken in and put out—re-introjected and re-projected. Fabian's greed, as can be gathered from the story, is reinforced by his self-hatred and the urge to escape from his own personality.

II

My interpretation of the novel implies that the author has presented fundamental aspects of emotional life on two planes: the experiences of the infant and their influence on the life of the adult. In the last few pages I have touched on some of the infantile emotions, anxieties, introjections and projections which I take to underlie Fabian's adult character and experiences.

I shall substantiate these assumptions by discussing some further episodes which I have not mentioned in the account of the novel. In assembling the various incidents from this particular angle, I shall not follow the chronological order either of the book or of Fabian's development. I am rather considering them as the expression of certain aspects of infantile development, and we have to remember that especially in infancy emotional experiences are not only consecutive but to a large extent simultaneous.

There is an interlude in the novel which seems to me of fundamental importance for understanding Fabian's early development. Fabian-Fruges has gone to sleep very depressed about his poverty, his inadequacy, and full of fear that he might not be able to change himself into someone else. On waking he sees that it is a bright, sunny morning. He dresses more carefully than usual, goes out and, sitting in the sunshine, becomes elated. All faces around him appear to be beautiful. He also thinks that in this admiration of beauty there is not 'any of that lustful covetousness which was so apt to poison even his moments of really serious contemplation; on the contrary, he simply admired and with a touch of almost religious respect'. However, he soon feels hungry because he has had no breakfast, and to this he attributes a slight giddiness which he experiences together with hopefulness and elation. He realizes, though, that this state of happiness is also dangerous because he must spur himself on to action so as to turn himself into somebody else; but first of all he is driven by hunger to find some food.[1] He goes into a baker's shop to buy a roll. The very smell of flour and warm bread always reminds Fruges of childhood holidays in the country in a house full of children. I believe that the whole shop turns in his mind into the feeding mother. He is engrossed in looking at a large basket of fresh rolls and stretches his hand out towards them when he hears a woman's voice asking him what he wants. At this he jumps 'like a sleepwalker who has been suddenly woken up'. She too smells good — 'like a wheat-field' — he longs to touch her and is surprised that he is afraid to do so. He is entranced by her beauty and feels that for her sake he could give up all his beliefs and hopes. In watching with delight all her movements when she hands him a roll, he focuses on her breasts, whose outlines he can see under her clothing. The whiteness of her skin intoxicates him and he is filled with an irresistible desire to put his hands round her waist. As soon as he has left the shop he is overwhelmed with misery. He suddenly has a strong impulse to throw the roll on the ground and trample on it with 'his shiny black shoes . . . in order to insult the sacredness of bread itself'. Then he remembers that the woman touched it and 'in a passion of thwarted desire he bit furiously into the thickest part of the roll'. He attacks even its remains by crushing them in his pocket and at the same time it seems to him as if a crumb were sticking like a stone in his throat. He is in agony. 'Something was beating and fluttering like a second heart just above his stomach but something large and heavy.' In thinking again of the woman, he concludes with bitterness that he has never been loved. All his affairs with girls had been sordid and he had never before encountered in a woman 'that fullness of breast the very thought of which was now torturing him with its persistent image'. He decides to return to the shop to have at least another look at her, for his desires seem to be 'burning him up'. He finds her even more desirable and feels that his looking at her almost amounts to touching her. Then he sees a man talking to her, with his hand laid affectionately on her 'milk-white' arm. The woman smiles at the man and they discuss plans for the evening. Fabian-Fruges is sure that he will never forget this scene, 'every detail being invested with tragic importance'. The words which the man had spoken to her still ring in his ears. He

[1] This state of elation is, I think, comparable to the wish-fulfilling hallucination (Freud) which the infant under the stress of reality, in particular of hunger, cannot maintain for long.

cannot 'stifle the sound of that voice which from somewhere within went on speaking yet'. In despair he covers his eyes with his hands. He cannot remember any occasion when he has suffered so acutely from his desires.

I see in the details of this episode Fabian's powerfully revived desire for his mother's breast with the ensuing frustration and hatred; his wish to trample on the bread with his black shoes expresses his anal-sadistic attacks, and his furiously biting into the roll his cannibalism and his oral-sadistic impulses. The whole situation appears to be internalized and all his emotions, with the ensuing disappointment and attacks, apply also to the internalized mother. This is shown by Fabian-Fruges furiously crushing the remains of the roll in his pocket, by his feeling that a crumb had stuck like a stone in his throat and (immediately afterwards) that a second and bigger heart above his stomach was fluttering inside him. In the very same episode the frustration experienced at the breast and in the earliest relation to the mother appears to be closely linked with the rivalry with the father. This represents a very early situation when the infant, deprived of the mother's breast, feels that someone else, above all the father, has taken it away from him and is enjoying it—a situation of envy and jealousy which appears to me part of the earliest stages of the Oedipus complex. Fabian-Fruges' passionate jealousy of the man who he believes possesses the baker-woman at night refers also to an internal situation, for he feels that he can hear inside him the man's voice speaking to the woman. I would conclude that the incident he has watched with such strong emotions represents the primal scene which he has internalized in the past. When, in this emotional state, he covers his eyes with his hand he is, I think, reviving the young infant's wish never to have seen and taken in the primal scene.

The next part of this chapter deals with Fabian-Fruges' sense of guilt about his desires which he feels he must destroy 'as rubbish is consumed by fire'. He goes into a church only to find that there is no holy water in the stoup, which is 'bone-dry', and is very indignant about such neglect of religious duties. He kneels down in a state of depression and thinks that it would need a miracle to relieve his guilt and sadness and solve his conflicts about religion which have reappeared at this moment. Soon his complaints and accusations turn against God. Why had He created him to be 'as sick and bedraggled as a poisoned rat'? Then he remembers an old book about the many souls who might have come to life but had remained unborn. It was thus a question of God's choice, and this thought comforts him. He even becomes elated because he is alive and 'he clasped his side with both hands as if to assure himself of the beating of his heart'. Then he reflects that these are childish ideas, but concludes that 'truth itself' is 'the conception of a child'. Immediately after that he places votive candles in all the vacant places in the stand. An internal voice tempts him again, saying how beautiful it would be to see the baker-woman in the light of all these little candles.

My conclusion is that his guilt and despair relate to the phantasied destruction of the external and internal mother and her breasts, and to the murderous rivalry with his father, that is to say to the feeling that his good internal and external objects had been destroyed by him. This depressive anxiety was linked with a persecutory one. For God, who stood for the father, was accused of having made him a bad and poisoned creature. He fluctuates between this accusation and a feeling of satisfaction that he had been created in preference to the unborn souls and is alive. I suggest that the souls which have never come to life stand for Fabian's unborn brothers and sisters. The fact that he was an only child was both a cause for guilt and— since he had been chosen to be born while they had not—for satisfaction and gratitude to the father. The religious idea that truth is 'the conception of a child' thus takes on another significance. The greatest act of creation is to create a child, for this means perpetuating life. I think that when Fabian-Fruges put candles in all the vacant places in the stand and lights them, this means making the mother pregnant and bringing to life the unborn babies. The wish to see the baker-woman in the light of the candles would thus express the desire to see her pregnant with all the children he would give her. Here we find the 'sinful' incestuous desire for the mother as well as the tendency to repair by giving her all the babies he had destroyed. In this connection his indignation about the 'bone-dry' stoup has not only a religious basis. I see in it the child's anxiety about the mother who is frustrated and neglected by the father, instead of being loved and made pregnant by him. This anxiety is particularly strong in youngest and only children because the reality that no other child has been born seems to confirm the guilty feeling that they have prevented the parents' sexual intercourse, the mother's pregnancy and the arrival of other babies by hatred and jealousy and by attacks on the mother's body.[1] Since I assume that Fabian-Fruges had expressed his destruction of the mother's breast in attacking the roll which the baker-woman gave him I conclude that the bone-dry' stoup also stands for the breast sucked dry and destroyed by his infantile greed.

---

[1] I touch here on one of the essential causes for guilt and unhappiness in the infantile mind. The very young child feels that his sadistic impulses and phantasies are omnipotent and therefore have taken, are taking, and will take effect. He feels similarly about his reparative desires and phantasies, but it appears that frequently the belief in his destructive powers far outweighs his confidence in his constructive abilities.

### III

It is significant that Fabian's first meeting with the Devil happens when he is feeling acutely frustrated because his mother, who insisted that he should go to communion next day, had thereby prevented him from embarking that evening on a new love affair; and when Fabian rebels and actually goes to meet the girl, she does not appear. At that moment the Devil steps in; he represents in this context, I think, the dangerous impulses which are stirred up in the young infant when his mother frustrates him. In this sense the Devil is the personification of the infant's destructive impulses.

This touches, however, only upon one aspect of the complex relation to the mother, an aspect illustrated by Fabian trying to project himself into the waiter who brings him his meagre breakfast (in the novel, his first attempt to assume another man's personality). Projective processes dominated by greed are, as I have repeatedly remarked, part of the baby's relation to the mother, but they are particularly strong where frustration is frequent.[1] Frustration reinforces both the greedy wish for unlimited gratification and the desires to scoop out the breast and to enter the mother's body in order to obtain by force the gratification she withholds. We have seen in the relation to the baker-woman Fabian-Fruges' impetuous desires for the breast and the hatred which frustration arouses in him. Fabian's whole character and his strong feelings of resentment and deprivation support the assumption that he had felt very frustrated in the earliest feeding relation. Such feelings would be revived in relation to the waiter if he stands for one aspect of the mother—the mother who fed him but did not really satisfy him. Fabian's attempt to turn himself into the waiter would thus represent a revival of the desire to intrude into his mother in order to rob her and thus get more food and satisfaction. It is also significant that the waiter—the first object into whom Fabian intended to transform himself—is the only person whose permission he asks (a permission which the waiter refuses). This would imply that the guilt which is so clearly expressed in the relation to the baker-woman is even present in relation to the waiter.[2]

In the episode with the baker-woman, Fabian-Fruges experiences the whole gamut of emotions in relation to his mother, *i.e.* oral desires,

[1] As I have pointed out in various connections, the urge for projective identification derives not only from greed but from a variety of causes.

[2] In putting forward this interpretation I am aware that this is not the only line on which this episode could be explained. The waiter could also be seen as the father who did not satisfy his oral expectations; and the baker-woman episode would thus mean a step further back to the mother relation with all its desires and disappointments.

frustration, anxieties, guilt, and the urge to make reparation; he also re-lives the development of his Oedipus complex. The combination of passionate physical desires, affection, and admiration indicates that there was a time when Fabian's mother represented to him both the mother towards whom he experiences oral and genital desires and the ideal mother, the woman who should be seen in the light of the votive candles, *i.e.* should be worshipped. It is true that he does not succeed in this worship in church, for he feels he cannot restrain his desires. Nevertheless, at times she represents the ideal mother who should have no sexual life.

In contrast to the mother who ought to be worshipped like the Madonna there is another aspect of her. I take the transformation into the murderer Esménard to be an expression of the infantile impulses to murder the mother, whose sexual relation with the father is not only felt to be a betrayal of the infant's love for her, but is altogether felt to be bad and unworthy. This feeling underlies the unconscious equation between the mother and a prostitute which is characteristic of adolescence. Berthe, who is obviously thought of as a promiscuous woman, approximates in Fabian-Esménard's mind to the prostitute type. Another instance of the mother as a bad sexual figure is the old woman in the dark shop, who sells obscene postcards which are hidden behind other articles. Fabian-Fruges experiences both disgust and pleasure in looking at obscene pictures, and also feels haunted by the noise of the rotating stand. I believe that this expresses the infant's desire to watch and listen to the primal scene as well as his revulsion against these desires. The guilt attached to such actual or phantasied observations, in which sounds overheard frequently play a part, derives from sadistic impulses against the parents in this situation and also relates to masturbation which frequently accompanies such sadistic phantasies.

Another figure representing the bad mother is the maid in Camille's home, who is a hypocritical old woman, plotting with the bad uncle against the young people. Fabian's own mother appears in a similar light when she insists on his going to confession. For Fabian is hostile towards the father-confessor and hates confessing his sins to him. His mother's demand is, therefore, bound to represent to him a conspiracy between the parents, allied against the child's aggressive and sexual desires. Fabian's relation to his mother, represented by these various figures, shows devaluation and hatred as well as idealization.

IV

There are only a few hints about Fabian's early relation to his father, but they are significant. In speaking of Fabian's introjective identifications I have suggested that his strong attachment to his father's watch, and the thoughts it aroused in him about his father's life and premature end, showed love and compassion for his father and sadness about his death. Referring to the author's remarks that Fabian had ever since childhood 'been haunted by a feeling of some inner presence . . .' I concluded that this inner presence represented the internalized father.

I think that the urge to make up for his father's early death and in a sense to keep him alive contributed much to Fabian's impetuous and greedy desire to live life to the full. I would say he was also greedy on his father's behalf. On the other hand, in his restless search for women and disregard of health, Fabian also re-enacted the fate of his father who was assumed to have died prematurely as a result of his dissolute life. This identification was reinforced by Fabian's bad health, for he had the same heart disease from which his father had suffered, and he had often been warned not to exert himself.[1] It would thus appear that in Fabian a drive towards bringing about his death was in conflict with a greedy need to prolong his life, and thereby his internalized father's life, by entering other people and actually stealing their lives. This inner struggle between seeking and combating death was part of his unstable and restless state of mind.

Fabian's relation to his internalized father focused, as we have just seen, on the need to prolong his father's life or to revive him. I wish to mention another aspect of the dead internal father. The guilt relating to the father's death—owing to death wishes against him—tends to turn the dead internalized father into a persecutor. There is an episode in Green's novel which points to Fabian's relation to death and the dead. Before Fabian has entered into the pact the Devil takes him at night on a journey to a sinister house where a strange company is assembled. Fabian finds himself the centre of intense attention and envy. What they envy him for is indicated by their murmuring 'It's for the gift . . .' The 'gift', as we know, is the Devil's magic formula which will give Fabian the power to transform himself into other people and, as it appears to him, to prolong his life indefinitely. Fabian is welcomed by the Devil's 'underling', a very seductive aspect of the Devil, succumbs to his charm and allows himself to be persuaded to accept the 'gift'. It seems that the assembled people are meant to represent the spirits of the dead who either did not receive the 'gift' or failed to use it well. The Devil's 'underling' speaks contemptuously of them, giving the impression that they have been incapable of living their lives to the full; perhaps he despises them because they sold themselves to the Devil, and in

[1] This is an instance of the mutual influence of physical (possibly inherited) and emotional factors.

vain. A likely conclusion is that these dissatisfied and envious people also stand for Fabian's dead father, because Fabian would have attributed to his father—who in fact had wasted his life—such feelings of envy and greed. His corresponding anxiety lest the internalized father would wish to suck out Fabian's life both added to Fabian's need to escape from his self and to his greedy wish (in identification with the father) to rob other people of their lives.

The loss of his father at an early age contributed much to his depression, but the roots of these anxieties can again be found in his infancy. For if we assume that Fabian's powerful emotion towards the baker-woman's lover are a repetition of his early Oedipus feelings, we would conclude that he experienced strong death-wishes against his father. As we know, death-wishes and hatred towards the father as a rival lead not only to persecutory anxiety but also—because they conflict with love and compassion—to severe feelings of guilt and depression in the young child. It is significant that Fabian, who possesses the power to transform himself into whomsoever he wishes, never even thinks of changing himself into the envied lover of the admired woman. It seems that were he to have effected such a transformation, he would have felt that he was usurping his father's place and giving free rein to his murderous hatred towards him. Both fear of the father and the conflict between love and hatred, *i.e.* both persecutory and depressive anxiety, would cause him to retreat from so undisguised an expression of his Oedipus wishes. I have already described his conflicting attitudes towards his mother—again a conflict between love and hatred—which contributed to his turning away from her as a love object and to repressing his Oedipus feelings.

Fabian's difficulties in relation to his father have to be considered in connection with his greed, his envy, and his jealousy. His transforming himself into Poujars is motivated by violent greed, envy, and hatred, such as the infant experiences towards his father who is adult and potent and who, in the child's phantasy, possesses everything because he possesses the mother. I have referred to the author's describing Fabian's envy of Poujars in the words: 'Ah! the sun. It often seemed to him that M. Poujars kept it hidden in his pocket.'[1]

Envy and jealousy, reinforced by frustrations, contribute to the infant's feelings of grievance and resentment towards his parents and

---

[1] One of the meanings of the sun in his pocket may be the good mother whom father has taken into himself. For the young infant, as I pointed out earlier, feels that when he is deprived of the mother's breast it is the father who receives it. The feeling that the father contains the good mother, thus robbing the infant of her, stirs up envy and greed and is also an important stimulus towards homosexuality.

stimulate the wish to reverse the rôles and deprive *them*. From Fabian's attitude, when he has changed places with Poujars and looks with a mixture of contempt and pity at his former unprepossessing self, we gather how much he enjoys having reversed the rôles. Another situation in which Fabian punishes a bad father-figure arises when he is Fabian-Camille: he insults and enrages Camille's old uncle before leaving the house.

In Fabian's relation to his father, as in the relation to his mother, we can detect the process of idealization and its corollary, the fear of persecutory objects. This becomes clear when Fabian has turned himself into Fruges, whose inner struggle between his love for God and his attraction to the Devil is very acute; God and the Devil clearly represent the ideal and the wholly bad father. The ambivalent attitude towards the father is also shown in Fabian-Fruges accusing God (father) of having created him as such a poor creature: yet he acknowledges gratitude for His having given life to him. From these indications I conclude that Fabian has always been searching for his ideal father and that this is a strong stimulus towards his projective identifications. But in his search for the ideal father he fails: he is bound to fail because he is driven by greed and envy. All the men into whom he transforms himself turn out to be contemptible and weak. Fabian hates them for disappointing him and he feels glee over the fate of his victims.

## v

I have suggested that some of the emotional experiences which occurred during Fabian's transformations throw light on his earliest development. Of his adult sexual life we gain a picture from the period preceding his encounter with the Devil, that is to say when he is still the original Fabian. I have already mentioned that Fabian's sexual relations were short-lived and ended in disappointment. He did not seem capable of genuine love for a woman. I interpreted the interlude with the baker-woman as a revival of his early Oedipus feelings. His unsuccessful dealing with these feelings and anxieties underlies his later sexual development. Without becoming impotent he had developed the division into two trends, described by Freud (1912) as 'heavenly and profane (or animal) love'.

Even this splitting process failed to achieve its aims, for he never actually found a woman whom he could idealize; but that such a person existed in his mind is shown by his wondering whether the old woman who could fully satisfy him would be 'a statue of ivory and gold'. As we have seen, in the rôle of Fabian-Fruges, he experienced a passionate admiration, amounting to idealization, for the baker-woman. He was, I should say, unconsciously searching all his life for the ideal mother whom he had lost.

The episodes in which Fabian turns himself into the rich Poujars or the physically powerful Esménard, or lastly into a married man (Camille who has a beautiful wife), suggest an identification with his father, based on his wish to be like him and to take his place as a man. In the novel there is no hint that Fabian was homosexual. An indication of homosexuality is to be found, however, in his strong physical attraction to the Devil's 'underling'—a young and handsome man whose persuasion overcomes Fabian's doubts and anxieties about entering into the pact with the Devil. I have already referred to Fabian's fear of what he imagines to be the Devil's sexual advances towards him. But the homosexual desire to be his father's lover manifests itself more directly in relation to Elise. His being attracted to Elise—to her longing eyes—was, as the author indicates, due to an identification with her. For one moment he is tempted to turn himself into her, if only he could be sure that the handsome Camille would love her. But he realizes that this could not happen and decides not to become Elise.

In this context Elise's unrequited love seems to express Fabian's inverted Oedipus situation. To place himself in the rôle of a woman loved by the father would mean displacing or destroying the mother and would arouse intense guilt; in fact, in the story Elise has the unpleasant but beautiful wife of Camille as her hated rival—another mother figure, I think. It is of interest that not until near the end did Fabian experience the wish to become a woman. This might be connected with the emergence of repressed desires and urges, and thereby with a lessening of the strong defences against his early feminine and passive-homosexual impulses.

From this material some conclusions can be drawn about the serious disabilities from which Fabian suffers. His relation to his mother was fundamentally disturbed. She is, as we know, described as a dutiful mother, concerned above all with his son's physical and moral welfare, but not capable of affection and tenderness. It seems likely that she had the same attitude to him when he was an infant. I have already mentioned that Fabian's character, the nature of his greed, envy, and resentment, indicate that his oral grievances had been very great and were never overcome. We may assume that these feelings of frustration extended to his father; for, in the young infant's phantasies, the father is the second object from whom oral gratifications are expected. In other words, the positive side of Fabian's homosexuality was also disturbed at the root.

Failure to modify the fundamental oral desires and anxieties has many consequences. Ultimately it means that the paranoid-schizoid position has not been successfully worked through. I think this was true of Fabian and therefore he had not dealt adequately with the depressive position either. For those reasons his capacity to make reparation had been impaired and he could not cope later on with his feelings of persecution and depression. In consequence his relations to his parents and to people in general were very unsatisfactory. All this implies, as my experience has shown me, that he was unable to establish securely the good breast, the good mother, in his inner world[1]—an initial failure which in turn prevented him from developing a strong identification with a good father. Fabian's excessive greed, to some extent derived from his insecurity about his good internal objects, influenced both his introjective and and projective processes and—since we are also discussing the adult Fabian—the processes of re-introjection and re-projection. All these difficulties contributed to his incapacity to establish a love relation with a woman, that is to say, to the disturbance in his sexual development. In my view he fluctuated between a strongly repressed homosexuality and an unstable heterosexuality.

I have already mentioned a number of external factors which played an important rôle in Fabian's unhappy development, such as his father's early death, his mother's lack of affection, his poverty, the unsatisfactory nature of his work, his conflict with his mother about religion and—a very important point—his physical illness. From these facts we can draw some further conclusions. The marriage of Fabian's parents was obviously an unhappy one, as is indicated by his father finding his pleasures elsewhere. The mother was not only unable to show warmth of feeling but was also, as we may assume, an unhappy woman who sought consolation in religion. Fabian was an only child and no doubt lonely. His father died when Fabian was still at school and this deprived him of his further education and of prospects for a successful career; it also had the effect of stirring up his feelings of persecution and depression.

We know that all the events from his first transformation to his return home are supposed to happen within three days. During these three days, as we learn at the end when Fabian-Camille rejoins his former self, Fabian had been lying in bed unconscious, looked after by his mother. As she tells him, he had collapsed in his employer's office after having misbehaved there, was brought home and had remained unconscious ever since. She thinks, when he refers to Camille's visit, that he has been delirious. Perhaps the author intends us to take the whole story as representing Fabian's phantasies during

[1] The secure internalization of a good mother—a process of fundamental importance—varies in degree and is never so complete that it cannot be shaken by anxieties from internal or external sources.

the illness preceding his death? This would imply that all the characters were figures of his inner world and again illustrate that introjection and projection were operating in him in closest interaction.

VI

The processes underlying projective identification are depicted very concretely by the author. One part of Fabian literally leaves his self and enters into his victim, an event which in both parties is accompanied by strong physical sensations. We are told that the split-off part of Fabian submerges in varying degrees in his objects and loses the memories and characteristics appertaining to the original Fabian. We should conclude therefore (in keeping with the author's very concrete conception of the projective process), that Fabian's memories and other aspects of his personality are left behind in the discarded Fabian who must have retained a good deal of his ego when the split occurred. This part of Fabian, lying dormant until the split-off aspects of his personality return, represents, in my view, that component of the ego which patients unconsciously feel they have retained while other parts are projected into the external world and lost.

The spatial and temporal terms in which the author describes these events are actually the ones in which our patients experience such processes. A patient's feeling that parts of his self are no longer available, are far away, or have altogether gone is of course a phantasy which underlies splitting processes. But such phantasies have far-reaching consequences and vitally influence the structure of the ego. They have the effect that those parts of his self from which he feels estranged, often including his emotions, are not at the time accessible either to the analyst or to the patient.[1] The feeling that he does not know where the parts of himself which he has dispersed into the external world have gone to, is a source of great anxiety and insecurity.[2]

[1] There is another side to such experiences. As Paula Heimann describes in her paper (1955) a patient's conscious feelings can also express his splitting processes.

[2] I suggested in 'Schizoid Mechanisms' that the fear of being imprisoned inside the mother as a consequence of projective identification underlies various anxiety situations and among them claustrophobia. I would now add that projective identification may result in the fear that the lost part of the self will never be recovered because it is buried in the object. In the story Fabian feels—after both his transformation into Poujars and into Fruges—that he is entombed and will never escape again. This implies that he will die inside his objects. There is another point I wish to mention here: besides the fear of being imprisoned inside the mother, I have found that another contributory factor to claustrophobia is the fear relating to the inside of one's own body and the dangers threatening there. To quote again Milton's lines, 'Thou art become (O worst imprisonment) the Dungeon of thyself'.

I shall next consider Fabian's projective identifications from three angles: (i) the relation of the split-off and projected parts of his personality to those he had left behind; (ii) the motives underlying the choice of objects into whom he projects himself; and (iii) how far in these processes the projected part of his self becomes submerged in the object or gains control over it.

(i) Fabian's anxiety that he is going to deplete his ego by splitting off parts of it and projecting them into other people is expressed, before he starts on his transformations, by the way he looks at his clothes heaped untidily on a chair: 'He had a horrible sensation in looking at them that he was seeing himself, but a self assassinated or in some way destroyed. The empty sleeves of his coat had, as they drooped limply to the ground, a forlorn suggestion of tragedy.'

We also learn that Fabian, when he turns himself into Poujars (that is to say, when the processes of splitting and projection have just occurred), is very concerned about his former person. He thinks he might wish to return to his original self, and being, therefore, anxious that Fabian should be taken home, writes out a cheque in his favour.

The importance attaching to Fabian's name also denotes that his identity was bound up with those parts of himself which were left behind and that they represented the core of his personality; the name was an essential part of the magic formula, and it is significant that the first thing which occurs to him when, under the influence of Elise, he experiences the urge to regain his former self, is the name 'Fabian'. I think that feelings of guilt about having neglected and deserted a precious component of his personality contributed to Fabian's longing to be himself again—a longing which irresistibly drove him home at the end of the novel.

(ii) The choice of his first intended victim, the waiter, becomes easily understandable if we assume, as I suggested above, that he stood for Fabian's mother; for the mother is the first object for the infant's identification both by introjection and by projection.

Some of the motives which impelled Fabian to project himself into Poujars have already been discussed; I suggested that he wished to turn himself into the wealthy and powerful father, thereby robbing him of all his possessions and punishing him. In doing so he was also actuated by a motive which in this connection I wish to emphasize. I think that Fabian's sadistic impulses and phantasies (expressed in the desire to control and punish his father) were something he felt he had in common with Poujars. Poujars' cruelty, as Fabian thought of it, also represented Fabian's own cruelty and lust for power.

The contrast between Poujars (who turned out to be ailing and miserable) and the virile young Esménard was only a contributing factor in Fabian's choice of the latter as an object for identification. I believe that the main cause for Fabian's decision to turn himself into Esménard, in spite of his being unprepossessing and repellent, was that Esménard stood for one part of Fabian's self, and that the murderous hatred which impels Fabian-Esménard to kill Berthe is a revival of the emotions which Fabian experienced in infancy towards his mother when she frustrated him, as he felt, orally and genitally. Esménard's jealousy of any man whom Berthe favoured renews in an extreme form Fabian's Oedipus complex and intense rivalry with his father. This part of himself which was potentially murderous was personified by Esménard. Fabian, by becoming Esménard, thus projected into another person and lived out some of his own destructive tendencies. Fabian's complicity in the murder is pointed out by the Devil who reminds him, after his transformation into Fruges, that the hands which strangled Berthe were only a few minutes ago his own.

Now we come to the choice of Fruges. Fabian has a good deal in common with Fruges, in whom, however, these characteristics are much more pronounced. Fabian is inclined to deny the hold religion (and that also means God—the father) has over him and attributes his conflicts about religion to his mother's influence. Fruges' conflicts about religion are acute, and, as the author describes, he is fully aware that the struggle between God and the Devil dominates his life. Fruges is constantly fighting against his desires for luxury and wealth; his conscience drives him to extreme austerity. In Fabian the wish to be as rich as the people he envies is also very pronounced, but he does not attempt to restrain it. The two also have in common their intellectual pursuits and a very marked intellectual curiosity.

These common characteristics would predispose Fabian to choose Fruges for projective identification. I think, however, that another motive enters into this choice. The Devil, playing here the rôle of a guiding super-ego, has helped Fabian to leave Esménard and warned him to beware of entering a person in whom he would submerge to such an extent that he could never escape again. Fabian is terrified of having turned himself into a murderer, which, I think, means having succumbed to the most dangerous part of himself—to his destructive impulses; he therefore escapes by changing rôles with somebody completely different from his previous choice. My experience has shown me that the struggle against an overwhelming identification—be it by introjection or projection—often drives people to identifications with objects which show the opposite characteristics. (Another consequence of such a struggle is an indiscriminate flight into a multitude of further identifications and fluctuations between them. Such conflicts and anxieties are often perpetuated, and further weaken the ego.)

Fabian's next choice, Camille, has hardly anything in common with him. But through Camille, it appears, Fabian identifies himself with Elise, the girl who is unhappily in love with Camille. As we have seen, Elise stood for the feminine side of Fabian, and her feelings towards Camille for his unfulfilled homosexual love for his father. At the same time Elise also represented the good part of his self which was capable of longing and loving. In my view Fabian's infantile love for his father, bound up as it was with his homosexual desires and his feminine position, had been disturbed at the root. I also pointed out that he was unable to change himself into a woman because this would have represented a realization of the deeply repressed feminine desires in the inverted Oedipus relation to his father. (I am not dealing in this context with other factors which impede the feminine identification, above all castration fear.) With the awakening of the capacity to love, Fabian can identify himself with Elise's unhappy infatuation with Camille; in my view he also becomes able to experience his love and desires towards his father. I would conclude that Elise had come to represent a good part of his self.

I would furthermore suggest that Elise also stands for an imaginary sister. It is well known that children have imaginary companions. They represent, particularly in the phantasy life of only children, older or younger brothers or sisters, or a twin, who have never been born. One may surmise that Fabian, who was an only child, would have gained much from the companionship of a sister. Such a relation would also have helped him to cope better with his Oedipus complex and to gain more independence from his mother. In Camille's family such a relationship actually exists between Elise and Camille's schoolboy brother.

We shall remember here that Fabian-Fruges' overwhelming feelings of guilt in church appeared to relate also to his having been chosen, whereas other souls never came to life. I interpreted his lighting votive candles and picturing the baker-woman surrounded by them both as an idealization of her (the mother as saint) and as an expression of his wish to make reparation by bringing to life the unborn brothers and sisters. Particularly youngest and only children often have a strong sense of guilt because they feel that their jealous and aggressive impulses have prevented their mother from giving birth to any more children. Such feelings are also bound up with fears of retaliation and persecution. I have repeatedly found that fear and suspicion of schoolmates or of other children were linked with phantasies that the unborn brothers and sisters had after all come to life and were represented by any children who appeared to be hostile. The longing for friendly brothers and sisters is strongly influenced by such anxieties.

So far I have not discussed why Fabian in the first place chose to identify himself with the Devil—a fact on which the plot is based. I pointed out earlier that the Devil stood for the seducing and dangerous father; he also represented parts of Fabian's mind, super-ego as well as id. In the novel the Devil is unconcerned about his victims; extremely greedy and ruthless, he appears as the prototype of hostile and evil projective identifications which in the novel are described as violent intrusions into people. I would say that he shows in an extreme form that component of infantile emotional life which is dominated by omnipotence, greed, and sadism, and that it is these characteristics which Fabian and the Devil have in common. Therefore Fabian identifies himself with the Devil and carries out all his behests.

It is significant—and I think expresses an important aspect of identification—that when changing himself into a new person Fabian to some extent retains his previous projective identifications. This is shown by the strong interest—an interest mixed with contempt—which Fabian-Fruges takes in the fate of his former victims, and also in his feeling that after all he is responsible for the murder he committed as Esménard. It shows most clearly at the end of the story, for his experiences in the characters into whom he had turned himself are all present in his mind before he dies and he is concerned about their fate. This would imply that he introjects his objects, as well as projects himself into them—a conclusion which is in keeping with my view restated in the introduction to this paper that projection and introjection interact from the beginning of life.

In singling out an important motive for the choice of objects for identification I have, for the purpose of presentation, described this as happening in two stages: (a) there is some common ground, (b) the identification takes place. But the process as we watch it in our analytic work is not so divided. For the individual to feel that he has a good deal in common with another person is concurrent with projecting himself into that person (and the same applies to introjecting him). These processes vary in intensity and duration and on these variations depend the strength and importance of such identifications and their vicissitudes. In this connection I wish to draw attention to the fact that while the processes I described often appear to operate simultaneously, we have to consider carefully in each state or situation whether, for instance, projective identification has the upper hand over introjective processes or vice versa.[1]

[1] This is of great importance in technique. For we have always to choose for interpretation the material which is the most urgent at the moment; and in this

I have suggested in my 'Notes on Some Schizoid Mechanisms' that the process of reintrojecting a projected part of the self includes internalizing a part of the object into whom the projection has taken place, a part which the patient may feel to be hostile, dangerous, and most undesirable to reintroject. In addition, since the projection of a part of the self includes the projection of internal objects, these too are re-introjected. All this has a bearing on how far in the individual's mind the projected parts of the self are able to retain their strength within the object into which they have intruded. I shall now make a few suggestions about this aspect of the problem, which takes me to my third point.

(iii) In the story, as I have pointed out earlier, Fabian succumbs to the Devil and becomes identified with him. Although Fabian seemed deficient in the capacity for love and concern even before that, as soon as he follows the Devil's lead he is completely ruled by ruthlessness. This implies that, in identifying himself with the Devil, Fabian fully succumbs to the greedy, omnipotent, and destructive part of his self. When Fabian has turned himself into Poujars, he retains some of his own attitudes, and particularly a critical opinion of the person whom he has entered. He dreads losing himself completely inside Poujars, and it is only because he has retained some of Fabian's initiative that he is able to bring about the next transformation. However, he comes near to losing his former self entirely when he turns himself into the murderer Esménard. Yet since the Devil, whom we assume to be also part of Fabian—here his super-ego—warns him and helps him to escape from the murderer, we should conclude that Fabian has not been entirely submerged in Esménard.[1]

The situation with Fruges is different: in this transformation the original Fabian remains much more active. Fabian is very critical of Fruges, and it is this greater capacity to keep something of his original self alive inside Fruges that makes it possible for him gradually to rejoin his depleted ego and become himself again. Generally speaking, I hold that the extent to which the individual feels his ego

---

context I would say that there are stretches of analysis during which some patients seem completely ruled by projection or by introjection. On the other hand, it is essential to remember that the opposite process remains always to some extent operative and therefore enters sooner or later again into the picture as the predominant factor.

[1] I would say that however strongly splitting and projection operate, the disintegration of the ego is never complete as long as life exists. For I believe that the urge towards integration, however disturbed—even at the root—is in some degree inherent in the ego. This is in keeping with my view that no infant could survive without possessing in some degree a good object. It is these facts which make it possible for the analysis to bring about some measure of integration sometimes even in very severe cases.

to be submerged in the objects with whom it is identified by introjection or projection is of greatest importance for the development of object relations and also determines the strength or weakness of the ego.

Fabian regains parts of his personality after his transformation into Fruges and at the same time something very important happens. Fabian-Fruges notices that his experiences have given him a better understanding of Poujars, Esménard, and even Fruges, and that he is now able to feel sympathy with his victims. Also through Fruges, who is fond of children, Fabian's affection for little George awakens. George, as the author describes him, is an innocent child, fond of his mother and longing to return to her. He awakens in Fabian-Fruges the memory of Fruges' childhood, and the impetuous desire arises to turn himself into George. I believe he is longing to recover the capacity for love, in other words an ideal childhood self.

This resurgence of feelings of love shows itself in various ways: he experiences passionate feelings for the baker-woman which, in my view, meant a revival of his early love life. Another step in this direction is his transforming himself into a married man and thereby entering into a family circle. But the one person whom Fabian finds likeable and of whom he becomes fond is Elise. I have already described the various meanings Elise has for him. In particular he has discovered in her that part of himself which is capable of love, and he is deeply attracted towards this side of his own personality; that is to say, he has also discovered some love for himself. Physically and mentally, by retracing the steps he has taken in his transformations, he is driven back with increasing urgency closer and closer to his home and to the ill Fabian whom he had forsaken and who by now has come to represent the good part of his personality. We have seen that the sympathy with his victims, the tenderness towards George, the concern for Elise, and the identification with her unhappy passion for Camille, as well as the wish for a sister—all these steps are an unfolding of his capacity to love. I suggest that this development was a precondition for Fabian's passionate need to find his old self again, that is to say for integration. Even before his transformations occurred, the longing to recover the best part of his personality—which because it had been lost, appeared to be ideal—had, as I suggested, contributed to his loneliness and restlessness; had given impetus to his projective identifications[1] and was complementary to his self-hatred, another factor impelling him to force

---

[1] The feeling of having dispersed goodness and good parts of the self into the external world adds to the sense of grievance and envy of others who are felt to contain the lost goodness.

himself into other people. The search for the lost ideal self,[1] which is an important feature of mental life, inevitably includes the search for lost ideal objects; for the good self is that part of the personality which is felt to be in a loving relation to its good objects. The prototype of such a relation is the bond between the baby and his mother. In fact, when Fabian rejoins his lost self, he also recovers his love for his mother.

With Fabian we note that he seemed incapable of an identification with a good or admired object. A variety of reasons would have to be discussed in this connection, but I wish to single out one as a possible explanation. I have already pointed out that in order to identify strongly with another person, it is essential to feel that there is within the self enough common ground with that object. Since Fabian had lost—so it seemed—his good self, he did not feel that there was enough goodness within him for identification with a very good object. There might also have been the anxiety, characteristic of such states of mind, lest an admired object should be taken into an inner world which is too much deprived of goodness. The good object is then kept outside (with Fabian, I think, the distant stars). But when he rediscovered his good self, then he found his good objects as well and could identify with them.

In the story, as we have seen, the depleted part of Fabian also longs to be re-united with the projected parts of his self. The nearer Fabian-Camille comes to the house, the more restless Fabian grows on his sickbed. He regains consciousness and walks to the door through which his other half, Fabian-Camille, utters the magic formula. According to the author's description, the two halves of Fabian are longing to be re-united. This means that Fabian was longing to integrate his self. As we have seen, this urge was bound up with a growing capacity to love. This corresponds to Freud's theory of synthesis as a function of the libido—ultimately of the life instinct.

I have suggested earlier that although Fabian was searching for a good father, he was unable to find him because envy and greed, increased by grievance and hatred, determined his choice of father-figures. When he becomes less resentful and more tolerant, his objects appear to him in a better light; but then he is also less demanding than he was in the past. It appears that he no longer claims that his parents should be ideal and therefore he can forgive them for

---

[1] Freud's concept of the ego ideal was, as we know, the precursor of his super-ego concept. But there are some features of the ego ideal which have not been fully taken over into his super-ego concept. My description of the ideal self which Fabian is trying to regain comes, I think, much closer to Freud's original views about the ego ideal than to his views about the super-ego.

their shortcomings. To his greater capacity for love corresponds a diminution of hatred, and this in turn results in a lessening of feelings of persecution—all of which has a bearing on the lessening of greed and envy. Self-hatred was one of the outstanding features in his character; together with the greater capacity for love and for tolerance towards others arose the greater tolerance and love towards his own self.

In the end Fabian recovers his love for his mother and makes his peace with her. It is significant that he recognizes her lack of tenderness but feels that she might have been better had *he* been a better son. He obeys his mother's injunction to pray and seems to have recovered after all his struggles his belief and trust in God. Fabian's last words are 'Our Father', and it would appear that at that moment, when he is filled with love for humanity, the love for his father returns. Those persecutory and depressive anxieties which were bound to be stirred up by the approach of death would to some extent be counteracted by idealization and elation.

As we have seen, Fabian-Camille is driven home by an irresistible impulse. It seems probable that his sense of impending death gives impetus to his urge to rejoin the deserted part of his self. For I believe that the fear of death which he has denied, although he knew of his severe illness, has come out in full force. Maybe he had denied this fear because its nature was so intensely persecutory. We know how full of grievance he was against fate and against his parents; how persecuted he felt by his own unsatisfactory personality. In my experience, the fear of death is very much intensified if death is felt as an attack by hostile internal and external objects or if it arouses depressive anxiety lest the good objects be destroyed by those hostile figures. (These persecutory and depressive phantasies may of course co-exist.) Anxieties of a psychotic nature are the cause for this excessive fear of death from which many individuals suffer throughout their lives; and the intense mental sufferings which, as a few observations have shown me, some people experience on their deathbed, are due in my view to the revival of infantile psychotic anxieties.

Considering that the author describes Fabian as a restless and unhappy person, full of grievances, one would expect that his death should be painful and give rise to the persecutory anxieties which I have just mentioned. However, this is not what happens in the story, for Fabian dies happily and at peace. Any explanation for this sudden ending can only be tentative. From the artistic point of view it was probably the author's best solution. But, in keeping with my conception of Fabian's experiences which I have put forward in this paper, I am inclined to explain the unexpected ending by the story presenting to us two sides of Fabian. Up to the point where the transformations begin, it is the adult Fabian whom we meet. In the course of his transformations we encounter the emotions, the persecutory and depressive anxieties which characterized, as I believe, his early development. But whereas in childhood he had not been able to overcome these anxieties and to achieve integration, in the three days covered by the novel, he successfully traverses a world of emotional experiences which in my view entails a working through of the paranoid-schizoid and the depressive positions. As a result of overcoming the fundamental psychotic anxieties of infancy, the intrinsic need for integration comes out in full force. He achieves integration concurrently with good object relations and thereby repairs what had gone wrong in his life.

# 10

# ENVY AND GRATITUDE[1]

## (1957)

I HAVE for many years been interested in the earliest sources of two attitudes that have always been familiar—envy and gratitude. I arrived at the conclusion that envy is a most potent factor in undermining feelings of love and gratitude at their root, since it affects the earliest relation of all, that to the mother. The fundamental importance of this relation for the individual's whole emotional life has been substantiated in a number of psycho-analytic writings, and I think that by exploring further a particular factor that can be very disturbing at this early stage, I have added something of significance to my findings concerning infantile development and personality formation.

I consider that envy is an oral-sadistic and anal-sadistic expression of destructive impulses, operative from the beginning of life, and that it has a constitutional basis, These conclusions have certain important elements in common with Karl Abraham's work, and yet imply some differences from it. Abraham found that envy is an oral trait, but—and this is where my views differ from his—he assumed that envy and hostility operate at a later period, which, according to his hypothesis, constituted a second, the oral-sadistic, stage. Abraham did not speak of gratitude, but he described generosity as an oral feature. He considered the anal elements as an important component in envy, and stressed their derivation from oral-sadistic impulses.

A further fundamental point of agreement is Abraham's assumption of a constitutional element in the strength of oral impulses, which he linked with the aetiology of manic-depressive illness.

Above all, both Abraham's work and my own brought out more fully and more deeply the significance of destructive impulses. In his 'Short History of the Development of the Libido, Viewed in the

[1] I wish to express my deep gratitude to my friend Lola Brook who has worked with me throughout the preparation of this book [*Envy and Gratitude*] as with many of my writings. She has a rare understanding of my work and has helped me with formulations and criticisms of the content at every stage. My thanks are also due to Dr Elliott Jaques who has made a number of valuable suggestions while the book was still in manuscript and has helped me by working on the proofs. I am indebted to Miss Judith Fay who took great trouble over making the index.

Light of Mental Disorders', written in 1924, Abraham did not mention Freud's hypothesis of the life and death instincts, although *Beyond the Pleasure Principle* had been published four years previously. However, in his book Abraham explored the roots of destructive impulses and applied this understanding to the aetiology of mental disturbances more specifically than had ever been done before. It appears to me that although he had not made use of Freud's concept of the life and death instincts, his clinical work, particularly the analysis of the first manic-depressive patients to be analysed, was based on insight which was taking him in that direction. I would assume that Abraham's early death prevented his realizing the full implications of his own findings and their essential connection with Freud's discovery of the two instincts.

As I am about to publish *Envy and Gratitude*, three decades after Abraham's death, it is a source of great satisfaction to me that my work has contributed to the growing recognition of the full significance of Abraham's discoveries.

I

Here I intend to make some further suggestions concerning the earliest emotional life of the infant and also to draw some conclusions about adulthood and mental health. It is inherent in Freud's discoveries that the exploration of the patient's past, of his childhood, and of his unconscious is a precondition for understanding his adult personality. Freud discovered the Oedipus complex in the adult and reconstructed from such material not only details of the Oedipus complex but also its timing. Abraham's findings have added considerably to this approach, which has become characteristic of the psycho-analytic method. We should also remember that, according to Freud, the conscious part of the mind develops out of the unconscious. Therefore, in tracing to early infancy material that I found first of all in the analysis of young children, and subsequently in that of adults, I followed a procedure now familiar in psycho-analysis. Observations of young children soon confirmed Freud's findings. I believe that some of the conclusions that I reached regarding a much earlier stage, the first years of life, can also be confirmed up to a point by observation. The right—indeed the necessity—to reconstruct from the material presented to us by our patients details and data about earlier stages is most convincingly described by Freud in the following passage:

'What we are in search of is a picture of the patient's forgotten years that shall be alike trustworthy and in all essential respects complete. . . . His [the psycho-analyst's] work of construction, or, if it is preferred, of reconstruction, resembles to a great extent an archaeologist's excavation of some dwelling-place that has been destroyed and buried or of some ancient edifice. The two processes are in fact identical, except that the analyst works under better conditions and has more material at his command to assist him, since what he is dealing with is not something destroyed but something that is still alive—and perhaps for another reason as well. But just as the archaeologist builds up the walls of the building from the foundations that have remained standing, determines the number and position of the columns from depressions in the floor and reconstructs the mural decorations and paintings from the remains found in the debris, so does the analyst proceed when he draws his inferences from the fragments of memories, from the associations and from the behaviour of the subject of the analysis. Both of them have an undisputed right to reconstruct by means of supplementing and combining the surviving remains. Both of them, moreover, are subject to many of the same difficulties and sources of error. . . . The analyst, as we have said, works under more favourable conditions than the archaeologist since he has at his disposal material which can have no counterpart in excavations, such as the repetition of reactions dating from infancy and all that is indicated by the transference in connection with these repetitions. . . . All of the essentials are preserved; even things that seem completely forgotten are present somehow and somewhere, and have merely been buried and made inaccessible to the subject. Indeed, it may, as we know, be doubted whether any psychical structure can really be the victim of total destruction. It depends only upon analytic technique whether we shall succeed in bringing what is concealed completely to light.'[1]

Experience has taught me that the complexity of the fully grown personality can only be understood if we gain insight into the mind of the baby and follow up its development into later life. That is to say, analysis makes its way from adulthood to infancy, and through intermediate stages back to adulthood, in a recurrent to-and-fro movement according to the prevalent transference situation.

Throughout my work I have attributed fundamental importance to the infant's first object relation—the relation to the mother's breast and to the mother—and have drawn the conclusion that if this primal object, which is introjected, takes root in the ego with relative security, the basis for a satisfactory development is laid. Innate factors contribute to this bond. Under the dominance of oral impulses, the breast is instinctively felt to be the source of nourishment and therefore, in a deeper sense, of life itself. This mental and physical closeness to the gratifying breast in some measure restores,

[1] Constructions in Analysis' (1937).

if things go well, the lost prenatal unity with the mother and the feeling of security that goes with it. This largely depends on the infant's capacity to cathect sufficiently the breast or its symbolic representative, the bottle; in this way the mother is turned into a loved object. It may well be that his having formed part of the mother in the pre-natal state contributes to the infant's innate feeling that there exists outside him something that will give him all he needs and desires. The good breast is taken in and becomes part of the ego, and the infant who was first inside the mother now has the mother inside himself.

While the pre-natal state no doubt implies a feeling of unity and security, how far this state is undisturbed must depend on the psychological and physical condition of the mother, and possibly even on certain still unexplored factors in the unborn infant. We might, therefore, consider the universal longing for the pre-natal state also partly as an expression of the urge for idealization. If we investigate this longing in the light of idealization, we find that one of its sources is the strong persecutory anxiety stirred up by birth. We might speculate that this first form of anxiety possibly extends to the unborn infant's unpleasant experiences which, together with the feeling of security in the womb, foreshadow the double relation to the mother: the good and the bad breast.

External circumstances play a vital part in the initial relation to the breast. If birth has been difficult, and in particular if it results in complications such as lack of oxygen, a disturbance in the adaptation to the external world occurs and the relation to the breast starts at a great disadvantage. In such cases the baby's ability to experience new sources of gratification is impaired and in consequence he cannot sufficiently internalize a really good primal object. Furthermore, whether or not the child is adequately fed and mothered, whether the mother fully enjoys the care of the child or is anxious and has psychological difficulties over feeding—all these factors influence the infant's capacity to accept the milk with enjoyment and to internalize the good breast.

An element of frustration by the breast is bound to enter into the infant's earliest relation to it, because even a happy feeding situation cannot altogether replace the pre-natal unity with the mother. Also, the infant's longing for an inexhaustible and ever-present breast stems by no means only from a craving for food and from libidinal desires. For the urge even in the earliest stages to get constant evidence of the mother's love is fundamentally rooted in anxiety. The struggle between life and death instincts and the ensuing threat of annihilation of the self and of the object by destructive impulses are fundamental factors in the infant's initial relation to his mother. For his desires imply that the breast, and soon the mother, should do away with these destructive impulses and the pain of persecutory anxiety.

Together with happy experiences, unavoidable grievances reinforce the innate conflict between love and hate, in fact, basically between life and death instincts, and result in the feeling that a good and a bad breast exist. As a consequence, early emotional life is characterized by a sense of losing and regaining the good object. In speaking of an innate conflict between love and hate, I am implying that the capacity both for love and for destructive impulses is, to some extent, constitutional, though varying individually in strength and interacting from the beginning with external conditions.

I have repeatedly put forward the hypothesis that the primal good object, the mother's breast, forms the core of the ego and vitally contributes to its growth, and have often described how the infant feels that he concretely internalizes the breast and the milk it gives. Also there is in his mind already some indefinite connection between the breast and other parts and aspects of the mother.

I would not assume that the breast is to him merely a physical object. The whole of his instinctual desires and his unconscious phantasies imbue the breast with qualities going far beyond the actual nourishment it affords.[1]

We find in the analysis of our patients that the breast in its good aspect is the prototype of maternal goodness, inexhaustible patience and generosity, as well as of creativeness. It is these phantasies and instinctual needs that so enrich the primal object that it remains the foundation for hope, trust, and belief in goodness.

This book deals with a particular aspect of earliest object relations and internalization processes that is rooted in orality. I am referring to the effects of envy on the development of the capacity for gratitude and happiness. Envy contributes to the infant's difficulties in building up his good object, for he feels that the gratification of which he was deprived has been kept for itself by the breast that frustrated him.[2]

---

[1] All this is felt by the infant in much more primitive ways than language can express. When these pre-verbal emotions and phantasies are revived in the transference situation, they appear as 'memories in feelings', as I would call them, and are reconstructed and put into words with the help of the analyst. In the same way, words have to be used when we are reconstructing and describing other phenomena belonging to the early stages of development. In fact we cannot translate the language of the unconscious into consciousness without lending it words from our conscious realm.

[2] In a number of my writings, *The Psycho-Analysis of Children*, 'Early Stages of the Oedipus Complex', and in 'The Emotional Life of the Infant,' I have referred to envy, arising from oral-, urethral-, and anal-sadistic sources, during

A distinction should be drawn between envy, jealousy, and greed. Envy is the angry feeling that another person possesses and enjoys something desirable—the envious impulse being to take it away or to spoil it. Moreover, envy implies the subject's relation to one person only and goes back to the earliest exclusive relation with the mother. Jealousy is based on envy, but involves a relation to at least two people; it is mainly concerned with love that the subject feels is his due and has been taken away, or is in danger of being taken away, from him by his rival. In the everyday conception of jealousy, a man or a woman feels deprived of the loved person by somebody else.

Greed is an impetuous and insatiable craving, exceeding what the subject needs and what the object is able and willing to give. At the unconscious level, greed aims primarily at completely scooping out, sucking dry, and devouring the breast: that is to say, its aim is destructive introjection; whereas envy not only seeks to rob in this way, but also to put badness, primarily bad excrements and bad parts of the self, into the mother, and first of all into her breast, in order to spoil and destroy her. In the deepest sense this means destroying her creativeness. This process, which derives from urethral- and anal-sadistic impulses, I have elsewhere defined[1] as a destructive aspect of projective identification starting from the beginning of life.[2] One essential difference between greed and envy, although no rigid dividing line can be drawn since they are so closely associated, would accordingly be that greed is mainly bound up with introjection and envy with projection.

According to the *Shorter Oxford Dictionary*, jealousy means that

---

the earliest stages of the Oedipus complex and connected it with the desire to spoil the mother's possessions, in particular the father's penis which in the infant's phantasy she contains. Already in my paper 'An Obsessional Neurosis in a Six-Year-Old Girl', which was read in 1924 but not published until it appeared in *The Psycho-Analysis of Children*, envy bound up with oral-, urethral-, and anal-sadistic attacks on her mother's body played a prominent rôle. But I had not related this envy specifically to the desire to take away and to spoil the mother's breasts, although I had come very near to these conclusions. In my paper 'On Identification' (1955). I discussed envy as a very important factor in projective identification. As far back as my *Psycho-Analysis of Children* I suggested that not only oral-sadistic but also urethral-sadistic and anal-sadistic trends are operative in very young infants.

[1] Notes on some Schizoid Mechanisms'.

[2] Dr Elliott Jaques has drawn my attention to the etymological root of *envy* in the Latin *invidia*, which comes from the verb *invideo*—to look askance at, to look maliciously or spitefully into, to cast an evil eye upon, to envy or grudge anything. An early use is given in the phrase from Cicero, the translation of which is: 'to produce misfortune by his evil eye'. This confirms the differentiation I made between envy and greed in laying emphasis on the projective character of envy.

somebody else has taken, or is given, 'the good' which by right belongs to the individual. In this context I would interpret 'the good' basically as the good breast, the mother, a loved person, whom somebody else has taken away. According to Crabb's *English Synonyms*, '. . . Jealousy fears to lose what it has; envy is pained at seeing another have that which it wants for itself. . . . The envious man sickens at the sight of enjoyment. He is easy only in the misery of others. All endeavours therefore to satisfy an envious man are fruitless.' Jealousy, according to Crabb, is 'a noble or an ignoble passion according to the object. In the former case it is emulation sharpened by fear. In the latter case it is greediness stimulated by fear. Envy is always a base passion, drawing the worst passions in its train.'

The general attitude to jealousy differs from that to envy. In fact, in some countries (particularly in France) murder prompted by jealousy carries a less severe sentence. The reason for this distinction is to be found in a universal feeling that the murder of a rival may imply love for the unfaithful person. This means, in the terms discussed above, that love for 'the good' exists and that the loved object is not damaged and spoilt as it would be by envy.

Shakespeare's Othello, in his jealousy, destroys the object he loves and this, in my view, is characteristic of what Crabb described as an 'ignoble passion of jealousy'—greed stimulated by fear. A significant reference to jealousy as an inherent quality of the mind occurs in the same play:

> *But jealous souls will not be answer'd so;*
> *They are not ever jealous for the cause,*
> *But jealous for they are jealous; 'tis a monster*
> *Begot upon itself, born on itself.*

It could be said that the very envious person is insatiable, he can never be satisfied because his envy stems from within and therefore always finds an object to focus on. This shows also the close connection between jealousy, greed and envy.

Shakespeare does not always seem to differentiate between envy and jealousy; the following lines from Othello fully show the significance of envy in the sense I have defined it here:

> *Oh beware my Lord of jealousy;*
> *It is the green-eyed monster which doth mock*
> *The meat it feeds on. . . .*

One is reminded of the saying 'to bite the hand which feeds one', which is almost synonymous with biting, destroying, and spoiling the breast.

My work has taught me that the first object to be envied is the feeding breast,[1] for the infant feels that it possesses everything he desires and that it has an unlimited flow of milk, and love which the breast keeps for its own gratification. This feeling adds to his sense of grievance and hate, and the result is a disturbed relation to the mother. If envy is excessive, this, in my view, indicates that paranoid and schizoid features are abnormally strong and that such an infant can be regarded as ill.

Throughout this section I am speaking of the primary envy of the mother's breast, and this should be differentiated from its later forms (inherent in the girl's desire to take her mother's place and in the boy's feminine position) in which envy is no longer focused on the breast but on the mother receiving the father's penis, having babies inside her, giving birth to them, and being able to feed them.

I have often described the sadistic attacks on the mother's breast as determined by destructive impulses. Here I wish to add that envy gives particular impetus to these attacks. This means that when I wrote about the greedy scooping out of the breast and of the mother's body, and the destruction of her babies, as well as putting bad excrements into the mother,[2] this adumbrated what I later came to recognize as the envious spoiling of the object.

If we consider that deprivation increases greed and persecutory anxiety, and that there is in the infant's mind a phantasy of an inexhaustible breast which is his greatest desire, it becomes understandable how envy arises even if the baby is inadequately fed. The infant's feelings seem to be that when the breast deprives him, it becomes bad because it keeps the milk, love, and care associated with the good breast all to itself. He hates and envies what he feels to be the mean and grudging breast.

It is perhaps more understandable that the satisfactory breast is also envied. The very ease with which the milk comes—though the infant feels gratified by it—also gives rise to envy because this gift seems something so unattainable.

We find this primitive envy revived in the transference situation. For instance: the analyst has just given an interpretation which brought the patient relief and produced a change of mood from despair to hope and trust. With some patients, or with the same

---

[1] Joan Riviere, in her paper 'Jealousy as a Mechanism of Defence' (1932), traced envy in women to the infantile desire to rob the mother of her breasts and to spoil them. According to her findings, jealousy is rooted in this primal envy. Her paper contains interesting material illustrating these views.

[2] Cf. my *Psycho-Analysis of Children*, where these concepts play a part in a number of connections.

patient at other times, this helpful interpretation may soon become the object of destructive criticism. It is then no longer felt to be something good he has received and has experienced as an enrichment. His criticism may attach itself to minor points; the interpretation should have been given earlier; it was too long, and has disturbed the patient's associations; or it was too short, and this implies that he has not been sufficiently understood. The envious patient grudges the analyst the success of his work; and if he feels that the analyst and the help he is giving have become spoilt and devalued by his envious criticism, he cannot introject him sufficiently as a good object nor accept his interpretations with real conviction and assimilate them. Real conviction, as we often see in less envious patients, implies gratitude for a gift received. The envious patient may also feel, because of guilt about devaluing the help given, that he is unworthy to benefit by analysis.

Needless to say, our patients criticize us for a variety of reasons, sometimes with justification. But a patient's need to devalue the analytic work which he has experienced as helpful is the expression of envy. In the transference we discover the root of envy if we trace back the emotional situations we encounter in earlier stages down to the primary one. Destructive criticism is particularly evident in paranoid patients who indulge in the sadistic pleasure of disparaging the analyst's work, even though it has given them some relief. In these patients envious criticism is quite open; in others it may play an equally important rôle but remains unexpressed and even unconscious. In my experience, the slow progress we make in such cases is also connected with envy. We find that their doubts and uncertainties about the value of the analysis persist. What happens is that the patient has split off the envious and hostile part of his self and constantly presents to the analyst other aspects that he feels to be more acceptable. Yet the split-off parts essentially influence the course of the analysis, which ultimately can only be effective if it achieves integration and deals with the whole of the personality. Other patients try to avoid criticism by becoming confused. This confusion is not only a defence but also expresses the uncertainty as to whether the analyst is still a good figure, or whether he and the help he is giving have become bad because of the patient's hostile criticism. This uncertainty I would trace back to the feelings of confusion that are one of the consequences of the disturbed earliest relation to the mother's breast. The infant who, owing to the strength of paranoid and schizoid mechanisms and the impetus of envy, cannot divide and keep apart successfully love and hate, and therefore the good and bad object, is liable to feel confused between what is good and bad in other connections.

In these ways envy, and the defences against it, play an important part in the negative therapeutic reaction, in addition to the factors discovered by Freud and further developed by Joan Riviere.[1]

For envy, and the attitudes it gives rise to, interfere with the gradual building up of a good object in the transference situation. If at the earliest stage the good food and the primal good object could not be accepted and assimilated, this is repeated in the transference and the course of the analysis is impaired.

In the context of the analytic material, it is possible by, working through former situations, to reconstruct the patient's feelings as a baby towards the mother's breast. For instance, the infant may have a grievance that the milk comes too quickly or too slowly;[2] or that he was not given the breast when he most craved for it, and therefore, when it is offered, he does not want it any more. He turns away from it and sucks his fingers instead. When he accepts the breast, he may not drink enough, or the feed is disturbed. Some infants obviously have great difficulty in overcoming such grievances. With others these feelings, even though based on actual frustrations, are soon overcome; the breast is taken and the feed is fully enjoyed. We find in analysis that patients who, according to what they have been told, took their food satisfactorily and showed no obvious signs of the attitudes I have just described, had split off their grievance, envy, and hate, which nevertheless form part of their character development. These processes become quite clear in the transference situation. The original wish to please the mother, the longing to be loved, as well as the urgent need to be protected from the consequences of their own destructive impulses, can be found in the analysis to underlie the co-operation of those patients whose envy and hate are split off but form part of the negative therapeutic reaction.

I have often referred to the infant's desire for the inexhaustible, ever-present breast. But as has been suggested in the previous section, it is not only food he desires; he also wants to be freed from destructive impulses and persecutory anxiety. This feeling that the mother is omnipotent and that it is up to her to prevent all pain and evils from internal and external sources is also found in the analysis of adults. In passing, I would say that the very favourable changes

[1] 'A Contribution to the Analysis of the Negative Therapeutic Reaction' (1936); also Freud, *The Ego and the Id*.

[2] The baby may in fact have received too little milk, did not receive it at the time it was most wanted, or did not get it in the right way, for instance the milk came too quickly or too slowly. The way the infant was held, whether comfortable or not, the mother's attitude towards feeding, her pleasure in it or anxiety about it, whether the bottle or breast was given—all these factors are in every case of great importance.

in feeding children which have come about in recent years, in contrast to the rather rigid way of feeding according to timetable, cannot altogether prevent the infant's difficulties, because the mother cannot eliminate his destructive impulses and persecutory anxiety. There is another point to be considered. A too anxious attitude on the part of the mother who, whenever the infant cries, at once presents him with food, is unhelpful to the infant. He feels the mother's anxiety and this increases his own. I have also met in adults the grievance that they had not been allowed to cry enough, and thereby missed the possibility of expressing anxiety and grief (and thus getting relief) so that neither aggressive impulses nor depressive anxieties could sufficiently find an outlet. It is of interest that Abraham mentions, among the factors which underlie manic-depressive illness, both excessive frustration and too great indulgence.[1] For frustration, if not excessive, is also a stimulus for adaptation to the external world and for the development of the sense of reality. In fact, a certain amount of frustration followed by gratification might give the infant the feeling that he has been able to cope with his anxiety. I have also found that the infant's unfulfilled desires—which are to some extent incapable of fulfilment—are an important contributory factor to his sublimations and creative activities. The absence of conflict in the infant, if such a hypothetical state could be imagined, would deprive him of enrichment of his personality and of an important factor in the strengthening of his ego. For conflict, and the need to overcome it, is a fundamental element in creativeness.

From the contention that envy spoils the primal good object, and gives added impetus to sadistic attacks on the breast, further conclusions arise. The breast attacked in this way has lost its value, it has become bad by being bitten up and poisoned by urine and faeces. Excessive envy increases the *intensity* of such attacks and their *duration*, and thus makes it more difficult for the infant to regain the lost good object; whereas sadistic attacks on the breast that are less determined by envy pass more quickly, and therefore do not, in the infant's mind, so strongly and lastingly destroy the goodness of the object: the breast that returns and can be enjoyed is felt as an evidence that it is not injured and that it is still good.[2]

The fact that envy spoils the capacity for enjoyment explains to

[1] A Short History of the Development of the Libido' (1924).

[2] Observations of babies show us something of these underlying unconscious attitudes. As I have said above, some infants who have been screaming with rage appear quite happy soon after they begin to feed. This means that they have temporarily lost but regained their good object. With others, the persisting grievance and anxiety—even though they are for the moment diminished by the feed—can be gathered by careful observers.

some extent why envy is so persistent.[1] For it is *enjoyment* and the *gratitude* to which it gives rise that mitigate destructive impulses, envy, and greed. To look at it from another angle: greed, envy, and persecutory anxiety, which are bound up with each other, inevitably increase each other. The feeling of the harm done by envy, the great anxiety that stems from this, and the resulting uncertainty about the goodness of the object, have the effect of increasing greed and destructive impulses. Whenever the object is felt to be good after all, it is all the more greedily desired and taken in. This applies to food as well. In analysis we find that when a patient is in great doubt about his object, and therefore also about the value of the analyst and the analysis, he may cling to any interpretations that relieve his anxiety, and is inclined to prolong the session because he wants to take in as much as possible of what at the time he feels to be good. (Some people are so afraid of their greed that they are particularly keen to leave on time.)

Doubts in the possession of the good object and the corresponding uncertainty about one's own good feelings also contribute to greedy and indiscriminate identifications; such people are easily influenced because they cannot trust their own judgement.

In contrast with the infant who, owing to his envy, has been unable to build up securely a good internal object, a child with a strong capacity for love and gratitude has a deep-rooted relation with a good object and can, without being fundamentally damaged, withstand temporary states of envy, hatred, and grievance, which arise even in children who are loved and well mothered. Thus, when these negative states are transient, the good object is regained time and time again. This is an essential factor in establishing it and in laying the foundations of stability and a strong ego. In the course of development, the relation to the mother's breast becomes the foundation for devotion to people, values, and causes, and thus some of the love which was originally experienced for the primal object is absorbed.

One major derivative of the capacity for love is the feeling of gratitude. Gratitude is essential in building up the relation to the good object and underlies also the appreciation of goodness in others and in oneself. Gratitude is rooted in the emotions and attitudes that arise in the earliest stage of infancy, when for the baby the mother is the one and only object. I have referred to this early bond[2] as the basis for all later relations with one loved person.

[1] It is clear that deprivation, unsatisfactory feeding, and unfavourable circumstances intensify envy because they disturb full gratification, and a vicious circle is created.

[2] 'The Emotional Life of the Infant' (1952).

While the exclusive relation to the mother varies individually in duration and intensity, I believe that, up to a point, it exists in most people. How far it remains undisturbed depends partly on external circumstances. But the internal factors underlying it—above all the capacity for love—appear to be innate. Destructive impulses, especially strong envy, may at an early stage disturb this particular bond with the mother. If envy of the feeding breast is strong, the full gratification is interfered with because, as I have already described, it is characteristic of envy that it implies robbing the object of what it possesses, and spoiling it.

The infant can only experience complete enjoyment if the capacity for love is sufficiently developed; and it is enjoyment that forms the basis for gratitude. Freud described the infant's bliss in being suckled as the prototype of sexual gratification.[1] In my view these experiences constitute not only the basis of sexual gratification but of all later happiness, and make possible the feeling of unity with another person; such unity means being fully understood, which is essential for every happy love relation or friendship. At best, such an understanding needs no words to express it, which demonstrates its derivation from the earliest closeness with the mother in the preverbal stage. The capacity to enjoy fully the first relation to the breast forms the foundation for experiencing pleasure from various sources.

If the undisturbed enjoyment in being fed is frequently experienced, the introjection of the good breast comes about with relative security. A full gratification at the breast means that the infant feels he has received from his loved object a unique gift which he wants to keep. This is the basis of gratitude. Gratitude is closely linked with the trust in good figures. This includes first of all the ability to accept and assimilate the loved primal object (not only as a source of food) without greed and envy interfering too much; for greedy internalization disturbs the relation to the object. The individual feels that he is controlling and exhausting, and therefore injuring it, whereas in a good relation to the internal and external object, the wish to preserve and spare it predominates. I have described in another connection[2] the process underlying the belief in the good breast as derived from the infant's capacity to invest the first external object with libido. In this way a good object is established,[3] which loves and protects the self and is loved and protected by the self. This is the basis for trust in one's own goodness.

[1] *Three Essays on the Theory of Sexuality.*

[2] 'On Observing the Behaviour of Young Infants' (1952).

[3] Cf. also Donald Winnicott's concept of the 'illusory breast' and his view that at the beginning the objects are created by the self ('Psychoses and Child Care', 1953).

The more often gratification at the breast is experienced and fully accepted, the more often enjoyment and gratitude, and accordingly the wish to return pleasure, are felt. This recurrent experience makes possible gratitude on the deepest level and plays an important rôle in the capacity to make reparation, and in all sublimations. Through processes of projection and introjection, through inner wealth given out and re-introjected, an enrichment and deepening of the ego comes about. In this way the possession of the helpful inner object is again and again re-established and gratitude can fully come into play.

Gratitude is closely bound up with generosity. Inner wealth derives from having assimilated the good object so that the individual becomes able to share its gifts with others. This makes it possible to introject a more friendly outer world, and a feeling of enrichment ensues. Even the fact that generosity is often insufficiently appreciated does not necessarily undermine the ability to give. By contrast, with people in whom this feeling of inner wealth and strength is not sufficiently established, bouts of generosity are often followed by an exaggerated need for appreciation and gratitude, and consequently by persecutory anxieties of having been impoverished and robbed.

Strong envy of the feeding breast interferes with the capacity for complete enjoyment, and thus undermines the development of gratitude. There are very pertinent psychological reasons why envy ranks among the seven 'deadly sins'. I would even suggest that it is unconsciously felt to be the greatest sin of all, because it spoils and harms the good object which is the source of life. This view is consistent with the view described by Chaucer in *The Parsons Tale*: 'It is certain that envy is the worst sin that is; for all other sins are sins only against one virtue, whereas envy is against all virtue and against all goodness.' The feeling of having injured and destroyed the primal object impairs the individual's trust in the sincerity of his later relations and makes him doubt his capacity for love and goodness.

We frequently encounter expressions of gratitude which turn out to be prompted mainly by feelings of guilt and much less by the capacity for love. I think the distinction between such guilty feelings and gratitude on the deepest level is important. This does not mean that some element of guilt does not enter into the most genuine feelings of gratitude.

My observations have shown me that significant changes in character, which at close quarters reveal themselves as character deterioration, are much more likely to happen in persons who have not established their first object securely and are not capable of maintaining gratitude towards it. When in those people persecutory anxiety increases for internal or external reasons, they lose completely their primal good object, or rather its substitutes, be it persons or values. The processes that underlie this change are a regressive return to early splitting mechanisms and disintegration. Since this is a matter of degree, such a disintegration, though ultimately it strongly affects character, does not necessarily lead to manifest illness. The craving for power and prestige, or the need to pacify persecutors at any cost, are among the aspects of the character changes I have in mind.

I have seen in some cases that when envy of a person arises, the feeling of envy from its earliest sources is activated. Since these primary feelings are of an omnipotent nature, this reflects on the current feeling of envy experienced towards a substitute figure and contributes, therefore, both to the emotions stirred by envy as well as to despondency and guilt. It seems likely that this activation of the earliest envy by a common experience is common to everyone, but both the degree and the intensity of the feeling, as well as the feeling of omnipotent destruction, vary with the individual. This factor may prove to be of great importance in the analysis of envy for only if it can reach down to its deeper sources is the analysis likely to take full effect.

No doubt, in every individual, frustration and unhappy circumstances rouse some envy and hate throughout life, but the strength of these emotions and the way in which the individual copes with them varies considerably. This is one of the many reasons why the capacity for enjoyment, bound up with a feeling of gratitude for goodness received, differs vastly in people.

III

To clarify my argument, some reference to my views on the early ego seems necessary. I believe that it exists from the beginning of post-natal life, though in a rudimentary form and largely lacking coherence. Already at the earliest stage it performs a number of important functions. It might well be that this early ego approximates to the unconscious part of the ego postulated by Freud. Though he did not assume that an ego exists from the beginning, he attributed to the organism a function which, as I see it, can only be performed by the ego. The threat of annihilation by the death instinct within is, in my view—which differs from Freud's on this point[1]—the primordial anxiety, and it is the ego which, in the service of the life instinct—possibly even called into operation by

[1] Freud stated that 'the unconscious seems to contain nothing that could give any content to the concept of the annihilation of life'. *Inhibitions, Symptoms and Anxiety*, S.E. **20**, 129.

the life instinct—deflects to some extent that threat outwards. This fundamental defence against the death instinct Freud attributed to the organism, whereas I regard this process as the prime activity of the ego.

There are other primal activities of the ego which, in my view, derive from the imperative need to deal with the struggle between life and death instincts. One of these functions is gradual integration which stems from the life instinct and expresses itself in the capacity for love. The opposite tendency of the ego to split itself and its objects occurs in part because the ego largely lacks cohesion at birth, and in part because it constitutes a defence against the primordial anxiety, and is therefore a means of preserving the ego. I have, for many years, attributed great importance to one particular process of splitting: the division of the breast into a good and a bad object. I took this to be an expression of the innate conflict between love and hate and of the ensuing anxieties. However, co-existing with this division, there appear to be various processes of splitting, and it is only in recent years that some of them have been more clearly understood. For instance, I found that concurrently with the greedy and devouring internalization of the object—first of all the breast—the ego in varying degrees fragments itself and its objects, and in this way achieves a dispersal of the destructive impulses and of internal persecutory anxieties. This process, varying in strength and determining the greater or lesser normality of the individual, is one of the defences during the paranoid-schizoid position, which I believe normally extends over the first three or four months of life.[1] I am not suggesting that during that period the infant is not capable of fully enjoying his feeds, the relation to his mother, and frequent states of physical comfort or well-being. But whenever anxiety arises, it is mainly of a paranoid nature and the defences against it, as well as the mechanisms used, are predominantly schizoid. The same applies, *mutatis mutandis*, to the infant's emotional life during the period characterized by the depressive position.

To return to the splitting process, which I take to be a pre-condition for the young infant's relative stability; during the first few months he predominantly keeps the good object apart from the bad one and thus, in a fundamental way, preserves it—which also means that the security of the ego is enhanced. At the same time, this primal division only succeeds if there is an adequate capacity for love and a relatively strong ego. My hypothesis is, therefore, that the capacity for love gives impetus both to integrating tendencies and to a successful primal splitting between the loved and hated

[1] Cf. my 'Notes on some Schizoid Mechanisms'; also Herbert Rosenfeld 'Analysis of a Schizophrenic State with Depersonalization' (1947).

object. This sounds paradoxical. But since, as I said, integration is based on a strongly rooted good object that forms the core of the ego, a certain amount of splitting is essential for integration; for it preserves the good object and later on enables the ego to synthesize the two aspects of it. Excessive envy, an expression of destructive impulses, interferes with the primal split between the good and bad breast, and the building up of a good object cannot sufficiently be achieved. Thus the basis is not laid for a fully developed and integrated adult personality; for the later differentiation between good and bad is disturbed in various connections. In so far as this disturbance of development is due to excessive envy, it derives from the prevalence, in the earliest stages, of paranoid and schizoid mechanisms which, according to my hypothesis, form the basis of schizophrenia.

In the exploration of early splitting processes, it is essential to differentiate between a good object and an idealized one, though this distinction cannot be drawn sharply. A very deep split between the two aspects of the object indicates that it is not the good and bad object that are being kept apart but an idealized and an extremely bad one. So deep and sharp a division reveals that destructive impulses, envy, and persecutory anxiety are very strong and that idealization serves mainly as a defence against these emotions.

If the good object is deeply rooted, the split is fundamentally of a different nature and allows the all-important process of ego integration and object synthesis to operate. Thus a mitigation of hatred by love can come about in some measure and the depressive position can be worked through. As a result, the identification with a good and whole object is the more securely established; and this also lends strength to the ego and enables it to preserve its identity as well as a feeling of possessing goodness of its own. It becomes less liable to identify indiscriminately with a variety of objects, a process that is characteristic of a weak ego. Furthermore, full identification with a good object goes with a feeling of the self possessing goodness of its own. When things go wrong, excessive projective identification, by which split-off parts of the self are projected into the object, leads to a strong confusion between the self and the object, which also comes to stand for the self.[1] Bound up with this is a weakening of the ego and a grave disturbance in object relations.

Infants whose capacity for love is strong feel less need for idealization than those in whom destructive impulses and persecutory

[1] I have dealt with the importance of this process in earlier writings and only wish to stress here that it seems to me a fundamental mechanism in the paranoid-schizoid position.

anxiety are paramount. Excessive idealization denotes that persecution is the main driving force. As I discovered many years ago in my work with young children, idealization is a corollary of persecutory anxiety—a defence against it—and the ideal breast is the counterpart of the devouring breast.

The idealized object is much less integrated in the ego than the good object, since it stems predominantly from persecutory anxiety and much less from the capacity for love. I also found that idealization derives from the innate feeling that an extremely good breast exists, a feeling which leads to the longing for a good object and for the capacity to love it.[1] This appears to be a condition for life itself, that is to say, an expression of the life instinct. Since the need for a good object is universal, the distinction between an idealized and a good object cannot be considered as absolute.

Some people deal with their incapacity (derived from excessive envy) to possess a good object by idealizing it. This first idealization is precarious, for the envy experienced towards the good object is bound to extend to its idealized aspect. The same is true of idealizations of further objects and the identification with them, which is often unstable and indiscriminate. Greed is an important factor in these indiscriminate identifications, for the need to get the best from everywhere interferes with the capacity for selection and discrimination. This incapacity is also bound up with the confusion between good and bad that arises in the relation to the primal object.

While people who have been able to establish the primal good object with relative security are capable of retaining their love for it in spite of its shortcomings, with others idealization is a characteristic of their love relations and friendships. This tends to break down and then one loved object may frequently have to be exchanged for another; for none can come fully up to expectations. The former idealized person is often felt as a persecutor (which shows the origin of idealization as a counterpart to persecution), and into him is projected the subject's envious and critical attitude. It is of great importance that similar processes operate in the internal world which in this way comes to contain particularly dangerous objects. All this leads to instability in relationships. This is another aspect of the weakness of the ego, to which I referred earlier in connection with indiscriminate identifications.

Doubts connected with the good object easily arise even in a secure child-mother relation; this is not only due to the fact that the infant

---

[1] I have already referred to the inherent need to idealize the pre-natal situation. Another frequent field for idealization is the baby-mother relation. It is particularly those people who were not able to experience sufficient happiness in this relation who idealize it in retrospect.

is very dependent on the mother, but also to the recurrent anxiety that his greed and his destructive impulses will get the better of him—an anxiety which is an important factor in depressive states. However, at any stage of life, under the stress of anxiety, the belief and trust in good objects can be shaken; but it is the *intensity* and *duration* of such states of doubt, despondency, and persecution that determine whether the ego is capable of re-integrating itself and of reinstating its good objects securely.[1] Hope and trust in the existence of goodness, as can be observed in everyday life, helps people through great adversity, and effectively counteracts persecution.

## IV

It appears that one of the consequences of excessive envy is an early onset of guilt. If premature guilt is experienced by an ego not yet capable of bearing it, guilt is felt as persecution and the object that rouses guilt is turned into a persecutor. The infant then cannot work through either depressive or persecutory anxiety because they become confused with each other. A few months later, when the depressive position arises, the more integrated and stronger ego has a greater capacity to bear the pain of guilt and to develop corresponding defences, mainly the tendency to make reparation.

The fact that in the earliest stage (*i.e.* during the paranoid-schizoid position) premature guilt increases persecution and disintegration, brings the consequence that the working-through of the depressive position also fails.[2]

This failure can be observed in both child and adult patients: as

[1] In this connection I refer to my paper on 'Mourning and its Relation to Manic-Depressive States' in which I defined the normal working-through of mourning as a process during which the early good objects are reinstated. I suggested that this working-through first takes place when the infant successfully deals with the depressive position.

[2] Whereas I have not altered my views on the depressive position setting in about the second quarter of the first year and coming to a climax at about six months, I have found that some infants seem to experience guilt transiently in the first few months of life (Cf. 'On the Theory of Anxiety and Guilt'). This does not imply that the depressive position has already arisen. I have elsewhere described the variety of processes and defences that characterize the depressive position, such as the relation to the whole object; stronger recognition of internal and external reality; defences against depression, in particular the urge for reparation, and the widening of object relations leading to the early stages of the Oedipus complex. In speaking about guilt transiently experienced in the first stage of life, I came closer to the view I held at the time when I wrote the *Psycho-Analysis of Children*, where I described guilt and persecution experienced by very young infants. When later on I defined the depressive position, I divided more clearly, and perhaps too schematically, guilt, depression, and the corresponding defences on the one hand, and the paranoid stage (which I later called the paranoid-schizoid position) on the other.

soon as guilt is felt, the analyst becomes persecutory and is accused on many grounds. In such cases we find that as infants they could not experience guilt without its simultaneously leading to persecutory anxiety with its corresponding defences. These defences appear later as projection on to the analyst and omnipotent denial.

It is my hypothesis that one of the deepest sources of guilt is always linked with the envy of the feeding breast, and with the feeling of having spoilt its goodness by envious attacks. If the primal object has been established with relative stability in early infancy, the guilt aroused by such feelings can be coped with more successfully because then envy is more transient and less liable to endanger the relation to the good object.

Excessive envy interferes with adequate oral gratification and so acts as a stimulus towards the intensification of genital desires and trends. This implies that the infant turns too early towards genital gratification, with the consequence that the oral relation becomes genitalized and the genital trends become too much coloured by oral grievances and anxieties. I have often contended that genital sensations and desires are possibly operative from birth onwards; for instance, it is well known that infant boys have erections at a very early stage. But in speaking of these sensations arising prematurely I mean that genital trends interfere with oral ones at a stage when normally the oral desires are uppermost.[1] Here again we have to consider the effects of early confusion, which expresses itself in a blurring of the oral, anal, and genital impulses and phantasies. An overlapping between these various sources both of libido and of aggressiveness is normal. But when the overlapping amounts to an incapacity to experience sufficiently the predominance of either of these trends at their proper stage of development, then both later sexual life and sublimations are adversely affected. Genitality based on a flight from orality is insecure because into it are carried over the suspicions and disappointments attaching to the impaired oral enjoyment. The interference with oral primacy by genital trends undermines the gratification in the genital sphere and often is the cause of obsessional masturbation and of promiscuity. For the lack of the primary enjoyment introduces into the genital desires compulsive elements and, as I have seen with some patients, may therefore lead to sexual sensations entering into all activities, thought processes, and interests. With some infants, the flight into genitality is also a defence against hating and injuring the first object

[1] I have reason to believe that this premature genitalization is often a feature in strong schizophrenic traits or in full-blown schizophrenia. Cf. W. Bion in 'Notes on the Theory of Schizophrenia' (1954) and 'Differentiation of the Psychotic from the Non-Psychotic Personalities' (1958).

towards which ambivalent feelings operate. I have found that the premature onset of genitality may be bound up with the early occurrence of guilt and is characteristic of paranoid and schizoid cases.[1]

When the infant reaches the depressive position, and becomes more able to face his psychic reality, he also feels that the object's badness is largely due to his own aggressiveness and the ensuing projection. This insight, as we can see in the transference situation, gives rise to great mental pain and guilt when the depressive position is at its height. But it also brings about feelings of relief and hope, which in turn make it less difficult to reunite the two aspects of the object and of the self and to work through the depressive position. This hope is based on the growing unconscious knowledge that the internal and external object is not as bad as it was felt to be in its split-off aspects. Through mitigation of hatred by love the object improves in the infant's mind. It is no longer so strongly felt to have been destroyed in the past and the danger of its being destroyed in the future is lessened; not being injured, it is also felt to be less vulnerable in the present and future. The internal object acquires a restraining and self-preservative attitude and its greater strength is an important aspect of its super-ego function.

In describing the overcoming of the depressive position, bound up with the greater trust in the good internal object, I do not intend to convey that such results cannot be temporarily undone. Strain of an internal or external nature is liable to stir up depression and distrust in the self as well as in the object. However, the capacity to emerge from such depressive states, and to regain one's feeling of inner security, is in my view the criterion of a well developed personality. By contrast, the frequent way of dealing with depression by hardening one's feelings and denying depression is a regression to the manic defences used during the infantile depressive position.

There is a direct link between the envy experienced towards the mother's breast and the development of jealousy. Jealousy is based on the suspicion of and rivalry with the father, who is accused of having taken away the mother's breast and the mother. This rivalry marks the early stages of the direct and inverted Oedipus complex, which normally arises concurrently with the depressive position in the second quarter of the first year.[2]

---

[1] Cf. 'The Importance of Symbol-Formation in the Development of the Ego' (1930) and 'A Contribution to the Psychogenesis of Manic-Depressive States' (1935); also *The Psycho-Analysis of Children*.

[2] I have pointed out elsewhere (e.g. in 'The Emotional Life of the Infant') the close connection between the phase in which the depressive position develops and the early stages of the Oedipus complex.

The development of the Oedipus complex is strongly influenced by the vicissitudes of the first exclusive relation with the mother, and when this relation is disturbed too soon, the rivalry with the father enters prematurely. Phantasies of the penis inside the mother, or inside her breast, turn the father into a hostile intruder. This phantasy is particularly strong when the infant has not had the full enjoyment and happiness that the early relation to the mother can afford him and has not taken in the first good object with some security. Such failure partly depends on the strength of envy.

When in earlier writings I described the depressive position, I showed that at that stage the infant progressively integrates his feelings of love and hatred, synthesizes the good and bad aspects of the mother, and goes through states of mourning bound up with feelings of guilt. He also begins to understand more of the external world and realizes that he cannot keep his mother to himself as his exclusive possession. Whether or not the infant can find help against that grief in the relation to the second object, the father, or to other people in his surroundings, largely depends on the emotions which he experiences towards his lost unique object. If that relation was well founded, the fear of losing the mother is less strong and the capacity to share her is greater. Then he can also experience more love towards his rivals. All this implies that he has been able to work through the depressive position satisfactorily, which in turn depends on envy towards the primal object not being excessive.

Jealousy is, as we know, inherent in the Oepidus situation and is accompanied by hate and death wishes. Normally, however, the gain of new objects who can be loved—the father and siblings—and other compensations which the developing ego derives from the external world, mitigate to some extent jealousy and grievance. If paranoid and schizoid mechanisms are strong, jealousy—and ultimately envy—remain unmitigated. The development of the Oedipus complex is essentially influenced by all these factors.

Among the features of the earliest stage of the Oedipus complex are the phantasies of the mother's breast and the mother containing the penis of the father, or the father containing the mother. This is the basis of the combined parent figure, and I have elaborated the importance of this phantasy in earlier writings.[1] The influence of the combined parent figure on the infant's ability to differentiate between the parents, and to establish good relations with each of

---

[1] *The Psycho-Analysis of Children* (particularly Chapter VIII) and 'The Emotional Life of the Infant'. I have pointed out there that these phantasies form normally part of the early stages of the Oedipus complex but I would now add that the whole development of the Oedipus complex is strongly influenced by the intensity of envy which determines the strength of the combined parent figure.

them, is affected by the strength of envy and the intensity of his Oedipus jealousy. For the suspicion that the parents are always getting sexual gratification from one another reinforces the phantasy —derived from various sources—that they are always combined. If these anxieties are strongly operative, and therefore unduly prolonged, the consequence may be a lasting disturbance in the relation to both parents. In very ill individuals, the inability to disentangle the relation to the father from the one to the mother, because of their being inextricably interlinked in the patient's mind, plays an important rôle in severe states of confusion.

If envy is not excessive, jealousy in the Oedipus situation becomes a means of working it through. When jealousy is experienced, hostile feelings are directed not so much against the primal object but rather against the rivals—father or siblings—which brings in an element of distribution. At the same time, when these relations develop, they give rise to feelings of love, and become a new source of gratification. Furthermore, the change from oral desires to genital ones reduces the importance of the mother as a giver of oral enjoyment. (As we know, the object of envy is largely oral.) With the boy, a good deal of hate is deflected on to the father who is envied for the possession of the mother; this is the typical Oedipus jealousy. With the girl, the genital desires for the father enable her to find another loved object. Thus jealousy to some extent supersedes envy; the mother becomes the chief rival. The girl desires to take her mother's place and to possess and take care of the babies which the loved father gives to the mother. The identification with the mother in this rôle makes a wider range of sublimations possible, It is essential also to consider that the working-through of envy by means of jealousy is at the same time an important defence against envy. Jealousy is felt to be much more acceptable and gives rise much less to guilt than the primary envy which destroys the first good object.

In analysis we can often see the close connection between jealousy and envy. For instance, a patient felt very jealous of a man with whom he thought that I was in close personal contact. The next step was a feeling that in any case I was probably in private life uninteresting and boring, and suddenly the whole of the analysis appeared to him as boring. The interpretation—in this case by the patient himself—that this was a defence led to the recognition of a devaluation of the analyst as a result of an upsurge of envy.

Ambition is another factor highly instrumental in stirring up envy. This frequently relates first to the rivalry and competition in the Oedipus situation; but if excessive, it clearly shows its root in the envy of the primal object. Failure to fulfil one's ambition is often aroused by the conflict between the urge to make reparation to the object injured by destructive envy and a renewed reappearance of envy.

Freud's discovery of penis-envy in women and its link with aggressive impulses was a basic contribution to the understanding of envy. When penis-envy and castration wishes are strong, the envied object, the penis, is to be destroyed and the man who owns it is to be deprived of it. In his 'Analysis Terminable and Interminable' Freud (1937) emphasized the difficulty arising in the analysis of women patients by the very fact that they can never acquire the penis that they desire. He stated that a woman patient feels 'an internal conviction that the analysis will be of no use and that nothing can be done to help her. And we can only agree that she is right, when we learn that her strongest motive in coming for treatment was the hope that, after all, she might still obtain a male organ, the lack of which was so painful to her.'

A number of factors contribute to penis-envy which I have discussed in other connections.[1] In this context I wish to consider the woman's penis-envy mainly in so far as it is of oral origin. As we know, under the dominance of oral desires, the penis is strongly equated with the breast (Abraham) and in my experience the woman's penis-envy can be traced back to envy of the mother's breast. I have found that if the penis-envy of women is analysed on these lines, we can see that its root lies in the earliest relation to the mother, in the fundamental envy of the mother's breast, and in the destructive feelings allied with it.

Freud has shown how vital is the attitude of the girl to her mother in her subsequent relations to men. When envy of the mother's breast has been strongly transferred to the father's penis, the outcome may be a reinforcing of her homosexual attitude. Another outcome is a sudden and abrupt turning to the penis away from the breast, because of the excessive anxieties and conflicts to which the oral relation gives rise. This is essentially a flight mechanism and

[1] 'The Oedipus Complex in the Light of Early Anxieties' (1945), *Writings*, **1**, p. 418. 'Penis envy and the castration complex play an essential part in the girl's development. But they are very much reinforced by frustration of her positive Oedipus desires. Though the little girl at one stage assumes that her mother possesses a penis as a male attribute, this concept does not play nearly as important a part in her development as Freud suggests. The unconscious theory that her mother contains the admired and desired penis of the father underlies, in my experience, many of the phenomena which Freud described as the relation of the girl to the phallic mother. The girl's oral desires for her father's penis mingle with her first genital desires to receive that penis. These genital desires imply the wish to receive the children from her father, which is also borne out by the equation "penis=child". The feminine desire to internalize the penis and to receive a child from her father invariably precedes the wish to possess a penis of her own.'

therefore does not lead to stable relations with the second object. If the main motive for this flight is envy and hatred experienced towards the mother, these emotions are soon transferred to the father, and therefore a lasting and loving attitude to him cannot be established. At the same time, the envious relation to the mother expresses itself in an excessive Oedipus rivalry. This rivalry is much less due to love of the father than to envy of the mother's possession of the father and his penis. The envy experienced towards the breast is then fully carried over into the Oedipus situation. The father (or his penis) has become an appendage to the mother and it is on these grounds that the girl wants to rob her mother of him. Therefore in later life, every success in her relation to men becomes a victory over another woman. This applies even where there is no obvious rival, because the rivalry is then directed against the man's mother, as can be seen in the frequent disturbances of the relation between daughter-in-law and mother-in-law. If the man is mainly valued because his conquest is a triumph over another woman, she may lose interest in him as soon as success has been achieved. The attitude towards the rival woman then implies: 'You (standing for the mother) had that wonderful breast which I could not get when you withheld it from me and which I still wish to rob you of; therefore I take from you that penis which you cherish.' The need to repeat this triumph over a hated rival often strongly contributes to the search for another and yet another man.

When hate and envy of the mother are not so strong, nevertheless disappointment and grievance may lead to a turning away from her; but an idealization of the second object, the father's penis and the father, may then be more successful. This idealization derives mainly from the search for a good object, a search which has not succeeded in the first place and therefore may fail again, but need not fail if the love for the father is dominant in the jealousy situation; for then the woman can combine some hatred against the mother and love for the father and later on for other men. In this case friendly emotions towards women are possible, as long as they do not too much represent a mother substitute. Friendship with women and homosexuality may then be based on the need to find a good object instead of the avoided primal object. The fact that such people—and this applies to men as well as to women—can have good object relations is therefore often deceptive. The underlying envy towards the primal object is split off but remains operative and is liable to disturb any relations.

In a number of cases I found that frigidity, occurring in different degrees, was a result of unstable attitudes to the penis, based mainly on a flight from the primal object. The capacity for full oral gratification, which is rooted in a satisfactory relation to the mother, is the basis for experiencing full genital orgasm (Freud).

In men, the envy of the mother's breast is also a very important factor. If it is strong and oral gratification thereby impaired, hatred and anxieties are transferred to the vagina. Whereas normally the genital development enables the boy to retain his mother as a love-object, a deep disturbance in the oral relation opens the way for severe difficulties in the genital attitude towards women. The consequence of a disturbed relation first to the breast and then to the vagina are manifold, such as impairment of genital potency, compulsive need for genital gratification, promiscuity, and homosexuality.

It appears that one source of guilt about homosexuality is the feeling of having turned away with hate from the mother and betrayed her by making an ally of the father's penis and of the father. Both during the Oedipus stage and in later life this element of betrayal of a loved woman may have repercussions, such as a disturbance in friendships with men, even if they are not of a manifest homosexual nature. On the other hand, I have observed that the guilt towards a loved woman and the anxiety implied in that attitude often reinforce the flight from her and increase homosexual tendencies.

Excessive envy of the breast is likely to extend to all feminine attributes, in particular to the woman's capacity to bear children. If development is successful, the man derives compensation for these unfulfilled feminine desires by a good relation to his wife or lover and by becoming the father of the children she bears him. This relation opens up experiences such as identification with his child which in many ways make up for early envy and frustrations; also the feeling that he has created the child counteracts the man's early envy of the mother's femininity.

In both male and female, envy plays a part in the desire to take away the attributes of the other sex, as well as to possess or spoil those of the parent of the same sex. It follows that paranoid jealousy and rivalry in the direct and inverted Oedipus situation are in both sexes, however divergent their development, based on excessive envy towards the primal object, the mother, or rather her breast.

The 'good' breast that feeds and initiates the love relation to the mother is the representative of the life instinct[1] and is also felt as the first manifestation of creativeness. In this fundamental relation the infant receives not only the gratification he desires but feels that he is being kept alive. For hunger, which rouses the fear of starvation — possibly even all physical and mental pain — is felt as the threat of

[1] See 'The Emotional Life of the Infant' and 'The Behaviour of Young Infants'.

death. If the identification with a good and life-giving internalized object can be maintained, this becomes an impetus towards creativeness. Though superficially this may manifest itself as a coveting of the prestige, wealth, and power which others have attained,[1] its actual aim is creativeness. The capacity to give and to preserve life is felt as the greatest gift and therefore creativeness becomes the deepest cause for envy. The spoiling of creativity implied in envy is illustrated in Milton's *Paradise Lost*[2] where Satan, envious of God, decides to become the usurper of Heaven. He makes war on God in his attempt to spoil the heavenly life and falls out of Heaven. Fallen, he and his other fallen angels build Hell as a rival to Heaven, and become the destructive force which attempts to destroy what God creates.[3] This theological idea seems to come down from St Augustine, who describes Life as a creative force opposed to Envy, a destructive force. In this connection, the First Letter to the Corinthians reads, 'Love envieth not'.

My psycho-analytic experience has shown me that envy of creativeness is a fundamental element in the disturbance of the creative process. To spoil and destroy the initial source of goodness soon leads to destroying and attacking the babies that the mother contains and results in the good object being turned into a hostile, critical, and envious one. The super-ego figure on which strong envy has been projected becomes particularly persecutory and interferes with thought processes and with every productive activity, ultimately with creativeness.

The envious and destructive attitude towards the breast underlies destructive criticism which is often described as 'biting' and 'pernicious'. It is particularly creativeness which becomes the object of such attacks. Thus Spenser in 'The Faerie Queene' describes envy as a ravenous wolf:

> He hated all good workes and vertuous deeds
>
> .   .   .   .   .
>
> And eke the verse of famous Poets witt
> He does backebite, and spightfull poison spues[4]
> From leprous mouth on all that ever writt.

[1] 'On Identification' (1955).

[2] Books I and II.

[3] But by the envy of the Devil, death entered into the world, and they that are of his portion make trial thereof. (Wisdom of Solomon, Ch. 3, v. 24.)

[4] In Chaucer also we find extensive references to this backbiting and destructive criticising which characterizes the envious person. He describes the sin of backbiting as arising from a compound of the envious person's unhappiness at other men's goodness and prosperity, and his joy in their harm. The sinful behaviour is characterized by 'the man who praises his neighbour but with wicked intent,

Constructive criticism has different sources; it aims at helping the other person and furthering his work. Sometimes it derives from a strong identification with the person whose work is under discussion. Maternal or fatherly attitudes may also enter, and often a confidence in one's own creativeness counteracts envy.

A particular cause of envy is the relative absence of it in others. The envied person is felt to possess what is at bottom most prized and desired—and this is a good object, which also implies a good character and sanity. Moreover, the person who can ungrudgingly enjoy other people's creative work and happiness is spared the torments of envy, grievance, and persecution. Whereas envy is a source of great unhappiness, a relative freedom from it is felt to underlie contented and peaceful states of mind—ultimately sanity. This is also in fact the basis of inner resources and resilience which can be observed in people who, even after great adversity and mental pain, regain their peace of mind. Such an attitude, which includes gratitude for pleasures of the past and enjoyment of what the present can give, expresses itself in serenity. In old people, it makes possible the adaptation to the knowledge that youth cannot be regained and enables them to take pleasure and interest in the lives of young people. The well-known fact that parents relive in their children and grand-children their own lives—if this is not an expression of excessive possessiveness and deflected ambition—illustrates what I am trying to convey. Those who feel that they have had a share in the experience and pleasures of life are much more able to believe in the continuity of life.[1] Such capacity for resignation without undue bitterness and yet keeping the power of enjoyment alive has its roots in infancy and depends on how far the baby had been able to enjoy the breast without excessively envying the mother for its possession. I suggest that the happiness experienced in infancy and the love for the good object which enriches the personality underlie the capacity for enjoyment and sublimation, and still make themselves felt in old age. When Goethe said, 'He is the happiest of men who can make the end of his life agree closely with the beginning', I

---

for he always put "but" at the end, and follows it with another of greater blame than is the worth of the person. Or, if a man is good and does or says things of good intent, the backbiter will turn all this goodness upside down to his own shrewd intent. Of if other men speak good of a man, then the backbiter will say that he is very good, but will point to someone else who is better, and will thus disparage he whom other men praise.'

[1] The belief in the continuity of life was significantly expressed in the remark of a boy in his fifth year whose mother was pregnant. He expressed the hope that the expected baby would be a girl, and added, 'then she will have babies, and her babies will have babies, and then it goes on forever'.

would interpret 'the beginning' as the early happy relation to the mother which throughout life mitigates hate and anxiety and still gives the old person support and contentment. An infant who has securely established the good object can also find compensations for loss and deprivation in adult life. All this is felt by the envious person as something he can never attain because he can never be satisfied, and therefore his envy is reinforced.

V

I shall now illustrate some of my conclusions by clinical material.[1] My first instance is taken from the analysis of a woman patient. She had been breast-fed, but circumstances had otherwise not been favourable and she was convinced that her babyhood and feeding had been wholly unsatisfactory. Her grievance about the past linked with hopelessness about the present and future. Envy of the feeding breast, and the ensuing difficulties in object relations, had already been extensively analysed prior to the material to which I am going to refer.

The patient telephoned and said that she could not come for treatment because of a pain in her shoulder. On the next day she rang me to say that she was still not well but expected to see me on the following day. When, on the third day, she actually came, she was full of complaints. She had been looked after by her maid, but nobody else had taken an interest in her. She described to me that at one moment her pain had suddenly increased, together with a sense of extreme coldness. She had felt an impetuous need for somebody to come at once and cover up her shoulder, so that it should get warm, and to go away again as soon as that was done. At that instant it occurred to her that this must be how she had felt as a baby when she wanted to be looked after and nobody came.

It was characteristic of the patient's attitude to people, and threw light on her earliest relation to the breast, that she desired to be looked after but at the same time repelled the very object which was to gratify her. The suspicion of the gift received, together with her impetuous need to be cared for, which ultimately meant a desire to be fed, expressed her ambivalent attitude towards the breast. I have referred to infants whose response to frustration is to make insufficient use of the gratification that the feed, even if delayed, could give them. I would surmise that though they do not give up their desires for a gratifying breast, they cannot enjoy it and therefore

---

[1] I am aware that in the following case material details of the patient's history, personality, age, and external circumstances would have been of value. Reasons of discretion make it impossible to go into such details and I can only attempt illustrations of my main themes by extracts from material.

repel it. The case under discussion illustrates some of the reasons for this attitude: suspicion of the gift she wished to receive because the object was already spoilt by envy and hatred, and at the same time deep resentment about every frustration. We also have to remember —and this applies to other adults in whom envy is marked—that many disappointing experiences, no doubt partly due to her own attitude, had contributed to her feeling that the desired care would not be satisfactory.

In the course of this session the patient reported a dream: she was in a restaurant, seated at a table; however nobody came to serve her. She decided to join a queue and fetch herself something to eat. In front of her was a woman who took two or three little cakes and went away with them. The patient also took two or three little cakes. From her associations I am selecting the following: the woman seemed very determined, and her figure was reminiscent of mine. There was a sudden doubt about the name of the cakes (actually *petits fours*) which she first thought were 'petit fru', which reminded her of 'petit frau' and thus of 'Frau Klein'. The gist of my interpretations was that her grievance about the missed analytic sessions related to the unsatisfactory feeds and unhappiness in babyhood. The two cakes out of the 'two or three' stood for the breast which she felt she had been twice deprived of by missing analytic sessions. There were 'two or three' because she was not sure whether she would be able to come on the third day. The fact that the woman was 'determined' and that the patient followed her example in taking the cakes pointed both at her identification with the analyst and at projection of her own greed on to her. In the present context, one aspect of the dream is most relevant. The analyst who went away with the two or three *petits fours* stood not only for the breast which was withheld, but also for the breast which was going to *feed itself*. (Taken together with other material, the 'determined' analyst represented not only a breast but a person with whose qualities, good and bad, the patient identified herself.)

To frustration had thus been added envy of the breast. This envy had given rise to bitter resentment, for the mother had been felt to be selfish and mean, feeding and loving herself rather than her baby. In the analytic situation I was suspected of having enjoyed myself during the time when she was absent, or of having given the time to other patients whom I preferred. The queue which the patient had decided to join referred to other more favoured rivals.

The response to the analysis of the dream was a striking change in the emotional situation. The patient now experienced a feeling of happiness and gratitude more vividly than in previous analytic sessions. She had tears in her eyes, which was unusual, and said that she felt as if she now had had an entirely satisfactory feed.[1] It also occurred to her that her breast-feeding and her infancy might have been happier than she had assumed. Also, she felt more hopeful about the future and the result of her analysis. The patient had more fully realized one part of herself, which was by no means unknown to her in other connections. She was aware that she was envious and jealous of various people but had not been able to recognize it sufficiently in the relation to the analyst because it was too painful to experience that she was envying and spoiling the analyst as well as the success of the analysis. In this session, after the interpretations referred to, her envy had lessened; the capacity for enjoyment and gratitude had come to the fore, and she was able to experience the analytic session as a happy feed. This emotional situation had to be worked through over and over again, both in the positive and negative transference, until a more stable result was achieved.

It was by enabling her gradually to bring the split-off parts of her self together in relation to the analyst, and by her recognizing how envious and therefore suspicious she was of me, and in the first place of her mother, that the experience of that happy feed came about. This was bound up with feelings of gratitude. In the course of the analysis envy was diminished and feelings of gratitude became much more frequent and lasting.

My second instance is taken from the analysis of a woman patient with strong depressive and schizoid features. She had suffered from depressive states over a long period. The analysis proceeded and made some headway, though the patient again and again expressed her doubts about the work. I had interpreted the destructive impulses against the analyst, parents, and siblings, and the analysis succeeded in making her recognize specific phantasies of destructive attacks on her mother's body. Such insight was usually followed by depression but not of an unmanageable nature.

It is remarkable that during the early part of her treatment the depth and severity of the patient's difficulties could not be seen. Socially, she gave an impression of being a pleasant person, though

[1] It is not only in children but also in adults that a full revival of the emotions felt during the earliest feeding experiences can come about in the transference situation. For instance, a feeling of hunger or thirst comes up very strongly during the session and has gone after the interpretation which was felt to have satisfied it. One of my patients, overcome by such feelings, got up from the couch and put his arms round one section of the arch which separated one part of my consulting room from the other. I have repeatedly heard the expression at the end of such sessions 'I have been well nourished'. The good object, in its earliest primitive form as the mother who takes care of the baby and feeds him, had been regained.

liable to be depressed. Her reparative tendencies and helpful attitude towards friends were quite genuine. However, the severity of her illness became apparent at one stage, partly due to the previous analytic work and partly to some external experiences. Several disappointments occurred; but it was an unexpected success in her professional career that brought more to the fore what I had been analysing for some years, namely, the intense rivalry with me and a feeling that she might in her own field become equal, or rather superior, to me. Both she and I came to recognize the importance of her destructive envy towards me; and, as always when we reach these deep strata, it appeared that whatever destructive impulses were there, they were felt to be omnipotent and therefore irrevocable and irremediable. I had until then analysed her oral-sadistic desires extensively, and that is also how we arrived at her partial realization of her destructive impulses towards her mother and myself. The analysis had also dealt with urethral- and anal-sadistic desires, but in this respect I felt that I had not made much headway and that her understanding of these impulses and phantasies was more of an intellectual nature. During the particular period I now want to discuss, urethral material appeared with increased strength.

A feeling of great elation about her success soon developed and was ushered in by a dream which showed the triumph over me and, underlying this, the destructive envy of me standing for her mother. In the dream she was up in the air on a magic carpet which supported her and was above the top of a tree. She was sufficiently high up to look through a window into a room where a cow was munching something which appeared to be an endless strip of blanket. In the same night she also had a bit of a dream in which her pants were wet.

The associations to this dream made it clear that being on top of the tree meant having outstripped me, for the cow represented myself, at whom she looked with contempt. Quite early on in her analysis she had had a dream in which I was represented by an apathetic cow-like woman, whereas she was a little girl who made a brilliant and successful speech. My interpretations at that time that she had made the analyst into a contemptible person, whereas she gave such a successful performance in spite of being so much younger, had only partly been accepted although she fully realized that the little girl was herself and the cow-woman was the analyst. This dream led gradually to a stronger realization of her destructive and envious attacks upon me and her mother. Ever since, the cow-woman, standing for myself, had been a well-established feature in the material, and therefore it was quite clear that in the new dream the cow in the room into which she was looking was the analyst. She

207

associated that the endless strip of blanket represented an endless stream of words, and it occurred to her that these were all the words I had ever said in the analysis and which I now had to swallow. The strip of blanket was a hit at the woolliness and worthlessness of my interpretations. Here we see the full devaluation of the primal object, significantly represented by the cow, as well as the grievance against the mother who had not fed her satisfactorily. The punishment inflicted on me by having to eat all my words throws light on the deep distrust and the doubts which had again and again assailed her in the course of the analysis. It became quite clear after my interpretations that the ill-treated analyst could not be trusted, and that she could also have no confidence in the devalued analysis. The patient was surprised and shocked at her attitude towards me, which prior to the dream she had for a long time refused to acknowledge in its full impact.

The wet pants in the dream and the association to them expressed (among other meanings) poisonous urethral attacks on the analyst which were to destroy her mental powers and change her into the cow-woman. Very soon she had another dream illustrating this particular point. She was standing at the bottom of a staircase, looking up at a young couple with whom something was very wrong. She threw a woollen ball up to them, which she herself described as 'good magic', and her associations showed that bad magic, and more specifically poison, must have given rise to the need to use good magic afterwards. The associations to the couple enabled me to interpret a strongly denied current jealousy situation and led us from the present back to earlier experiences, ultimately of course to the parents. The destructive and envious feeling towards the analyst, and in the past towards her mother, turned out to underlie the jealousy and envy towards the couple in the dream. The fact that this light ball never reached the couple implied that her reparation did not succeed; and the anxiety about such failure was an important element in her depression.

This is only an extract from the material which convincingly proved to the patient her poisonous envy of the analyst and of her primal object. She succumbed to depression of a depth such as she had never had before. The main cause of this depression, which followed on her state of elation, was that she had been made to realize a completely split-off part of herself which so far she had been unable to acknowledge. As I said earlier, it was very difficult to help her to realize her hate and agressiveness. But when we came to this particular source of destructiveness, her envy, as the impetus towards damaging and humiliating the analyst, whom in another part of her mind she highly valued, she could not bear to see herself in that light. She did not appear to be particularly boastful or conceited, but by means of a variety of splitting processes and manic defences she had clung to an idealized picture of herself. As a consequence of the realization, which at that stage of the analysis she could no longer deny, that she felt bad and despicable, the idealization broke down and distrust of herself as well as guilt about irrevocable harm done in the past and in the present came up. Her guilt and depression focused on her feeling of ingratitude towards the analyst who, she knew, had helped her and was helping her, and towards whom she felt contempt and hate: ultimately on the ingratitude towards her mother, whom she unconsciously saw as spoilt and damaged by her envy and destructive impulses.

The analysis of her depression led to an improvement which after some months was followed by a renewed deep depression. This was caused by the patient recognizing more fully her virulent anal-sadistic attacks on the analyst, and in the past on her family, and confirmed her feeling both of illness and of badness. It was the first time that she was able to see how strongly urethral- and anal-sadistic features had been split off. Each of these had involved important parts of the patient's personality and interests. The steps towards integration which took place following the analysis of the depression implied regaining these lost parts, and the necessity to face them was the cause of her depression.

The next instance is of a woman patient whom I would describe as fairly normal. She had in the course of time become more and more aware of envy experienced both towards an older sister and towards her mother. The envy of the sister had been counteracted by a feeling of strong intellectual superiority which had a basis in fact, and by an unconscious feeling that the sister was extremely neurotic. The envy of the mother was counteracted by very strong feelings of love and appreciation of her goodness.

The patient reported a dream in which she was alone in a railway carriage with a woman, of whom she could only see the back, who was leaning towards the door of the compartment in great danger of falling out. The patient held her strongly, grasping her by the belt with one hand; with the other hand she wrote a notice to the effect that a doctor was engaged with a patient in this compartment and should not be disturbed, and she put up this notice on the window.

From the associations to the dream I select the following: the patient had a strong feeling that the figure on whom she kept a tight grip was part of herself, and a mad one. In the dream she had a conviction that she should not let her fall out through the door but should keep her in the compartment and deal with her. The analysis of the dream revealed that the compartment stood for herself. The associations to the hair, which was only seen from behind, were to the older sister. Further associations led to recognition of rivalry and envy in relation to her, going back to the time when the patient was still a child, while her sister was already being courted. She then spoke of a dress which her mother wore and which as a child the patient had both admired and coveted. This dress had very clearly shown the shape of the breasts, and it became more evident than ever before, though none of this was entirely new, that what she originally envied and spoiled in her phantasy was the mother's breast.

This recognition gave rise to increased feelings of guilt, towards both her sister and her mother, and led to a further revision of her earliest relations. She arrived at a much more compassionate understanding of the deficiencies of this sister and felt that she had not loved her sufficiently. She also discovered that she had loved her in her early childhood more than she had remembered.

I interpreted that the patient felt that she had to keep a grip on a mad, split-off part of herself, which was also linked with the internalization of the neurotic sister. Following the interpretation of the dream, the patient, who had reasons for regarding herself as fairly normal, had a feeling of strong surprise and shock. This case illustrates a conclusion that is becoming increasingly familiar, namely, that a residue of paranoid and schizoid feelings and mechanisms, often split-off from the other parts of the self, exists even in normal people.[1]

The patient's feeling that she had to keep a firm hold on that figure implied that she should also have helped her sister more, prevented her, as it were, from falling; and this feeling was now re-experienced in connection with her as an internalized object. The revision of her earliest relations was bound up with changes in feelings towards her primal introjected objects. The fact that her sister also represented the mad part of herself turned out to be partly a projection of her own schizoid and paranoid feelings on to her sister. It was together with this realization that the split in her ego diminished.

I now wish to refer to a man patient and report a dream which had a strong effect in making him recognize not only destructive impulses towards the analyst and towards his mother, but envy as a very specific factor in his relation to them. Up till then, and with strong

[1] Freud's *Interpretation of Dreams* shows clearly that some of this residue of madness finds expression in dreams, and that they are therefore a most valuable safeguard for sanity.

feelings of guilt, he had already recognized in some measure his destructive impulses, but still did not realize envious and hostile feelings directed against the creativeness of the analyst, and of his mother in the past. He was aware, though, that he experienced envy towards other people and that, together with a good relation to his father, he had also feelings of rivalry and jealousy. The following dream brought a much stronger insight into his envy of the analyst and threw light on his early desires to possess all the feminine attributes of his mother.

In the dream the patient had been fishing; he was wondering whether he should kill the fish he caught in order to eat it, but decided to put it into a basket and let it die. The basket in which he was carrying the fish was a woman's laundry basket. The fish suddenly turned into a beautiful baby and there was something green about the baby's clothes. Then he noticed—and at that point he became very concerned—that the baby's intestines were protruding because it had been damaged by the hook which it had swallowed in its fish state. The association to green was the cover of the books in the *International Psycho-Analytical Library* series, and the patient remarked that the fish in the basket stood for one of my books which he had obviously stolen. Further associations, however, showed that the fish was not only my work and my baby but also stood for myself. My swallowing the hook, which meant having swallowed the bait, expressed his feeling that I had thought better of him than he deserved and not recognized that there were also very destructive parts of his self operative in relation to me. Although the patient still could not fully acknowledge that the way he treated the fish, the baby, and myself meant destroying me and my work out of envy, he unconsciously realized it. I also interpreted that the laundry basket in this connection expressed his desire to be a woman, to have babies, and deprive his mother of them. The effect of this step in integration was a strong onset of depression due to his having to face the aggressive components of his personality. Although this had been foreshadowed in the earlier part of his analysis, he now experienced it as a shock and as horror of himself.

The following night the patient dreamed of a pike, to which he associated whales and sharks, but he did not feel in the dream that the pike was a dangerous creature. It was old and looked tired and very worn. On it was a suckerfish, and he at once suggested that the suckerfish does not suck the pike or the whale but sucks itself on to its surface and is thus protected from attacks by other fish. The patient recognized that this explanation was a defence against the feeling that he was the suckerfish and I was the old and worn-out pike and was in that state because I had been so badly treated in the dream of the previous night, and because he felt I had been sucked dry by him. This had made me not only into an injured but also into a dangerous object. In other words, persecutory as well as depressive anxiety had come to the fore; the pike associated to whales and sharks showed the persecutory aspects, whereas its old and worn-out appearance expressed the patient's sense of guilt about the harm he felt he had been doing and was doing to me.

The strong depression which followed this insight lasted for several weeks, more or less uninterrupted, but did not interfere with the patient's work and family life. He described this depression as different from any he had experienced formerly and much deeper. The urge for reparation, expressed in physical and mental work, was increased by the depression and paved the way to an overcoming of it. The result of this phase in the analysis was very noticeable. Even when the depression had lifted after having been worked through, the patient was convinced that he would never see himself again in the way he had done before, though this no longer implied a feeling of dejection but a greater knowledge of himself as well as greater tolerance of other people. What the analysis had achieved was an important step in integration, bound up with the patient being capable of facing his psychic reality. In the course of his analysis, however, there were times when this attitude could not be maintained. That is to say, as in every case, the working-through was a gradual process.

Although his observation and judgement of people had previously been fairly normal, there was definite improvement as a result of this stage of his treatment. A further consequence was that memories of childhood and attitude to siblings came up with greater strength and led back to the early relation to the mother. During the state of depression I have referred to, he had, as he recognized, lost to a large extent the pleasure and interest in the analysis; but he regained them completely when the depression lifted. He soon brought a dream which he himself saw as mildly belittling the analyst, but which turned out in the analysis to express strong devaluation. In the dream he had to deal with a delinquent boy, but was not satisfied with the way in which he had handled the situation. The boy's father suggested taking the patient by car to his destination. He noticed that he was being taken further and further away from where he wanted to go. After a while he thanked the father and got out of his car; but he was not lost because he kept, as usual, a general sense of direction. In passing, he looked at a rather extraordinary building which, he thought, looked interesting and suitable for an exhibition but would not be pleasant to live in. His associations to it linked with some aspect of my appearance. Then he spoke of that building having two wings and remembered the expression 'taking somebody under one's wing'. He recognized that the delinquent boy in whom he had taken an interest stood for himself and the continuation of the dream showed why he was delinquent: when the father, representing the analyst, was taking him more and more away from his destination, this expressed doubts he made use of partly in order to devalue me; he queried whether I was taking him in the right direction, whether it was necessary to go so deep, and whether I was doing harm to him. When he referred to his keeping a sense of direction and to his not feeling lost, this implied the contrary of the accusations against the boy's father (the analyst): he knew that the analysis was very valuable to him and that it was his envy of me which increased his doubts.

He also understood that the interesting building, which he would not like to live in, represented the analyst. On the other hand, he felt that by analysing him I had taken him under my wing and was protecting him against his conflicts and anxieties. The doubts and the accusations against me in the dream were used as devaluation and related not only to envy but also to despondency about the envy and to his feelings of guilt because of his ingratitude.

There was another interpretation of this dream, which was also confirmed by later ones, and which was based on the fact that in the analytic situation I often stood for the father, changing quickly into the mother, and at times representing both parents simultaneously. This interpretation was that the accusation against the father for taking him in the wrong direction was linked with his early homosexual attraction towards the father. This attraction had proved during the analysis to be bound up with intense feelings of guilt, because I was able to show the patient that the strongly split-off envy and hatred of his mother and her breast had contributed to his turning towards the father, and that his homosexual desires were felt to be a hostile alliance against the mother. The accusation that the father took him in the wrong direction linked with the general feeling we so often find in patients that he had been seduced into homosexuality. Here we have the projection of the individual's own desires on to the parent.

The analysis of his sense of guilt had various effects; he experienced a deeper love for his parents; he also realized—and these two facts are closely linked—that there had been a compulsive element in his need to make reparation. An over-strong identification with the object harmed in phantasy—originally the mother—had impaired his capacity for full enjoyment and thereby to some extent impoverished his life. It became clear that even in his earliest relation to his mother, though there was no reason to doubt that he had been happy in the suckling situation, he had not been able to enjoy it completely because of his fear of exhausting or depriving the breast. On the other hand, the interference with his enjoyment gave cause for grievance and increased his feelings of persecution. This is an instance of the process I described in a previous section by which in the early stages of development guilt—in particular guilt about destructive envy of the mother and the analyst—is liable to change into persecution. Through the analysis of primary envy and a corresponding lessening of depressive and persecutory anxiety, his capacity for enjoyment and gratitude at a deep level increased.

I shall now mention the case of another man patient in whom a tendency to depression also went with a compulsive need for reparation; his ambition, rivalry, and envy, co-existing with many good character traits, had been gradually analysed. Nevertheless, it was some years[1] before the envy of the breast and of its creativeness and the desire to spoil it, which was very much split off, were fully experienced by the patient. Early on in his analysis he had a dream that he described as 'ludicrous': he was smoking his pipe and it was filled with my papers which had been torn out of one of my books. He first expressed great surprise about this because 'one does not smoke printed papers'. I interpreted that this was only a minor feature of the dream; the main meaning was that he had torn up my work and was destroying it. I also pointed out that the destruction of my papers was of an anal-sadistic nature, implied in smoking them. He had denied these aggressive attacks; for, together with the strength of his splitting processes, he had a great capacity for denial. Another aspect of this dream was that persecutory feelings came up in connection with the analysis. Previous interpretations had been resented and felt as something which he had to 'put into his pipe and smoke'. The analysis of his dream helped the patient to recognize his destructive impulses against the analyst, and also that they had been stimulated by a jealousy situation which had arisen on the previous day; it centred on the feeling that somebody else was more valued by me than himself. But the insight gained did not lead to an understanding of his envy of the analyst, though it was interpreted to him. I have no doubt, however, that this paved the way for

[1] Experience has shown me that when the analyst becomes fully convinced of the importance of a new aspect of emotional life, he becomes able to interpret it earlier in the analysis. By thus giving it sufficient emphasis whenever the material allows it, he may bring the patient much sooner to the realization of such processes and in this way the effectiveness of the analysis may be enhanced.

material in which destructive impulses and envy gradually became more and more clear.

A climax was reached at a later stage in his analysis when all these feelings in relation to the analyst came home to the patient in full force. The patient reported a dream which once again he described as 'ludicrous': he was moving along with great speed, as if in a motor car. He was standing on a semi-circular contraption which was made either out of wire or some 'atomic stuff'. As he put it, 'this kept me going'. Suddenly he noticed that the thing he was standing on was falling to pieces, and he was much distressed. He associated to the semi-circular object the breast and the erection of the penis, implying his potency. His sense of guilt about not making the right use of his analysis and about his destructive impulses towards me entered into this dream. He felt in his depression that I could not be preserved and there were many links to similar anxieties, partly even conscious, that he had not been able to protect his mother when his father was away during the war and later on. His feeling of guilt in relation to his mother and to myself had been extensively analysed by then. But recently he had come more specifically to feel that it was his envy that was destructive of me. His feelings of guilt and unhappiness were all the greater because in one part of his mind he was grateful to the analyst. The phrase 'this kept me going' implied how essential the analysis was to him and that it was a pre-condition for his potency in the widest sense, that is to say for the success of all his aspirations.

The realization of his envy and hate towards me came as a shock and was followed by strong depression and a feeling of unworthiness. I believe that this kind of shock, which I have now reported in several cases, is the result of an important step in the healing of the split between parts of the self, and thus a stage of progress in ego-integration.

A still fuller realization of his ambition and envy came in a session following the second dream. He spoke of his knowing his limitations and, as he put it, he did not expect that he would cover himself and his profession with glory. At this moment, and still under the influence of the dream, he understood that this way of putting it showed the strength of his ambition and his envious comparison with me. After an initial feeling of surprise, this recognition carried full conviction.

VI

I have often described my approach to anxiety as a focal point of my technique. However, from the very beginning, anxieties cannot be encountered without the defences against them. As I pointed out in an earlier section, the first and foremost function of the ego is to deal with anxiety. I even think it is likely that the primordial anxiety, engendered by the threat of the death instinct within, might be the explanation why the ego is brought into activity from birth onwards. The ego is constantly protecting itself against the pain and tension to which anxiety gives rise, and therefore makes use of defences from the beginning of post-natal life. I have for many years held the view that the greater or lesser capacity of the ego to bear anxiety is a constitutional factor that strongly influences the development of defences. If its capacity to cope with anxiety is inadequate, the ego may return regressively to earlier defences, or even be driven to the excessive use of those appropriate to its stage. As a result, persecutory anxiety and the methods of dealing with it can be so strong that subsequently the working-through of the depressive position is impaired. In some cases, particularly of a psychotic type, we are confronted from the beginning with defences of such an apparently impenetrable nature that it may for some time seem impossible to analyse them.

I shall now enumerate some of the defences against envy that I have encountered in the course of my work. Some of the earliest defences often described before, such as omnipotence, denial, and splitting, are reinforced by envy. In an early section I have suggested that *idealization* not only serves as a defence against persecution but also against envy. In infants, if the normal splitting between the good and the bad object does not initially succeed, this failure, bound up with excessive envy, often results in splitting between an omnipotently idealized and a very bad primal object. Strongly exalting the object and its gifts is an attempt to diminish envy. However, if envy is very strong, it is likely, sooner or later, to turn against the primal idealized object and against other people who, in the course of development, come to stand for it.

As suggested earlier, when the fundamental normal splitting into love and hate and into the good and the bad object is not successful, *confusion* between the good and bad object may arise.[1] I believe this to be the basis of any confusion—whether in severe confusional states or in milder forms such as indecision—namely a difficulty in coming to conclusions and a disturbed capacity for clear thinking. But confusion is also used defensively: this can be seen on all levels of development. By becoming confused as to whether a substitute for the original figure is good or bad, persecution as well as the guilt about spoiling and attacking the primary object by envy is to some extent counteracted. The fight against envy takes on another character when, together with the depressive position, severe feelings of guilt

[1] Cf. Rosenfeld, 'Notes on the Psychopathology of Confusional States in Chronic Schizophrenias' (1950).

set in. Even with people in whom envy is not excessive, the concern for the object, the identification with it, and the fear of its loss and of the harm done to its creativeness, is an important factor in the difficulty of working through the depressive position.

The *flight from the mother to other people*, who are admired and idealized in order to avoid hostile feelings towards that most important envied (and therefore hated) object, the breast, becomes a means of preserving the breast—which means also preserving the mother.[1] I have often pointed out that the way in which the turning from the first to the second object, the father, is carried out is of major importance. If envy and hatred are predominant, these emotions are to some degree transferred to the father or to siblings, and later to other people, and thereafter the flight mechanism fails.

Bound up with the turning away from the primal object is dispersal of the feeling towards it which, at a later stage of development, might lead to promiscuity. The widening of object relations in infancy is a normal process. In so far as the relation to new objects is in some part a substitute for love for the mother, and not predominantly a flight from the hate of her, the new objects are helpful, and a compensation for the unavoidable feeling of loss of the unique first object—a loss arising with the depressive position. Love and gratitude are then in varying degrees preserved in the new relations, though these emotions are to some extent cut off from the feelings towards the mother. However, if the dispersal of emotions is predominantly used as a defence against envy and hatred, such defences are not a basis for stable object relations because they are influenced by the persistent hostility to the first object.

Defence against envy often takes the form of *devaluation of the object*. I have suggested that spoiling and devaluing are inherent in envy. The object which has been devalued need not be envied any more. This soon applies to the idealized object, which is devalued and therefore no longer idealized. How quickly this idealization breaks down depends on the strength of envy. But devaluation and ingratitude are resorted to at every level of development as defences against envy, and in some people remain characteristic of their object relations. I have referred to those patients who, in the transference situation, after having been decidedly helped by an interpretation, criticize it, until at last nothing good is left of it. To give an instance: a patient, who during an analytic session had arrived at a satisfactory solution of an external problem, started the next session by saying that he felt very annoyed with me: I had roused great anxiety on the previous day in making him face this particular problem. It also appeared that he felt accused and devalued by me because, until the

[1] Cf. 'The Emotional Life of the Infant'.

217

problem was analysed, the solution had not occurred to him. It was only on reflection that he acknowledged that the analysis had actually been helpful.

A defence particular to more depressive types is *devaluation of the self*. Some people may be unable to develop their gifts and use them in a successful way. In other cases this attitude only comes up on certain occasions, whenever there is danger of rivalry with an important figure. By devaluing their own gifts they both deny envy and punish themselves for it. In analysis it can be seen, however, that devaluation of the self again stirs up envy of the analyst, who is felt to be superior, particularly because the patient has strongly devalued himself. Depriving oneself of success has, of course, many determinants, and this applies to all the attitudes I am referring to.[1] But I found as one of the deepest roots of this defence the guilt and unhappiness about not having been able to preserve the good object because of envy. People who have rather precariously established their good object suffer under anxiety lest it be spoilt and lost by competitive and envious feelings, and therefore have to avoid success and competition.

Another defence against envy is closely linked with greed. By *internalizing the breast so greedily* that in the infant's mind it becomes entirely his possession and controlled by him, he feels that all the good that he attributes to it will be his own. This is used to counteract envy. It is the very greed with which this internalization is carried out that contains the germ of failure. As I said earlier, a good object which is well established, and therefore assimilated, not only loves the subject but is loved by it. This, I believe, is characteristic of the relation to a good object, but does not apply, or only in a minor degree, to an idealized one. By powerful and violent possessiveness, the good object is felt to turn into a destroyed persecutor and the consequences of envy are not sufficiently prevented. By contrast, if tolerance towards a loved person is experienced, it is also projected on to others, who thus become friendly figures.

A frequent method of defence is *to stir up envy in others* by one's own success, possessions, and a good fortune, thereby reversing the situation in which envy is experienced. The ineffectiveness of this method derives from the persecutory anxiety to which it gives rise. Envious people, and in particular the envious internal object, are felt to be the worst persecutors. Another reason why this defence is precarious derives ultimately from the depressive position. The desire to make other people, particularly loved ones, envious and to triumph over them gives rise to guilt and to the fear of harming them. The anxiety

[1] Cf. Freud, 'Some Character-Types Met with in Psycho-Analytic Work' (1915).

stirred up impairs the enjoyment of one's own possessions and again increases envy.

There is another, and not infrequent defence, the *stifling of feelings of love and corresponding intensifying of hate*, because this is less painful than to bear the guilt arising from the combination of love, hate, and envy. This may not express itself as hate but takes on the appearance of indifference. An allied defence is to withdraw from contact with people. The need for independence, which, as we know, is a normal phenomenon of development, may be reinforced in order to avoid gratitude or guilt about ingratitude and envy. In analysis, we find that unconsciously this independence is actually quite spurious: the individual remains dependent on his internal object.

Herbert Rosenfeld[1] has described a particular method of dealing with the situation when split-off parts of the personality, including the most envious and destructive parts, come together, and steps in integration occur. He showed that 'acting out' is used in order to avoid the undoing of the split; in my view *acting out* in so far as it is used to avoid integration, becomes a defence against the anxieties aroused by accepting the envious part of the self.

I have by no means described all the defences against envy because their variety is infinite. They are closely interlinked with the defences against destructive impulses and persecutory and depressive anxiety. How successful they are depends on many external and internal factors. As has been mentioned, when envy is strong, and therefore likely to reappear in all object relations, defences against it seem to be precarious; those against destructive impulses not dominated by envy appear to be much more effective, though they might imply inhibitions and limitations of the personality.

When schizoid and paranoid features are in the ascendant, defences against envy cannot be successful, for the attacks on the subject lead to an increased feeling of persecution that can only be dealt with by renewed attacks, that is to say, by reinforcing the destructive impulses. In this way is set up a vicious circle that impairs the ability to counteract envy. This applies particularly to schizophrenic cases and explains to some extent the difficulties in the way of curing them.[2]

The outcome is more favourable when, in some measure, a relation to a good object exists, for this also means that the depressive position has been partially worked through. The experience of depression

---

[1] 'An Investigation of the Need of Neurotic and Psychotic Patients to Act Out during Analysis' (1955).

[2] Some of my colleagues who analyse schizophrenic cases have told me that the emphasis they are now laying on envy as a spoiling and destructive factor proves of great importance both in understanding and in treating their patients.

and guilt implies the wish to spare the loved object and to restrict envy.

The defences I have enumerated, and many others, form part of the negative therapeutic reaction because they are a powerful obstacle to the capacity to take in what the analyst has to give. I have referred earlier to some of the forms taken by envy of the analyst. When the patient is able to experience gratitude—and this means that at such times he is less envious—he is in a much better position to benefit by the analysis and to consolidate the gain already achieved. In other words, the more depressive features predominate over schizoid and paranoid features, the better are the prospects of the cure.

The urge to make reparation and the need to help the envied object are also very important means of counteracting envy. Ultimately this involves counteracting destructive impulses by mobilizing feelings of love.

Since I have referred several times to confusion, it may be useful to summarize some of the important states of confusion as they normally arise at different stages of development and in various connections. I have often pointed out[1] that from the beginning of post-natal life urethral and anal (and even genital) libidinal and aggressive desires are operative—though under the dominance of the oral—and that within a few months the relation to part-objects overlaps with that to whole people.

I have already discussed those factors—in particular strong paranoid-schizoid features and excessive envy—which from the beginning blur the distinction, and impair successful splitting, between the good and bad breast; thus confusion in the infant is reinforced. I believe it essential in analysis to trace all states of confusion in our patients, even the most severe in schizophrenia, to this early inability to distinguish between the good and bad primal object, though the defensive use of confusion against envy and destructive impulses must also be considered.

To enumerate a few consequences of this early difficulty: the premature onset of guilt, the infant's incapacity to experience separately guilt and persecution, and the resulting increase in persecutory anxiety, have already been mentioned above; I have also drawn attention to the importance of the confusion between the parents resulting from an intensification by envy of the combined parent figure. I linked the premature onset of genitality with the flight from orality leading to an increased confusion between oral, anal, and genital trends and phantasies.

[1] Cf. *The Psycho-Analysis of Children*, Chapter VIII.

Other factors that make a very early contribution to confusion and perplexed states of mind are projective and introjective identification because they may temporarily have the effect of blurring the distinction between the self and objects, and between the internal and external world. Such confusion interferes with the recognition of psychic reality, which contributes to the understanding and realistic perception of external reality. Distrust and fear of taking in mental food goes back to the distrust of what the envied and spoiled breast offered. If, primarily, the good food is confused with the bad, later the ability for clear thinking and for developing standards of values is impaired. All these disturbances, which in my view are also bound up with defence against anxiety and guilt, and which are aroused by hate and envy, express themselves in inhibitions in learning and development of the intellect. I am leaving out of account here the various other factors that contribute to such difficulties.

The states of confusion that I have briefly summarized, to which the intense conflict between destructive (hate) and integrating (love) trends contributes, are up to a point normal. It is with growing integration and by working successfully through the depressive position which includes a greater clarification of internal reality, that the perception of the external world becomes more realistic—a result which is normally well on the way in the second half of the first year and the beginning of the second year.[1] These changes are essentially bound up with a decrease in projective identification, which forms part of paranoid-schizoid mechanisms and anxieties.

## VII

I shall now attempt a brief description of the difficulties that characterize progress during an analysis. To enable the patient to face primary envy and hate only becomes possible after long and painstaking work. Although feelings of competition and envy are familiar to most people, their deepest and earliest implications, experienced in the transference situation, are extremely painful, and therefore difficult, for the patient to accept. The resistance we find in both male and female cases in analysing their Oedipus jealousy and hostility, though very strong, is not as intense as that which we encounter in analysing the envy and hate of the breast. To help a patient to go through these deep conflicts and sufferings is the most effective means of furthering his stability and integration, because it enables him, by means of the transference, to establish more securely

---

[1] I have suggested (cf. my 1952 papers) that in the second year of life obsessional mechanisms come to the fore and ego organization occurs under the dominance of anal impulses and phantasies.

his good object and his love for it and to gain some confidence in himself. Needless to say, the analysis of this earliest relation involves the exploration of his later ones, and enables the analyst to understand more fully the patient's adult personality.

In the course of the analysis we have to be prepared to encounter fluctuations between improvement and setbacks. This may show in many ways. For instance, the patient has experienced gratitude and appreciation for the analyst's skill. This very skill, the cause for admiration, soon gives way to envy; envy may be counteracted by pride in having a good analyst. If pride stirs up possessiveness, there may by a revival of infantile greed, which could be expressed in the following terms: I have everything I want; I have the good mother all to myself. Such a greedy and controlling attitude is liable to spoil the relation to the good object and gives rise to guilt, which may soon lead to another defence: for instance, I do not want to injure the analyst-mother, I would rather refrain from accepting her gifts. In this situation the early guilt about rejecting milk and love offered by the mother is revived, because the analyst's help is not accepted. The patient also experiences guilt because he is depriving himself (the good part of his self) of improvement and help, and he reproaches himself for putting too great a burden on the analyst by not sufficiently co-operating; in this way he feels that he is exploiting the analyst. Such attitudes alternate with the persecutory anxiety of being robbed of his defences and emotions, of his thoughts and all his ideals. In states of great anxiety there seems to exist in the patient's mind no other alternative but that he is robbing or being robbed.

Defences, as I have suggested, remain operative even when more insight comes about. Every step nearer to integration, and the anxiety stirred up by this, may lead to early defences appearing with greater strength, and even to new ones. We must also expect that primary envy will come up again and again, and we are therefore confronted with repeated fluctuations in the emotional situation. For instance, when the patient feels despicable, and therefore inferior to the analyst, to whom at that moment he attributes goodness and patience, very soon envy of the analyst reappears. His own unhappiness and the pain and conflicts he goes through are contrasted with what he feels to be the analyst's peace of mind—actually his sanity—and this is a particular cause for envy.

The incapacity of the patient to accept with gratitude an interpretation which in some parts of his mind he recognizes as helpful is one aspect of the negative therapeutic reaction. Under the same heading there are many other difficulties, a few of which I shall now mention. We must be prepared to find that whenever the patient makes progress in integration, that is to say, when the envious, hating and hated part of the personality has come closer together with other parts of the self, intense anxieties might come to the fore, and increase the patient's distrust in his loving impulses. The stifling of love, which I have described as a manic defence during the depressive position, is rooted in the danger threatening from destructive impulses and persecutory anxiety. In an adult, dependence on a loved person revives the helplessness of the infant and is felt to be humiliating. But there is more to it than infantile helplessness: the child can be excessively dependent on the mother, if his anxiety lest his destructive impulses change her into a persecutory or damaged object is too great; and this over-dependence can be revived in the transference situation. The anxiety lest, if one gives way to love, greed should destroy the object, is another cause for stifling loving impulses. There is also the fear that love will lead to too much responsibility and that the object will make too many demands. The unconscious knowledge that hate and destructive impulses are operative may make the patient feel more sincere in not admitting love either to himself or others.

Since no anxiety can arise without the ego using whatever defences it can produce, splitting processes play an important rôle as methods against experiencing persecutory and depressive anxiety. When we interpret such splitting processes, the patient becomes more conscious of a part of himself of which, because he feels it to be the representative of destructive impulses, he is terrified. With patients in whom early splitting processes (always bound up with schizoid and paranoid features) are less dominant, *repression* of impulses is stronger, and therefore the clinical picture is different. That is to say, we deal then with the more neurotic type of patient, who has succeeded to some extent in overcoming early splitting, and in whom repression has become the main defence against emotional disturbances.

Another difficulty impeding the analysis for long periods is the tenacity with which the patient clings to a strong positive transference; this may to some extent be deceptive because it is based on idealization and covers up the hate and envy which are split off. It is characteristic that oral anxieties are then often avoided and genital elements are in the foreground.

I have tried to show in various connections that destructive impulses, the expression of the death instinct, are first of all felt to be directed against the ego. Confronted with them, even though it has happened gradually, the patient feels exposed to destruction while he is in the process of accepting these impulses as aspects of himself and integrating them. That is to say, the patient at certain times faces several great dangers as a result of integration: his ego may be overwhelmed; the ideal part of his self may be lost when the existence of the split-off, destructive, and hated part of the personality is recognized; the analyst may become hostile and retaliate for the patient's destructive impulses which are no longer repressed, thus also becoming a dangerous super-ego figure; the analyst, in so far as he stands for a good object, is threatened with destruction. The danger to the analyst, which contributes to the strong resistance we meet in attempting to undo splitting and to bring about steps in integration, becomes understandable if we remember that the infant feels his primal object to be the source of goodness and life, and therefore irreplaceable. His anxiety lest he has destroyed it is the cause of major emotional difficulties and enters prominently into the conflicts arising in the depressive position. The feeling of guilt resulting from the realization of destructive envy may lead temporarily to an inhibition of the patient's capacities.

We encounter a very different situation when, as a defence against integration, omnipotent and even megalomanic phantasies increase. This can be a critical stage because the patient may take refuge in reinforcing his hostile attitudes and projections. Thus he thinks himself superior to the analyst, whom he accuses of undervaluing him, and whom in this way he finds some justification for hating. He takes credit for everything so far achieved in the analysis. To go back to the early situation, as an infant, the patient may have had phantasies of being more powerful than his parents, and even that he or she created, as it were, the mother or gave birth to her and possessed the mother's breast. Accordingly it would be the mother who robbed the patient of the breast and not the patient who robbed her. Projection, omnipotence, and persecution are then at their highest. Some of these phantasies are operative whenever feelings of priority in scientific or other work are very strong. There are other factors as well which might stir up the craving for priority such as ambition from various sources, and in particular the feeling of guilt, basically bound up with envy and destruction of the primary object or its later substitutes. For such guilt about robbing the primal object may lead to denial, which takes the form of claiming complete originality and thereby excluding the possibility of having taken or accepted anything from the object.

In the last paragraph I stressed the difficulties arising at certain points in the analysis of patients whose envy is constitutionally strong. However, the analysis of those deep and severe disturbances is in many cases a safeguard against potential danger of psychosis resulting from excessively envious and omnipotent attitudes. But it is essential not to attempt to hurry these steps in integration. For if the realization of the division in his personality were to come suddenly, the patient would have great difficulties in coping with it.[1] The more strongly had the envious and destructive impulses been split off, the more dangerous the patient feels them to be when he becomes conscious of them. In analysis we should make our way slowly and gradually towards the painful insight into the divisions in the patient's self. This means that the destructive sides are again and again split off and regained, until greater integration comes about. As a result, the feeling of responsibility becomes stronger, and guilt and depression are more fully experienced. When this happens, the ego is strengthened, omnipotence of destructive impulses is diminished, together with envy, and the capacity for love and gratitude, stifled in the course of splitting processes, is released. Therefore the split-off aspects gradually become more acceptable and the patient is increasingly able to repress destructive impulses towards loved objects instead of splitting the self. This implies that the projection on the analyst, which turns him into a dangerous and retaliating figure, also diminishes, and that the analyst in turn finds it easier to help the patient towards further integration. That is to say, the negative therapeutic reaction is losing in strength.

It makes great demands on the analyst and on the patient to analyse splitting processes and the underlying hate and envy in both the positive and negative transference. One consequence of this difficulty is the tendency of some analysts to reinforce the positive and avoid the negative transference, and to attempt to strengthen feelings of love by taking the rôle of the good object which the patient had not been able to establish securely in the past. This procedure differs essentially from the technique which, by helping the patient to achieve a better integration of his self, aims at a mitigation of hatred by love. My observations have demonstrated to me that techniques based on reassurance are seldom successful; in particular their results are not lasting. There is indeed an ingrained need for reassurance in everybody, which goes back to the earliest relation to the mother. The infant expects her to attend not only to all his needs, but also craves for signs of her love whenever he experiences anxiety. This longing for reassurance is a vital factor in the analytic situation and we must not underrate its importance in our patients, adults and children alike. We find that though their conscious, and often unconscious, purpose is to be analysed, the patient's strong desire to receive evidence of love and appreciation from the analyst, and thus to be reassured, is never completely given up. Even the

[1] It might well be that a person who unexpectedly commits a crime or has a psychotic breakdown had suddenly become aware of the split-off dangerous parts of his self. Cases are known of people trying to be arrested in order to prevent themselves from committing a murder.

patient's co-operation, which allows for an analysis of very deep layers of the mind, of destructive impulses, and of persecutory anxiety, may up to a point be influenced by the urge to satisfy the analyst and to be loved by him. The analyst who is aware of this will analyse the infantile roots of such wishes; otherwise, in identification with his patient, the early need for reassurance may strongly influence his counter-transference and therefore his technique. This identification may also easily tempt the analyst to take the mother's place and give in to the urge immediately to alleviate his child's (the patient's) anxieties.

One of the difficulties of bringing about steps in integration arises when the patient says: 'I can understand what you are telling me but I do not *feel* it.' We are aware that we are in fact referring to a part of the personality which, to all intents and purposes, is not sufficiently accessible either to the patient or to the analyst at that time. Our attempts to help the patient to integrate only carry conviction if we can show him, in the material both present and past, how and why he is again and again splitting off parts of his self. Such evidence is often also provided by a dream preceding the session, and it may be gathered from the whole context of the analytic situation. If an interpretation of splitting is sufficiently supported in the way I described, it might be confirmed in the next session by the patient reporting a bit of a dream or bringing some more material. The cumulative result of such interpretations gradually enables the patient to make some progress in integration and insight.

The anxiety that prevents integration has to be fully understood and interpreted in the transference situation. I have earlier pointed out the threat, both to the self and to the analyst, arising in the patient's mind if split-off parts of the self are regained in the analysis. In dealing with this anxiety one should not underrate the loving impulses when they can be detected in the material. For it is these which in the end enable the patient to mitigate his hate and envy.

However much the patient may at a given moment feel that the interpretation does not strike home, this may often be an expression of resistance. If we have from the beginning of the analysis paid sufficient attention to the ever-repeated attempts to split off destructive parts of the personality, in particular hate and envy, we have in fact, at least in most cases, enabled the patient to make some steps towards integration. It is only after painstaking, careful, and consistent work on the part of the analyst that we can expect a more stable integration in the patient.

I shall now illustrate this phase in the analysis by two dreams.

The second male patient I referred to, at a later stage of his analysis, when greater integration and improvement in various ways had occurred, reported the following dream, which shows the fluctuations in the process of integration caused by the pain of depressive feelings. He was in an upstairs flat and 'X', a friend of a friend of his, was calling him from the street suggesting a walk together. The patient did not join 'X', because a black dog in the flat might get out and be run over. He stroked the dog. When he looked out of the window, he found that 'X' had 'receded'.

Some of the associations brought the flat into connection with mine and the black dog with my black cat, which he described as 'she'. The patient never liked 'X', who was an old fellow-student of his. He described him as suave and insincere; 'X' also often borrowed money (though he returned it later) and did so in a manner which suggested that he had every right to ask for such favours. 'X' turned out, however, to be very good in his profession.

The patient recognized that 'a friend of his friend' was one aspect of himself. The gist of my interpretations was that he had come closer to realizing an unpleasant and frightening part of his personality; the danger to the dog-cat—the analyst—was that she would be run over (that is to say, injured) by 'X'. When 'X' had been asking him to join him for a walk, this symbolized a step towards integration. At this stage a hopeful element entered into the dream by the association that 'X', in spite of his faults, had turned out to be good in his profession. It is also characteristic of progress that the side of himself to which he came closer in this dream was not so destructive and envious as in previous material.

The patient's concern with the safety of the dog-cat expressed the wish to protect the analyst against his own hostile and greedy tendencies, represented by 'X', and led to a temporary widening of the split that had already partly been healed. When, however, 'X', the rejected part of himself, 'receded', this showed that he had not altogether gone and that the process of integration was only temporarily disturbed. The mood of the patient at that time was characterized by depression; guilt towards the analyst and the wish to preserve her were prominent. In this context, the fear of integration was caused by the feeling that the analyst must be protected from the patient's repressed greedy and dangerous impulses. I had no doubt that he was still splitting off a part of his personality, but the *repression* of greedy and destructive impulses had become more noticeable. The interpretation, therefore, had to deal both with splitting and with repression.

The first man patient also brought at a later stage of his analysis a dream that showed rather more advanced steps in integration. He dreamed that he had a delinquent brother who committed a serious crime. He had been received in a house and had killed the inhabitants and robbed them. The patient was deeply disturbed by this but felt that he must be loyal to his brother and save him. They fled together and found themselves in a boat. Here the patient associated *Les Misérables* by Victor Hugo, and mentioned Javert who had persecuted an innocent person all his life and even followed him right into the sewers of Paris where he was hiding. But Javert ended by committing suicide because he had recognized that he had spent his whole life in the wrong way.

The patient then went on with his account of the dream. He and his brother were arrested by a policeman who looked kindly at him, and so the patient hoped he would not be executed after all; he seemed to leave his brother to his fate.

The patient realized at once that the delinquent brother was part of himself. He had recently used the expression 'delinquent' referring to very minor matters in his own conduct. We shall also remember here that in a previous dream he had referred to a delinquent boy with whom he could not deal.

The step in integration to which I am referring was shown by the patient taking the responsibility for the delinquent brother and by being with him in 'the same boat'. I interpreted the crime of murdering and robbing the people who had kindly received him as his phantasied attacks on the analyst, and referred to his often-expressed anxiety lest his greedy wish to get as much out of me as possible would harm me. I linked this with the early guilt in relation to his mother. The kindly policeman stood for the analyst who would not judge him harshly and would help him to get rid of the bad part of himself. I pointed out, moreover, that in the process of integration the use of splitting—both of the self and of the object—had reappeared. This was shown by the analyst figuring in a double rôle: as the kindly policeman and the persecutory Javert, who in the end took his own life, and on whom the patient's 'badness' was also projected. Although the patient had understood his responsibility for the 'delinquent' part of his personality, he was still splitting his self. For he was represented by the 'innocent' man, whereas the sewers into which he was pursued meant the depths of his anal and oral destructiveness.

The recurrence of splitting was caused not only by persecutory but also by depressive anxiety, for the patient felt that he could not confront the analyst (when she appeared in a kindly rôle) with the bad part of himself without harming her. This was one of the reasons why he resorted to uniting with the policeman against the bad part of himself, which at that moment he wished to annihilate.

\* \* \*

Freud early accepted that some individual variations in development are due to constitutional factors: for instance, he expressed in
'Character and Anal Erotism' (1908) the view that strong anal
erotism is in many people constitutional.[1] Abraham discovered an
innate element in the strength of oral impulses, which he connected
with the aetiology of manic-depressive illness. He said that '. . . what
really is constitutional and inherited is an over-accentuation of oral
erotism in the same way that in certain families anal erotism seems
to be a preponderant factor from the very beginning.'[2]

I have previously suggested that greed, hate, and persecutory
anxieties in relation to the primal object, the mother's breast, have
an innate basis. In this discussion, I have added that envy too, as a
powerful expression of oral- and anal-sadistic impulses, is constitutional. The variations in the intensity of these constitutional factors
are in my view linked with the preponderance of the one or other instinct in the fusion of the life and death instincts postulated by Freud.
I believe there is a connection between the preponderance of the one
or other instinct and the strength or weakness of the ego. I have
often referred to the strength of the ego in relation to the anxieties
it has to cope with as a constitutional factor. Difficulties in bearing
anxiety, tension, and frustration are an expression of an ego which,
from the beginning of post-natal life, is weak in proportion to the
intense destructive impulses and persecutory feelings it experiences.
These strong anxieties imposed on a weak ego lead to an excessive
use of defences such as denial, splitting, and omnipotence, which to
some extent are always characteristic of earliest development. In
keeping with my thesis, I would add that a constitutionally strong
ego does not easily become a prey to envy and is more capable of
effecting the splitting between good and bad which I assume to be a
precondition for establishing the good object. The ego is then less
liable to those splitting processes which lead to fragmentation and
are part of marked paranoid-schizoid features.

Another factor that influences development from the beginning is
the variety of external experiences through which the infant goes.
This in some measure explains the development of his early anxieties,
which would be particularly great in a baby who had a difficult
birth and unsatisfactory feeding. My accumulated observations, however, have convinced me that the impact of these external experiences is in proportion to the constitutional strength of the innate
destructive impulses and the ensuing paranoid anxieties. Many
infants have not had very unfavourable experiences and yet suffer

---

[1] 'From these indications we infer that the erotogenic significance of the anal
zone is intensified in the innate sexual constitution of these persons.'
[2] 'A Short History of the Development of the Libido' (1924).

from serious difficulties in feeding and sleeping, and we can see in them every sign of great anxiety for which external circumstances do not account sufficiently.

It is also well known that some infants are exposed to great deprivations and unfavourable circumstances, and yet do not develop excessive anxieties, which would suggest that their paranoid and envious traits are not predominant; this is often confirmed by their later history.

I have had many opportunities in my analytic work to trace the origin of character formation to variations in innate factors. There is much more to be learnt about pre-natal influences; but even greater knowledge about them would not detract from the importance of inborn elements in determining the strength of the ego and of instinctual drives.

The existence of the innate factors referred to above points to the limitations of psycho-analytic therapy. While I fully realize this, my experience has taught me that nevertheless we are able in a number of cases to produce fundamental and positive changes, even where the constitutional basis was unfavourable.

## CONCLUSION

For many years the envy of the feeding breast as a factor which adds intensity to the attacks on the primal object has been part of my analyses. It is, however, only more recently that I have laid particular emphasis on the spoiling and destructive quality of envy in so far as it interferes with the building up of a secure relation to the good external and internal object, undermines the sense of gratitude, and in many ways blurs the distinction between good and bad.

In all the cases I have described, the relation to the analyst as an internal object was of fundamental importance. This I found to be true generally. When anxiety about envy and its consequences reaches a climax, the patient in varying degrees feels persecuted by the analyst as an internal grudging and envious object, disturbing his work, life, and activities. When this occurs, the good object is felt to be lost, and with it inner security. My observations have shown me that when, at any stage in life, the relation to the good object is seriously disturbed—a disturbance in which envy plays a prominent rôle—not only are inner security and peace interfered with but character deterioration sets in. The prevalence of internal persecutory objects reinforces destructive impulses; whereas, if the good object is well established, the identification with it strengthens the capacity for love, constructive impulses, and gratitude. This is in keeping with the hypothesis I put forward at the beginning of this contribution: if the good object is deeply rooted, temporary disturbances may be withstood and the foundation of mental health, of character formation, and of successful ego development is laid.

I have described in other connections the importance of the earliest internalized persecutory object—the retaliating, devouring, and poisonous breast. I would now assume that the projection of the infant's envy lends a particular complexion to his anxiety about the primal and later internal persecution. The 'envious super-ego' is felt to disturb or annihilate all attempts at reparation and creativeness. It is also felt to make constant and exorbitant demands on the individual's gratitude. For to persecution are added the guilt feelings that the persecutory internal objects are the result of the individual's own envious and destructive impulses which have primarily spoilt the good object. The need for punishment, which finds satisfaction by the increased devaluation of the self, leads to a vicious circle.

As we all know, the ultimate aim of psycho-analysis is the integration of the patient's personality. Freud's conclusion that where id was, ego shall be, is a pointer in that direction. Splitting processes arise in the earliest stages of development. If they are excessive, they form an integral part of severe paranoid and schizoid features which may be the basis of schizophrenia. In normal development, these schizoid and paranoid trends (the paranoid-schizoid position) are, to a large extent, overcome during the period which is characterized by the depressive position, and integration develops successfully. The important steps towards integration introduced during that stage prepare the capacity of the ego for repression which I believe increasingly operates in the second year of life.

In 'The Emotional Life of the Infant' I suggested that the young child is able to deal with emotional difficulties by repression if splitting processes in the early stages have not been too powerful, and therefore a consolidation of the conscious and unconscious parts of the mind has come about. In the earliest stages splitting and other defence mechanisms are always paramount. Already, in *Inhibition, Symptoms and Anxiety*, Freud had suggested that there may be methods of defence earlier than repression. In the present work I have not dealt with the vital significance of repression for normal development, because the effect of primary envy and its close connection with splitting processes have been my main subject matter.

As regards technique, I have attempted to show that by analysing over and over again the anxieties and defences bound up with envy and destructive impulses, progress in integration can be achieved. I have always been convinced of the importance of Freud's finding that 'working-through' is one of the main tasks of the analytic procedure, and my experience in dealing with splitting processes and tracing them back to their origin has made this conviction even stronger.

The deeper and more complex the difficulties we are analysing, the greater is the resistance we are likely to encounter, and this has a bearing on the necessity to give adequate scope to 'working-through'.

This necessity arises particularly with regard to envy of the primary object. Patients might recognize their envy, jealousy, and competitive attitudes towards other people, even the wish to harm their faculties, but only the analyst's perseverance in analysing these hostile feelings in the transference, and thereby enabling the patient to re-experience them in his earliest relation, can lead to the splitting within the self being diminished.

My experience has shown me that when the analysis of these fundamental impulses, phantasies, and emotions fails, this is partly because the pain and depressive anxiety made manifest, in some people outweigh the desire for truth and, ultimately, the desire to be helped. I believe that a patient's co-operation has to be based on a strong determination to discover the truth about himself if he is to accept and assimilate the analyst's interpretations relating to these early layers of the mind. For these interpretations, if deep enough, mobilize a part of the self that is felt as an enemy to the ego as well as to the loved object, and has, therefore, been split off and annihilated. I have found that the anxieties aroused by interpretations of hate and envy toward the primal object, and the feeling of persecution by the analyst whose work stirs up those emotions, are more painful than any other material we interpret.

These difficulties apply particularly to patients with strong paranoid anxieties and schizoid mechanisms, for they are less able to experience, side by side with the persecutory anxiety stirred up by interpretations, a positive transference and trust in the analyst—ultimately they are less capable of maintaining feelings of love. At the present stage of our knowledge, I am inclined to the view that these are the patients, not necessarily of a manifest psychotic type, with whom success is limited, or may not be achieved.

When the analysis can be carried to these depths, envy and the fear of envy diminish, leading to a greater trust in constructive and reparative forces, actually in the capacity for love. The result is also greater tolerance towards one's own limitations, as well as improved object relations and a clearer perception of internal and external reality.

The insight gained in the process of integration makes it possible, in the course of the analysis, for the patient to recognize that there are potentially dangerous parts of his self. But when love can be sufficiently brought together with the split-off hate and envy, these emotions become bearable and diminish, because they are mitigated by love. The various anxiety contents mentioned earlier are also lessened, such as the danger of being overwhelmed by a split-off, destructive part of the self. This danger seems all the greater because, as a consequence of excessive early omnipotence, the harm done in phantasy appears irrevocable. The anxiety lest hostile feelings destroy the loved objects diminishes when these feelings become better known and are integrated in the personality. The pain the patient experiences during the analysis is also gradually lessened by improvements bound up with progress in integration, such as regaining some intiative, becoming able to make decisions he was previously unable to reach and, in general, using his gifts more freely. This is linked up with a lessening inhibition of his capacity to make reparation. His power of enjoyment increases in many ways, and hope reappears, though it may still alternate with depression. I have found that creativeness grows in proportion to being able to establish the good object more securely, which in successful cases is the result of the analysis of envy and destructiveness.

Similarly, as in infancy, repeated happy experiences of being fed and loved are instrumental in establishing securely the good object, so during an analysis repeated experiences of the effectiveness and truth of the interpretations given lead to the analyst—and retrospectively the primal object—being built up as good figures.

All these changes amount to an enrichment of the personality. Together with hate, envy, and destructiveness, other important parts of the self which had been lost are regained in the course of the analysis. There is also considerable relief in feeling more of a whole person, in gaining control over one's self, and in a deeper sense of security in relation to the world in general. In 'Some Schizoid Mechanisms' I have suggested that the sufferings of the schizophrenic, due to his feelings of being split in bits, are most intense. These sufferings are underrated because his anxieties appear in a different form from those of the neurotic. Even when we are not dealing with psychotics, but are analysing people whose integration had been disturbed and who feel uncertain about both themselves and others, similar anxieties are experienced and are relieved when fuller integration is achieved. Complete and permanent integration is in my view never possible. For under strain from external or internal sources, even well integrated people may be driven to stronger splitting processes, even though this may be a passing phase.

In the paper, 'On Identification', I suggested how important it is for the development of mental health and personality that in the early splitting processes fragmentation should not dominate. I wrote there: 'The feeling of containing an unharmed nipple and breast—although co-existing with phantasies of a breast devoured and therefore in bits—has the effect that splitting and projecting are not *predominantly* related to fragmented parts of the personality but to more coherent parts of the self. This implies that the ego is not exposed to a fatal weakening by dispersal and for this reason is more capable of repeatedly undoing splitting and achieving integration and synthesis in its relation to objects.'[1]

I believe this capacity to regain the split-off parts of the personality to be a precondition for normal development. This implies that splitting is to some extent overcome during the depressive position and that repression of impulses and phantasies gradually takes its place.

Character analysis has always been an important and very difficult part of analytic therapy.[2] It is, I believe, through tracing back certain aspects of character formation to the early processes I have described that we can, in a number of cases, effect far-reaching changes in character and personality.

We can consider from another angle the aspects of technique which I have tried to convey here. From the beginning, all emotions attach themselves to the first object. If destructive impulses, envy, and paranoid anxiety are excessive, the infant grossly distorts and magnifies every frustration from outer sources, and the mother's breast turns externally and internally predominantly into a persecutory object. Then even actual gratifications cannot sufficiently counteract persecutory anxiety. In taking the analysis back to earliest infancy, we enable the patient to revive fundamental situations—a revival which I have often spoken of as 'memories in feeling'. In the course of this revival, it becomes possible for the patient to develop a different attitude to his early frustrations. There is no doubt that if the infant was actually exposed to very unfavourable conditions, the retrospective establishing of a good object cannot undo bad early experiences. However, the introjection of the analyst as a good object, if not based on idealization has, to some extent, the effect of providing an internal good object where it has been largely lacking. Also, the weakening of projections, and therefore the achieving of greater tolerance, bound up with less resentment, make it possible for the patient to find some features and to revive pleasant memories of the past, even when the early situation was very unfavourable. The means by which this is achieved is the analysis of the negative and

---

[1] pp. 144–45 above.

[2] The most fundamental contributions to this topic have been made by Freud, Jones, and Abraham. Cf. for instance, Freud 'Character and Anal Erotism' (1908), Jones 'Hate and Anal-Erotism in the Obsessional Neuroses' (1913) and 'Anal-Erotic Character Traits' (1918), and Abraham 'Contributions to the Theory of the Anal Character' (1921), 'The Influence of Oral Erotism on Character Formation' (1924), and 'Character Formation on the Genital Level of Libido Development' (1925).

positive transference which takes us back to earliest object relations. All this becomes possible because the integration resulting from the analysis has strengthened the ego, which was weak at the beginning of life. It is on these lines that the psycho-analysis of psychotics may also succeed. The more integrated ego becomes capable of experiencing guilt and feelings of responsibility, which it was unable to face in infancy; object synthesis, and therefore a mitigation of hate by love, come about, and greed and envy, which are corollaries of destructive impulses, lose in power.

To express it in another way, persecutory anxiety and schizoid mechanisms are diminished, and the patient can work through the depressive position. When his initial inability to establish a good object is, to some extent, overcome, envy is diminished and his capacity for enjoyment and gratitude increases step by step. These changes extend to many aspects of the patient's personality and range from earliest emotional life to adult experiences and relations. In the analysis of the effects of early disturbances on the whole development, lies, I believe, our greatest hope of helping our patients.

# ON THE DEVELOPMENT OF
# MENTAL FUNCTIONING

## (1958)

THE paper I present here is a contribution to merapsychology, an attempt to carry further Freud's fundamental theories on this subject in the light of conclusions derived from progress in psycho-analytic practice.

Freud's formulation of mental structure in terms of id, ego and super-ego has become the basis for all psycho-analytic thinking. He made it clear that these parts of the self are not sharply separated from one another and that the id is the foundation of all mental functioning. The ego develops out of the id, but Freud gave no consistent indication at which stage this happens; throughout life the ego reaches deep down into the id and is therefore under the constant influence of unconscious processes.

Moreover, his discovery of the life and death instincts, with their polarity and fusion operating from birth onwards, was a tremendous advance in the understanding of the mind. I recognized, in watching the constant struggle in the young infant's mental processes between an irrepressible urge to destroy as well as to save himself, to attack his objects and to preserve them, that primordial forces struggling with each other were at work. This gave me a deeper insight into the vital *clinical* importance of Freud's concept of life and death instincts. When I wrote *The Psycho-Analysis of Children*[1], I had already come to the conclusion that under the impact of the struggle between the two instincts, one of the ego's main functions—the mastery of anxiety—is brought into operation from the very beginning of life.[2]

Freud assumed that the organism protects itself against the danger arising from the death instinct working within by deflecting it outwards, while that portion of it which cannot be deflected is bound by the libido. He considered in *Beyond the Pleasure Principle* (1922)

---

[1] Cf. pp. 126-28.

[2] In 'Notes on some Schizoid Mechanisms' (1946), I suggested that some of the functions—in particular that of dealing with anxiety—which we know from the later ego, are already operative at the beginning of life. The anxiety arising from the operation of the death instinct within the organism, and felt as fear of annihilation (death), takes the form of persecution.

the operation of the life and death instincts as biological processes. But it has not been sufficiently recognized that Freud in some of his writings based his *clinical* considerations on the concept of the two instincts, as for example in 'The Economic Problem of Masochism' (1924). May I recall the last few sentences of that paper. He said: 'Thus moral masochism becomes a classical piece of evidence for the existence of fusion of instinct. Its danger lies in the fact that it originates from the death instinct and corresponds to that part of the instinct which has escaped being turned outwards as an instinct of destruction. But since, on the other hand, it has the value of an erotic component, even the subject of destruction of himself cannot take place without libidinal satisfaction.' (*S.E.* **19,** p. 170). In the *New Introductory Lectures* (1933), he put the psychological aspect of his new discovery in even stronger terms. He said: 'This hypothesis opens a prospect to us of investigations which may some day be of great importance for the understanding of pathological processes. For fusions may also come apart, and we may expect that functioning will be most gravely affected by defusions of such a kind. But these conceptions are still too new; no one has yet tried to apply them in our work.' (*S.E.* **22,** p. 105). I would say that in so far as Freud took the fusion and defusion of the two instincts as underlying the *psychological* conflict between aggressive and libidinal impulses, it would be the ego, and not the organism, which deflects the death instinct.

Freud stated that no fear of death exists in the unconscious, but this does not seem compatible with his discovery of the dangers arising from the death instinct working within. As I see it, the primordial anxiety which the ego fights is the threat arising from the death instinct. I pointed out in 'The Theory of Anxiety and Guilt' (1948)[1] that I do not agree with Freud's view that 'the unconscious seems to contain nothing that would lend substance to the concept of the annihilation of life' and that, therefore, 'the fear of death should be regarded as analogous to the fear of castration'. In 'The Early Development of Conscience in the Child' (1933), I referred to Freud's theory of the two instincts, according to which at the outset of life the instinct of aggression, or the death instinct, is being opposed and bound by the libido or life instinct—the Eros—and said: 'The danger of being destroyed by this instinct of aggression sets up, I think, an excessive tension in the ego, which is felt by it as an anxiety, so that it is faced at the very beginning of its development with the task of mobilizing libido against its death-instinct.' I concluded that the danger of being destroyed by the death instinct thus gives rise to primordial anxiety in the ego.[2]

[1] See pp. 28–30 in this volume.

[2] Joan Riviere (1952) refers to 'Freud's decisive rejection of the possibility of an

The young infant would be in danger of being flooded by his self-destructive impulses if the mechanism of projection could not operate. It is partly in order to perform this function that the ego is called into action at birth by the life instinct. The primal process of projection is the means of deflecting the death instinct outwards.[1] Projection also imbues the first object with libido. The other primal process is introjection, again largely in the service of the life instinct; it combats the death instinct because it leads to the ego taking in something life-giving (first of all food) and thus binding the death instinct working within.

From the beginning of life the two instincts attach themselves to objects, first of all the mother's breast.[2] I believe, therefore, that some light may be thrown on the development of the ego in connection with the functioning of the two instincts by my hypothesis that the introjection of the mother's feeding breast lays the foundation for all internalization processes. According to whether destructive impulses or feelings of love predominate, the breast (for which the bottle can symbolically come to stand) is felt at times to be good, at times to be bad. The libidinal cathexis of the breast, together with gratifying experiences, builds up in the infant's mind the primal good object, the projection on the breast of destructive impulses the primal bad object. Both these aspects are introjected and thus the life and death instincts, which had been projected, again operate within the ego. The need to master persecutory anxiety gives impetus to splitting the breast and mother, externally and internally, into a helpful and loved and, on the other hand, a frightening and hated object. These are the prototypes of all subsequent internalized objects.

The strength of the ego—reflecting the state of fusion between the two instincts—is, I believe, constitutionally determined. If in the fusion the life instinct predominates, which implies an ascendancy of

---

unconscious fear of death'; she goes on to conclude that 'the helplessness and dependence of human children must, in conjunction with their phantasy life, presuppose that the fear of death is even part of their experience.'

[1] Here I differ from Freud is so far as it seems that Freud understood by deflection only the process whereby the death instinct directed against the self is turned into aggression against the object. In my view, two processes are involved in that particular mechanism of deflection. Part of the death instinct is projected into the object, the object thereby becoming a persecutor; while that part of the death instinct which is retained in the ego causes aggression to be turned against that persecutory object.

[2] In 'Notes on some Schizoid Mechanisms', I said: 'The fear of the destructive impulse seems to attach itself at once to an object—or rather it is experienced as the fear of an uncontrollable overpowering object. Other important sources of primary anxiety are the trauma of birth (separation anxiety) and frustration of bodily needs; these experiences too are from the beginning felt as being caused by objects.'

the capacity for love, the ego is relatively strong, and is more able to bear the anxiety arising from the death instinct and to counteract it.

To what extent the strength of the ego can be maintained and increased is in part affected by external factors, in particular the mother's attitude towards the infant. However, even when the life instinct and the capacity for love predominate, destructive impulses are still deflected outwards and contribute to the creation of persecutory and dangerous objects which are reintrojected. Furthermore, the primal processes of introjection and projection lead to constant changes in the ego's relation to its objects, with fluctuations between internal and external, good and bad ones, according to the infant's phantasies and emotions as well as under the impact of his actual experiences. The complexity of these fluctuations engendered by the perpetual activity of the two instincts underlies the development of the ego in its relation to the external world as well as the building up of the internal world.

The internalized good object comes to form the core of the ego around which it expands and develops. For when the ego is supported by the internalized good object, it is more able to master anxiety and preserve life by binding with libido some portions of the death instinct operative within.

However, a part of the ego, as Freud described in the *New Introductory Lectures* (1933), comes to 'stand over' against the other part as a result of the ego splitting itself. He made it clear that this split-off part performing many functions is the super-ego. He also stated that the super-ego consists of certain aspects of the introjected parents and is largely unconscious.

With these views I agree. Where I differ is in placing at birth the processes of introjection which are the basis of the super-ego. The super-ego precedes by some months the beginning of the Oedipus complex,[1] a beginning which I date, together with that of the depressive position, in the second quarter of the first year. Thus the early introjection of the good and bad breast is the foundation of the super-ego and influences the development of the Oedipus complex. This conception of super-ego formation is in contrast to Freud's explicit statements that the identifications with the parents are the heir of the Oedipus complex and only succeed if the Oedipus complex is successfully overcome.

---

[1] For a more detailed picture of how my views on the early Oedipus complex have developed, see 'Early Stages of the Oedipus Conflict' (1928), *The Psycho-Analysis of Children* (1932), (particularly Chapter VIII), 'The Oedipus Complex in the Light of Early Anxieties' (1945), and 'Some Theoretical Conclusions Regarding the Emotional Life of the Infant' (1952, p. 218).

In my view, the splitting of the ego, by which the super-ego is formed, comes about as a consequence of conflict in the ego, engendered by the polarity of the two instincts.[1] This conflict is increased by their projection as well as by the resulting introjection of good and bad objects. The ego, supported by the internalized good object and strengthened by the identification with it, projects a portion of the death instinct into that part of itself which it has split off—a part which thus comes to be in opposition to the rest of the ego and forms the basis of the super-ego. Accompanying this deflection of a portion of the death instinct is a deflection of that portion of the life instinct which is fused with it. Along with these deflections, parts of the good and bad objects are split off from the ego into the super-ego. The super-ego thus acquires both protective and threatening qualities. As the process of integration—present from the beginning in both the ego and the super-ego—goes on, the death instinct is bound, up to a point, by the super-ego. In the process of binding, the death instinct influences the aspects of the good objects contained in the super-ego, with the result that the action of the super-ego ranges from restraint of hate and destructive impulses, protection of the good object and self-criticism, to threats, inhibitory complaints and persecution. The super-ego—being bound up with the good object and even striving for its preservation—comes close to the actual good mother who feeds the child and takes care of it, but since the super-ego is also under the influence of the death instinct, it partly becomes the representative of the mother who frustrates the child, and its prohibitions and accusations arouse anxiety. To some extent, when development goes well, the super-ego is largely felt as helpful and does not operate as too harsh a conscience. There is an inherent need in the young child—and, I assume, even in the very young infant—to be protected as well as to be submitted to certain prohibitions, which amounts to a control of destructive impulses. I have suggested in *Envy and Gratitude* (pp. 179-80 above), that the infantile wish for an ever-present, inexhaustible breast includes the desire that the breast should do away with or control the infant's destructive impulses and in this way protect his good object as well as safeguard him against persecutory anxieties. This function pertains to the super-ego. However, as soon as the infant's destructive impulses and his anxiety are aroused, the super-ego is felt to be strict and over-bearing and the ego then, as Freud described it, 'has to serve three harsh masters', the id, the super-ego, and external reality.

When at the beginning of the twenties I embarked on the new

[1] Cf. for instance 'The Theory of Anxiety and Guilt' (1948), this volume pp. 31-32.

venture of analysing by play technique children from their third year onwards, one of the unexpected phenomena I came across was a very early and savage super-ego. I also found that young children introject their parents—first of all the mother and her breast'—in a phantastic way, and I was led to this conclusion by observing the terrifying character of some of their internalized objects. These extremely dangerous objects give rise, in early infancy, to conflict and anxiety within the ego; but under the stress of acute anxiety they, and other terrifying figures, are split off in a manner different from that by which the super-ego is formed, and are relegated to the deeper layers of the unconscious. The difference in these two ways of splitting—and this may perhaps throw light on the many as yet obscure ways in which splitting processes take place—is that in the splitting-off of frightening figures defusion seems to be in the ascendant; whereas super-ego formation is carried out with a predominance of fusion of the two instincts. Therefore the super-ego is normally established in close relation with the ego and shares different aspects of the same good object. This makes it possible for the ego to integrate and accept the super-ego to a greater or less extent. In contrast, the extremely bad figures are not accepted by the ego in this way and are constantly rejected by it.

However, with young infants, and I assume that this is more strongly the case the younger the infant is, the boundaries between split-off figures and those less frightening and more tolerated by the ego are fluid. Splitting normally succeeds only temporarily or partially. When it fails, the infant's persecutory anxiety is intense, and this is particularly the case in the first stage of development characterized by the paranoid-schizoid position, which I assume to be at its height in the first three or four months of life. In the very young infant's mind the good breast and the bad devouring breast alternate very quickly, possibly are felt to exist simultaneously.

The splitting-off of persecutory figures which go to form part of the unconscious is bound up with splitting off idealized figures as well. Idealized figures are developed to protect the ego against the terrifying ones. In these processes the life instinct appears again and asserts itself. The contrast between persecutory and idealized, between good and bad objects—being an expression of life and death instincts and forming the basis of phantasy life—is to be found in every layer of the self. Among the hated and threatening objects, which the early ego tries to ward off, are also those which are felt to have been injured or killed and which thereby turn into dangerous persecutors. With the strengthening of the ego and its growing capacity for integration and synthesis, the stage of the depressive position is reached. At this stage the injured object is no longer predominantly felt as a persecutor but as a loved object towards whom a feeling of guilt and the urge to make reparation are experienced.[1] This relation to the loved injured object goes to form an important element in the super-ego. According to my hypothesis, the depressive position is at its height towards the middle of the first year. From then onwards, if persecutory anxiety is not excessive and the capacity for love is strong enough, the ego becomes increasingly aware of its psychic reality and more and more feels that it is its own destructive impulses which contribute to the spoiling of its objects. Thus injured objects, which were felt to be bad, improved in the child's mind and approximate more to the real parents; the ego gradually develops its essential function of dealing with the external world.

The success of these fundamental processes and the subsequent integration and strengthening of the ego depend, as far as internal factors are concerned, on the ascendancy of the life instinct in the interaction of the two instincts. But splitting processes continue; throughout the stage of the infantile neurosis (which is the means of expressing as well as working through early psychotic anxieties) the polarity between the life and death instincts makes itself strongly felt in the form of anxieties arising from persecutory objects which the ego attempts to cope with by splitting and later by repression.

With the beginning of the latency period, the organized part of the super-ego, although often very harsh, is much more cut off from its unconscious part. This is the stage in which the child deals with his strict super-ego by projecting it on to his environment—in other words, externalizing it—and trying to come to terms with those in authority. However, although in the older child and in the adult these anxieties are modified, changed in form, warded off by stronger defences, and therefore are also less accessible to analysis than in the young child, when we penetrate to deeper layers of the unconscious, we find that dangerous and persecutory figures still co-exist with idealized ones.

To return to my concept of primal splitting processes, I have recently put forward the hypothesis that it is essential for normal development that a division between the good and bad object, between love and hate, should take place in earliest infancy. When such a division is not too severe, and yet sufficient to differentiate between good and bad, it forms in my view one of the basic elements for stability and mental health. This means that the ego is strong enough not to be overwhelmed by anxiety and that, side by side with splitting, some integration is going on (though in a rudimentary

---

[1] For clinical material illustrating this particular point, see 'A Contribution to the Psychogenesis of Manic-Depressive States (1934). *Writings*, **1**, pp. 273-74.

form) which is only possible if in the fusion the life instinct predominates over the death instinct. As a result, integration and synthesis of objects can eventually be better achieved. I assume, however, that even under such favourable conditions, terrifying figures in the deep layers of the unconscious make themselves felt when internal or external pressure is extreme. People who are on the whole stable — and that means that they have firmly established their good object and therefore are closely identified with it — can overcome this intrusion of the deeper unconscious into their ego and regain their stability. In neurotic, and still more in psychotic individuals, the struggle against such dangers threatening from the deep layers of the unconscious is to some extent constant and part of their instability or their illness.

Since clinical developments in recent years have made us more aware of the psycho-pathological processes in schizophrenics, we can see more clearly that in them the super-ego becomes almost indistinguishable from their destructive impulses and internal persecutors. Herbert Rosenfeld (1952) in his paper on the super-ego of the schizophrenic, has described the part which such an overwhelming super-ego plays in schizophrenia. The persecutory anxieties these feelings engender I found also at the root of hypochondria.[1] I think the struggle and its outcome is different in manic depressive illnesses, but must satisfy myself here with these hints.

If, owing to a predominance of destructive impulses which goes with excessive weakness of the ego, the primary splitting processes are too violent, at a later stage integration and synthesis of objects are impeded and the depressive position cannot be worked through sufficiently.

I have emphasized that the dynamics of the mind are the result of the working of the life and death instincts, and that in addition to these forces the unconscious consists of the unconscious ego and soon of the unconscious super-ego. It is part of this concept that I regard the id as identical with the two instincts. Freud has in many places spoken about the id, but there are some inconsistencies in his definitions. In at least one passage, however, he defines the id in terms of instincts only; he says in the *New Introductory Lectures*: 'Instinctual cathexes seeking discharge—that, in our view, is all there is in the id.

---

[1] As I mentioned, for instance, in the footnote on p. 63 of this volume, 'the anxiety relating to attacks by internalized objects—first of all part-objects—is in my view the basis of hypochondriasis. I put forward this hypothesis in my book *The Psycho-Analysis of Children*, pp. 144, 264, 273.' Similarly in 'The Theory of Intellectual Inhibition' (1931), I pointed out, on p. 238, that 'a person's fear of his faeces as a persecutor is ultimately derived from his sadistic phantasies. . . . These fears give rise to a terror of having a number of persecutors inside his body and of being poisoned, as well as to hypochondriacal fears.'

It even seems that the energy of these instinctual impulses is in a state different from that in the other regions of the mind.' (*S.E.* **22,** p. 74).

My concept of the id, from the time I wrote *The Psycho-Analysis of Children* (1933), has been in accordance with the definition contained in the above quotation; it is true that I have occasionally used the term id more loosely in the sense of representing the death instinct only or the unconscious.

Freud stated that the ego differentiates itself from the id by the repression-resistance barrier. I have found that splitting is one of the initial defences and precedes repression, which I assume begins to operate in about the second year. Normally no splitting is absolute, any more than repression is absolute. The conscious and unconscious parts of the ego are therefore not separated by a rigid barrier; as Freud described it, in speaking of the different areas of the mind, they are shaded off into each other.

When, however, there is a very rigid barrier produced by splitting, the implication is that development has not proceeded normally. The conclusion would be that the death instinct is dominant. On the other hand, when the life instinct is in the ascendant, integration and synthesis can successfully progress. The nature of splitting determines the nature of repression.[1] If splitting processes are not excessive, the conscious and unconscious remain permeable to one another. However, whereas splitting performed by an ego which is still largely unorganized cannot adequately lead to modification of anxiety, in the older child and in the adult repression is a much more successful means both of warding off anxieties and modifying them. In repression the more highly organized ego divides itself off against the unconscious thoughts, impulses, and terrifying figures more effectively.

Although my conclusions are based on Freud's discovery of the instincts and their influence on the different parts of the mind, the additions I have suggested in this paper have involved a number of differences, upon which I would now make some concluding remarks.

---

[1] Cf. my paper 'Some Theoretical Conclusions Regarding the Emotional Life of the Infant' (pp. 86–87 of this volume) where I said: 'The mechanism of splitting underlies repression (as implied in Freud's concept); but in contrast to the earliest forms of splitting which lead to states of disintegration, repression does not normally result in a disintegration of the self. Since at this stage there is greater integration, within both the conscious and the unconscious parts of the mind, and since in repression the splitting predominantly effects a division between conscious and unconscious, neither part of the self is exposed to the degree of disintegration which may arise in previous stages. However, the extent to which splitting processes are resorted to in the first few months of life vitally influences the use of repression at a later stage.'

You may recall that Freud's emphasis on the libido was much greater than that on aggression. Although long before he discovered the life and death instincts he had seen the importance of the destructive component of sexuality in the form of sadism, he did not give sufficient weight to aggression in its impact on emotional life. Perhaps, therefore, he never fully worked out his discovery of the two instincts and seemed reluctant to extend it to the whole of mental functioning. Yet, as I pointed out earlier, he applied this discovery to clinical material to a greater extent than has been realized. If, however, Freud's conception of the two instincts is taken to its ultimate conclusion, the interaction of the life and death instincts will be seen to govern the whole of mental life.

I have already suggested that the formation of the super-ego precedes the Oedipus complex and is initiated by the introjection of the primal object. The super-ego maintains its connection with the other parts of the ego through having internalized different aspects of the same good object, a process of internalization which is also of the greatest importance in the organization of the ego. I attribute to the ego from the beginning of life a need and capacity not only to split but also to integrate itself. Integration, which gradually leads to a climax in the depressive position, depends on the preponderance of the life instinct and implies in some measure the acceptance by the ego of the working of the death instinct. I see the formation of the ego as an entity to be largely determined by the alternation between splitting and repression on the one hand, and integration in relation to objects on the other.

Freud stated that the ego constantly enriches itself from the id. I have said earlier that in my view the ego is called into operation and developed by the life instinct. The way in which this is achieved is through its earliest object relations. The breast, on which the life and death instincts are projected, is the first object which by introjection is internalized. In this way both instincts find an object to which they attach themselves and thereby by projection and re-introjection the ego is enriched as well as strengthened.

The more the ego can integrate its destructive impulses and synthesize the different aspects of its objects, the richer it becomes; for the split-off parts of the self and of impulses which are rejected because they arouse anxiety and give pain also contain valuable aspects of the personality and of the phantasy life which is impoverished by splitting them off. Though the rejected aspects of the self and of internalized objects contribute to instability, they are also at the source of inspiration in artistic productions and in various intellectual activities.

My conception of earliest object relations and super-ego development is in keeping with my hypothesis of the operation of the ego at least from birth onwards, as well as of the all-pervading power of the life and death instincts.

# 12

# OUR ADULT WORLD AND ITS ROOTS IN INFANCY

## (1959)

IN considering from the psycho-analytic point of view the behaviour of people in their social surroundings, it is necessary to investigate how the individual develops from infancy into maturity. A group — whether small or large—consists of individuals in a relationship to one another; and therefore the understanding of personality is the foundation for the understanding of social life. An exploration of the individual's development takes the psycho-analyst back, by gradual stages, to infancy; and I shall first enlarge, therefore, on fundamental trends in the young child.

The various signs of difficulties in the infant—states of rage, lack of interest in his surroundings, incapacity to bear frustration, and fleeting expressions of sadness—did not formerly find any explanation except in terms of physical factors. For until Freud made his great discoveries there was a general tendency to regard childhood as a period of perfect happiness, and the various disturbances displayed by children were not taken seriously. Freud's findings have, in the course of time, helped us to understand the complexity of the child's emotions and have revealed that children go through serious conflicts. This has led to a better insight into the infantile mind and its connection with the mental processes of the adult.

The play technique that I developed in the psycho-analysis of very young children, and other advances in technique resulting from my work, allowed me to draw new conclusions about very early stages of infancy and deeper layers of the unconscious. Such retrospective insight is based on one of the crucial findings of Freud, the transference situation, that is to say the fact that in a psycho-analysis the patient re-enacts in relation to the psycho-analyst earlier—and, I would add, even very early—situations and emotions. Therefore the relationship to the psycho-analyst at times bears, even in adults, very childlike features, such as over-dependence and the need to be guided, together with quite irrational distrust. It is part of the technique of the psycho-analyst to deduce the past from these manifestations. We know that Freud first discovered the Oedipus complex in the adult and was able to trace it back to childhood. Since I had the good fortune to analyse very young children, I was able to gain an even closer insight into their mental life, which led me back to an understanding of the mental life of the baby. For I was enabled by the meticulous attention I paid to the transference in the play technique to come to a deeper understanding of the ways in which—in the child and later also in the adult—mental life is influenced by earliest emotions and unconscious phantasies. It is from this angle that I shall describe with the use of as few technical terms as possible what I have concluded about the emotional life of the infant.

I have put forward the hypothesis that the newborn baby experiences, both in the process of birth and in the adjustment to the postnatal situation, anxiety of a persecutory nature. This can be explained by the fact that the young infant, without being able to grasp it intellectually, feels unconsciously every discomfort as though it were inflicted on him by hostile forces. If comfort is given to him soon—in particular warmth, the loving way he is held, and the gratification of being fed—this gives rise to happier emotions. Such comfort is felt to come from good forces and, I believe, makes possible the infant's first loving relation to a person or, as the psycho-analyst would put it, to an object. My hypothesis is that the infant has an innate unconscious awareness of the existence of the mother. We know that young animals at once turn to the mother and find their food from her. The human animal is not different in that respect, and this instinctual knowledge is the basis for the infant's primal relation to his mother. We can also observe that at an age of only a few weeks the baby already looks up to his mother's face, recognizes her footsteps, the touch of her hands, the smell and feel of her breast or of the bottle that she gives him, all of which suggest that some relation, however primitive, to the mother has been established.

He not only expects food from her but also desires love and understanding. In the earliest stages, love and understanding are expressed through the mother's handling of her baby, and lead to a certain unconscious oneness that is based on the unconscious of the mother and of the child being in close relation to each other. The infant's resultant feeling of being understood underlies the first and fundamental relation in his life—the relation to the mother. At the same time, frustration, discomfort and pain, which I suggested are experienced as persecution, enter as well into his feelings about his mother, because in the first few months she represents to the child the whole of the external world; therefore both good and bad come in his mind from her, and this leads to a twofold attitude toward the mother even under the best possible conditions.

Both the capacity to love and the sense of persecution have deep roots in the infant's earliest mental processes. They are focused first of all on the mother. Destructive impulses and their concomitants — such as resentment about frustration, hate stirred up by it, the incapacity to be reconciled, and envy of the all-powerful object, the mother, on whom his life and well-being depend — these various emotions arouse persecutory anxiety in the infant. *Mutatis mutandis* these emotions are still operative in later life. For destructive impulses towards anybody are always bound to give rise to the feeling that that person will also become hostile and retaliatory.

Innate aggressiveness is bound to be increased by unfavourable external circumstances and, conversely, is mitigated by the love and understanding that the young child receives; and these factors continue to operate throughout development. But although the importance of external circumstances is by now increasingly recognized, the importance of internal factors is still underrated. Destructive impulses, varying from individual to individual, are an integral part of mental life, even in favourable circumstances, and therefore we have to consider the development of the child and the attitudes of the adults as resulting from the interaction between internal and external influences. The struggle between love and hate — now that our capacity to understand babies has increased — can to some extent be recognized through careful observation. Some babies experience strong resentment about any frustration and show this by being unable to accept gratification when it follows on deprivation. I would suggest that such children have a stronger innate aggressiveness and greed than those infants whose occasional outbursts of rage are soon over. If a baby shows that he is able to accept food and love, this means that he can overcome resentment about frustration relatively quickly and, when gratification is again provided, regains his feelings of love.

Before continuing my description of the child's development, I feel that I should briefly define from the psycho-analytic point of view the terms *self* and *ego*. The ego, according to Freud, is the organized part of the self, constantly influenced by instinctual impulses but keeping them under control by repression; furthermore it directs all activities and establishes and maintains the relation to the external world. The self is used to cover the whole of the personality, which includes not only the ego but the instinctual life which Freud called the *id*.

My work has led me to assume that the ego exists and operates from birth onwards and that in addition to the functions mentioned above it has the important task of defending itself against anxiety stirred up by the struggle within and by influences from without. Furthermore it initiates a number of processes from which I shall first of all select *introjection* and *projection*. To the no less important process of *splitting*, that is to say dividing, impulses and objects I shall turn later.

We owe to Freud and Abraham the great discovery that introjection and projection are of major significance both in severe mental disturbances and in normal mental life. I have here to forgo even the attempt to describe how in particular Freud was led from the study of manic-depressive illness to the discovery of introjection which underlies the super-ego. He also expounded the vital relation between super-ego and ego and the id. In the course of time these basic concepts underwent further development. As I came to recognize in the light of my psycho-analytic work with children, introjection and projection function from the beginning of post-natal life as some of the earliest activities of the ego, which in my view operates from birth onwards. Considered from this angle, introjection means that the outer world, its impact, the situations the infant lives through, and the objects he encounters, are not only experienced as external but are taken into the self and become part of his inner life. Inner life cannot be evaluated even in the adult without these additions to the personality that derive from continuous introjection. Projection, which goes on simultaneously, implies that there is a capacity in the child to attribute to other people around him feelings of various kinds, predominantly love and hate.

I have formed the view that love and hate towards the mother are bound up with the very young infant's capacity to project all his emotions on to her, thereby making her into a good as well as dangerous object. However, introjection and projection, though they are rooted in infancy, are not only infantile processes. They are part of the infant's phantasies, which in my view also operate from the beginning and help to mould his impression of his surroundings; and by introjection this changed picture of the external world influences what goes on in his mind. Thus an inner world is built up which is partly a reflection of the external one. That is to say, the double process of introjection and projection contributes to the interaction between external and internal factors. This interaction continues throughout every stage of life. In the same way introjection and projection go on throughout life and become modified in the course of maturation; but they never lose their importance in the individual's relation to the world around him. Even in the adult, therefore, the judgement of reality is never quite free from the influence of his internal world.

I have already suggested that from one angle the processes of projection and introjection that I have been describing have to be considered as unconscious phantasies. As my friend the late Susan

Isaacs put it in her paper (1952) on this subject 'Phantasy is (in the first instance) the mental corollary, the psychic representative of instinct. There is no impulse, no instinctual urge or response which is not experienced as unconscious phantasy. . . . A phantasy represents the particular content of the urges or feelings (for example, wishes, fears, anxieties, triumphs, love or sorrow) dominating the mind at the moment.'

Unconscious phantasies are not the same as day-dreams (though they are linked with them) but an activity of the mind that occurs on deep unconscious levels and accompanies every impulse experienced by the infant. For instance, a hungry baby can temporarily deal with his hunger by hallucinating the satisfaction of being given the breast, with all the pleasures he normally derives from it, such as the taste of the milk, the warm feel of the breast, and being held and loved by the mother. But unconscious phantasy also takes the opposite form of feeling deprived and persecuted by the breast which refuses to give this satisfaction. Phantasies — becoming more elaborate and referring to a wider variety of objects and situations — continue throughout development and accompany all activities; they never stop playing a great part in mental life. The influence of unconscious phantasy on art, on scientific work, and on the activities of every-day life cannot be overrated.

I have already mentioned that the mother is introjected, and that this is a fundamental factor in development. As I see it, object relations start almost at birth. The mother in her good aspects — loving, helping, and feeding the child — is the first good object that the infant makes part of his inner world. His capacity to do so is, I would suggest, up to a point innate. Whether the good object becomes sufficiently part of the self depends to some extent on persecutory anxiety — and accordingly resentment — not being too strong; at the same time a loving attitude on the part of the mother contributes much to the success of his process. If the mother is taken into the child's inner world as a good and dependable object, an element of strength is added to the ego. For I assume that the ego develops largely round this good object, and the identification with the good characteristics of the mother becomes the basis for further helpful identifications. The identification with the good object shows externally in the young child's copying the mother's activities and attitudes; this can be seen in his play and often also in his behaviour towards younger children. A strong identification with the good mother makes it easier for the child to identify also with a good father and later on with other friendly figures. As a result, his inner world comes to contain predominantly good objects and feelings, and these good objects are felt to respond to the infant's love. All this contributes to a stable personality and makes it possible to extend sympathy and friendly feelings to other people. It is clear that a good relation of the parents to each other and to the child, and a happy home atmosphere, play a vital rôle in the success of this process.

Yet, however good are the child's feelings towards both parents, aggressiveness and hate also remain operative. One expression of this is the rivalry with the father which results from the boy's desires towards the mother and all the phantasies linked with them. Such rivalry finds expression in the Oedipus complex, which can be clearly observed in children of three, four, or five years of age. This complex exists, however, very much earlier and is rooted in the baby's first suspicions of the father taking the mother's love and attention away from him. There are great differences in the Oedipus complex of the girl and of the boy, which I shall characterize only by saying that whereas the boy in his genital development returns to his original object, the mother, and therefore seeks female objects, with consequent jealousy of the father and men in general, the girl to some extent has to turn away from the mother and find the object of her desires in the father and later on in other men. I have, however, stated this in an over-simplified form, because the boy is also attracted towards the father and identifies with him; and therefore an element of homosexuality enters into normal development. The same applies to the girl, for whom the relation to the mother, and to women in general, never loses its importance. The Oedipus complex is thus not a matter only of feelings of hate and rivalry towards one parent and love towards the other, but feelings of love and the sense of guilt also enter in connection with the rival parent. Many conflicting emotions therefore centre upon the Oedipus complex.

We turn now again to projection. By projecting oneself or part of one's impulses and feelings into another person, an identification with that person is achieved, though it will differ from the identification arising from introjection. For if an object is taken into the self (introjected), the emphasis lies on acquiring some of the characteristics of this object and on being influenced by them. On the other hand, in putting part of oneself into the other person (projecting), the identification is based on attributing to the other person some of one's own qualities. Projection has many repercussions. We are inclined to attribute to other people—in a sense, to put into them— some of our own emotions and thoughts; and it is obvious that it will depend on how balanced or persecuted we are whether this projection is of a friendly or a hostile nature. By attributing part of our feelings to the other person, we understand their feelings, needs, and satisfactions; in other words, we are putting ourselves into the other person's shoes. There are people who go so far in this direction that they lose themselves entirely in others and become incapable of objective judgement. At the same time excessive introjection endangers the strength of the ego because it becomes completely dominated by the introjected object. If projection is predominantly hostile, real empathy and understanding of others is impaired. The character of projection is, therefore, of great importance in our relations to other people. If the interplay between introjection and projection is not dominated by hostility or over-dependence, and is well balanced, the inner world is enriched and the relations with the external world are improved.

I referred earlier to the tendency of the infantile ego to split impulses and objects, and I regard this as another of the primal activities of the ego. This tendency to split results in part from the fact that the early ego largely lacks coherence. But—here again I have to refer to my own concepts—persecutory anxiety reinforces the need to keep separate the loved object from the dangerous one, and therefore to split love from hate. For the young infant's self-preservation depends on his trust in a good mother. By splitting the two aspects and clinging to the good one he preserves his belief in a good object and his capacity to love it; and this is an essential condition for keeping alive. For without at least some of this feeling, he would be exposed to an entirely hostile world which he fears would destroy him. This hostile world would also be built up inside him. There are, as we know, babies in whom vitality is lacking and who cannot be kept alive, probably because they have not been able to develop their trusting relation to a good mother. By contrast, there are other babies who go through great difficulties but retain sufficient vitality to make use of the help and food offered by the mother. I know of an infant who underwent a prolonged and difficult birth and was injured in the process, but when put to the breast, took it avidly. The same has been reported of babies who had serious operations soon after birth. Other infants in such circumstances are not able to survive because they have difficulties in accepting nourishment and love, which implies that they have not been able to establish trust and love towards the mother.

The process of splitting changes in form and content as development goes on, but in some ways it is never entirely given up. In my view omnipotent destructive impulses, persecutory anxiety, and splitting are predominant in the first three to four months of life. I have described this combination of mechanisms and anxieties as the paranoid-schizoid position, which in extreme cases becomes the basis of paranoia and schizophrenic illness. The concomitants of destructive feelings at this early stage are of great importance, and I shall single out greed and envy as very disturbing factors, first of all in the relation to the mother and later on to other members of the family, in fact throughout life.

Greed varies considerably from one infant to another. There are babies who can never be satisfied because their greed exceeds everything they may receive. With greed goes the urge to empty the mother's breast and to exploit all the sources of satisfaction without consideration for anybody. The very greedy infant may enjoy whatever he receives for the time being; but as soon as the gratification has gone, he becomes dissatisfied and is driven to exploit first of all the mother and soon everybody in the family who can give him attention, food, or any other gratification. There is no doubt that greed is increased by anxiety—the anxiety of being deprived, of being robbed, and of not being good enough to be loved. The infant who is so greedy for love and attention is also insecure about his own capacity to love; and all these anxieties reinforce greed. This situation remains in fundamentals unchanged in the greed of the older child and of the adult.

As regards envy, it is not easy to explain how the mother who feeds the infant and looks after him can also be an object of envy. But whenever he is hungry or feels neglected, the child's frustration leads to the phantasy that the milk and love are deliberately withheld from him, or kept by the mother for her benefit. Such suspicions are the basis of envy. It is inherent in the feeling of envy not only that possession is desired, but that there is also a strong urge to spoil other people's enjoyment of the coveted object—an urge which tends to spoil the object itself. If envy is very strong, its spoiling quality results in a disturbed relation to the mother as well as later to other people; it also means that nothing can be fully enjoyed because the desired thing has already been spoiled by envy. Furthermore, if envy is strong, goodness cannot be assimilated, become part of one's inner life, and so give rise to gratitude. By contrast, the capacity to enjoy fully what has been received, and the experience of gratitude towards the person who gives it, influence strongly both the character and the relations with other people. It is not for nothing that in saying grace before meals, Christians use the words, 'For what we are about to receive may the Lord make us truly thankful.' These words imply that one asks for the one quality—gratitude—which will make one happy and free from resentment and envy. I heard a little girl say that she loved her mother most of all people, because what would she have done if her mother had not given birth to her and had not fed her? This strong feeling of gratitude was linked with her capacity for enjoyment and showed itself in her character and relations to other people, particularly in generosity and consideration.

Throughout life such capacity for enjoyment and gratitude makes a variety of interests and pleasures possible.

In normal development, with growing integration of the ego, splitting processes diminish, and the increased capacity to understand external reality, and to some extent to bring together the infant's contradictory impulses, leads also to a greater synthesis of the good and bad aspects of the object. This means that people can be loved in spite of their faults and that the world is not seen only in terms of black and white.

The super-ego—the part of the ego that criticizes and controls dangerous impulses, and that Freud first placed roughly in the fifth year of childhood—operates, according to my views, much earlier. It is my hypothesis that in the fifth or sixth month of life the baby becomes afraid of the harm his destructive impulses and his greed might do, or might have done, to his loved objects. For he cannot yet distinguish between his desires and impulses and their actual effects. He experiences feelings of guilt and the urge to preserve these objects and to make reparation to them for harm done. The anxiety now experienced is of a predominantly depressive nature; and the emotions accompanying it, as well as the defences evolved against them, I recognized as part of normal development, and termed the 'depressive position'. Feelings of guilt, which occasionally arise in all of us, have very deep roots in infancy, and the tendency to make reparation plays an important rôle in our sublimations and object relations.

When we observe young infants from this angle, we can see that at times, without any particular external cause, they appear depressed. At this stage they try to please the people around them in every way available to them—smiles, playful gestures, even attempts to feed the mother by putting a spoon with food into her mouth. At the same time this is also a period in which inhibitions over food and nightmares often set in, and all these symptoms come to a head at the time of weaning. With older children, the need to deal with guilt feelings expresses itself more clearly; various constructive activities are used for this purpose and in the relation to parents or siblings there is an excessive need to please and to be helpful, all of which expresses not only love but also the need to make reparation.

Freud has postulated the process of *working through* as an essential part of psycho-analytic procedure. To put it in a nutshell, this means enabling the patient to experience his emotions, anxieties, and past situations over and over again both in relation to the analyst and to different people and situations in the patient's present and past life. There is, however, a working through occurring to some extent in normal individual development. Adaptation to external reality increases and with it the infant achieves a less phantastic picture of the world around him. The recurring experience of the mother going away and coming back to him makes her absence less frightening, and therefore his suspicion of her leaving him diminishes. In this way he gradually works through his early fears and comes to terms with his conflicting impulses and emotions. Depressive anxiety at this stage predominates and persecutory anxiety lessens. I hold that many apparently odd manifestations, inexplicable phobias, and idiosyncrasies that can be observed in young children are indications of, as well as ways of, working through the depressive position. If the feelings of guilt arising in the child are not excessive, the urge to make reparation and other processes that are part of growth bring relief. Yet depressive and persecutory anxieties are never entirely overcome; they may temporarily recur under internal or external pressure, though a relatively normal person can cope with this recurrence and regain his balance. If, however, the strain is too great, the development of a strong and well-balanced personality may be impeded.

Having dealt—though I am afraid in an over-simplified way—with paranoid and depressive anxieties and their implications, I should like to consider the influence of the processes I have described on social relations. I have spoken of introjection of the external world and have hinted that this process continues throughout life. Whenever we can admire and love somebody—or hate and despise somebody—we also take something of them into ourselves and our deepest attitudes are shaped by such experiences. In the one case it enriches us and becomes a foundation for precious memories; in the other case we sometimes feel that the outer world is spoilt for us and the inner world is therefore impoverished.

I can here only touch on the importance of actual favourable and unfavourable experiences to which the infant is from the beginning subjected, first of all by his parents, and later on by other people. External experiences are of paramount importance throughout life. However, much depends, even in the infant, on the ways in which external influences are interpreted and assimilated by the child, and this in turn largely depends on how strongly destructive impulses and persecutory and depressive anxieties are operative. In the same way our adult experiences are influenced by our basic attitudes, which either help us to cope better with misfortunes or, if we are too much dominated by suspicion and self-pity, turn even minor disappointments into disasters.

Freud's discoveries about childhood have increased the understanding of problems of upbringing, but these findings have often been misinterpreted. Though it is true that a too disciplinarian upbringing reinforces the child's tendency to repression, we have to remember that too great indulgence may be almost as harmful for the child as too much restraint. The so-called 'full self-expression' can have great disadvantages both for the parents and for the child. Whereas in former times the child was often the victim of the parents' disciplinarian attitude, the parents may now become the victims of their offspring. It is an old joke that there was a man who never tasted breast of chicken; for when he was a child, his parents ate it, and when he grew up, his children were given it. When dealing with our children, it is essential to keep a balance between too much and too little discipline. To turn a blind eye to some of the smaller misdeeds is a very healthy attitude. But if these grow into persistent lack of consideration, it is necessary to show disapproval and to make demands on the child.

There is another angle from which the parents' excessive indulgence must be considered: while the child may take advantage of his parents' attitude, he also experiences a sense of guilt about exploiting them and feels a need for some restraint which would give him security. This would also make him able to feel respect for his parents, which is essential for a good relation towards them and for developing respect for other people. Moreover, we must also consider that parents who are suffering too much under the unrestrained self-expression of the child—however much they try to submit to it—are bound to feel some resentment which will enter into their attitude towards the child.

I have already described the young child who reacts strongly against every frustration—and there is no upbringing possible without some unavoidable frustration—and who is apt to resent bitterly any failings and shortcomings in his environment and to underrate goodness received. Accordingly he will project his grievances very strongly on to the people around him. Similar attitudes are well known in adults. If we contrast the individuals who are capable of bearing frustration without too great resentment and can soon regain their balance after a disappointment with those who are inclined to put the whole blame on to the outer world, we can see the detrimental effect of hostile projection. For projection of grievance rouses in other people a counter-feeling of hostility. Few of us have the tolerance to put up with the accusation, even if it is not expressed in words, that we are in some ways the guilty party. In fact, it very often makes us dislike such people, and we appear all the more as enemies to them; in consequence they regard us with increased persecutory feelings and suspicions, and relations become more and more disturbed.

One way of dealing with excessive suspicion is to try to pacify the supposed or actual enemies. This is rarely successful. Of course, some people can be won over by flattery and appeasement, particularly if their own feelings of persecution make for the need to be appeased. But such a relation easily breaks down and changes into mutual hostility. In passing, I would mention the difficulties that such fluctuations in the attitudes of leading statesmen may produce in international affairs.

Where persecutory anxiety is less strong, and projection, mainly attributing to others good feelings, thereby becomes the basis of empathy, the response from the outer world is very different. We all know people who have the capacity to be liked; for we have the impression that they have some trust in us, which evokes on our part a feeling of friendliness. I am not speaking of people who are trying to make themselves popular in an insincere way. On the contrary, I believe it is the people who are genuine and have the courage of their convictions who are in the long run respected and even liked.

An interesting instance of the influence of early attitudes throughout life is the fact that the relation to early figures keeps reappearing and problems that remain unresolved in infancy or early childhood are revived though in modified form. For example, the attitude towards a subordinate or a superior repeats up to a point the relation to a younger sibling or to a parent. If we meet a friendly and helpful older person, unconsciously the relation to a loved parent or grandparent is revived; while a condescending and unpleasant older individual stirs up anew the rebellious attitudes of the child towards his parents. It is not necessary that such people should be physically, mentally, or even in actual age similar to the original figures; something in common in their attitude is enough. When somebody is entirely under the sway of his early situation and relations, his judgement of people and events is bound to be disturbed. Normally such revival of early situations is limited and rectified by objective judgement. That is to say, we are all capable of being influenced by irrational factors, but in normal life we are not dominated by them.

The capacity for love and devotion, first of all to the mother, in many ways develops into devotion to various causes that are felt to be good and valuable. This means that the enjoyment which in the past the baby was able to experience because he felt loved and loving, in later life becomes transferred not only to his relations to people, which is very important, but also to his work and to all that he feels worth striving for. This means also an enrichment of the personality and capacity to enjoy his work, and opens up a variety of sources of satisfaction.

In this striving to further our aims, as well as in our relation to other people, the early wish to make reparation is added to the capacity for love. I have already said that in our sublimations, which grow out of the earliest interests of the child, constructive activities gain more impetus because the child unconsciously feels that in this way he is restoring loved people whom he had damaged. This impetus never loses its strength, though very often it is not recognized in ordinary life. The irrevocable fact that none of us is ever entirely free from guilt has very valuable aspects because it implies the never fully exhausted wish to make reparation and to create in whatever way we can.

All forms of social service benefit by this urge. In extreme cases, feelings of guilt drive people towards sacrificing themselves completely to a cause or to their fellow beings, and may lead to fanaticism. We know, however, that some people risk their own lives in order to save others, and this is not necessarily of the same order. It is not so much guilt which might be operative in such cases as the capacity for love, generosity, and an identification with the endangered fellow being.

I have emphasized the importance of the identification with the parents, and subsequently with other people, for the young child's development and I now wish to stress one particular aspect of successful identification which reaches into adulthood. When envy and rivalry are not too great, it becomes possible to enjoy vicariously the pleasures of others. In childhood the hostility and rivalry of the Oedipus complex are counteracted by the capacity to enjoy vicariously the happiness of the parents. In adult life, parents can share the pleasures of childhood and avoid interfering with them because they are capable of identifying with their children. They become able to watch without envy their children growing up.

This attitude becomes particularly important when people grow older and the pleasures of youth become less and less available. If gratitude for past satisfactions has not vanished, old people can enjoy whatever is still within their reach. Furthermore, with such an attitude, which gives rise to serenity, they can identify themselves with young people. For instance, anyone who is looking out for young talents and who helps to develop them—be it in his function as teacher or critic, or in former times as patron of the arts and of culture—is only able to do so because he can identify with others; in a sense he is repeating his own life, sometimes even achieving vicariously the fulfilment of aims unfulfilled in his own life.

At every stage the ability to identify makes possible the happiness of being able to admire the character or achievements of others. If we cannot allow ourselves to appreciate the achievements and qualities of other people—and that means that we are not able to bear the thought that we can never emulate them—we are deprived of sources of great happiness and enrichment. The world would be in our eyes a much poorer place if we had no opportunities of realizing that greatness exists and will go on existing in the future. Such admiration also stirs up something in us and increases indirectly our belief in ourselves. This is one of the many ways in which identifications derived from infancy become an important part of our personality.

The ability to admire another person's achievements is one of the factors making successful team work possible. If envy is not too great, we can take pleasure and pride in working with people who sometimes outstrip our capacities, for we identify with these outstanding members of the team.

The problem of identification is, however, very complex. When Freud discovered the super-ego, he saw it as part of the mental structure derived from the influence of the parents on the child—an influence that becomes part of the child's fundamental attitudes. My work with young children has shown me that even from babyhood onwards the mother, and soon other people in the child's surroundings, are taken into the self, and this is the basis of a variety of identifications, favourable and unfavourable. I have above given instances of identifications that are helpful both to the child and to the adult. But the vital influence of early environment has also the effect that unfavourable aspects of the attitudes of the adult towards the child are detrimental to his development because they stir up in him hatred and rebellion or too great submissiveness. At the same time he internalizes this hostile and angry adult attitude. Out of such experiences, an excessively disciplinarian parent, or a parent lacking in understanding and love, by identification influences the character formation of the child and may lead him to repeat in later life what he himself has undergone. Therefore a father sometimes uses the same wrong methods towards his children that his father used towards him. On the other hand, the rebellion against the wrongs experienced in childhood can lead to the opposite reaction of doing everything differently from the way the parents did it. This would lead to the other extreme, for instance to over-indulgence of the child, to which I have referred earlier. To have learnt from our experiences in childhood and therefore to be more understanding and tolerant towards our own children, as well as towards people outside the family circle, is a sign of maturity and successful development. But tolerance does not mean being blind to the faults of others. It means recognizing those faults and nevertheless not losing one's ability to co-operate with people or even to experience love towards some of them.

In describing the child's development I have emphasized particularly the importance of greed. Let us consider now what part greed plays in character formation and how it influences the attitudes of the adult. The rôle of greed can be easily observed as a very destructive element in social life. The greedy person wants more and more, even at the expense of everybody else. He is not really capable of consideration and generosity towards others. I am not speaking here only of material possessions but also of status and prestige.

The very greedy individual is liable to be ambitious. The rôle of ambition, both in its helpful and in its disturbing aspects, shows itself wherever we observe human behaviour. There is no doubt that ambition gives impetus to achievement, but, if it becomes the main driving force, co-operation with others is endangered. The highly ambitious person, in spite of all his successes, always remains dissatisfied, in the same way as a greedy baby is never satisfied. We know well the type of public figure who, hungry for more and more success, appears never to be content with what he had achieved. One feature in this attitude—in which envy also plays an important rôle —is the inability to allow others to come sufficiently to the fore. They may be allowed to play a subsidiary part as long as they do not challenge the supremacy of the ambitious person. We find also that such people are unable and unwilling to stimulate and encourage younger people, because some of them might become their successors. One reason for the lack of satisfaction they derive from apparently great success results from the fact that their interest is not so much devoted to the field in which they are working as to their personal prestige. This description implies the connection between greed and envy. The rival is seen not only as someone who has robbed and deprived one of one's own position or goods, but also as the owner of valuable qualities which stir up envy and the wish to spoil them.

Where greed and envy are not excessive, even an ambitious person finds satisfaction in helping others to make their contribution. Here we have one of the attitudes underlying successful leadership. Again, to some extent, this is already observable in the nursery. An older child may take pride in the achievements of a younger brother or sister and do everything to help them. Some children even have an integrating effect on the whole family life; by being predominantly friendly and helpful they improve the family atmosphere. I have seen that mothers who were very impatient and intolerant of difficulties have improved through the influence of such a child. The same applies to school life where sometimes only as few as one or two children have a beneficial effect on the attitude of all the others by a kind of moral leadership which is based on a friendly and co-operative relation to the other children without any attempt to make them feel inferior.

To return to leadership: if the leader—and that may also apply to any member of a group—suspects that he is the object of hate, all his antisocial attitudes are increased by this feeling. We find that the person who is unable to bear criticism because it touches at once on his persecutory anxiety is not only a prey to suffering but also has difficulties in relation to other people and may even endanger the cause for which he is working, in whatever walk of life it may be; he will show an incapacity to correct mistakes and to learn from others.

If we look at our adult world from the viewpoint of its roots in infancy, we gain an insight into the way our mind, our habits, and our views have been built up from the earliest infantile phantasies and emotions to the most complex and sophisticated adult manifestations. There is one more conclusion to be drawn, which is that nothing that ever existed in the unconscious completely loses its influence on the personality.

A further aspect of the child's development to be discussed is his character formation. I have given some instances of how destructive impulses, envy and greed, and the resulting persecutory anxieties disturb the child's emotional balance and his social relations. I have also referred to the beneficial aspects of an opposite development and attempted to show how they arise. I have tried to convey the importance of the interaction between innate factors and the influence of the environment. In giving full weight to this interplay we get a deeper understanding of how the child's character develops. It has always been a most important aspect of psycho-analytic work that, in the course of a successful analysis, the patient's character undergoes favourable changes.

One consequence of a balanced development is integrity and strength of character. Such qualities have a far-reaching effect both on the individual's self-reliance and on his relations to the outside world. The influence of a really sincere and genuine character on other people is easily observed. Even people who do not possess the same qualities are impressed and cannot help feeling some respect for integrity and sincerity. For these qualities arouse in them a picture of what they might themselves have become or perhaps even still might become. Such personalities give them some hopefulness about the world in general and greater trust in goodness.

I have concluded this paper by discussing the importance of character, because in my view character is the foundation for all human achievement. The effect of a good character on others lies at the root of healthy social development.

## POSTSCRIPT

When I discussed my views on character development with an anthropologist, he objected to the assumption of a general foundation for character development. He quoted his experience that in his fieldwork he had come across an entirely different evaluation of character. For instance, he had worked in a community where it was regarded as admirable to cheat other people. He also described, in answer to some of my questions, that in that community it was considered as a weakness to show mercy to an adversary. I inquired whether there were no circumstances in which mercy would be shown. He replied that if a person could place himself behind a woman in such a way that he would be up to a point covered by her skirt, his life would be spared. In answer to further questions he told me that if the enemy managed to get into a man's tent, he would not be killed; and that there was also safety within a sanctuary.

The anthropologist agreed when I suggested that the tent, the woman's skirt, and the sanctuary were symbols of the good and protective mother. He also accepted my interpretation that the mother's protection was extended to a hated sibling—the man hiding behind the woman's skirt—and that the ban on killing within one's own tent linked with the rules of hospitality. My conclusion about the last point is that fundamentally hospitality links with family life, with the relation of children to one another, and in particular to the mother. For, as I suggested earlier, the tent represents the mother who protects the family.

I am quoting this instance to suggest possible links between cultures that appear to be entirely different, and to indicate that these links are found in the relation to the primal good object, the mother, whatever may be the forms in which distortions of character are accepted and even admired.

# 13

# A NOTE ON DEPRESSION
# IN THE SCHIZOPHRENIC
## (1960)

In this contribution I shall concentrate mainly on depression as experienced by the paranoid schizophrenic. My first point arises from my contention, expressed in 1935, that the paranoid position (which I later termed the paranoid-schizoid position) is bound up with splitting processes and contains the fixation points for the group of schizophrenias, while the depressive position contains the fixation points for manic-depressive illness. I also held and still hold the view that paranoid and schizoid anxieties and depressive feelings, as they may occur in more normal people under external or internal pressure, go back to these early positions which are revived in such situations.

The often-observed connection between the groups of schizophrenic and manic-depressive illnesses can in my view be explained by the developmental link existing in infancy between the paranoid-schizoid and depressive positions. The persecutory anxieties and splitting processes characteristic of the paranoid-schizoid position continue, though changed in strength and form, into the depressive position. Emotions of depression and guilt, which develop more fully at the stage when the depressive position arises, are already (according to my newer concepts) in some measure operative during the paranoid-schizoid phase. The link between these two positions—with all the changes in the ego which they imply—is that they are both the outcome of the struggle between the life and death instincts. In the earlier stage (extending over the first three or four months of life) the anxieties arising from this struggle take on a paranoid form, and the still incoherent ego is driven to reinforce splitting processes. With the growing strength of the ego, the depressive position arises. During this stage paranoid anxieties and schizoid mechanisms diminish and depressive anxiety gains in strength. Here, too, we can see the working of the conflict between life and death instincts. The changes which have taken place are the result of alterations in the states of fusion between the two instincts.

Already in the first phase the primal object, the mother, is internalized in her good and bad aspects. I have often maintained that without the good object at least to some extent becoming part of the ego, life cannot continue. The relation to the object, however, changes in the second quarter of the first year and the preservation of this good object is the essence of depressive anxieties. The splitting processes, too, change. Whereas at the beginning there is a splitting between the good and bad object, this happens side by side with strong fragmentation both of the ego and of the object. As the fragmentation processes become less, the division between the injured or dead object and the live one comes more into the foreground. The lessening of fragmentation and the focusing on the object go along with steps towards integration which implies a growing fusion of the two instincts in which the life instinct predominates.

In what follows I shall put forward some indications of why depressive features in paranoid schizophrenics are not experienced in a form which is as easily recognized as in manic-depressive states, and I shall suggest some explanations for the difference in the nature of depression as experienced in these two groups of illnesses. In the past I have laid emphasis on the distinction between paranoid anxiety, which I defined as being centred on the preservation of the ego, and depressive anxiety, which focuses on the preservation of the good internalized and external object. As I see it now, this distinction is too schematic. For I have for many years put forward the view that from the beginning of post-natal life the internalization of the object is the basis of developmen. This implies that some internalization of the good object also occurs in the paranoid schizophrenic. From birth onwards, however, in an ego lacking in strength and subjected to violent splitting processes the internalization of the good object differs in nature and strength from that of the manic-depressive. It is less permanent, less stable, and does not allow for a sufficient identification with it. Nevertheless, since some internalization of the object does occur, anxiety on behalf of the ego—that is to say, paranoid anxiety—is bound to include also some concern for the object.

There is another new point to add: depressive anxiety and guilt (defined by me as experienced in relation to the internalized good object), in so far as they already occur in the paranoid-schizoid position, refer also to a part of the ego, namely that part which is felt to contain the good object and therefore to be the good part. That is to say, the guilt of the schizophrenic applies to destroying something good in himself and also to weakening his ego by splitting processes.

There is a second reason why the sense of guilt is experienced by the schizophrenic in a very particular form and is therefore difficult to detect. Owing to processes of fragmentation—and I shall remind

you here of Schreber's capacity to divide himself into sixty souls —
and to the violence with which this splitting takes place in the
schizophrenic, depressive anxiety and guilt are very strongly split off.
Whereas paranoid anxiety is experienced in most parts of the split
ego and therefore predominates, guilt and depression are only experienced in some parts which are felt by the schizophrenic to be out
of reach, until the analysis brings them into consciousness.

Moreover, since depression is mainly a result of synthesizing the
good and bad object and goes with a stronger integration of the ego,
the nature of the depression in the schizophrenic is bound to differ
from that of the manic-depressive.

A third reason why depression is so difficult to detect in the
schizophrenic is that projective identification, which is very strong
in him, is used to project depression and guilt into an object — during
the analytic procedure mainly into the analyst. Since re-introjection
follows projective identification, the attempt towards a lasting projection of depression does not succeed.

Interesting instances of how in schizophrenics projective identification deals with depression have been given by Hanna Segal in a
recent paper (1956). In that paper the author exemplifies the process
of improvement in schizophrenics by helping them, by the analysis
of deep layers, to diminish splitting and projection and therefore to
come nearer to experiencing the depressive position, with ensuing
guilt and urge for reparation.

It is only in the analysis of deep layers of the mind that we come
across the schizophrenic's feelings of despair about being confused and
in bits. Further work enables us in some cases to get access to the
feeling of guilt and depression about being dominated by destructive
impulses and about having destroyed oneself and one's good object
by splitting processes. As a defence against such pain we might
find that fragmentation occurs again; it is only by repeated experiences of such pain and the analysis of it that progress can be
made.

I wish here quite briefly to refer to the analysis of a very ill boy
of nine who was incapable of learning and was deeply disturbed in his
object relations. In one session he experienced strongly a feeling of
despair and guilt about having fragmented himself and destroyed
what was good in him, and the affection for his mother, as well as
inability to express it, came up. At that moment he took his beloved
watch out of his pocket, threw it on the floor and stamped on it until
it was in little pieces. That meant that he both expressed and repeated
the fragmentation of his self. I would now conclude that this fragmentation appeared also as a defence against the pain of integration.
I have had similar experiences in the analysis of adults, only with

the difference that they were not expressed by destroying a loved possession.

If the drive to make reparation is mobilized by the analysis of destructive impulses and splitting process, steps towards improvement—and sometimes towards a cure—can be made. The means of strengthening the ego, of enabling the schizophrenic to experience the split-off goodness both of himself and of the object, are based on healing the splitting process in some measure and therefore diminishing the fragmentation, which means that the lost parts of the self become more accessible to him. By contrast, I believe that although therapeutic methods of helping the schizophrenic by enabling him to perform constructive activities are useful, they are not as lasting as the analysis of deep layers of the mind and of splitting processes.

# 14

# ON MENTAL HEALTH

## (1960)

A well-integrated personality is the foundation for mental health. I shall begin by enumerating a few elements of an integrated personality: emotional maturity, strength of character, capacity to deal with conflicting emotions, a balance between internal life and adaptation to reality, and a successful welding into a whole of the different parts of the personality.

To some extent infantile phantasies and desires persist even in an emotionally mature person. If phantasies and desires have been freely experienced and successfully worked through—first of all in the play of the child—they are a source of interests and activities and thereby enrich the personality. But if grievance about unfulfilled desires has remained too potent and their working-through is therefore impeded, personal relations and enjoyment from various sources are disturbed, it becomes difficult to accept those substitutes which would be more appropriate to later stages of development, and the sense of reality is impaired.

Even if development is satisfactory and leads to enjoyment from various sources, some feeling of mourning for irretrievably lost pleasures and unfulfilled possibilities can still be found in the deeper layers of the mind. While regret that childhood and youth will never return is often consciously experienced by people near to middle age, in psycho-analysis we find that even infancy and its pleasures are still unconsciously longed for. Emotional maturity means that these feelings of loss can up to a point be counteracted by the ability to accept substitutes, and infantile phantasies do not disturb adult emotional life. Being able to enjoy pleasures which are available is bound up at any age with a relative freedom from envy and grievances. One way in which contentment at a later stage in life can therefore be found is to enjoy vicariously the pleasures of young people, particularly of our children and grandchildren. Another source of gratification, even before old age, is the richness of memories which keep the past alive.

Strength of character is based on some very early processes. The first and fundamental relation in which the child experiences feelings of love as well as of hate is the relation to the mother. Not only does she figure as an external object, but the infant also takes into himself (introjects, according to Freud) aspects of her personality. If the good aspects of the introjected mother are felt to dominate over the frustrating ones—this internalized mother becomes a foundation for strength of character, because the ego can develop its potentialities on that basis. For, if she can be felt to be guiding and protecting but not dominating, the identification with her makes possible inner peace. The success of this first relation extends to relations with other members of the family, first of all to the father, and is reflected in adult attitudes, both in the family circle and towards people in general.

The internalization of the good parents and the identification with them underlie loyalty towards people and causes and the ability to make sacrifices for one's convictions. Loyalty towards what is loved or felt to be right implies that hostile impulses bound up with anxieties (which are never entirely eliminated) are turned towards those objects which endanger what is felt to be good. This process never fully succeeds and the anxiety remains that destructiveness may also endanger the good internalized object as well as the external one.

Many apparently well-balanced people have no strength of character. They make life easy for themselves by avoiding inner and external conflicts. As a consequence they aim at what is successful or expedient and they cannot develop deep-rooted convictions.

However, a strong character, if it is not mitigated by consideration for others, is not characteristic of a balanced personality. Understanding of other people, compassion, sympathy and tolerance, enrich our experience of the world, and make us feel more secure in ourselves and less lonely.

Balance depends upon some insight into the variety of our contradictory impulses and feelings and the capacity to come to terms with these inner conflicts. An aspect of balance is the adaptation to the external world—an adaptation which does not interfere with the freedom of our own emotions and thoughts. This implies an interaction: inner life always influences the attitudes towards external reality and in turn is influenced by the adjustment to the world of reality. Already the infant internalizes his first experiences and the people who surround him and these internalizations influence his inner life. If the goodness of the object predominates in these processes and becomes part of the personality, his attitude towards the experiences coming from the external world is in turn favourably influenced. It is not necessarily a perfect world which such an infant perceives, but it is certainly a world much more worth while because his internal situation is a happier one. A successful interaction of this kind contributes to balance and to a good relation to the external world.

Balance does not mean the avoidance of conflict; it implies the strength to live through painful emotions and to cope with them. If painful emotions are excessively split off, this restricts the personality and leads to inhibitions of various kinds. In particular the repression of phantasy life has strong repercussions on development, for it results in inhibition of talents and of intellect; it also impedes the appreciation of other people's achievements and the enjoyment which could be derived from them. Lack of enjoyment in work and leisure and in contacts with other people leaves the personality barren and stirs up anxieties and dissatisfactions. Such anxieties, both of a persecutory and depressive nature, are—if excessive—a foundation for mental illness.

The fact that some people go through life fairly smoothly, particularly if they are successful, does not exclude their liability to mental illness if they have never come to terms with their deeper conflicts. These unsolved conflicts may make themselves felt in particular at certain critical phases, such as adolescence, middle age or old age, whereas people who are mentally healthy are much more likely to remain balanced at any stage of life and are less dependent on external success.

It is evident from my description that mental health is not compatible with shallowness. For shallowness is bound up with denial of inner conflict and of external difficulties. Denial is resorted to excessively because the ego is not strong enough to cope with pain. Although in some situations denial appears to be part of a normal personality, if it is predominant it leads to lack of depth because it prevents insight into one's inner life and therefore real understanding of others. One of the satisfactions lost is the ability to give and take —to experience gratitude and generosity.

The insecurity which underlies strong denial is also a cause oι lack of trust in ourselves because, unconsciously, insufficient insight results in parts of the personality remaining unknown. To escape from that insecurity there is a turning to the external world; however, if misfortune or failure in achievements and in relations to people should arise, such individuals are incapable of dealing with them.

By contrast, a person who can deeply experience sorrow when it arises is also able to share other people's grief and misfortune. At the same time, not to be overwhelmed by grief or by other people's unhappiness and to regain and maintain a balance is part of mental health. The first experience of sympathizing with other people's sorrows is in relation to those closest to the young child--parents and siblings. In adulthood parents who can understand their children's conflicts and share their occasional sadness have a deeper insight into the complexities of the child's inner life. This means that they are also able to share fully the child's pleasures and derive happiness from this close bond.

Some striving for external success is quite compatible with a strong character if it does not become the focus on which satisfaction in life rests. In my observation, if that is the main aim and the other attitudes which I have mentioned earlier are not developed, mental balance is insecure. External satisfactions do not make up for the lack of peace of mind. This can only come about if inner conflicts are reduced and therefore trust in oneself and in others has been established. If such peace of mind is lacking, the individual is liable to respond to any external reverses with strong feelings of being persecuted and deprived.

The description of mental health I have given shows its many-sided and complex nature. For, as I have tried to indicate, it is based on an interplay between the fundamental sources of mental life—the impulses of love and hate—an interplay in which the capacity for love is predominant.

In order to throw light on the origin of mental health, I shall give a short outline of the emotional life of the infant and young child. The young infant's good relation to the mother and to the food, love and care she provides is the basis for a stable emotional development. However, even at this early stage, and even under very favourable conditions, the conflict between love and hate (or, to put it in Freud's terms, between destructive impulses and libido) plays an important rôle in this relation. Frustrations, which to some extent are unavoidable, strengthen hate and aggressiveness. By frustration I do not only mean that the infant is not always fed when he wants to be; we find in analysis retrospectively that there are unconscious desires —not always perceptible in the behaviour of the infant—which focus on the continuous presence of the mother and her exclusive love. It is part of the emotional life of the infant that he is greedy and desires more than even the best external situation can fulfil. Together with destructive impulses the infant also experiences feelings of envy which reinforce his greed and interfere with his being able to enjoy the available satisfactions. Destructive feelings give rise to fear of retaliation and persecution, and this is the first form anxiety takes in the infant.

This struggle has the effect that in so far as the infant wants to preserve the loved aspects of the good mother, internal and external, he must continue to split love from hate and thus to maintain the division of the mother into a good one and a bad one. This enables him to derive a certain amount of security from his relation to the loved mother and therefore to develop his capacity for love. If splitting is not too deep, and integration and synthesis at a later stage are not impeded, this is a precondition for a good relation to the mother and for normal development.

I have mentioned persecutory feelings as the first form of anxiety. But feelings of a depressive nature also are sporadically experienced from the beginning of life. They gain in strength with the growth of the ego and increasing sense of reality and come to a head about the second half of the first year (depressive position). At that stage the infant experiences more fully depressive anxiety and a sense of guilt about his aggressive impulses towards his loved mother. Many problems which arise in young children with varying severity—such as disturbed sleep, difficulties over eating, inability to be contented by themselves, and constant demands for attention and the presence of the mother—are fundamentally an outcome of this conflict. At a later stage another outcome increases difficulties in adapting to the demands of upbringing.

Together with the more developed sense of guilt, a wish to make reparation is experienced, and this tendency brings relief to the infant because by pleasing his mother he feels that he undoes the harm which in his aggressive phantasies he is inflicting on her. The ability —however primitive in the very young child—to give effect to this urge forms one of the main factors in helping him to some extent to overcome his depression and guilt. If he cannot feel and express his wish for reparation, which would mean that his capacity for love is not strong enough, the infant may resort to increased splitting processes. As a result he may appear to be excessively good and submissive. But such splitting may impair gifts and talents because they are often repressed together with the painful feelings which underlie the child's conflicts. Thus not to be able as an infant to experience painful conflicts implies also losing a great deal in other ways, such as the development of interests and the capacity to appreciate people and to experience pleasures of various kinds.

In spite of all these internal and external difficulties, the young child normally finds a way of coping with his fundamental conflicts, and this allows him at other times to experience enjoyment and gratitude for happiness received. If he is lucky enough to have understanding parents, his problems can be diminished, and—on the other hand—a too strict or too lenient upbringing may increase them. The child's capacity to cope with his conflicts continues into adolescence and adulthood and is the foundation for mental health. Mental health is thus not only a product of the mature personality but in some way applies to every stage in the individual's development.

I have mentioned the importance of the child's background, but this is only one aspect of a very complex interplay between internal and external factors. By internal factors I mean that some children from the beginning have a greater capacity for love than others, which is bound up with a stronger ego, and that their phantasy life is richer and allows interests and gifts to develop. We may, therefore, find that children under favourable circumstances do not acquire the balance which I take to be the foundation for mental health, whereas sometimes children under unfavourable conditions are able to do so.

Certain attitudes which are prominent in the early stages continue in varying measure into adult life. It is only if they are sufficiently modified that mental health is possible. For instance, there is a feeling of omnipotence in the infant which makes both his hating and his loving impulses appear extremely powerful to him. Remnants of this attitude can easily be observed also in the adult, though normally the better adaptation to reality diminishes the feeling that what has been wished has taken effect.

Another factor in early development is denial of what is painful, and here again we are aware that in adult life this attitude has not entirely vanished. The urge to idealize both the self and the object is a result of the infant's need to split good from bad, both in himself and in his objects. There is a close correlation between the need to idealize and persecutory anxiety. Idealization has the effect of a reassurance, and in so far as this process remains operative in the adult, it still serves the purpose of counteracting persecutory anxieties. The fear of enemies and of hostile attacks is mitigated by increasing the power of goodness of other people.

The more all these attitudes have been modified in childhood and in adulthood, the greater will be mental balance. When judgement is not blurred by persecutory anxiety and idealization, a mature outlook is possible.

The attitudes I have enumerated, since they are never completely overcome, play a part in the manifold defences which the ego uses in order to combat anxiety. For instance, splitting is one way of preserving the good object and the good impulses against the dangerous and frightening destructive impulses which create retaliatory objects, and this mechanism is reinforced whenever anxiety is increased. I have also found in analysing young children how strongly they reinforce omnipotence when they are frightened Projection and introjection, which are fundamental processes, are other mechanisms which can be used defensively. The child feels himself to be bad and he attempts to escape from guilt by attributing his own badness to others, which means that he reinforces his persecutory

273

anxieties. A way in which introjection is used as a defence is to take into the self objects which one hopes will be a protection against the bad ones. A corollary of persecutory anxiety is idealization, for the greater the persecutory anxiety the stronger the need to idealize. The idealized mother thus becomes a help against the persecutory one. Some element of denial is bound up with all these defences because it is the means of coping with every frightening or painful situation.

The more the ego develops, the more intricate are the defences used and the better they dovetail, but they are less rigid. When insight is not stifled by defences, mental health is possible. A mentally healthy person can become aware of his need to see any unpleasant situation in a more pleasant light and can correct his tendency to embellish it. In this way he is less exposed to the painful experience of idealization breaking down and persecutory and depressive anxieties getting the upper hand, just as he is more able to cope with painful experiences derived from the external world.

One important element in mental health that I have so far not dealt with is the integration which finds expression in the welding together of the different parts of the self. The need for integration derives from the unconscious feeling that parts of the self are unknown, and there is a sense of impoverishment due to the self being deprived of some of its parts. The unconscious feeling that parts of the self are unknown increases the urge for integration. The need for integration, moreover, derives from the unconscious knowledge that hate can only be mitigated by love; and if the two are kept apart, this mitigation cannot succeed. In spite of this urge, integration always implies pain, because the split-off hate and its consequences are extremely painful to face; the incapacity to bear this pain re-awakens a tendency to split off the threatening and disturbing parts of impulses. In a normal person, in spite of these conflicts, a considerable amount of integration can take place, and when it is disturbed for external or internal reasons a normal person can find his way back to it. Integration also has the effect of tolerance towards one's own impulses and therefore also towards other people's defects. My experience has shown me that complete integration never exists, but the nearer he reaches towards it, the more will the individual have insight into his anxieties and impulses, the stronger will be his character, and the greater will be his mental balance.

# 15

# SOME REFLECTIONS ON
## 'THE ORESTEIA'
### (1963)

THE following discussion is based on Gilbert Murray's famous translation of the *Oresteia*. The main angle from which I intend to consider this trilogy is the variety of symbolic rôles in which the characters appear.

Let me first give a brief outline of the three plays. In the first, *Agamemnon*, the hero returns triumphant after the sack of Troy. He is received by Clytemnestra, his wife, with false praise and admiration, and she persuades him to walk into the house over a precious tapestry. There are some hints that she uses the same tapestry later to envelop Agamemnon in his bath and to make him helpless. She kills him with her battle-axe and appears before the Elders in a state of great triumph. She justifies her murder as a revenge for the sacrifice of Iphigenia. For Iphigenia had been killed on Agamemnon's command in order to make the winds favourable for the voyage to Troy.

Clytemnestra's revenge on Agamemnon, however, is not only caused by the grief for her child. She has, during his absence, taken his arch-enemy as her lover, and is therefore confronted with the fear of Agamemnon's revenge. It is clear that either Clytemnestra and her lover will be killed, or that she has to kill her husband. Over and above these motives, she gives the impression of deeply hating him, which appears clearly when she speaks to the Elders and voices her triumph about his death. These feelings are soon followed by depression. She restrains Aegisthus, who wants immediately to suppress the opposition among the Elders by violence, and begs him: 'let us not stain ourselves with blood'.

The next part of the trilogy, the *Cheophoroe*, deals with Orestes who had been sent away by his mother when he was a young child. He meets Electra by the funeral mound of their father. Electra, who burns with hostility against her mother, has come with the slave women sent by Clytemnestra after a very frightening dream to bring libations to Agamemnon's tomb. It is the leader of these libation bearers who suggests to Electra and Orestes that full revenge would imply killing Clytemnestra as well as Aegisthus. Her words confirm for Orestes the command given to him by the Delphic Oracle—a command which ultimately came from Apollo himself.

Orestes disguises himself as a travelling merchant, and accompanied by his friend Pylades, goes to the Palace, where, relying on not being recognized, he tells Clytemnestra that Orestes has died. Clytemnestra gives expression to grief. However, that she is not fully convinced is shown by her sending for Aegisthus with the message that he should come with his spearmen. The leader of the slave women suppresses this message; Aegisthus arrives alone and unarmed, and Orestes kills him. A slave informs Clytemnestra of Aegisthus' death, and she feels herself to be in danger and calls for her battle-axe. Orestes actually threatens to kill her; but instead of fighting him, she implores him to spare her life. She also warns him that the Erinnyes would punish him. In spite of her warnings, he kills his mother, and the Erinnyes at once appear to him.

Years have passed when the third play (the *Eumenides*) opens— years in which Orestes has been hunted by the Erinnyes and kept away from his home and from his father's throne. He tries to reach Delphi where he hopes to be pardoned. Apollo advises him to appeal to Athena, who represents justice and wisdom. Athena arranges for a tribunal to which she calls the wisest men of Athens, and before which Apollo, Orestes and the Erinnyes give evidence. The votes cast for and against Orestes are equal, and Athena, who has the casting vote, supports the pardon for Orestes. In the course of the proceedings, the Erinnyes maintain stubbornly that Orestes must be punished and that they are not going to give up their prey. However, Athena promises them that she will share with them her power over Athens and that they will remain the guardians of law and order for ever and as such will be honoured and loved. Her promises and arguments produce a change in the Erinnyes who become the Eumenides, the 'kindly ones'. They agree to Orestes being pardoned, and he returns to his native town to become his father's successor.

Before attempting to discuss those aspects of the *Oresteia* which are of particular interest to me, I wish to restate some of my findings about early development. In the analysis of young children, I discovered a ruthless and persecuting super-ego, co-existing with the relation to the loved and even idealized parents. Retrospectively I found that during the first three months, in which destructive impulses, projection and splitting are at their height, frightening and persecuting figures are part of the infant's emotional life. To begin with they represent the frightening aspects of the mother and threaten the infant with all evils which he in states of hate and rage directs against his primal object. Although these figures are counteracted by love towards the mother, they are nevertheless the cause of great anxieties.[1] From the beginning, introjection and projection are operative and are the basis for the internalization of the first and fundamental object, the mother's breast and the mother, both in her frightening and in her good aspects. It is this internalization which is the foundation of the super-ego. I tried to show that even the child who has a loving relation with his mother has also unconsciously a terror of being devoured, torn up and destroyed by her.[2] These anxieties, though modified by a growing sense of reality, go on to a greater or lesser extent throughout early childhood.

Persecutory anxieties of this nature are part of the paranoid-schizoid position which characterizes the first few months of life. It includes a certain amount of schizoid withdrawal; also strong destructive impulses (the projection of which creates persecutory objects) and a splitting of the mother figure into a very bad part and an idealized good one. There are many other processes of splitting, such as fragmentation and a strong impetus to relegate the terrifying figures into the deep layers of the unconscious.[3] Among the mechanisms at their height during this stage is the denial of all frightening situations; this is bound up with idealization. From the earliest stage onwards these processes are reinforced by repeated experiences of frustration, which can never be completely avoided.

It is part of the young infant's anxiety situation that the terrifying figures cannot be completely split off. Moreover, projection of hate and destructive impulses can succeed only up to a point, and the division between the loved and the hated mother cannot be fully maintained. Therefore the infant is unable to escape altogether from feelings of guilt, though in the early stages these are only evanescent.

All these processes are bound up with the infant's drive towards symbol formation and form part of his phantasy life. Under the impact of anxiety, frustration and his insufficient ability to express his emotions towards his loved objects, he is driven to transfer his emotions and anxieties on to the objects by which he is surrounded. This transfer occurs first of all to parts of his own body as well as parts of his mother's body.

The conflicts which the child experiences from birth are derived from the struggle between life and death instincts which express themselves in conflict between loving impulses and destructive ones. Both of them take on manifold forms and have many ramifications. Thus, for instance, resentment increases the feelings of deprivation

[1] My first descriptions of these anxieties are contained in my paper 'Early Stages of the Oedipus Conflict' (1928).

[2] I have dealt with this more fully and given instances of these anxieties in my *Psycho-Analysis of Children*.

[3] See my paper 'On the Development of Mental Functioning' (1958).

which are never missing in any infant's life. While the mother's capacity to feed is a source of admiration, envy of this capacity is a strong stimulus towards destructive impulses. It is inherent in envy that it aims at spoiling and destroying the mother's creativeness, on which at the same time the infant depends; and this dependence reinforces hate and envy. As soon as the relation to the father enters, there is admiration for the father's potency and power, which again leads to envy. Phantasies of reversing the early situation and triumphing over the parents are elements in the emotional life of the young infant. Sadistic impulses from oral and urethral and anal sources find expression in these hostile feelings directed against the parents, and in turn give rise to greater persecution and fear of retaliation by them.

I found that the frequent nightmares and phobias of young children derive from the terror of persecutory parents who by internalization form the basis of the relentless super-ego. It is a striking fact that children, in spite of love and affection on the part of the parents, produce threatening internalized figures; as I have already pointed out, I found the explanation for this phenomenon in the projection on to the parents of the child's own hate, increased by resentment about being in the parents' power. This view at one time seemed contradictory to Freud's concept of the super-ego as mainly due to the introjection of the punishing and restraining parents. Freud later on agreed with my concept that the child's hate and aggressiveness projected on to the parents plays an important part in the development of the super-ego.

I came in the course of my work to see more clearly that a corollary to the persecutory aspects of the internalized parents is their idealization. From the beginning, under the influence of the life instinct, the infant also introjects a good object, and the pressure of anxiety leads to the tendency to idealize this object. This has repercussion on the development of the super-ego. We are reminded here of Freud's (1928) view, expressed in his paper on 'Humour,' (*S.E.* **21**, p. 166) that the kind attitude of the parents enters into the child's super-ego.

When persecutory anxiety is still in the ascendant, early feelings of guilt and depression are to some extent experienced as persecution. Gradually, with increasing strength of the ego, greater integration and progress in the relation to whole objects, persecutory anxiety loses in power and depressive anxiety dominates. Greater integration implies that hate in some measure becomes mitigated by love, that the capacity for love gains in strength, and that the split between hated and therefore terrifying objects, and loved ones, diminishes. Evanescent feelings of guilt, linked with a feeling of incapacity to prevent destructive impulses from harming the loved objects, increase and become more poignant. I have described this stage as the depressive position, and my psycho-analytic experience with children and adults has confirmed my findings that to go through the depressive position results in very painful feelings. I cannot here discuss the manifold defences the stronger ego develops to deal with depression and guilt.

At this stage the super-ego makes itself felt as conscience; it forbids murderous and destructive tendencies and links with the child's need for guidance and some restraint by his actual parents. The super-ego is the basis for the moral law which is ubiquitous in humanity. However, even in normal adults, under strong internal and external pressure, the split-off impulses and the split-off dangerous and persecutory figures reappear temporarily and influence the super-ego. The anxieties then experienced approximate to the terrors of the infant, though in a different form.

The stronger the neurosis of the child, the less he is able to effect the transition to the depressive position, and its working through is impeded by a vacillation between persecutory and depressive anxiety. Throughout this early development a regression to the paranoid-schizoid stage may take place, whereas a stronger ego and a greater capacity to bear suffering results in a greater insight into his psychic reality and enables him to work through the depressive position. This does not mean, as I have pointed out, that at this stage he has no persecutory anxiety. In fact, persecutory anxiety, though depressive feelings dominate, is part of the depressive position.

The experiences of suffering, depression and guilt, linked with the greater love for the object, stir up the urge to make reparation. This urge diminishes the persecutory anxiety relating to the object and therefore makes it more trustworthy. All these changes, which express themselves in hopefulness, are bound up with the diminished harshness of the super-ego.

If the depressive position is being successfully worked through— not only during its climax in infancy but throughout childhood and in adulthood—the super-ego is mainly felt to be guiding and restraining the destructive impulses and some of its severity will have been mitigated. When the super-ego is not excessively harsh, the individual is supported and helped by its influence, for it strengthens the loving impulses and furthers the tendency towards reparation. A counterpart of this internal process is the encouragement by parents when the child shows more creative and constructive tendencies and his relation to his environment improves.

Before turning to the *Oresteia* and the conclusions I shall draw from it as far as mental life is concerned, I should like to deal with the Hellenic concept of *hubris*. In Gilbert Murray's definition, 'the typical sin which all things, so far as they have life, commit is in poetry *Hubris*, a word generally translated "insolence" or "pride". . . . Hubris grasps at more, bursts bounds and breaks the order; it is followed by *Dike*, Justice, which re-establishes them. This rhythm— *Hubris-Dike*, Pride and its fall, Sin and Chastisement—is the commonest burden of those philosophical lyrics which are characteristic of Greek tragedy. . . .'

In my view the reason why *hubris* appears to be so sinful is that it is based on certain emotions which are felt to be dangerous to others and to the self. One of the most important of these emotions is greed, first of all experienced in relation to the mother; it is accompanied by the expectation of being punished by the mother who has been exploited. Greed links with the concept of *moria*, expounded in the Introduction by Gilbert Murray. *Moira* represents the portion allotted to each man by the gods. When *moira* is overstepped, punishment by the gods follows. The fear of such punishment goes back to the fact that greed and envy are first of all experienced towards the mother who is felt to be injured by these emotions and who by projection turns in the child's mind into a greedy and resentful figure. She is therefore feared as a source of punishment, the prototype of God. Any overstepping of *moira* is also felt to be closely bound up with envy of the possessions of others; as a sequel, by projection, persecutory fear is aroused that others will envy and destroy one's own achievements or possessions.

> '. . . For not many men, the proverb saith,
> Can love a friend who fortune prospereth
> Unenvying; and about the envious brain
> Cold poison clings and doubles all the pain
> Life brings him. His own woundings he must nurse,
> And feels another's gladness like a curse.'

Triumph over everybody else, hate, the wish to destroy others, to humiliate them, the pleasure in their destruction because they have been envied, all these early emotions which are first experienced in connection with parents and siblings form part of *hubris*. Every child at times has some envy and wants to possess the attributes and capacities, first of all of the mother, and then of the father. Envy is primarily directed towards the mother's breast and the food she can produce, actually towards her creativeness. One of the effects of strong envy is the wish to reverse the situation, to make the parents helpless and infantile and to derive sadistic pleasure from this reversal. When the infant feels dominated by these hostile impulses and in his mind destroys the mother's goodness and love, he feels not only persecuted by her, but also guilty and bereft of good objects. One of the reasons why these phantasies have such an impact on emotional life is that they are experienced in an omnipotent way. In other words, in the infant's mind, they have taken effect, or might take effect, and he becomes responsible for all troubles or illness which befall his parents. This leads to a constant fear of loss which increases persecutory anxiety and underlies the fear of punishment for *hubris*.

Later on, competitiveness and ambition, which are components of *hubris*, may become deep causes of guilt, if envy and destructiveness predominate in them. This guilt may be overlaid by denial, but behind denial the reproaches which derive from the super-ego remain operative. I would suggest that the processes I have described are the reason why *hubris* is felt to be so strongly forbidden and punished according to Hellenic belief.

The infantile anxiety lest triumph over others and destruction of their capacities make them envious and dangerous has important consequences in later life. Some people deal with this anxiety by inhibiting their own gifts. Freud (1916) has described a type of individual who cannot bear success because it arouses guilt, and he connected this guilt in particular with the Oedipus complex. In my view, such people originally meant to outshine and destroy the mother's fertility. Some of these feelings are transferred to the father and to siblings, and later on to other people whose envy and hate are then feared; guilt in this connection may lead to strong inhibitions of talent and potentialities. There is a pertinent statement by Clytemnestra which sums up this fear: 'Who feareth envy, feareth to be great.'

I shall now substantiate my conclusions by some instances from the analysis of young children. When a child in his play expresses his rivalry with his father by making a small train move faster than a bigger one, or makes the small train attack the larger one, the sequel is often a feeling of persecution and guilt. In *Narrative of a Child Analysis*, I describe how every session for some time ended with what the boy called a 'disaster' and which consisted in all the toys being knocked over. Symbolically this meant to the child that he had been powerful enough to destroy his world. For a number of sessions there was usually one survivor—himself—and the sequel to the 'disaster' was a feeling of loneliness, anxiety and a longing for the return of his good object.

Another instance derives from the analysis of an adult. A patient who throughout life had restrained his ambition and his wish to be superior to other people, and therefore had been unable adequately to develop his gifts, dreamed of a flag-staff by which he stood, surrounded by children. He himself was the only adult. The children attempted in turn to climb to the top of the flag-staff but failed. He thought in the dream that if he were to try to climb but also failed that would amuse the children. Nevertheless, against his will, he achieved the feat and found himself on top.

This dream confirmed and strengthened his insight, derived from former material, that his ambition and competitiveness were much greater and more destructive than he had formerly allowed himself to know. He had in the dream contemptuously changed his parents, the analyst and all potential rivals into incompetent and helpless children. He alone was an adult. At the same time he attempted to prevent himself from having success because his success would mean hurting and humiliating people whom he also loved and respected and who would turn into envious and dangerous persecutors—the children who would be amused by his failure. However, as the dream showed, the attempt to inhibit his gifts failed. He reached the top and was afraid of the consequences.

In the *Oresteia*, Agamemnon displays *hubris* in full measure. He experiences no sympathy with the people of Troy whom he has destroyed, and seems to feel he had a right to destroy them. Only when speaking to Clytemnestra about Cassandra does he refer to the precept that the conqueror should have pity for the conquered. Since Cassandra, however, was obviously his lover, it is not only compassion that he is expressing but also the wish to preserve her for his own pleasure. Otherwise, it is clear that he is proud of the terrible destruction he has wrought. But the prolonged war which he waged has also meant suffering for the people of Argos, because many women have been widowed and many mothers mourn their sons; his own family suffered by being deserted for ten years. Thus ultimately some of the destruction of which he is so proud when he returns, damaged the people towards whom he can be assumed to have had some love. His destructiveness, involving those nearest to him, could be interpreted as being directed against his early loved objects. The ostensible reason for committing all those crimes was to avenge the insult against his brother to help him to regain Helen. It is made clear, however, by Aeschylus that Agamemnon was driven by ambition as well, and being acclaimed 'the King of Kings' satisfied his *hubris*.

Yet his successes not only satisfied his *hubris*; they increased it and led to a hardening and deterioration of his character. We learn that the Watchman was devoted to him, that the members of his household and the Elders loved him, and that his subjects were craving for his return. This would indicate that in the past he had been more humane than after his victories. Agamemnon reporting his triumphs and the destruction of Troy seems neither lovable nor able to love. I shall again quote Aeschylus.

'Sin lies that way.
For visibly Pride doth breed its own return
On prideful men, who, when their houses swell
With happy wealth, breathe ever wrath and blood.'

His unrestrained destructiveness and glorying in power and cruelty point in my view to a regression. At an early age the young child—in particular the boy—admires not only goodness but also power and cruelty, and attributes these qualities to the potent father with whom he identifies but whom at the same time he fears. In an adult, regression can revive this infantile attitude and diminish compassion.

Considering the excessive *hubris* which Agamemnon displays, Clytemnestra in a sense is the tool of justice, *dike*. In a very telling passage in the *Agamemnon* she describes to the Elders, before her husband arrives, her vision of the sufferings of the people of Troy, and does so with sympathy and without any expression of admiration for Agamemnon's achievements. In turn, at the moment when she has murdered him, *hubris* dominates her feelings and there are no signs of remorse. When she again speaks to the Elders, she is proud of the murder she has committed and triumphant about it. She supports Aegisthus in usurping Agamemnon's regal powers.

Agamemnon's *hubris* was thus followed by *dike* and in turn by Clytemnestra's *hubris*, which again was punished by *dike*, represented by Orestes.

I should like to put forward some suggestions about the change in Agamemnon's attitude towards his subjects and his family as a result of his successful campaigns. As I have mentioned earlier, his lack of sympathy with the sufferings his prolonged war has inflicted on the people of Troy is striking. Yet he is frightened of the gods and of the impending doom, and therefore only unwillingly agrees to enter the house treading on beautiful tapestries which Clytemnestra's maids had spread out for him. When he argues that one should be careful not to attract the wrath of the gods, he expresses only his persecutory anxiety and no guilt. Perhaps the regression which I mentioned earlier was possible because kindness and sympathy had never been sufficiently established as part of his character.

By contrast, Orestes is subject to feelings of guilt as soon as he has committed the murder of his mother. This is the reason why I believe that in the end Athena is able to help him. While he feels no guilt about his murder of Aegisthus, he is in severe conflict about killing his mother. His motives for doing so are duty and also love for his dead father with whom he is identified. There is very little to show that he wanted to triumph over his mother. This would indicate that *hubris* and its concomitants were not excessive in him. We know that it was partly Electra's influence and Apollo's command which led him to commit the murder of his mother. Immediately after he has killed her, remorse and horror of himself arise, symbolized by the Furies who at once attack him. The leader of the slave women, who very much encouraged the killing of his mother, and who cannot see the Furies, tries to comfort him by pointing out that he was justified in what he has done and that order has been restored. The fact that nobody but Orestes can see the Furies shows that this persecutory situation is an internal one.

As we know, in killing his mother, Orestes follows Apollo's command given at Delphi. This too can be considered as part of his internal situation. Apollo in one aspect here represents Orestes' own cruelty and vengeful urges, and thus we discover Orestes' feelings of destructiveness. However, the main elements which *hubris* includes, such as envy and the need to triumph, appear not to be dominant in him.

It is significant that Orestes sympathizes strongly with the neglected, unhappy and mournful Electra. For his own destructiveness had been stimulated by his resentment of his neglect by his mother. She had sent him away to strangers; in other words, she gave him too little love. The primary motive for Electra's hate is that apparently she had not been loved sufficiently by her mother and that her longing to be loved by her had been frustrated. Electra's hate against her mother—although intensified by the murder of Agamemnon—contains also the rivalry of the daughter with the mother, which focuses on not having had her sexual desires gratified by the father. These early disturbances of the girl's relation to her mother are an important factor in the development of her Oedipus complex.[1]

Another aspect of the Oedipus complex is shown by the hostility between Cassandra and Clytemnestra. Their direct rivalry concerning Agamemnon illustrates one feature of the daughter and mother relation—the rivalry between two women for the sexual gratification by the same man. Because Cassandra had been Agamemnon's lover, she could also feel like a daughter who had actually succeeded in taking away the father from the mother and therefore expects punishment from her. It is part of the Oedipus

---

[1] Cf. *The Psycho-Analysis of Children*, Chapter XI.

situation that the mother responds—or is felt to respond—with hatred to the oedipal desires of the daughter.

If we consider Apollo's attitude, there are indications that his complete obedience to Zeus is bound up with hatred of women and with his inverted Oedipus complex. The following passages are characteristic of his contempt for women's fertility:

'No nursling of the darkness of the womb,
But such a flower of life as goddess ne'er
Hath borne. . . .'          (speaking of Athena)

The mother to the child that men call hers
Is not true life-begetter, but a nurse
Of live seed. 'Tis the sower of the seed
Alone begetteth. . . .'

His hatred of women also enters into his command that Orestes should kill his mother, and into the persistence with which he persecutes Cassandra, whatever her failing towards him might have been. The fact that he is promiscuous is in no contradiction to his inverted Oedipus complex. By contrast, he praises Athena who has hardly any feminine attributes and is completely identified with her father. At the same time his admiration for the older sister may also indicate a positive attitude towards the mother figure. That is to say, some signs of the direct Oedipus complex are not altogether missing.

The good and helpful Athena has no mother, having been produced by Zeus. She shows no hostility towards women, but I would suggest that this lack of rivalry and hate has some connection with her having appropriated the father; he returns her devotion, for she has a particular position among all the gods and is known to be the favourite of Zeus. Her complete submission and devotion to Zeus can be considered as an expression of her Oedipus complex. Her apparent freedom from conflict may be explained by her having turned her whole love towards one object only.

Orestes' Oedipus complex can also be gathered from various passages in the Trilogy. He reproaches his mother for having neglected him and expresses his resentment against her. Nevertheless, there are hints that his relation to his mother was not entirely negative. The libations which Clytemnestra offers to Agamemnon are obviously valued by Orestes because he believes that they are reviving the father. When she tells him that she had nourished and loved him as a baby, he wavers in his decision to kill her and turns to his friend Pylades for advice. There are also indications of his jealousy which point at a positive Oedipus relation. Clytemnestra's grief about Aegisthus' death and her love for him rouse Orestes to fury. It is a frequent experience that the hate towards the father in the Oedipus situation can be deflected towards another person; for instance, Hamlet's hate for his uncle.[1] Orestes idealizes his father, and it is often easier to restrain rivalry and hate towards a dead father than towards a living one. His idealization of the greatness of Agamemnon—an idealization which Electra also experiences—leads him to deny that Agamemnon had sacrificed Iphigenia and showed utter ruthlessness towards the sufferings of the Trojans. In admiring Agamemnon, Orestes also identifies with the idealized father, and this is the way in which many a son overcomes his rivalry with the father's greatness and his envy of him. These attitudes, increased by his mother's neglect as well as by her murder of Agamemnon, form part of Orestes' inverted Oedipus complex.

I have mentioned above that Orestes was relatively free from *hubris* and, in spite of his identification with his father, more liable to a sense of guilt. His suffering following the murder of Clytemnestra represents, in my view, persecutory anxiety and the feelings of guilt which form part of the depressive position. The interpretation seems to suggest itself that Orestes was suffering from manic-depressive illness—Gilbert Murray calls him mad—because of his excessive feelings of guilt (represented by the Furies). On the other hand, we may assume that Aeschylus shows in a magnified form an aspect of normal development. For certain features which are the basis of manic-depressive illness are not strongly operative in Orestes. In my view he shows the mental state which I take to be characteristic of the transition between the paranoid-schizoid and the depressive position, a stage when guilt is essentially experienced as persecution. When the depressive position is reached and worked through— which is symbolized in the Trilogy by Orestes' changed demeanour at the Areopagus—guilt becomes predominant and persecution diminishes.

The play suggests to me that Orestes can overcome his persecutory anxieties and work through the depressive position because he never gives up the urge to cleanse himself of his crime and to return to his people whom presumably he wishes to govern in a benevolent way. These intentions point to the drive for reparation which is characteristic of the overcoming of the depressive position. His relation to Electra who stirs up his pity and love, the fact that he never gives up hopefulness in spite of suffering and his whole attitude towards the gods, in particular his gratitude towards Athena—all this suggests that his internalization of a good object was relatively stable and a basis for normal development had been laid. We can only

[1] Cf. Ernest Jones, *Hamlet and Oedipus* (1949).

guess that in the earliest stage these feelings entered in some way into the relation to his mother, because when Clytemnestra reminds him:

> 'My child, dost thou not fear
> To strike this breast? Hast thou not slumbered here,
> Thy gums draining the milk that I did give?'

Orestes lowers his sword and hesitates. The warmth which the nurse shows for him suggests love given and received in infancy. The nurse could have been a mother substitute; but up to a point this loving relation may have applied to the mother as well. Orestes' mental and physical suffering when being driven from place to place are a vivid picture of sufferings experienced when guilt and persecution are at their height. The furies who persecute him are the personification of bad conscience and make no allowance for the fact that he was commanded to commit the murder. I have suggested above that when Apollo gave that command he represented Orestes' own cruelty, and looking at it from this angle we understand why the Furies make no allowance for the fact that Apollo ordered him to commit the murder; for it is characteristic of a relentless super-ego that it will not forgive destructiveness.

The unforgiving nature of the super-ego, and the persecutory anxieties it arouses, find expression, I believe, in the Hellenic myth that the power of the Furies continues even after death. This is seen as a way of punishing the sinner and is an element common to most religions. In the *Eumenides* Athena says:

> '. . . Most potent hands
> Hath great Erinyes, in the lands
> Where dwell the deathless and the dead.'

The Furies also claim that

> 'Mine until death He wandereth,
> And freedom never more shall win,
> Not when dead. . . .'

Another point which is specific to the Hellenic beliefs is the need of the dead to be avenged if death has been violent. I would suggest that this demand for revenge derives from early persecutory anxieties which are increased by the child's death wishes against the parents and undermine his security and contentment. The attacking enemy thus becomes an embodiment of all the evils which the infant expects in retaliation for his destructive impulses.

I have dealt elsewhere[1] with the excessive fear of death in people

[1] 'On Identification' (1955b).

287

for whom death is a persecution by internal and external enemies as well as a threat of destruction to the good internalized object. If this fear is particularly intense, it may extend to terrors which threaten in after-life. In Hades revenge for the harm suffered preceding death is essential for peace after death. Orestes and Electra are both convinced that their dead father supports them in the task of revenge; and Orestes, in describing his conflict to the Areopagus, points out that Apollo foretold punishment for him if he did not avenge his father. Clytemnestra's ghost urging the Erinnyes to resume their pursuit of Orestes, complains of the contempt to which she is exposed in Hades because her murderer has not been punished. She is obviously moved by continuing hate against Orestes, and it could be concluded that hate continuing beyond the grave underlies the need for revenge after death. It may also be that the feeling attributed to the dead of being despised while their murderer remains unpunished derives from the suspicion that their descendants do not care enough for them.

Another reason why the dead call for revenge is hinted at in the Introduction where Gilbert Murray refers to the belief that Mother Earth is polluted by the blood which is split on her and that she and the Chtonian people (the dead) inside her call out for vengeance. I would interpret the Chtonian people as the unborn babies inside the mother whom the child feels he has destroyed in his jealous and hostile phantasies. Abundant material in psycho-analysis shows the deep feelings of guilt about a miscarriage which the mother had or the fact that she did not have another child after the individual's birth,[1] and the fears that this injured mother will retaliate.

Yet Gilbert Murray also speaks of Mother Earth as giving life and fruitfulness to the innocent. In that aspect, she represents the kind, feeding and loving mother. The splitting of the mother into a good and a bad one I have taken for many years to be one of the earliest processes in relation to her.

The Hellenic concept that the dead do not disappear but continue a kind of shadowy existence in Hades and exert an influence on those who are left alive recalls the belief in ghosts who are driven to persecute the living because they can find no peace until they are avenged. We may also link this belief of dead people influencing and controlling live ones, with the concept that they continue as internalized objects who are simultaneously felt to be dead and active within the self in good ways or in bad ways. The relation to the good internal object—in the first place the good mother—implies that it is felt to be helpful and guiding. It is particularly in grief and in the process of mourning that the individual struggles to preserve the good

[1] Cf. *Narrative of a Child Analysis* (1961).

relation which previously existed and to feel strength and comfort through this internal companionship. When mourning fails—and there may be many reasons for this—it is because this internalization cannot succeed and helpful identifications are interfered with. The appeal of Electra and Orestes for the dead father under the mound to support and strengthen them corresponds to the wish to be united with the good object who has been lost externally through death and has to be established internally. This good object whose help is implored, is part of the super-ego in its guiding and helping aspects. This good relation to the internalized object is the basis for an identification which proves of great importance for the stability of the individual.

The belief that libation can 'open the parched lips' of the dead, derives, I think, from the fundamental feeling that milk given by the mother to the baby is a means of keeping alive not only the baby but also his internal object. Since the internalized mother (first of all the breast) becomes part of the child's ego, and he senses that his life is bound up with her life, the milk, love, and care given by the external mother to the child are in one sense felt to benefit the internal mother as well. This also applies to other internalized objects. The libation given in the play by Clytemnestra is taken by Electra and Orestes to be a sign that by feeding the internalized father she revives him, in spite of her being a bad mother as well.

We find in psycho-analysis the feeling that the internal object participates in whatever pleasure the individual experiences. This is also a means of reviving a loved dead object. The phantasy that the dead internalized object, when it is loved, keeps a life of its own— helpful, comforting, guiding—is in keeping with the conviction of Orestes and Electra that they will be helped by the revived dead father.

I suggested that the unavenged dead stand for *internalized* dead objects and become threatening internalized figures. They complain about the harm which the subject in his hate has done to them. With ill people these terrifying figures form part of the super-ego and are closely linked with the belief in fate which drives to evil and then punishes the evildoer.

> 'Wer . . . . . . . . . . . . . . . .
> . . . . . . . . . . . . . . . . . . .
> Der kennt euch nich, ihr himmlischen Mächte!
>
> Ihr führt in's Leben uns hinein,
> Ihr lasst den Armen schuldig werden,
> Dann überlasst ihr ihn der Pein:
> Denn alle Schuld rächt sich auf Erden.'
>
> (Goethe, *Mignon*)

These persecuting figures are also personified in the Erinnyes. In early mental life, even normally, splitting never fully succeeds, and therefore the frightening internal objects remain up to a point operative. That is to say, the child experiences psychotic anxieties which vary individually in degree. According to the talion principle, based on projection, the child is tortured by the fear that what he in phantasy did to the parents is being done to him; and this may be an incentive towards reinforcing the cruel impulses. Because he feels persecuted internally and externally, he is driven to project the punishment outwards and in doing so tests by external reality his internal anxieties and fears of actual punishment. The more guilty and persecuted a child feels—that is to say, the more ill he is—the more aggressive he often may become. We have to believe that similar processes are operative in the delinquent or criminal.

Because the destructive impulses are primarily directed against the parents, the sin which is felt to be most fundamental is the murder of the parents. That is clearly expressed in the *Eumenides* when, following Athena's intervention, the Erinnyes describe the situation of chaos that would arise if they were no longer to act as a deterrent against the sins of matricide and patricide and punish them if they have taken place.

> 'Yea, for parents hereafter there is guile
> That waiteth and great anguish; by a knife
> In a child's hand their bosom shall be torn.'

I have said earlier that the cruel and destructive impulses of the infant create the primitive and terrifying super-ego. There are various hints about the way in which the Erinnyes carry out their attacks:

> 'Living, from every vein,
> Thine own blood, rich and red,
> For our parched mouths to drain,
> Till my righteous heart be fed
> With thy blood and thy bitter pain;
> Till I waste thee like the dead,
> And cast thee among the slain. . . .'[1]

The tortures with which the Erinnyes threaten Orestes are of the most primitive oral- and anal-sadistic nature. We are told that their breath is 'as a fire flung far and wide' and that from their bodies poisonous vapours emanate. Some of the earliest means of destruc-

---

[1] This description of sucking out the blood of the victim recalls Abraham's (1924) suggestion that in the oral sucking stage cruelty also enters; he spoke of 'vampire-like sucking'.

tion which in his mind the baby uses are attacks by flatus and faeces by which he feels he poisons his mother, as well as burning her with his urine—the fire. As a consequence the early super-ego threatens him with the same destruction. When the Erinnyes fear that their power will be taken away by Athena, they express their anger and apprehension in the following words: 'Shall not mine injury turn and crush this people? Shall not poison rain upon them, even the poison of this pain wherewith my heart doth burn?' This reminds us of the way in which the child's resentment about frustration, and the pain caused by it, increases his destructive impulses and drives him to intensify his aggressive phantasies.

The cruel Erinnyes, however, also link with that aspect of the super-ego which is based on complaining injured figures. We are told that they have blood dropping from their eyes and from their lips, which shows that they themselves are tortured. These internalized injured figures are felt by the infant to be revengeful and threatening and he tries to split them off. They nevertheless enter into his early anxieties and nightmares and play a part in all his phobias. Because Orestes has injured and killed his mother, she has become one of those injured objects whose revenge the child fears. He speaks of the Erinnyes as his mother's 'wrathful hounds'.

It would seem that Clytemnestra is not persecuted by the super-ego, for the Erinnyes do not pursue her. However, after her triumphant and elated speech following her killing of Agamemnon, she shows signs of depression and guilt. Hence her words, 'Let us not stain ourselves with blood.' She also experiences persecutory anxiety which clearly appears in her dream about the monster she feeds at her breast; it bites her so violently that blood and milk are mingled. As a result of the anxiety expressed by this dream she sends libations to the tomb of Agamemnon. Therefore, although she is not pursued by the Erinnyes, persecutory anxiety and guilt are not lacking.

Another aspect of the Erinnyes is that they cling to their own mother—the Night—as their only protector, and they repeatedly appeal to her against Apollo, the sun god, the enemy of the night, who wants to deprive them of their power and by whom they feel persecuted. From this angle we get an insight into the part which the inverted Oedipus complex plays even in the Erinnyes. I would suggest that the destructive impulses towards their mother are to some extent displaced on to the father—on to men in general—and that the idealization of the mother and their inverted Oedipus complex can only be maintained by this displacement. They are particularly concerned with any harm done to a mother, and seem to avenge matricide only. This is the reason why they do not persecute Clytemnestra who has murdered her husband. They argue that she did not kill a blood relation and therefore her crime was not important enough for them to persecute her. I think there is a great deal of denial in this argument. What is denied is that any murder derives ultimately from the destructive feelings against the parents and that no murder is permissible.

It is of interest that it is the influence of a woman—Athena—which brings about the change in the Erinnyes from relentless hate to milder feelings. However, they have had no father; or rather, Zeus, who might have stood for a father, had turned against them. They say that because of the terror which they spread 'and the world's hate that we bear, God has cast us from his Hall'. Apollo, full of contempt, tells them that they have never been kissed by man or god.

I suggest that their inverted Oedipus complex was increased by the absence of a father, or by his hating and neglecting them. Athena promises them that they will be loved and honoured by the Athenians, that is to say, by men as well as by women. The Areopagus, consisting of men, accompanies them to the place they will inhabit in Athens. My speculation would be that Athena, representing here the mother and now sharing with the daughters the love of men, i.e. of father figures, brings about a change in their feelings and impulses and in their whole character.

Taking the Trilogy as a whole, we find the super-ego represented by a variety of figures. For instance, Agamemnon, who is felt to be revived and supporting his children, is an aspect of the super-ego that is based on love and admiration for the father. The Erinnyes are described as belonging to the period of the old gods, the Titans who reigned in a barbarous and violent way. In my view they link with the earliest and most relentless super-ego and represent the terrifying figures which are predominantly the result of the child projecting his destructive phantasies on to his objects. They are however, counteracted—though in a split-off way—by the relation to the good object or the idealized one. I have already suggested that the relation of the mother to the child—and to a large extent the father's relation towards him—has an influence on the development of the super-ego because it affects the internalization of the parents. In Orestes the internalization of the father, which is based on admiration and on love, proves to be of greatest significance for his further actions; the dead father is a very important part of Orestes' super-ego.

When I first defined the concept of the depressive position, I suggested that the injured internalized objects complain and contribute thereby to guilt feelings and thus to the super-ego. According to views which I developed later on, such guilt feelings—though evanescent and not yet forming the depressive position—are in some measure operative during the paranoid-schizoid position. It can be observed that there are babies who refrain from biting the breast, who even wean themselves at an age of about four to five months for no external reasons, whereas others, by injuring the breast, make it impossible for the mother to feed them. Such restraint, I think, indicates that there is an unconscious awareness in the young baby of the desire to inflict harm on his mother by his greed. As a result the infant feels that the mother has been injured and emptied by his greedy sucking or biting and therefore in his mind he contains the mother or her breast in an injured state. There is much evidence, gained retrospectively in the psycho-analysis of children and even of adults, that the mother is very early on felt to be an injured object, internalized and external.[1] I would suggest that this complaining injured object is part of the super-ego.

The relation to this injured and loved object includes not only guilt but also compassion, and is the fundamental source of all sympathy with others and consideration for them. In the Trilogy this aspect of the super-ego is represented by the unhappy Cassandra. Agamemnon, who has wronged her and is delivering her into Clytemnestra's power, feels compassion and exhorts Clytemnestra to have pity on her. (It is the only occasion when he shows compassion.) Cassandra's part as the injured aspect of the super-ego links with the fact that she is a renowned prophetess whose main task is to issue warnings. The leader of the Elders is touched by her fate and tries to comfort her, at the same time standing in awe of her prophecies.

Cassandra as a super-ego, predicts ill to come and warns that punishment will follow and grief arise. She knows in advance both her own fate and the general disaster which will befall Agamemnon and his house; but nobody heeds her warnings, and this disbelief is attributed to Apollo's curse. The Elders, who are very sympathetic towards Cassandra, partly believe her; yet in spite of realizing the validity of the dangers she prophesizes for Agamemnon, for herself and for the people of Argos, they deny her prophesies. Their refusal to believe what at the same time they know expresses the universal tendency towards denial. Denial is a potent defence against the persecutory anxiety and guilt which result from destructive impulses never being completely controlled. Denial, which is always bound up with persecutory anxiety, may stifle feelings of love and guilt, undermine sympathy and consideration both with the internal and external objects, and disturb the capacity for judgement and the sense of reality.

[1] Cf. *The Psycho-Analysis of Children*, Chapter VIII.

As we know, denial is a ubiquitous mechanism and is also very much used for justification of destructiveness. Clytemnestra justifies her murder of her husband by the fact that he had killed their daughter, and denies that she has other motives for killing him. Agamemnon, who destroyed even the temples of the gods in Troy, feels justified in his cruelty by his brother's having lost his wife. Orestes has every reason, he feels, to kill not only the usurper Aegisthus but even his mother. The justification which I referred to is part of powerful denial of guilt and destructive impulses. People who have more insight into their inner processes and therefore use much less denial are less liable to give in to their destructive impulses; as a result they are more tolerant also towards others.

There is another interesting angle from which Cassandra's rôle as a super-ego can be considered. In the *Agamemnon* she is in a dream state and at first cannot collect herself. She overcomes that state and says clearly what she has been trying to convey previously in a confused way. We may assume that the unconscious part of the super-ego has become conscious, which is an essential step before it can be felt as conscience.

Another aspect of the super-ego is represented by Apollo who, as I suggested above, stands for Orestes' destructive impulses projected on to the super-ego. This aspect of the super-ego drives Orestes to violence and threatens to punish him if he does not kill his mother. Since Agamemnon would bitterly resent not being avenged, Apollo and the father both represent the cruel super-ego. This demand for revenge is in keeping with the relentlessness with which Agamemnon has destroyed Troy, showing no pity even for the sufferings of his own people. I have already referred to the connection between the hellenic belief that revenge is a duty laid on the descendants and the rôle of the super-ego as driving to crime. It is paradoxical that at the same time the super-ego treats revenge as a crime, and therefore the descendants are punished for the murder they committed though it was a duty.

The repeated sequence of crime and punishment, *hubris* and *dike*, is exemplified by the demon of the house, who, as we are told, lives on from generation to generation until he comes to rest when Orestes is forgiven and returns to Argos. The belief in the demon of the house springs from a vicious circle which is the consequence of hate, envy and resentment directed against the object; these emotions increase persecutory anxiety because the attacked object is felt to be retaliatory, and then further attacks on it are provoked. That is to say, destructiveness is increased by persecutory anxiety, and feelings of persecution are increased by destructiveness.

It is of interest that the demon, who since Pelops' time exerted a reign of terror in the royal house of Argos, comes to rest—so the legend goes—when Orestes has been forgiven and suffering no more, returns, as we may assume, to a normal and useful life. My interpretation would be that guilt and the urge to make reparation, the working through of the depressive position, breaks up the vicious circle because destructive impulses and their sequel of persecutory anxiety have diminished and the relation to the loved object has been re-established.

Apollo, however, who reigns at Delphi, represents in the Trilogy more than the destructive impulses and the cruel super-ego of Orestes. Through the priestess at Delphi he is also, as Gilbert Murray puts it 'god's prophet' as well as being the sun god. In the *Agamemnon* Cassandra refers to him as 'Light of the ways of men' and 'Light of all that is'. Nevertheless, not only his relentless attitude towards Cassandra but also the words used by the Elders about him, 'It is writ, He loves not grief nor lendeth ear to it,' point to the fact that he is not able to experience compassion and sympathy with suffering, in spite of his saying that he represents Zeus's thought. From this angle Apollo, the Sun God, reminds one of the people who turn away from any sadness as a defence against feelings of compassion, and make excessive use of denial of depressive feelings. It is typical of such people that they have no sympathy with the old and helpless ones. The leader of the Furies describes Apollo in the following words:

> 'Women are we, and old; and thou dost ride
> Above us, trampling, in thy youth and pride.'

These lines can also be considered from another point of view; if we look at their relation to Apollo, the Erinnyes appear as the old mother who is ill-treated by the young and ungrateful son. This lack of compassion links with the rôle of Apollo as the ruthless and unmitigated part of the super-ego, which I have described above.

There is another and very dominant aspect of the super-ego represented by Zeus. He is the father (the Father of the Gods) who has learnt through suffering to be more tolerant towards his children. We are told that Zeus, who had sinned against his own father and suffered guilt because of this, is therefore kind towards the supplicant. Zeus stands for an important part of the super-ego, the introjected mild father, and represents a stage in which the depressive position has been worked through. To have recognized and understood one's destructive tendencies directed against loved parents makes for greater tolerance towards oneself and towards deficiencies in others, for a better capacity for judgement and altogether greater wisdom.

As Aeschylus puts it,

> 'Man by suffering shall learn.
> So the heart of him, again
> Aching with remembered pain,
> Bleeds and sleepeth not, until
> Wisdom comes against his will.'

Zeus also symbolizes the ideal and omnipotent part of the self, the ego-ideal, a concept which Freud (1914) formulated before he fully developed his views on the super-ego. As I see it the idealized part of the self and of the internalized object is split off from the bad part of the self and from the bad part of the object, and the individual maintains this idealization in order to deal with his anxieties.

There is another aspect of the Trilogy which I wish to discuss, and that is the relation between internal and external happenings. I have described the Furies as symbolizing internal processes, and Aeschylus has shown this by the following lines:

> 'Times there be when Fear is good,
> And the Watcher in the breast
> Needs must reign in masterhood.'

In the Trilogy, however, the Furies appear as external figures.

The personality of Clytemnestra as a whole illustrates how Aeschylus—while penetrating deeply into the human mind—is also concerned with the characters as external figures. He gives us several hints that Clytemnestra was actually a bad mother. Orestes accuses her of lack of love, and we know that she banished her little son and ill-treated Electra. Clytemnestra is driven by her sexual desires towards Aegisthus and neglects her children. It is not said in so many words in the Trilogy, but it is obvious that Clytemnestra has got rid of Orestes because she saw in him the avenger of his father because of her relation to Aegisthus. In fact, when she doubts Orestes' story, she calls for Aegisthus to come with his spearmen. As soon as she learns that Aegisthus is killed she asks for her axe:

> 'No, there, mine axe of battle! Let us try
> Who conquereth and who falleth, he or I. . . .'

and threatens to kill Orestes.

There are, nevertheless, indications that Clytemnestra was not always a bad mother. She fed her son as a baby, and her mourning for her daughter Iphigenia might have been sincere. But altered external situations brought about a change in her character. I would conclude that early hate and grievances, stirred up by external situations, reawaken destructive impulses; they come to predominate

296

over loving ones, and this involves a change in the states of fusion between the life and death instincts.

The change from the Erinnyes to the Eumenides is also to some extent influenced by an external situation. They are very worried lest they lose their power and are reassured by Athena who tells them that in their modified rôle they will exert an influence over Athens and help to preserve law and order. Another instance of the effect of external situations is the change in the character of Agamemnon because he has become the 'King of Kings' through his successes in the expedition. Success, particularly if its greatest value lies in an increase in prestige, is—as we can see in life in general—often dangerous because it reinforces ambition and competitiveness and interferes with feelings of love and humility.

Athena represents, as she so often says—the thoughts and feelings of Zeus. She is the wise and mitigated super-ego in contrast to the early super-ego, symbolized by the Erinnyes.

We have seen Athena in many rôles; she is the mouthpiece of Zeus and expresses his thoughts and wishes; she is a mitigated super-ego; she is also the daughter without a mother and in this way avoids the Oedipus complex. But she also has another and very fundamental function; she makes for peace and balance. She expresses the hope that the Athenians will avoid internal strife, symbolically representing the avoidance of hostility within the family. She achieves a change in the Furies towards forgiveness and peacefulness. This attitude expresses the tendency towards reconciliation and integration.

These features are characteristic of the internalized good object—primarily the good mother—who becomes the carrier of the life instinct. In this way Athena as the good mother is contrasted with Clytemnestra who represents the bad aspect of the mother. This rôle enters also into Apollo's relation to her. She is the only woman figure he looks up to. He speaks of her with great admiration and fully submits to her judgement. Although she seems only to represent an older sister, particularly favoured by the father, I would suggest that she also represents to him the good aspect of the mother.

If the good object is sufficiently established in the infant, the super-ego becomes milder; the drive for integration, which I assume to work from the beginning of life, and which leads to hate becoming mitigated by love, gains in strength. But even the mild super-ego demands the control of destructive impulses and aims at a balance between destructive and loving feelings. We therefore find Athena representing a mature stage of the super-ego which aims at reconciliation between contrasting impulses; this is bound up with establishing the good object more securely and forms the basis for integration. Athena expresses the need to control destructive impulses in the following words:

> 'And casting away Fear, yet cast not all;
> For who that hath no fear is safe from sin?
> That Fear which is both Rule and Law within
> Be yours, and round your city. . . .'

Athena's attitude as guiding but not dominating, characteristic of the mature super-ego built round the good object, is shown in her not assuming the right to decide over the fate of Orestes. She calls together the Areopagus and chooses the wisest men of Athens, gives them all the full freedom to vote, and reserves for herself only the casting vote. If I consider this part of the Trilogy again as representing internal processes, I would conclude that the opposing votes show that the self is not easily united, that destructive impulses drive one way, love and the capacity for reparation and compassion in other ways. Internal peace is not easily established.

The integration of the ego is accomplished by the different parts of the ego—represented in the Trilogy by the members of the Areopagus—being able to come together in spite of their conflicting tendencies. This does not mean that they can ever become identical with each other, because destructive impulses on the one hand, and love and the need to make reparation on the other, are contradictory. But the ego at its best is capable of acknowledging these different aspects and bringing them closer together, whereas they had been strongly split off in infancy. Nor is the power of the super-ego eliminated; for even in its more mitigated form it can still produce feelings of guilt. Integration and balance are the basis of a fuller and richer life. In Aeschylus this state of mind is shown by the songs of joy with which the Trilogy ends.

Aeschylus presents to us a picture of human development from its roots to its most advanced levels. One of the ways in which his understanding of the depths of human nature is expressed are the various symbolic rôles which in particular the gods come to play. This variety corresponds to the diverse, often conflicting, impulses and phantasies which exist in the unconscious and which ultimately derive from the polarity of the life and death instincts in their changing states of fusion.

In order to understand the part which symbolism plays in mental life, we have to consider the many ways in which the growing ego deals with conflicts and frustration. The means of expressing feelings of resentment and satisfaction, and the whole gamut of infantile emotions, alter gradually. Since phantasies pervade mental life from the beginning, there is a powerful drive to attach them to various objects—real and phantasied—which become symbols and provide an outlet for the infant's emotions. These symbols first represent part-objects and within a few months whole objects (that is to say, people). The child puts his love and hate, his conflicts, his satisfactions and his longing into the creation of these symbols, internal and external, which become part of his world. The drive to create symbols is so strong because even the most loving mother cannot satisfy the infant's powerful emotional needs. In fact no reality situation can fulfil the often contradictory urges and wishes of the child's phantasy life. It is only if in childhood, symbol formation is able to develop in full strength and variety and is not impeded by inhibitions, that the artist later can make use of the emotional forces which underlie symbolism. In an early paper (1923b) I have discussed the pervading importance of symbol formation in infantile mental life and implied that if symbol formation is particularly rich, it contributes to the development of talent or even of genius.

In the analysis of adults we find that symbol formation is still operative; the adult, too, is surrounded by symbolic objects. At the same time, however, he is more able to differentiate between phantasy and reality and to see people and things in their own right.

The creative artist makes full use of symbols; and the more they serve to express the conflicts between love and hate, between destructiveness and reparation, between life and death instincts, the more they approach universal form. He thus condenses the variety of infantile symbols, while drawing on the full force of emotions and phantasies which are expressed in them. The dramatist's capacity to transfer some of these universal symbols into the creation of his characters, and at the same time to make them into real people, is one of the aspects of his greatness. The connection between symbols and artistic creation has often been discussed, but my main concern is to establish the link between the earliest infantile processes and the later productions of the artist.

Aeschylus in his Trilogy makes the gods appear in a variety of symbolic rôles and I have tried to show how this adds to the richness and meaning of his plays. I shall conclude with the tentative suggestion that the greatness of Aeschylus's tragedies—and this might have a general application as far as other great poets are concerned—derives from his intuitive understanding of the inexhaustible depth of the unconscious and the ways in which this understanding influences the characters and situations he creates.

# 16

# ON THE SENSE OF LONELINESS

## (1963)

In the present paper an attempt will be made to investigate the
source of the sense of loneliness. By the sense of loneliness I am referring not to the objective situation of being deprived of external
companionship. I am referring to the inner sense of loneliness—the
sense of being alone regardless of external circumstances, of feeling
lonely even when among friends or receiving love. This state of
internal loneliness, I will suggest, is the result of a ubiquitous
yearning for an unattainable perfect internal state. Such loneliness,
which is experienced to some extent by everyone, springs from
paranoid and depressive anxieties which are derivatives of the
infant's psychotic anxieties. These anxieties exist in some measure
in every individual but are excessively strong in illness; therefore
loneliness is also part of illness, both of a schizophrenic and depressive nature.

In order to understand how the sense of loneliness arises we have
—as with other attitudes and emotions—to go back to early infancy
and trace its influence on later stages of life. As I have frequently
described, the ego exists and operates from birth onwards. At first
it is largely lacking in cohesion and dominated by splitting mechanisms. The danger of being destroyed by the death instinct directed
against the self contributes to the splitting of impulses into good and
bad; owing to the projection of these impulses on to the primal
object, it too is split into good and bad. In consequence, in the
earliest stages, the good part of the ego and the good object are in
some measure protected, since aggression is directed away from
them. These are the particular splitting processes which I have
described as the basis of relative security in the very young infant,
in so far as security can be achieved at this stage; whereas other
splitting processes, such as those leading to fragmentation, are
detrimental to the ego and its strength.

Together with the urge to split there is from the beginning of life
a drive towards integration which increases with the growth of the
ego. This process of integration is based on the introjection of the
good object, primarily a part object—the mother's breast, although
other aspects of the mother also enter into even the earliest relation.

If the good internal object is established with relative security, it becomes the core of the developing ego.

A satisfactory early relation to the mother (not necessarily based on breast feeding since the bottle can also symbolically stand for the breast) implies a close contact between the unconscious of the mother and of the child. This is the foundation for the most complete experience of being understood and is essentially linked with the preverbal stage. However gratifying it is in later life to express thoughts and feelings to a congenial person, there remains an unsatisfied longing for an understanding without words—ultimately for the earliest relation with the mother. This longing contributes to the sense of loneliness and derives from the depressive feeling of an irretrievable loss.

Even at best, however, the happy relation with the mother and her breast is never undisturbed, since persecutory anxiety is bound to arise. Persecutory anxiety is at its height during the first three months of life—the period of the paranoid-schizoid position; it emerges from the beginning of life as the result of the conflict between the life and death instincts and the experience of birth contributes to it. Whenever destructive impulses arise strongly, the mother and her breast, owing to projection, are felt to be persecutory, and therefore the infant inevitably experiences some insecurity. This paranoid insecurity is one of the roots of loneliness.

When the depressive position arises—ordinarily in the middle of the first half of the first year of life—the ego is already more integrated. This is expressed in a stronger sense of wholeness so that the infant is better able to relate itself to the mother, and later to other people, as a whole person. Then paranoid anxiety, as a factor in loneliness, increasingly gives way to depressive anxiety. But the actual process of integration brings in its train new problems, and I shall discuss some of these and their relation to loneliness.

One of the factors which stimulates integration is that the splitting processes by which the early ego attempts to counteract insecurity are never more than temporarily effective and the ego is driven to attempt to come to terms with the destructive impulses. This drive contributes towards the need for integration. For integration, if it could be achieved, would have the effect of mitigating hate by love and in this way rendering destructive impulses less powerful. The ego would then feel safer not only about its own survival but also about the preservation of its good object. This is one of the reasons why lack of integration is extremely painful.

However, integration is difficult to accept. The coming together of destructive and loving impulses, and of the good and bad aspects of the object, arouses the anxiety that destructive feelings may overwhelm the loving feelings and endanger the good object. Thus, there is conflict between seeking integration as a safeguard against destructive impulses and fearing integration lest the destructive impulses endanger the good object and the good parts of the self. I have heard patients express the painfulness of integration in terms of feeling lonely and deserted, through being completely alone with what to them was a bad part of the self. And the process becomes all the more painful when a harsh super-ego has engendered a very strong repression of destructive impulses and tries to maintain it.

It is only step by step that integration can take place and the security achieved by it is liable to be disturbed under internal and external pressure; and this remains true throughout life. Full and permanent integration is never possible for some polarity between the life and death instincts always persists and remains the deepest source of conflict. Since full integration is never achieved, complete understanding and acceptance of one's own emotions, phantasies and anxieties is not possible and this continues as an important factor in loneliness. The longing to understand oneself is also bound up with the need to be understood by the internalized good object. One expression of this longing is the universal phantasy of having a twin—a phantasy to which Bion drew attention in an unpublished paper. This twin figure as he suggested, represents those un-understood and split off parts which the individual is longing to regain, in the hope of achieving wholeness and complete understanding; they are sometimes felt to be the ideal parts. At other times the twin also represents an entirely reliable, in fact, idealized internal object.

There is one further connection between loneliness and the problem of integration that needs consideration at this point. It is generally supposed that loneliness can derive from the conviction that there is no person or group to which one belongs. This not belonging can be seen to have a much deeper meaning. However much integration proceeds, it cannot do away with the feeling that certain components of the self are not available because they are split off and cannot be regained. Some of these split-off parts, as I shall discuss in more detail later, are projected into other people, contributing to the feeling that one is not in full possession of one's self, that one does not fully belong to oneself or, therefore, to anybody else. The lost parts too, are felt to be lonely.

I have already suggested that paranoid and depressive anxieties are never entirely overcome, even in people who are not ill, and are the foundation for some measure of loneliness. There are considerable individual differences in the way in which loneliness is experienced. When paranoid anxiety is relatively strong, though still within the range of normality, the relation to the internal good object is liable to be disturbed and trust in the good part of the self is impaired. As a consequence, there is an increased projection of paranoid feelings and suspicions on others, with a resulting sense of loneliness.

In actual schizophrenic illness these factors are necessarily present but much exacerbated; the lack of integration which I have so far been discussing within the normal range, is now seen in its pathological form—indeed, all the features of the paranoid-schizoid position are present to an excessive degree.

Before going on to discuss loneliness in the schizophrenic it is important to consider in more detail some of the processes of the paranoid-schizoid position, particularly splitting and projective identification. Projective identification is based on the splitting of the ego and the projection of parts of the self, into other people; first of all the mother or her breast. This projection derives from the oral–anal–urethral impulses, the parts of the self being omnipotently expelled in the bodily substances into the mother in order to control and take possession of her. She is not then felt to be a separate individual but an aspect of the self. If these excrements are expelled in hatred the mother is felt to be dangerous and hostile. But it is not only bad parts of the self that are split off and projected, but also good parts. Ordinarily, as I have discussed, as the ego develops, splitting and projection lessen and the ego becomes more integrated. If, however, the ego is very weak, which I consider to be an innate feature, and if there have been difficulties at birth and the beginning of life, the capacity to integrate—to bring together the split-off parts of the ego—is also weak, and there is in addition a greater tendency to split in order to avoid anxiety aroused by the destructive impulses directed against the self and external world. This incapacity to bear anxiety is thus of far-reaching importance. It not only increases the need to split the ego and object excessively, which can lead to a state of fragmentation, but also makes it impossible to work through the early anxieties.

In the schizophrenic we see the result of these unresolved processes. The schizophrenic feels that he is hopelessly in bits and that he will never be in possession of his self. The very fact that he is so fragmented results in his being unable to internalize his primal object (the mother) sufficiently as a good object and therefore in his lacking the foundation of stability; he cannot rely on an external and internal good object, nor can he rely on his own self. This factor is bound up with loneliness, for it increases the feeling of the schizophrenic that he is left alone, as it were, with his misery. The sense of being surrounded by a hostile world, which is characteristic of the paranoid aspect of schizophrenic illness, not only increases all his anxieties but vitally influences his feelings of loneliness.

Another factor which contributes to the loneliness of the schizophrenic is confusion. This is the result of a number of factors, particularly the fragmentation of the ego, and the excessive use of projective identification, so that he constantly feels himself not only to be in bits, but to be mixed up with other people. He is then unable to distinguish between the good and bad parts of the self, between the good and bad object, and between external and internal reality. The schizophrenic thus, cannot understand himself or trust himself. These factors allied with his paranoid distrust of others, result in a state of withdrawal which destroys his ability to make object relations and to gain from them the reassurance and pleasure which can counteract loneliness by strengthening the ego. He longs to be able to make relationships with people, but cannot.

It is important not to underrate the schizophrenic's pain and suffering. They are not so easily detected because of his constant defensive use of withdrawal and the distraction of his emotions. Nevertheless, I and some of my colleagues, of whom I shall only mention Dr Davidson, Dr Rosenfeld and Dr Hanna Segal, who have treated or are treating schizophrenics, retain some optimism about the outcome. This optimism is based on the fact that there is an urge towards integration, even in such ill people, and that there is a relation, however undeveloped, to the good object and the good self.

I now wish to deal with the loneliness characteristic of a prevalence of depressive anxiety, first of all within the range of normality. I have often referred to the fact that early emotional life is characterized by the recurrent experiences of losing and regaining. Whenever the mother is not present, she may be felt by the infant to be lost, either because she is injured or because she has turned into a persecutor. The feeling that she is lost is equivalent to the fear of her death. Owing to introjection, the death of the external mother means the loss of the internal good object as well, and this reinforces the infant's fear of his own death. These anxieties and emotions are heightened at the stage of the depressive position, but throughout life the fear of death plays a part in loneliness.

I have already suggested that the pain which accompanies processes of integration also contributes to loneliness. For it means facing one's destructive impulses and hated parts of the self, which at times appear uncontrollable and which therefore endanger the good object. With integration and a growing sense of reality, omnipotence is bound to be lessened, and this again contributes to the pain of integration, for it means a diminished capacity for hope.

While there are other sources of hopefulness which derive from the strength of the ego and from trust in oneself and others, an element of omnipotence is always part of it.

Integration also means losing some of the idealization—both of the object and of a part of the self—which has from the beginning coloured the relation to the good object. The realization that the good object can never approximate to the perfection expected from the ideal one brings about de-idealization: and even more painful is the realization that no really ideal part of the self exists. In my experience, the need for idealization is never fully given up, even though in normal development the facing of internal and external reality tends to diminish it. As a patient put it to me, while admitting the relief obtained from some steps in integration, 'the glamour has gone'. The analysis showed that the glamour which had gone was the idealization of the self and of the object, and the loss of it led to feelings of loneliness.

Some of these factors enter in a greater degree into the mental processes characteristic of manic-depressive illness. The manic-depressive patient has already made some steps towards the depressive position, that is to say, he experiences the object more as a whole, and his feelings of guilt, though still bound up with paranoid mechanisms, are stronger and less evanescent. More, therefore, than the schizophrenic, he feels the longing to have the good object safely inside to preserve it and protect it. But this he feels unable to do since, at the same time, he has not sufficiently worked through the depressive position, so that his capacity for making reparation, for synthesizing the good object, and achieving integration of the ego, have not sufficiently progressed. In so far as, in his relation to his good object, there is still a great deal of hatred and, therefore, fear, he is unable sufficiently to make reparation to it, therefore his relation to it brings no relief but only a feeling of being unloved, and hated, and again and again he feels that it is endangered by his destructive impulses. The longing to be able to overcome all these difficulties in relation to the good object is part of the feeling of loneliness. In extreme cases this expresses itself in the tendency towards suicide.

In external relations similar processes are at work. The manic-depressive can only at times, and very temporarily, get relief from a relation with a well-meaning person, since, as he quickly projects his own hate, resentment, envy and fear, he is constantly full of distrust. In other words, his paranoid anxieties are still very strong. The feeling of loneliness of the manic-depressive centres, therefore, more on his incapacity to keep an inner and external companionship with a good object and less on his being in bits.

I shall discuss some further difficulties in integration and shall deal particularly with the conflict between male and female elements in both sexes. We know that there is a biological factor in bi-sexuality, but I am concerned here with the psychological aspect. In women there is universally the wish to be a man, expressed perhaps most clearly in terms of penis envy; similarly, one finds in men the feminine position, the longing to possess breasts and to give birth to children. Such wishes are bound up with an identification with both parents and are accompanied by feelings of competitiveness and envy, as well as admiration of the coveted possessions. These identifications vary in strength and also in quality, depending on whether admiration or envy is the more prevalent. Part of the desire for integration in the young child is the urge to integrate these different aspects of the personality. In addition, the super-ego makes the conflicting demand for identification with both parents, prompted by the need to make reparation for early desires to rob each of them and expressing the wish to keep them alive internally. If the element of guilt is predominant it will hamper the integration of these identifications. If, however, these identifications are satisfactorily achieved they become a source of enrichment and a basis for the development of a variety of gifts and capacities.

In order to illustrate the difficulties of this particular aspect of integration and its relation to loneliness, I shall quote the dream of a male patient. A little girl was playing with a lioness and holding out a hoop for her to jump through, but on the other side of the hoop was a precipice. The lioness obeyed and was killed in the process. At the same time, a little boy was killing a snake. The patient himself recognized, since similar material had come up previously, that the little girl stood for his feminine part and the little boy for his masculine part. The lioness had a strong link with myself in the transference, of which I shall only give one instance. The little girl had a cat with her and this led to associations to my cat, which often stood for me. It was extremely painful to the patient to become aware that, being in competition with my femininity, he wanted to destroy me, and in the past, his mother. This recognition that one part of himself wanted to kill the loved lioness–analyst, which would thus deprive him of his good object, led to a feeling not only of misery and guilt but also of loneliness in the transference. It was also very distressing for him to recognize that the competition with his father led him to destroy the father's potency and penis, represented by the snake.

This material led to further and very painful work about integration. The dream of the lioness which I have mentioned was preceded by a dream in which a woman committed suicide by throwing herself from a very high building, and the patient, contrary to his usual attitude, experienced no horror. The analysis which was, at that time, very much occupied with his difficulty over the feminine position, which was then at its height, showed that the woman represented his feminine part and that he really wished it to be destroyed. He felt that not only would it injure his relation to women, but would also damage his masculinity and all its constructive tendencies, including reparation to the mother, which became clear in relation to myself. This attitude of putting all his envy and competitiveness into his feminine part turned out to be one way of splitting, and at the same time seemed to overshadow his very great admiration and regard for femininity. Moreover, it became clear that while he felt masculine aggression to be comparatively open and, therefore, more honest, he attributed to the feminine side envy and deception, and since he very much loathed all insincerity and dishonesty, this contributed to his difficulties in integration.

The analysis of these attitudes, going back to his earliest feelings of envy towards the mother led to a much better integration of both the feminine and masculine parts of his personality and to the diminution of envy in both the masculine and feminine rôle. This increased his competence in his relationships and thus helped to combat a sense of loneliness.

I shall now give another instance, from the analysis of a patient, a man who was not unhappy or ill, and who was successful in his work and in his relationships. He was aware that he had always felt lonely as a child and that this feeling of loneliness had never entirely gone. Love of nature had been a significant feature in this patient's sublimations. Even from earliest childhood he found comfort and satisfaction in being out of doors. In one session he described his enjoyment of a journey which led him through hilly country and then the revulsion he felt when he entered the town. I interpreted as I had done previously, that to him nature represented not only beauty, but also goodness, actually the good object that he had taken into himself. He replied after a pause that he felt that was true, but that nature was not only good because there is always much aggression in it. In the same way, he added, his own relation to the countryside was also not wholly good, instancing how as a boy, he used to rob nests, while at the same time he had always wanted to grow things. He said that in loving nature he had actually, as he put it, 'taken in an integrated object'.

In order to understand how the patient had overcome his loneliness in relation to the countryside, while still experiencing it in connection with the town, we have to follow up some of his associations referring both to his childhood and to nature. He had told me that he was supposed to have been a happy baby, well fed by his mother; and much material—particularly in the transference situation—supported this assumption. He had soon become aware of his worries about his mother's health, and also his resentment about her rather disciplinarian attitude. In spite of this his relation to her was in many ways happy, and he remained fond of her; but he felt himself hemmed in at home and was aware of an urgent longing to be out of doors. He seemed to have developed a very early admiration for the beauties of nature; and as soon as he could get more freedom to be out of doors, this became his greatest pleasure. He described how he, together with other boys, used to spend his free time wandering in the woods and fields. He confessed to some aggression in connection with nature, such as robbing nests and damaging hedges. At the same time he was convinced that such damage would not be lasting because nature always repaired itself. Nature he regarded as rich and invulnerable, in striking contrast to his attitude towards his mother. The relation to nature seemed to be relatively free from guilt, whereas in his relation to his mother for whose frailty he felt responsible for unconscious reasons, there was a great deal of guilt.

From his material I was able to conclude that he had to some extent introjected the mother as a good object and had been able to achieve a measure of synthesis between his loving and hostile feelings towards her. He also reached a fair level of integration but this was disturbed by persecutory and depressive anxiety in relation to his parents. The relation to the father had been very important for his development, but it does not enter into this particular piece of material.

I have referred to this patient's obsessional need to be out of doors, and this was linked with his claustrophobia. Claustrophobia, as I have elsewhere suggested, derives from two main sources: projective identification into the mother leading to an anxiety of imprisonment inside her; and reintrojection resulting in a feeling that inside oneself one is hemmed in by resentful internal objects. With regard to this patient, I would conclude that his flight into nature was a defence against both these anxiety-situations. In a sense his love for nature was split off from his relation to his mother; his de-idealization of the latter having led to his transferring his idealization on to nature. In connection with home and mother he felt very lonely, and it was this sense of loneliness which was at the root of his revulsion against town. The freedom and enjoyment which nature gave him were not only a source of pleasure, derived from a strong sense of beauty and linked with appreciation of art, but also a means of counteracting the fundamental loneliness which had never entirely gone.

In another session the patient reported a feeling of guilt that on a trip into the country he had caught a field-mouse and put it in a box in the boot of his car, as a present for his young child who, he thought, would enjoy having this creature as a pet. The patient forgot about the mouse, remembering it only a day later. He made unsuccessful efforts to find it because it had eaten its way out of the box and hidden itself in the farthest corner of the boot where it was out of reach. Eventually, after renewed efforts to get hold of it, he found that it had died. The patient's guilt about having forgotten the field-mouse and thus caused its death led in the course of subsequent sessions to associations about dead people for whose death he felt to some extent responsible though not for rational reasons.

In the subsequent sessions there was a wealth of associations to the field-mouse which appeared to play a number of rôles; it stood for a split-off part of himself, lonely and deprived. By identification with his child he moreover felt deprived of a potential companion. A number of associations showed that throughout childhood the patient had longed for a playmate of his own age—a longing that went beyond the actual need for external companions and was the result of feeling that split-off parts of his self could not be regained. The field-mouse also stood for his good object, which he had enclosed in his inside—represented by the car—and about which he felt guilty and also feared that it might turn retaliatory. One of his other associations, referring to neglect, was that the field-mouse also stood for a neglected woman. This association came after a holiday and implied that not only had he been left alone by the analyst but that the analyst had been neglected and lonely. The link with similar feelings towards his mother became clear in the material, as did the conclusion that he contained a dead or lonely object, which increased his loneliness.

This patient's material supports my contention that there is a link between loneliness and the incapacity sufficiently to integrate the good object as well as parts of the self which are felt to be inaccessible.

I shall now go on to examine more closely the factors which normally mitigate loneliness. The relatively secure internalization of the good breast is characteristic of some innate strength of the ego. A strong ego is less liable to fragmentation and therefore more capable of achieving a measure of integration and a good early relation to the primal object. Further, a successful internalization of the good object is the root of an identification with it which strengthens the feeling of goodness and trust both in the object and in the self. This identification with the good object mitigates the destructive impulses and in this way also diminishes the harshness of the super-ego. A milder super-ego makes less stringent demands on the ego; this leads to tolerance and to the ability to bear deficiencies in loved objects without impairing the relation to them,

A decrease in omnipotence, which comes about with progress in integration and leads to some loss of hopefulness, yet makes possible a distinction between the destructive impulses and their effects; therefore aggressiveness and hate are felt to be less dangerous. This greater adaptation to reality leads to an acceptance of one's own shortcomings and in consequence lessens the sense of resentment about past frustrations. It also opens up sources of enjoyment emanating from the external world and is thus another factor which diminishes loneliness.

A happy relation to the first object and a successful internalization of it means that love can be given and received. As a result the infant can experience enjoyment not only at times of feeding but also in response to the mother's presence and affection. Memories of such happy experiences are a stand-by for the young child when he feels frustrated, because they are bound up with the hope of further happy times. Moreover, there is a close link between enjoyment and the feeling of understanding and being understood. At the moment of enjoyment anxiety is assuaged and the closeness to the mother and trust in her are uppermost. Introjective and projective identification, when not excessive, play an important part in this feeling of closeness, for they underlie the capacity to understand and contribute to the experience of being understood.

Enjoyment is always bound up with gratitude; if this gratitude is deeply felt it includes the wish to return goodness received and is thus the basis of generosity. There is always a close connection between being able to accept and to give, and both are part of the relation to the good object and therefore counteract loneliness. Furthermore, the feeling of generosity underlies creativeness, and this applies to the infant's most primitive constructive activities as well as to the creativeness of the adult.

The capacity for enjoyment is also the precondition for a measure of resignation which allows for pleasure in what is available without too much greed for inaccessible gratifications and without excessive resentment about frustration. Such adaptation can already be observed in some young infants. Resignation is bound up with tolerance and with the feeling that destructive impulses will not overwhelm love, and that therefore goodness and life may be preserved.

A child who, in spite of some envy and jealousy, can identify himself with the pleasures and gratifications of members of his family circle, will be able to do so in relation to other people in later life.

In old age he will then be able to reverse the early situation and identify himself with the satisfactions of youth. This is only possible if there is gratitude for past pleasures without too much resentment because they are no longer available.

All the factors in development which I have touched upon, though they mitigate the sense of loneliness, never entirely eliminate it; therefore they are liable to be used as defences. When these defences are very powerful and dovetail successfully, loneliness may often not be consciously experienced. Some infants use extreme dependence on the mother as a defence against loneliness, and the need for dependence remains as a pattern throughout life. On the other hand, the flight to the internal object, which can be expressed in early infancy in hallucinatory gratification, is often used defensively in an attempt to counteract dependence on the external object. In some adults this attitude leads to a rejection of any companionship, which in extreme cases is a symptom of illness.

The urge towards independence, which is part of maturation, can be used defensively for the purpose of overcoming loneliness. A lessening of dependence on the object makes the individual less vulnerable and also counteracts the need for excessive internal and external closeness to loved people.

Another defence, particularly in old age, is the preoccupation with the past in order to avoid the frustrations of the present. Some idealization of the past is bound to enter into these memories and is put into the service of defence. In young people, idealization of the future serves a similar purpose. Some measure of idealization of people and causes is a normal defence and is part of the search for idealized inner objects which is projected on to the external world.

Appreciation by others and success—originally the infantile need to be appreciated by the mother—can be used defensively against loneliness. But this method becomes very insecure if it is used excessively since trust in oneself is then not sufficiently established. Another defence, bound up with omnipotence and part of manic defence, is a particular use of the capacity to wait for what is desired; this may lead to over-optimism and a lack of drive and may be linked with a defective sense of reality.

The denial of loneliness, which is frequently used as a defence, is likely to interfere with good object relations, in contrast to an attitude in which loneliness is actually experienced and becomes a stimulus towards object relations.

Finally, I want to indicate why it is so difficult to evaluate the balance between internal and external influences in the causation of loneliness. I have so far in this paper dealt mainly with internal aspects—but these do not exist *in vacuo*. There is a constant interaction between internal and external factors in mental life, based on the processes of projection and introjection which initiate object relations.

The first powerful impact of the external world on the young infant is the discomfort of various kinds which accompanies birth and which is attributed by him to hostile persecutory forces. These paranoid anxieties become part of his internal situation. Internal factors also operate from the beginning; the conflict between life and death instincts engenders the deflection of the death instinct outwards and this, according to Freud, initiates the projection of destructive impulses. I hold, however, that at the same time the urge of the life instinct to find a good object in the external world leads to the projection of loving impulses as well. In this way the picture of the external world—represented first by the mother, and particularly by her breast, and based on actual good and bad experiences in relation to her—is coloured by internal factors. By introjection this picture of the external world affects the internal one. However, it is not only that the infant's feelings about the external world are coloured by his projection, but the mother's actual relation to her child is in indirect and subtle ways, influenced by the infant's response to her. A contented baby who sucks with enjoyment, allays his mother's anxiety; and her happiness expresses itself in her way of handling and feeding him, thus diminishing his persecutory anxiety and affecting his ability to internalize the good breast. In constrast, a child who has difficulties over feeding may arouse the mother's anxiety and guilt and thus unfavourably influence her relation to him. In these varying ways there is constant interaction between the internal and external world persisting throughout life.

The interplay of external and internal factors has an important bearing on increasing or diminishing loneliness. The internalization of a good breast which can only result from a favourable interplay between internal and external elements, is a foundation for integration which I have mentioned as one of the most important factors in diminishing the sense of loneliness. In addition, it is well recognized that in normal development, when feelings of loneliness are strongly experienced there is a great need to turn to external objects, since loneliness is partially allayed by external relations. External influences, particularly the attitude of people important to the individual, can in other ways, diminish loneliness. For example, a fundamentally good relation to the parents makes the loss of idealization and the lessening of the feeling of omnipotence more bearable. The parents, by accepting the existence of the child's destructive impulses and showing that they can protect themselves against his aggressiveness, can diminish his anxiety about the effects of his hostile wishes. As a result, the internal object is felt to be less vulnerable and the self less destructive.

I can here only touch on the importance of the super-ego in connection with all these processes. A harsh super-ego can never be felt to forgive destructive impulses; in fact, it demands that they should not exist. Although the super-ego is built up largely from a split-off part of the ego on to which impulses are projected, it is also inevitably influenced by the introjection of the personalities of the actual parents and of their relation to the child. The harsher the super-ego, the greater will be loneliness, because its severe demands increase depressive and paranoid anxieties.

In conclusion I wish to restate my hypothesis that although loneliness can be diminished or increased by external influences, it can never be completely eliminated, because the urge towards integration, as well as the pain experienced in the process of integration, spring from internal sources which remain powerful throughout life.

# SHORT CONTRIBUTIONS

## The Importance of Words in Early Analysis (1927)

I pointed out in my papers and lectures that the child differs in its mode of expression from the adult by the fact that it acts and dramatizes its thoughts and phantasies. But that does not mean that the word is not of great importance in so far as the child commands it. I will give an example. A little boy of five with very great repression about his phantasies has already gone through a certain part of analysis. He has brought forward a lot of material mostly through play, but he shows the tendency not to realize this. One morning he asked me to play shop and that I should be the one who sells. Now I used a technical measure which is important for the small child who is often not prepared to tell his associations. I asked him who I should be, a lady or a gentleman, as he would have to speak my name on coming into the shop. He told me I was to be 'Mr Cookey-Caker', and we found very soon that he meant someone who cooks cakes. I had to sell engines, which represented for him the new penis. He called himself 'Mr Kicker', which he quickly realized as kicking somebody. I asked him where Mr Cookey-Caker had gone. He answered: 'He has gone away somewhere.' He soon realized that Mr Cookey-Caker had been killed by his kicking him. 'Cooking cakes' represented for him making children in an oral and anal way. He realized after this interpretation his aggression against his father and this phantasy opened the way to others in which the person he was fighting against was always Mr Cookey-Caker. The word 'Cookey-Caker' is the bridge to reality which the child avoids as long as he brings forth his phantasies only by playing. It always means progress when the child has to acknowledge the reality of the objects through his own words.

# Note on 'A Dream of Forensic Interest' (1928)

IN order to support my remarks on the dream communicated by Dr Bryan I must refer to certain theoretical propositions which I brought forward in my paper for the last Congress,[1] and which I accounted for in greater detail in the lectures which I delivered here last autumn. In one of the early stages of the Oedipus conflict the desire to have intercourse with the mother and to engage in a contest with the father expresses itself in terms of the oral- and anal-sadistic instinctual impulses, which are predominant in this phase of development. The idea is that the boy, by penetrating the mother's womb, destroys it and gets rid of the father's penis which, according to a typical infantile sexual theory, is assumed to be permanently present in the womb (the father's penis at this stage being the complete embodiment of the father), and the way he destroys it is by devouring it. Mingling with this tendency, and yet recognizable as one distinct in itself, is another tendency, whose aim is the same, namely, to destroy the mother's womb and to devour the penis, but whose basis is an oral- and anal-sadistic identification with the mother. From this proceeds the boy's desire to rob the mother's body of faeces, children and the father's penis. The anxiety which ensues on this level is extraordinarily acute, for it has reference to the union of father and mother, represented by the womb and the father's penis, and I pointed out that this anxiety is the essential foundation of severe mental diseases.

From the analyses of little children I have learnt that the dread of the woman with the penis (which has so marked an influence in disturbances of potency in the male) is really dread of the mother, whose body is assumed always to contain the father's penis. The dread of the father (or of his penis), who is thus located within the mother, is here displaced on to dread of the mother herself. By this displacement the anxiety which really has reference to her and which proceeds from the destructive tendencies directed against her body receives an overwhelming reinforcement.

In the exceedingly interesting case reported by Dr Bryan this anxiety finds clear expression. The mother who in the dream overpowers the patient demands back the money which he has stolen from her, and the fact that it was only from women that he took money shows plainly the compulsion to steal the contents of the womb. Of special significance, too, is the use to which he put the stolen money. It seems evident that the patient took the money for

[1] 'Early Stages of the Oedipus Conflict', *Writings*, I.

315

the purpose of throwing it down the lavatory pan, and the obsessional nature of this behaviour is to be explained by his anxiety to make reparation, to restore to the mother (or the womb), represented by the lavatory-pan, that which he had stolen.

One of my female patients, whose grave neurosis proved to be due to her anxiety lest her own body should be destroyed by her mother, had the following dream: 'She was in a bathroom, and hearing steps, she threw the contents of a basket (representing, as we discovered, faeces, children and the penis) quickly into the lavatory pan. She succeeded in getting the pan flushed before her mother came in. Her mother had injured her anus and she was helping her with dressing the wound'. In this case the destructive impulses against the mother had mainly found expression in phantasy in the form of injury done to the anus.

Not only, then, were the thefts of the money a repetition of the early anal-sadistic desires to rob the mother, but they were also brought about by the compulsion, motivated by anxiety, to make reparation for these early thefts and to restore that which had been stolen. This latter desire is expressed by throwing away the money into the lavatory pan.

The part played by the father in the patient's anxiety is less immediately obvious, but it can, nevertheless, be demonstrated. As I have said, the dread which appears to have reference only to the mother implies also dread of the father (penis). Moreover, the thefts followed on a conversation with the patient's employer on the subject of embezzlement in general, in which the chief expressed his very special reprobation of misdemeanours of this class. This shows clearly how largely the very need for punishment by the father contributed to the patient's committing these offences. Further, what led to his making reparation at the last moment was the fact that he was faced with detection by another man, a new clerk; this man again represented the father, and what prevented the patient from forcibly bringing about a struggle with (punishment by) the father, to which his intolerable anxiety was impelling him, was thus precisely his anxiety of him.

To these remarks, which I made at the meeting when the dream was reported, I should like to add a few more relating to the history of this patient which I have since learnt. The boy's infantile dread of the witch on the broomstick, who he thought would injure his body with some instrument and make him blind, deaf and dumb, represents his dread of the mother with the penis. In his fugue he travelled to Scotland to the witch, ostensibly because his now unbearable anxiety impelled him to try to set matters right with her. How largely, however, this attempt at reconciliation really had reference to the father within the mother is clear from the fact that, before the journey, he had the phantasy of defending a girl against sexual assault by a man. The real object of his journey was in fact to reach the witch's 'hat' (the penis). But, just as later on the occasion of the thefts he was at the last moment restrained by his dread of the other man, so on this journey he did not reach his ultimate goal: a contest with the father's penis. On reaching Edinburgh he fell ill. His associations showed that this city stood for the witch's genitals: the meaning was, then, that he might not penetrate further. This anxiety is in accordance also with the patient's impotence.

As Dr Bryan pointed out, the anxiety-dream which followed on the visit to the dentist was based on an identification with the mother. Here the dread of some terrible destruction, of an explosion, was due to the anal-sadistic nature of this identification. Since the patient assumed that the incapacity to bear children himself involved his destroying and robbing his mother's womb, he anticipated similar destruction for his own body. Castration by the father, which is bound up with this identification with the mother, is represented by the dentist's actions. It shows also in the recollection which emerged when the patient related his dream. The place where he saw himself standing was a certain spot in a park, against which his mother had particularly warned him. She told him that bad men might attack him and, he himself concluded, they might steal his watch.

The patient's doubt about whether and how he could or ought to leave the park is related, as Dr Bryan in conclusion points out, to his anxiety lest he should be attacked by the father during coitus with the mother—attacked, that is, within as well as outside the mother's body.

# Theoretical Deductions from an
## Analysis of Dementia Praecox in Early Infancy (1929)[1]

THE case of a four-year-old boy who was demented is the basis of my investigation which showed that the premature and excessive defence of the ego against sadism under certain conditions prevents the development of the ego and the establishment of reality relations.


# Review of *Woman's Periodicity* by Mary Chadwick (1933)[1]

To begin with, the author takes the reader back to prehistoric times and shows the rôle which menstruation plays for man and woman, for the closer and the extended family, for the smaller and also for the wider communities. Menstruation has always been looked upon by men as a dangerous event against which they reacted with fear, anxiety and disdain. The belief prevailed that contact with a menstruating woman is dangerous and therefore severe restrictions were imposed in order to separate the 'impure' woman from the community for several days. The form in which the woman was excluded varied with the character of the tribes. The exile of the menstruating woman is a short repetition of the exclusion of adolescent girls from the community in connection with the puberty rites which may last from several months to years, and this is found even nowadays among primitive peoples.

Chadwick showed very convincingly that the primitives' fear of the menstruating woman is fear of the revenge of certain demons which ultimately is identical with castration anxiety. In addition she showed how other group phenomena in later periods have similar roots, for instance fear of witches which even led to their being burned. Even today certain religious demands and prohibitions have the same motivation. This anxiety also finds expression in certain superstitions, such as the commonly held idea that flowers touched by a menstruating woman will fade.

After this introduction the author turns to the present generation and to single individuals and again she shows that everyone has to cope with similar anxieties. These are based on the recognition of the difference between the sexes and the 'threatening' signs of the female cycle of regular haemorrhages. Sooner or later every child discovers the fact that the sexes differ and women menstruate.

[1] Translated from the German.

Consciously or unconsciously this knowledge works in the child and provokes anxious ideas about the wholesomeness of its own genitals. Everyone reacts to this knowledge according to his own constitution, state of development and possible neurosis.

Chadwick describes in detail what occurs in women, in men, in children and in employees—manifestly or latently—in regular cycles, either before, during or after the period of the woman. She emphasizes quarrels between the various members of the family caused by the tendency to depression and by the general nervous tension of the menstruating woman. This book describes very dramatically how the common and neurotic attitudes of man and woman to menstruation is transmitted to children and in turn, how they again show the same kind of disturbances when they are grown up—mechanisms of identification play the main part in this phenomenon—and how they transmit the same problems again to the new generation: in this way neurosis is transmitted from generation to generation. This book can provide parents and educators with much interesting information and can help them towards a better understanding of this problem and change their attitudes, which may prevent further damage to the coming generation.

## Some Psychological Considerations: A Comment (1942)

Dr Karin Stephen has stated lucidly some aspects of the psycho-analytic position. There are, however, sides of this problem which she did not cover, and which seem to me pertinent both to the understanding of the origin of the super-ego and to Dr Waddington's thesis.

Here in brief outline are some of the facts which have become clear to me in my psycho-analytic work with young children, and which I wish to bring to your notice. The feeling of 'good', in the baby's mind, first arises from the experience of *pleasurable* sensations, or, at least, freedom from painful internal and external stimuli. (Food is therefore particularly good, producing, as it does, gratification and relief from discomfort.) Evil is that which causes the baby *pain* and tension, and fails to satisfy his needs and desires. Since the differentiation between 'me' and 'not-me' hardly exists at the beginning, goodness within and goodness without, badness within and badness without, are almost identical to the child. Soon, however, the conception (though this abstract word does not fit these largely unconscious and highly emotional processes) of 'good' and 'evil' extends to the actual people around him. The parents also become embued with goodness and badness according to the child's feelings about them, and then are retaken into the ego, and, within the mind, their influence determines the individual conception of good and evil. This movement to and fro between projection and introjection is a continuous process, by which, in the first years of childhood, relationships with actual people are established and the various aspects of the super-ego are at the same time built up within the mind.

The child's mental capacity to establish people, in the first place his parents, within his own mind, as if they were part of himself, is determined by two facts: on the one hand, stimuli from without and from within, being at first almost undifferentiated become interchangeable; and on the other, the baby's greed, his wish to take in external good, enhances the process of introjection in such a way that certain experiences of the external world become almost simultaneously part of his inner world.

The baby's inherent feelings of love as well as of hatred are in the first place focused on his mother. Love develops in response to her love and care; hatred and aggression are stimulated by frustrations and discomfort. At the same time she becomes the object upon whom he projects his *own* emotions. By attributing to his parents his own sadistic tendencies he develops the cruel aspect of his super-ego (as Dr Stephen has already pointed out); but he also projects on to the people around him his feelings of love, and by these means develops the image of kind and helpful parents. From the first day of life, these processes are influenced by the actual attitudes of the people who look after him, and experiences of the actual outer world and inner experiences constantly interact. In endowing his parents with his feelings of love and thus building up the later ego-ideal, the child is driven by imperative physical and mental needs; he would perish without his mother's food and care, and his whole mental wellbeing and development depend on his establishing securely in his mind the existence of kind and protective figures.

The various aspects of the super-ego derive from the way in which, throughout successive stages of development, the child conceives of his parents. Another powerful element in the formation of the super-ego is the child's own feelings of revulsion against his own aggressive tendencies—a revulsion which he experiences unconsciously as early as in the first few months of life. How are we to explain this early turning of one part of the mind against the other —this inherent tendency to self-condemnation, which is the root of conscience? One imperative motive can be found in the unconscious fear of the child, in whose mind desires and feelings are omnipotent, that should his violent impulses prevail, they would bring about the destruction both of his parents and of himself, since the parents in his mind have become an integral part of his self (super-ego).

The child's overwhelming fear of losing the people he loves and most needs initiates in his mind not only the impulse to restrain his aggression but also a drive to preserve the very objects whom he attacks in phantasy, to put them right and to make amends for the injuries he may have inflicted on them. This drive to make reparation adds impetus and direction to the creative impulse and to all constructive activities. Something is now added to the early conception of good and evil: 'Good' becomes the preserving, repairing or re-creating of those objects which are endangered by his hatred or have been injured by it; 'Evil' becomes his own dangerous hatred.

Constructive and creative activities, social and co-operative feelings, are then felt to be morally good, and they are therefore the most important means of keeping at bay or overcoming the sense of guilt. When the various aspects of the super-ego have become unified (which is the case with mature and well-balanced people), the feeling of guilt has not been put out of action, but has become, together with the means of counteracting it, integrated in the personality. If guilt is too strong and cannot be dealt with adequately, it may lead to actions which create more guilt still (as in the criminal) and become the cause for abnormal development of all kinds.

When the imperatives: 'Thou shalt not kill' (primarily the loved object), and 'Thou shalt save from destruction' (again the loved objects, and in the first place from the infant's own aggression) have taken root in the mind, an ethical pattern is set up which is universal and the rudiment of all ethical systems, notwithstanding the fact that it is capable of manifold variations and distortions, and even of complete reversal. The originally loved object may be replaced by anything in the wide field of human interests: an abstract principle, or even a single problem, can come to stand for it, and this interest may seem to be remote from ethical feelings. (A collector, an inventor or a scientist might even feel capable of committing murder in order to further his purpose.) Yet this particular problem or interest represents in his unconscious mind the original loved person, and must therefore be saved or re-created; anything which stands in the way of his objective is then evil to him.

An instance of distortion, or rather reversal, of the primary pattern which at once presents itself to the mind is the Nazi attitude. Here the aggressor and aggression have become loved and admired objects, and the attacked objects have turned into evil and must therefore be exterminated. The explanation of such a reversal can be found in the early unconscious relation towards the first persons attacked or injured in phantasy. The object then turns into a potential persecutor, because retaliation by the same means by which it had been harmed is feared. The injured person is, however, also identical with the loved person, who should be protected and restored. Excessive early fears tend to increase the conception of the injured object as an enemy, and if this is the outcome, hatred will prevail in its struggle against love; moreover, the remaining love may be distributed in the particular ways which lead to the depravation of the super-ego.

There is one more step in the evolution of good and evil in the individual mind which should be mentioned. Maturity and mental health are 'good', as Dr Stephen pointed out. (Harmonious maturity, however, though a great 'good' in itself, is by no means the only condition for the feeling of adult 'goodness', for there are various kinds and orders of goodness, even among people whose balance is at times badly disturbed.) Harmony and mental balance—furthermore happiness and contentment—imply that the super-ego has been integrated by the ego; which in turn means that the conflicts between super-ego and ego have greatly diminished, and that we are at peace with the super-ego. This amounts to our having achieved harmony with the people whom we first loved and hated, and from whom the super-ego derives. We have travelled a long way from our early conflicts and emotions, and the objects of our interest and our goals have changed many times, becoming more and more elaborated and transformed in the process. However far we feel removed from our original dependencies, however much satisfaction we derive from the fulfilment of our adult ethical demands, in the depths of our minds our first longings to preserve and save our loved parents, and to reconcile ourselves with them, persist. There are many ways of gaining ethical satisfaction; but whether this be through social and co-operative feelings and pursuits, or even through interests which are further removed from the external world—whenever we have the feeling of moral goodness, in our unconscious minds this primary longing for reconciliation with the original objects of our love and hatred is fulfilled.

# EXPLANATORY NOTES[1]

## NOTES ON SOME SCHIZOID MECHANISMS (1946)

THIS is one of Melanie Klein's most important works. It presents for the first time a detailed account of the psychic processes that occur in the first three months of life. This first period, called formerly the paranoid position, and here renamed the paranoid-schizoid position (see her note on p. 2), had been only broadly outlined in 'A Contribution to the Psychogenesis of Manic-Depressive States' (1935) as a contrast to the depressive position. Melanie Klein now sets out the characteristics of the early ego, the form of its object relations and anxieties, and thereby illuminates the nature of—to name the most important—schizoid states, idealization, ego disintegration, and projective processes connected with splitting, for which she introduces the term 'projective identification', a concept discussed below. Furthermore, a new era is opened in the understanding, of schizophrenia. The paper provides the first detailed account of the mental processes, particularly the schizoid mechanisms, which result in states of schizophrenic dissociation and depersonalization. It also includes a valuable discussion on the technique of analysing schizoid states, a subject she returns to in a later work, *Envy and Gratitude*.

In this account of the paranoid-schizoid position, splitting is a key concept. It may be of interest to trace the development over the years of Melanie Klein's ideas on splitting. Splitting occurs in various forms. In her first published paper 'The Development of a Child' she remarked on the phenomenon of splitting off a bad aspect of an object in order to preserve it as a good object; she observed of a small boy that his witch figure is 'obtained by division of the mother imago' which is 'split off from his beloved mother, in order to maintain her as she is' (*Writings*, 1, p. 42). In *The Psycho-Analysis of Children* (1932) this type of splitting is seen as a relatively mature process which occurs as sadism declines. It enables the child to make restitution to his good object and turn away from bad frightening objects. In 1935 Melanie Klein placed this type of splitting, occurring on increasingly realistic planes, among the processes that belong to the normal working through of the depressive position (*Writings*, 1, p. 288).

There is a second main stream of ideas from her early writings. In 'Early Stages of the Oedipus Conflict' (1928) she drew attention to the existence of early phantasies of intrusion into the mother's body. She also

[1] These notes were prepared on behalf of the Melanie Klein Trustees by Mrs Edna O'Shaughnessy in consultation with the general editor of the *Writings*, Mr R. E. Money-Kyrle, and other members of the Editorial Board, Dr Hanna Segal and Miss Betty Joseph. See the Preface and the editor's Introduction to *Writings*, 1 (p. vii–xi).

described in 'Personification in the Play of Children' (1929) how anxiety may lead to a splitting or splitting up of the super-ego into its component figures followed by the projection of particular figures in order to reduce anxiety. The following year, in 'The Importance of Symbol Formation in the Development of the Ego', she took this idea further, and, without using the word 'splitting' or 'projection' described the expulsion of parts of the self. She suggested that the ego's first defence against anxiety is not repression, which comes later, but expulsion—a violent expulsion of sadism both to relieve the ego and to attack the persecuting objects. These earlier ideas all form part of the broader concept of projective identification which Melanie Klein introduces in the present paper. Projective identification is an overall name for a number of distinct yet related processes connected with splitting and projection. Melanie Klein shows that the leading defence against anxiety in the paranoid-schizoid position is projective identification, and further, that projective identification constructs the narcissistic object relations characteristic of this period, in which objects become equated with split-off and projected parts of the self. She also describes the anxieties attendant on phantasies of forceful entry and control of the object, as well as the impoverishing effect on the ego of the excessive use of projective identification. In 'On Identification' (1955) she studies at length another form of projective identification in which a pseudo-identity is acquired.

To continue the review of splitting. Melanie Klein first described the primal splitting of both emotions and the first object relations, which is the foundation of the paranoid-schizoid position, in 1935 in 'A Contribution to the Psychogenesis of Manic-Depressive States'. Love and hate are split, and object relations are correspondingly split into good and bad. In the present paper the details of this primal splitting are elaborated. Melanie Klein also draws attention for the first time to two further forms of splitting which affect the state of the ego. Under fear of annihilation the ego splits itself into minute parts, a mechanism which she thinks underlies states of disintegration in schizophrenia. She also suggests that when the object is taken sadistically it will be split in pieces and that this will result in an ego which is split; indeed, in this paper she underlines the fact that the ego cannot split the object without itself being split, again a fact of significance for schizophrenia.

In her subsequent work she made one or two additions to these basic findings on splitting. In 'Some Theoretical Conclusions Regarding the Emotional Life of the Infant' (1952) she describes the splitting which is characteristic of the depressive position. As a defence against depressive anxiety the ego makes a split between an uninjured live object and an injured dying or dead object. In the same paper she discusses the general effects of splitting on processes of integration. In 'On the Development of Mental Functioning' (1958) there is a sudden change in Melanie Klein's thinking: in addition to the split between ego and super-ego, she posits another structural split in the mind, a split-off area in the deep unconscious for the earliest and most terrifying figures.

The present paper is like the first map of a region before known only in general outline, and much remains to be filled in. Above all, the pathology of the paranoid-schizoid position is not delineated. Although Melanie Klein describes the detrimental effects of excessive splitting and states of persistent withdrawal in infancy, it is only later, in *Envy and Gratitude*, from the study of the effects of pronounced envy on development, that she was able to begin effectively to differentiate the normal from the abnormal form of the paranoid-schizoid position. She made two later modifications to her present account: in 'Anxiety and Guilt' (1948) and 'Depression in the Schizophrenic' (1960) she described very early forms of guilt and depression which antedate the depressive position and belong to the paranoid-schizoid position.

Taken together with 'A Contribution to the Psychogenesis of Manic-Depressive States' and 'Mourning and its Relation to Manic-Depressive States' which contain the account of the infantile depressive position, this paper completes the introduction into psycho-analysis of a new theory of development. It is a theory in which the nodal notion is development as a task for an active ego in relation to an object through two main positions, and the theory brings into psycho-analysis new concepts and hypotheses in terms of which Melanie Klein formulated and explained a wide range of psychological phenomena.

## ON THE THEORY OF ANXIETY AND GUILT (1948)

A series of Controversial Discussions on Melanie Klein's work was organized in the British Psycho-Analytical Society during 1943 and 1944. Her views were represented by four papers; one given by herself on 'The Emotional Life and Ego Development of the Infant with Special Reference to the Depressive Position', and three others given by two colleagues— 'The Nature and Function of Phantasy' by Susan Isaacs, 'Some Aspects of the Rôle of Introjection and Projection' by Paula Heimann, and a paper on 'Regression' given jointly by Susan Isaacs and Paula Heimann. From the paper that Melanie Klein delivered on that occasion three papers eventually emerged: this one, 'On the Theory of Anxiety and Guilt' and also 'Some Theoretical Conclusions Regarding the Emotional Life of the Infant' and 'On Observing the Behaviour of Young Infants'. These three together with 'Notes on Some Schizoid Mechanisms', which Melanie Klein delivered to the British Society in 1946, were published in 1952 in *Developments in Psycho-Analysis*, which included also expanded versions of the papers given in the Controversial Discussions by Susan Isaacs and Paula Heimann as well as two papers by Joan Riviere. The book is therefore a permanent record of Kleinian theory at that time.

The interest of the present paper is not new views, since aside from one emendation, noted below, all views stated here come from earlier writings which Melanie Klein herself refers to in the text. Rather, it is the fact that although for twenty-five years she saw anxiety as a crucial psychological factor and gave much thought and work to understanding it, this is her first and only paper entirely on the subject. This makes the present paper a welcome assembling of all her theories about anxiety and guilt, including points of derivation, agreement and difference with Freud. A full discussion of the fear of death occurs here in which she maintains against Freud that the fear of death is the most fundamental anxiety of all.

There is an emendation—the first of a series—to the account of guilt given in 'A Contribution to the Psychogenesis of Manic-Depressive States' (1935) where she maintains that guilt occurs first in the depressive position in relation to whole objects. Her new view is that guilt is experienced before this in transient states of integration in relation to part objects. Later, in *Envy and Gratitude*, she suggests that excessive envy leads to a premature sense of guilt, which confuses the working through of the anxieties of the paranoid-schizoid position, and in 'A Note on Depression in the Schizophrenic' (1960) she describes a form of early guilt and depression specific for schizophrenia. Thus, her final conception of the paranoid-schizoid position includes subsidiary depressive anxieties, the analogue of her view that the depressive position involves also paranoid anxieties.

## ON THE CRITERIA FOR THE TERMINATION OF A PSYCHO-ANALYSIS (1950)

Already in 1923 Melanie Klein noted that 'every time the anxiety was resolved, the analysis made a big step forward' ('Early Analysis', **1**, p. 78), and from then on it was her view that the key to analytic progress was the analysis of anxiety. Here this view is expressed with formality and precision in terms of her theory of early development. Her thesis is that the termination of a psycho-analysis, which in itself reactivates anxiety, is reached when persecutory and depressive anxieties are sufficiently reduced by working through the infantile paranoid-schizoid and depressive positions. Her further contention is that this criterion is connected to, and underlies, other generally accepted indications for termination.

This paper has two versions, a short and a long.

## THE ORIGINS OF TRANSFERENCE (1952)

This is Melanie Klein's only paper on the subject of transference and it brings together several ideas which she frequently stated and clinically illustrated in her writings. Her conception of transference is a rich one, involving what she calls 'total situations'. In her view, interpretations should cover both early object relations which are relived and evolve further in the transference, as well as the unconscious elements in experiences in the patient's current life. In *Envy and Gratitude* (1957) she records

(p. 180n) her use of the expression 'memories in feelings' for the occurrence in the transference of preverbal emotions and phantasies.

For many years now Melanie Klein had held the view that object relations begin at birth, a view which implies that narcissism and auto-erotism are not states prior to object relations, but rather are states contemporaneous with the first object relations. The present paper contains her only—and even here it is brief—discussion of primary narcissism, including an account of the relation of her views to Freud's. The reader will notice that in this discussion Melanie Klein is describing narcissistic states, which are states of withdrawal into internal objects. In her terminology narcissistic states are distinct from narcissistic object relations, which result from projective identification in the way described in 'Notes on some Schizoid Mechanisms', p. 13.

## THE MUTUAL INFLUENCES IN THE DEVELOPMENT OF EGO AND ID (1952)

This short paper was Melanie Klein's contribution to a symposium on the subject. Another and far more important discussion of metapsychology will be found in 'The Development of Mental Functioning' (1958).

## SOME THEORETICAL CONCLUSIONS REGARDING THE EMOTIONAL LIFE OF THE INFANT (1952)

As explained in the Explanatory Note to 'Anxiety and Guilt', this paper is one of three which had its origin in a paper Melanie Klein contributed to the Controversial Discussions of 1943–44.

On the completion of her early work twenty years before, Melanie Klein had attempted a detailed account of development in Part II of *The Psycho-Analysis of Children*. In the time intervening she formulated the theory of the infantile paranoid-schizoid and depressive positions. The considerable interest of the present paper is that it is the first, and a very full, survey of the period from birth to latency in the light of this new theory. Compared with her earlier account, there is here an impressive advance in scientific organization, understanding and consistency. Except for primary envy, which she described in *Envy and Gratitude* in 1957, it is Melanie Klein's final picture of early development.

Among the points of more specific interest in the present paper, is the account of splitting which adds to what she said before in two ways. (A general discussion of splitting is in the Explanatory Note to 'Notes on Some Schizoid Mechanisms'.) First she clarifies (pp. 86–7) the relationship between splitting and repression, and secondly she describes (p. 74) the particular form in which splitting occurs in the depressive position, a matter left unspecified in 1946. In this paper there is also the first explicit reference (p. 79, note 2) to separate internal parents related to one another in a happy way as the satisfactory evolution of the primitive figure of combined hostile parents. Lastly, one assumption in her earlier work, rejected by her subsequent theory, was that a phase of maximal sadism occurs in the middle of the first year. This is discussed in Chapter Note 4, p. 92, where Melanie Klein states her revised chronology of infantile aggression. This correction of her earlier view is also in her Preface to the Third Edition of *The Psycho-Analysis of Children*.

## ON OBSERVING THE BEHAVIOUR OF YOUNG INFANTS
(1952)

This paper, which developed out of Melanie Klein's contribution to the 1943–44 Controversial Discussions, forms with the preceding paper an important pair. 'Some Theoretical Conclusions Regarding the Emotional Life of the Infant' sets out Melanie Klein's final theory of early development, except for her work on primary envy which she added in 1957. In the present paper the feelings and the details of behaviour observed in young infants and small children are explained and illuminated by means of this theory.

A point of theoretical interest is the explicit statement in the first of the Notes appended to the paper of an hypothesis long presupposed in Melanie Klein's work, viz., that the infant has innate unconscious knowledge of a unique and good object, the mother's breast.

## THE PSYCHO-ANALYTIC PLAY TECHNIQUE: ITS HISTORY AND SIGNIFICANCE (1955[1953])

This is the closest Melanie Klein came to writing a professional auto-biography and it puts on record the history of her early days as a child analyst. There are two versions of this paper. The first version contained examples of the interpretation of children's play, which were replaced in the second and longer version by an account of child cases; the latter version is the one in this volume. Some further historical information will be found in the Preface to the First Edition of *The Psycho-Analysis of Children*. Most interesting of all in the present paper is Melanie Klein's account of the particular discovery each early child case enabled her to make.

## ON IDENTIFICATION (1955)

This is the second of Melanie Klein's three papers on literary material, the others being 'Infantile Anxiety Situations Reflected in a Work of Art and in the Creative Impulse' (1929) and 'Some Reflections on *The Oresteia*' (1963).

329

The present work treats Fabian, the main character in a novel by Julian Green—in Melanie Klein's words—'almost as if he were a patient', and the chief and very considerable interest of this paper is that it explores new aspects of projective identification. Formulated in 'Notes on Some Schizoid Mechanisms' (1946) the concept of projective identification embraces several distinct but related processes. In 1946 Melanie Klein described the type of object relations formed by projective identification in which the object becomes equated with split-off parts of the self. Here she studies not the change in the object brought about by projective identification, but the change in the identity of the subject; by intrusion into the object the subject takes possession of, and acquires the identity of, the object. Melanie Klein uses the story of Fabian, who enters and becomes a succession of different people to discuss the motives for the acquisition of a pseudo-identity in this way. She also discusses the question of the choice of object for projective identification, and the ego's states and anxieties which result, including the fate of parts of the personality which are felt to remain outside the new identity. She also describes briefly (p. 144) the beneficial governing effect that an intact good internal object has on splitting and projection.

## ENVY AND GRATITUDE (1957)

This is Melanie Klein's last major theoretical work. Before its appearance, envy was sporadically recognized by psycho-analysts as an important emotion—but only in situations of deprivation, and only one of its forms, penis envy, had been studied in detail. Melanie Klein's own previous references to envy begin with her description of the deep effect of envy on the development of Erna, an early case reported in an unpublished paper read to the First Conference of German Psycho-Analysts in 1924, which became the basis of Chapter III of *The Psycho-Analysis of Children*. In the intervening years, she noted envy as a factor of importance; she lists her past references in a footnote on pages 180–81, forgetting, however, her own anticipation of the present work in 'Some Theoretical Conclusions Regarding the Emotional Life of the Infant' (1952), where she says 'envy appears to be inherent in oral greed . . . envy (alternating with feelings of love and gratification) is first directed towards the feeding breast . . .' (p. 79).

In this monograph Melanie Klein charts an extensive area of which only a small sector had been known before. She posits that envy and gratitude are opposite and interacting feelings normally operative from birth and that the first object of envy, as of gratitude, is the feeding breast. She describes the influence of both envy and gratitude on the earliest object relations and studies the operation of envy not only in situations of deprivation, but also in situations of gratification where it interferes with normal gratitude. The effects of envy, particularly unconscious envy, on character formation are studied, including—and these are of prime importance—the nature of the defences erected against envy. The technique of analysing splitting processes is also discussed; this forms an important supplement to the discussion in 'Notes on Some Schizoid Mechanisms'.

Melanie Klein also examines abnormally pronounced envy. In 'Notes on Some Schizoid Mechanisms', though she noted several abnormalities of early functioning, for example, the introjection of objects fragmented by hate, the excessive use of splitting mechanisms and the persistence of narcissistic states, the psychopathology of the paranoid-schizoid position stayed largely unknown. Here she sets out in detail the abnormal formation of the paranoid-schizoid position which results from excessive envy; among other things she describes the confusion which comes from a failure in splitting, and shows the significance of an absence of idealization. She also outlines the abnormal structure of the depressive position and the Oedipus complex that then follows. She also posits that the feeding breast is perceived by the infant as a source of creativity and describes the damaging effects of undue envy on the capacity for creativeness. Throughout, her contentions both theoretical and clinical are illustrated by case material which is of particular interest in that it shows how she worked in this late period.

This work throws new light on the negative therapeutic reaction, studied as the effect of envy. Melanie Klein considers that although envy can to some extent be analysed, it sets a limit to analytic success. This fact, therefore, places the final curb on the high optimism of her early papers of the 'twenties.

## ON THE DEVELOPMENT OF MENTAL FUNCTIONING (1958)

Melanie Klein discusses two basic metapsychological principles that she has accepted from Freud: his structural theory and his theory of the life and death instincts. She states her additions to the theory of the life and death instincts and also her disagreements with Freud over certain particulars. She emphasizes that she employs the life and death instincts not as general concepts of the behaviour of the biological organism, but as the basis of love and hate, which are mental rather than biological phenomena. Her emphasis on the mental, however, is not just a particularized view of the theory of the instincts. It is her distinctive orientation in psycho-analysis. Her general approach, and her theory of the paranoid-schizoid and depressive positions, forms a theory of *mental* functioning. Note, for instance, the title of this paper.

While her discussion of the life and death instincts assembles long-held views, this is not the case with the discussion of mental structure, more specifically the super-ego. Here Melanie Klein has a sudden change of view. In contrast to emphatic earlier views (see the Explanatory Note to 'The Early Development of Conscience in the Child') that the hallmark of the normal early super-ego is its extreme and terrifying nature, she here suggests that the super-ego develops with the two instincts predominantly in a state of fusion, and that the terrifying internal figures which result from intense destructiveness do not form part of the super-ego. These exist in a separate area of the mind in the deep unconscious, split off both from the ego and the super-ego, where they remain unintegrated and unmodified by normal processes of growth; if an abnormal situation arises and there is a failure to maintain a split these terrifying objects become a source of acute anxiety and a threat to mental stability. She also suggests, as against earlier views, that there is a close accord between the ego and the super-ego from the beginning.

While her contention that the most terrifying figures in the psyche persist unchanged is at variance with many previous passages—for example, in 'Some Theoretical Conclusions Regarding the Emotional Life of the Infant' (1952), p. 87, she describes the modifying and integrative effects of the depressive position on the extreme severity of the early super-ego figures—it is nonetheless also a return to an old idea. In 'Symposium on Child Analysis' (1927) Melanie Klein wrote (p. 155) 'I am led to believe from the analysis of children that their super-ego is a highly resistant product, at heart unalterable . . .' and again in the same paper (p. 157) she refers to the super-ego 'whose nature is immutable'.

As was often her habit in such matters, Melanie Klein did not comment on or formally work out the implication of her changed views. Did her radical reclassification of the most terrifying figures out of the super-ego alter her view of their impact on the infant in the paranoid-schizoid position? The present paper and subsequent accounts of the infant's experiences in the first months of life in 'Our Adult World and Its Roots in Infancy' and 'The Oresteia' would seem to indicate that her conception of their impact on the infant remains the same, since the splitting off (see p. 241) of these terrifying figures would in the beginning often fail. On the other hand, her account of the super-ego development in, for example, schizophrenia would now seem to be different; before (see e.g. 'Personification in the Play of Children' (1929)) she considered that schizophrenia was characterized by the abnormal persistence and ascendency of the normal early severe super-ego; now her view is that (see p. 243) part of the schizophrenic process is an abnormal development of the super-ego itself in which it becomes indistinguishable from the most terrifying objects.

## OUR ADULT WORLD AND ITS ROOTS IN INFANCY (1959)

This is the last of Melanie Klein's papers for a wide rather than a specifically analytic audience, the others being 'On Weaning' (1936) and 'Love, Guilt and Reparation' (1937). With a minimum of technical terms she gives a broad survey of her findings and theories, stressing the continuing influence of early development on adult life, individual and social.

## A NOTE ON DEPRESSION IN THE SCHIZOPHRENIC (1960)

The last International Congress of Psycho-Analysis that Melanie Klein attended was the Twenty-First Congress in Copenhagen in 1959. She made two contributions: this short paper and 'On the Sense of Loneliness'. This paper was part of a symposium on depressive illness and deals with depression in schizophrenia. Melanie Klein here modifies some of her earlier views.

Before describing the paper, it may be useful to assemble her work on the subject, as schizophrenia, indeed the psychoses, interested her all her working life. Several ideas were present from the start. She thought that psychotic processes occur at a much younger age than commonly supposed, and in two separate ways: in normal infants as part of normal development, and, in a proliferated and abnormal form, in psychoses even in childhood itself. Also, she thought that psychotic processes are connected with sadism, and that they arise from acute anxiety which brings an excessive and damaging use of certain otherwise normal defences.

These ideas had their first rough-hewn expression in a group of papers published between 1927 and 1929. In 'Criminal Tendencies in Normal Children' (1927) she drew attention to the fact that a flight from reality is both one of the normal defences of childhood and also, if it pervades the personality, a basis of childhood psychosis. In 'Early Stages of the Oedipus Conflict' (1928) she described the interior world of horror and psychosis that results from phantasy attacks on the mother's inside. In 'Personification in the Play of Children' (1929) she listed signs of childhood schizophrenia, specifying the characteristic type of play, and concluded from her work on the early super-ego in which she was engaged at the time, that a central factor in psychosis is the acute anxiety caused by the early super-ego formed in the image of the child's sadistic phantasies. The next paper 'The Importance of Symbol Formation in the Development of the Ego' (1930) records both the first analysis of a psychotic child and also the existence of a defence mechanism prior to and distinct from repression. Melanie Klein describes how the ego uses this early mechanism to expel its own sadism and attack hostile objects, and the devastating effect on development if this mechanism (which as yet had no name) is used to excess to eliminate all sadism and anxiety—the ego then lacks the means for further development and remains in a psychotic condition. In these ideas there are the precursors of the concept of projective identification formulated in 'Notes on Some Schizoid Mechanisms' (1946).

By 1930, summarized in a brief paper, 'The Psychotherapy of the Psychoses' the lineaments of the psychotic's reality as a reflection of his hostile instinctual life had been drawn, as well as the general nature of his anxieties and defences. In *The Psycho-Analysis of Children* (1932) Melanie Klein expounds these views more fully. Her discovery that the earliest anxieties are psychotic rather than neurotic led her in this work to redefine the infantile neurosis as a composite of psychotic and neurotic trends, a statement not far short of her ultimate definition of the infantile neurosis given in 'Some Theoretical Conclusions Regarding the Emotional Life of the Infant' (1952): 'the infantile neurosis can be regarded as a combination of processes by which anxieties of a psychotic nature are bound, worked through and modified' (p. 81).

These early ideas became, in a more developed and more exact form, part of her theory of the paranoid-schizoid and depressive positions, expounded in three main papers, 'A Contribution to the Psychogenesis of Manic-depressive States' (1935), 'Mourning and Its Relation to Manic-Depressive States' (1940) and 'Notes on Some Schizoid Mechanisms' (1946). In 1935 she distinguished for the first time the two forms of anxiety, persecutory and depressive, a fundamental distinction which in itself illuminates the nature of psychotic anxiety. In the same paper she connects schizophrenia with the psychotic persecutory anxieties of the first three months of life, and gives also a detailed account, completed in her 1940 paper, of the connection between manic-depressive illness and the unresolved persecutory and depressive anxieties of the infantile depressive position which begins at four to five months. In 1946 she described in detail the many splitting mechanisms by which the ego defends itself against persecutory anxiety, and which form the basis of the dissociated and disintegrated condition of the schizophrenic. The connection between oral sadism and the fragmentation of the schizophrenic's mind is explained: when the object is introjected sadistically, the ego has at its call not an intact object but an object reduced to bits in the process of incorporation, and so would be itself in bits. As the dominant mechanisms of this period she posited projective identification, a new concept, which, as remarked before, formalized and extended her ideas about the existence of an early mechanism of defence, distinct from and antedating repression. Other aspects of psychoses were clarified in these papers of 1935, 1940 and 1946, including the well-known clinical fact of the existence of combinations of schizophrenia, mania and depression, which Melanie Klein explained in terms of the interaction both by development and regression between the infantile paranoid-schizoid and depressive positions.

The technique of analysing dissociated states was discussed in 1946 and again in *Envy and Gratitude* (1957). The main contribution of *Envy and Gratitude*, however, to the understanding of psychosis was the uncovering of excessive envy as a determinant of severe pathology in the paranoid-schizoid position. Lastly, in 'The Development of Mental Functioning' (1958) there was a reclassification. Until then Melanie Klein had always ascribed to the super-ego the terrifying figures whose dominance over the psyche is characteristic of psychosis. In 1958, however, she suggested that the earliest and most terrifying figures do not belong to the super-ego but are split off into an area in the deep unconscious, which remains apart from normal developmental processes, and which, in situations of stress, may infiltrate the ego and overwhelm it.

To come now to the background of the present paper. In 1935 Melanie Klein characterized the difference between the anxieties and feelings of the schizophrenic and the depressive in the following way: the schizophrenic suffers from persecutory anxiety over the preservation of his ego, while the depressive suffers from a mixture of anxieties, persecution, depression and guilt, over the preservation not only of the self, but of the good object with which it is identified. This accorded with her contention at that time that guilt begins in relation to whole objects in the depressive position. In 'A Contribution to the Theory of Anxiety and Guilt' (1948) her ideas about guilt changed; she considered that guilt occurs transiently before the depressive position in relation to part objects. In the present short paper she modifies her account of the difference between schizophrenia and depression. She states that the paranoid-schizophrenic, in addition to persecutory anxiety, suffers also depression and guilt about destroying the good parts of his ego and the good object it is felt to contain, and she describes the specific nature of his depression which differs in content, form and manifestation from the depression of the manic-depressive.

In her last paper 'On the Sense of Loneliness' (1963) Melanie Klein draws attention to the loneliness of the mentally ill. This is another aspect of the schizophrenic's sufferings, which she had commented on before in 'Notes on Some Schizoid Mechanisms'.


## ON MENTAL HEALTH (1960)

Melanie Klein died in London on 22 September 1960, as this paper went to press, and a short obituary was printed at its end. Melanie Klein had written the paper not long before, and perhaps for this reason, although she gives a general survey of the topic, the paper lacks her usual vigour.


## SOME REFLECTIONS ON 'THE ORESTEIA' (1963)

This was published posthumously from a manuscript that was an early draft and not yet corrected. Her two other papers on literary material had been written under the impress of new ideas — 'Infantile Anxiety Situations Reflected in a Work of Art and in the Creative Impulse' (1929) expounded her new picture of early anxieties, and 'On Identification' (1955) illustrated her new concept of projective identification. Here her aim is different. She sets out to discuss the symbolic rôles of the characters in the *Oresteia*, but the paper, in its still unrevised form, leaves a confused impression.


## ON THE SENSE OF LONELINESS (1963)

In this, her last paper, Melanie Klein opens a new topic: the inner sense of loneliness, which, she suggests, is part of the human condition. Linking

335

it to her theory of development she describes how paranoid insecurity as well as processes of integration lead in the normal course of development to inevitable loneliness. She also describes the loneliness of schizophrenia and manic-depressive illness, adding to her former account of the sufferings of the psychotic in 'Notes on Some Schizoid Mechanisms' (1946). She discusses the factors which mitigate loneliness, and the need also for an acceptance of loneliness. In the general atmosphere of the paper, though nowhere is it specified, there is a premonition of approaching death.

It must be remembered that Melanie Klein had not offered this paper for publication before she died—the present version was published posthumously after some slight editorial work—presumably because she did not consider it ready, and indeed it would have benefited from further work; it seems in places incomplete and its thought is not altogether resolved.

## SHORT CONTRIBUTIONS

Though they fall within its time span Melanie Klein did not include these five short pieces when she collected her writings for *Contributions to Psycho-Analysis 1921–1945*; whether she forgot them or thought them unsuitable is not known. The first, 'The Importance of Words in Early Analysis' is a short illustration of a point of technique in child analysis. The second, 'Note on the Preceding Communication', is a comment on 'A Dream of Forensic Interest' by Douglas Bryan, which appeared in the *Int. J. Psycho-Anal.*, **9,** 1928. Melanie Klein discusses the combined parents in the dream; she had first described the figure of combined parents the year before in 'Early Stages of the Oedipus Conflict' (1928). The third is a four-line report to the *Int. Z. f. Psychoanal.*, **15,** of her findings on 'The Importance of Symbol Formation in the Development of the Ego' (1930). The fourth is a review of a book, *Women's Periodicity* by Mary Chadwick. Of most interest is the last, 'Some Psychological Considerations: A comment', which appeared in *Science and Ethics*. This was a small volume edited by C. H. Waddington containing contributions from several well-known figures of the day. Melanie Klein, in a short and non-technical account, describes the formation and development of the super-ego.

# APPENDIX

## INTRODUCTORY NOTES BY ERNEST JONES TO PREVIOUS EDITIONS OF MELANIE KLEIN'S WORKS

### Introduction to *Contributions to Psycho-Analysis, 1921–45* (1948)

WHEN, more than twenty years ago, I invited Melanie Klein first to give a course of lectures and subsequently to settle in London I knew I was securing an extremely valuable recruit to the British Psycho-Analytical Society. But I had no perception at that time of what commotion this simple act would result in.[1] Until then, and for a while afterwards, our Society had been a model of co–operative harmony. For a time Mrs Klein was given an attentive hearing and aroused great interest. Soon—perhaps, I like to think, aided a little by my influence which was manifestly exerted in her favour—she began to win adherents and devoted followers. Before long, however, cries began to be raised that in the views she rather vehemently presented she was 'going too far', which I think simply meant she was going too fast. Not that it was easy at first to detect anything radically new in these views or methods of work. The trouble was that she was pursuing them with a novel rigour and consistent recklessness that evoked in some members of the Society at first uneasiness and gradually an intense opposition. Other members who championed her work with a certain degree of fanaticism found this opposition hard to bear, and in the course of time two extreme groups developed who between them vociferously, and therefore easily, restricted the quieter scientific endeavours of cooler members.

The division in the British Society will, presently, I doubt not, be reproduced in all other psycho-analytical societies, and in the absence of colleagues with first-hand experience of Mrs Klein's work she must expect adverse critics to be in the majority. In England itself the storm was heightened by the advent of our Viennese colleagues whose life in their homeland had become literally impossible. They added to the other criticisms the opinion that Mrs Klein's conclusions not only diverged from but were incompatible with Freud's. This I find myself a grossly exaggerated statement. Not that it should be in any event a decisive consideration, if experience showed that her conclusions were nearer the truth; I yield to no one in my admiration of Freud's genius, but on several occasions I have not hesitated to put forward reasons for thinking that certain of his inferences were imperfect. We had, however, become so accustomed to regard on good grounds, various analysts who had separated from Freud, such as Adler, Jung, Stekel and Rank, as being influenced by subjective motives—a rationalization of inner resistances—

[1] Hebbel's line, 'Er hat an den Frieden der Welt gerührt', which has been applied to Freud, might well be applied to Mrs Klein as well.

rather than by a profounder insight, that it seemed to many less presumptuous, and certainly easier, to place Mrs Klein in the same class. Yet, if psycho-analysis is to remain a branch of science it is evident that, now that Freud's ability to continue his magnificent impetus has been extinguished, advance beyond the limits he reached is inevitable.

Now what is all this storm about? Will the opposition to Mrs Klein's work be evanescent or has she raised winds that will rage with increasing reverberations? Her writings, displayed in the present volume as in her previous momentous work *The Psycho-Analysis of Children*, must of course speak for themselves, but perhaps it would not be out of place for me to take this opportunity of summarizing some of the most striking of them, and of commenting on them, as I see them.

Freud's investigation of the unconscious mind, which is essentially that of the young infant, had revealed unexpected aspects of childhood, but before Mrs Klein there had been little attempt to confirm these discoveries by the direct study of childhood. To her, therefore, is due the credit of carrying psycho-analysis to where it principally belongs—the heart of the child. There were stupendous difficulties to be overcome: the elaboration of special techniques, the overcoming of parental prejudices and fears of the unknown effects on the child's development, and so on. Dr Hug-Hellmuth in Vienna had suggested that the spontaneous play of young children might be used to supplement, or even replace, the material provided by adults in the form of free associations, but she evidently had not the ability to put the idea into effective practice. Mrs Klein, with the high psychological gifts and the amazing moral courage that so distinguish her, was not to be deterred by any difficulties. She developed fearlessly the play-technique of interpretation, using it in combination with various other devices, and was soon in a position to confirm at first hand all that Freud had inferred from adult material concerning the hitherto unknown unconscious mind of the child. Encouraged by this she exploited to the full the favourable opportunity she had created for herself and determined to pursue her investigations to their uttermost limit.

Now Freud had shown that the child's mind contained in its depths much besides the innocence and freshness that so entrance us. There were dark fears of possibilities that the most gruesome fairy tale had not dared to explore, cruel impulses where hate and murder rage freely, irrational phantasies that mock at reality in their extravagance: in short a world that reminds us of Belsen or of Walt Disney at his most grotesque. Of the world outcry at this derogation of smiling infancy this is not the place to speak; Mrs Klein is still experiencing much of the aftermath. I am reminded here of a patient who in a moment of sudden illumination exclaimed: 'I knew that Freud's theories were true, but I did not know that they were *so* true.'. Mrs Klein's unsparing presentation of the cutting, tearing, gouging, devouring phantasies of infants is apt to make most people recoil with a similar exclamation. She went further than this by maintaining that the Cimmerian picture Freud had drawn of the unconscious mind of a three-year-old was at least as valid of an infant of the first months of life. Thus, for example, it had been surmised that the oral erotism of such an infant could be divided into two stages: first a sucking one, then a biting one; and the name oral-sadistic or cannibalistic had been given to the latter one. Devouring or cannibalistic phantasies had been observed and traced to perhaps the age of three. But Mrs Klein ruthlessly maintains that they occur during the so-called cannibalistic stage of infancy itself, which after all seems what one would have expected.

Again, we had long been familiar with the concept of introjection formulated by Ferenczi in 1909, and with the much older psychiatric one of projection. But Mrs Klein has taught us much more about these mechanisms than was previously known. Not only do they apparently operate from the beginning of life, as was indeed implicit in Freud's description of the 'pleasure-ego', but they alternate and are interwoven with each other to such an extraordinary extent that the greater part of early infantile development can be described in terms of them. It is indeed becoming increasingly difficult to distinguish clearly between the processes of introjection, incorporation and identification. The whole theory of 'internal objects', 'good' and 'bad', has thus been enormously extended, with important results both for our understanding of early development and for our daily therapeutic practice.

Mrs Klein's boldness did not stop at the study of normal and neurotic infantile development. She has extended it into the field of insanity itself, no doubt somewhat to the dismay of those psychiatrists who regard this field as the last preserve of the medical profession. But the extension was unescapable. The resemblance between certain infantile processes and those so blatant in paranoia, schizophrenia and manic-depressive insanity could not be overlooked by someone of Mrs Klein's perspicacity, and she did not hesitate to appropriate terms from those fields and apply them, in of course a modified form, to various phases of infantile development, e.g. paranoid, depressive, and so on. Furthermore, the resemblance cannot be merely an external one. There must be an inner relation between these psychotic-like reactions and phases in the infant and the efflorescence of them in actual insanity. I am confident that Mrs Klein's work will prove as fruitful in this field as it has already shown itself to be in the more familiar one of neurotic and normal development.

Although I have not concealed my cordial agreement with the lines of Mrs Klein's investigations and the soundness of the principles on which they are based, I shall not be expected to underwrite every one of her conclusions and formulations: they will stand on their own merits without any support being needed from me. It would, it is true, be tempting to explain all criticisms of her work as a flinching from the rigorous and uncompromising penetration of psycho-analysis into the utmost depths of the child's mind, and indeed some of them often remind me of the very same phrases that were applied to Freud's own work in its inception: words like 'far-fetched', 'one-sided', 'arbitrary', have a familiar ring to me. But, however much truth there may actually be in this suggeston, it is not only a consideration that has to be excluded from scientific discussion but would certainly be unfair to most of the critics in question.

They have adduced a number of arguments that have to be dealt with very seriously, and indeed already have been by Dr Heimann, Mrs Isaacs, Mrs Riviere and others besides Mrs Klein. Nevertheless some of Mrs Klein's more abstract formulations will no doubt be modified in the future theoretic structure of psycho-analysis. What seems to me a probable example of this is her literal application to clinical findings of Freud's philosophical concept of a 'death-impulse', about which I have serious misgivings. I quote it not for this reason, however, but because I find it a little odd that I should be criticizing her for a too faithful adherence to Freud's views, and odder still that certain Viennese analysts see in it a divergence from his views. All of which shows that psycho-analytical theorizing continues to be a very lively activity. And in this activity Mrs Klein's work is playing, and is likely to play, a very central part.

ERNEST JONES

## Preface to *Developments in Psycho-Analysis* (1952)

Stupendous as was his output, both in quantity and in quality, so productive was Freud in original ideas and discoveries that it was not possible for even such a worker as he was to explore all their potential ramifications. Many collaborators have assisted in this gigantic task. A footnote of his was expanded into a book on Hamlet, and many light hints have been developed into essays or even books. This work will continue for many years to come, so fruitful were his inspirations. Furthermore, the use of the methods he devised must in the nature of things lead to fresh discoveries beyond those he made himself and to hypotheses that extend or even rectify his own—a procedure he unhesitatingly applies himself.

There comes a point, however, where such endeavours raise a difficult problem. Bitter experience has taught us that resistance against the unconscious can be so subtle that it may distort the analytic findings and reinterpret them in support of some personal defence. How can this disturbing state of affairs be distinguished from a true development, a deepening of our knowledge of the unconscious? The sole criterion that can legitimately be employed is that valid for all science, a consensus of conclusions reached by *adequately qualified* workers using the same method in similar conditions. What is certainly illegitimate is the Procrustean principle of assessing all conclusions with those reached by Freud, however great our respect for the latter may and should be.

Mrs Klein's work of the past thirty years, which is the theme of the present volume, illustrates the problem just stated. It has been attacked and defended with almost equal vehemence, but in the long run its value can be satisfactorily estimated only by those who themselves make comparable investigations. Mrs Riviere in her introductory chapter has dealt very faithfully with the various criticisms and objections that have been expressed by those disagreeing with Mrs Klein's work, and it would be out of place for me to discuss them further here. I will venture only one personal comment. As is well known, I have from the beginning viewed Mrs Klein's work with the greatest sympathy, especially as many of the conclusions coincided with those I reached myself; and I have all along been struck by the observation that many of the criticisms have been close echoes of those with which I had been made familiar in the earliest days of psycho-analysis. A good many of her findings and conclusions had been adumbrated in quite early days, by Freud, Rank and others, but what is so distinctive and admirable in her work is the courage and unshakable integrity with which she has quite unsparingly worked out the implications and consequences of those earlier hints, thereby making important fresh discoveries in her course. Her mind is very alien from those who accept the findings of psycho-analysis provided they are not taken too seriously.

ERNEST JONES

## Preface to *New Directions in Psycho-Analysis* (1955)

Mrs Klein's work of the past thirty years has been attacked and defended with almost equal vehemence, but in the long run its value can be satisfactorily estimated only by those who themselves make comparable investigations. As is well known, I have from the beginning viewed Mrs Klein's work with the greatest sympathy, especially as many of the conclusions coincided with those I reached myself; and I have all along been struck by the observation that many of the criticisms have been close echoes of those with which I had been made familiar in the earliest days of psycho-analysis. A good many of her findings and conclusions had been adumbrated in quite early days by Freud, Rank and others, but what is so distinctive and admirable in her work is the courage and unshakable integrity with which she has quite unsparingly worked out the implications and consequences of those earlier hints, thereby making important fresh discoveries in her course.

It is a matter for wide satisfaction as well as for personal congratulation that Mrs Klein has lived to see her work firmly established. So long as it was simply deposited in what she herself had published there was always the hope, but by no means the certainty, that it would be taken up by future students. The situation has now moved beyond that stage; her work is firmly established. As a result of her personal instruction, combined with the insight of those who decided to accept it, she has a considerable number of colleagues and pupils who follow her lead in exploring the deepest depths. To the papers that many of them have contributed to *New Directions in Psycho-Analysis* I have the pleasure of adding this *envoi*.

ERNEST JONES

# BIBLIOGRAPHY

Abraham, K. (1911). 'Notes on the Psycho-Analytical Investigation and Treatment of Manic-Depressive Insanity and Allied Conditions.' In: *Selected Papers on Psycho-Analysis* (London: Hogarth, 1927).

—— (1921). 'Contribution to the Theory of the Anal Character.' *ibid.*

—— (1924a). 'The Influence of Oral Erotism on Character Formation' *ibid.*

—— (1924b). 'A Short Study of the Development of the Libido, Viewed in the Light of Mental Disorders.' *ibid.*

—— (1925). 'Character-Formation on the Genital Level of the Libido.' *ibid.*

Balint, M. (1937). 'Early Developmental States of the Ego. Primary Object-Love.' In: *Primary Love and Psycho-Analytic Technique* (London: Hogarth, 1952).

Bernfeld, S. (1929). *Psychology of the Infant* (London: Kegan Paul).

Bion, W. R. (1954). 'Notes on the Theory of Schizophrenia.' *Int. J. Psycho-Anal.*, **35.**

—— (1958). 'Differentiation of the Psychotic from the Non-Psychotic Personalities.' *Int. J. Psycho-Anal.*, **39.**

Chadwick, Mary (1933). *Woman's Periodicity* (London: Noel Douglas)

Fairbairn, W. R. D. (1941). 'A Revised Psychopathology of the Psychoses and Psychoneuroses.' *Int. J. Psycho-Anal.*, **22.**

—— (1944). 'Endopsychic Structure Considered in Terms of Object Relationships.' *Int. J. Psycho-Anal.*, **25.**

Ferenczi, S. (1925). 'Psycho-Analysis of Sexual Habits.' In: *Further Contributions to the Theory and Technique of Psycho-Analysis* (London: Hogarth, 1926).

—— (1930). 'Notes and Fragments.' In: *Final Contributions to the Problems and Methods of Psycho-Analysis* (London: Hogarth).

Freud, A. (1927). *The Psycho-Analytical Treatment of Children* (London: Imago, 1946).

—— (1937). *The Ego and the Mechanisms of Defence* (London: Hogarth).

Freud, S. (1905). *Three Essays on the Theory of Sexuality. S.E.* **7.**

—— (1908). 'Character and Anal Erotism.' *S.E.* **9.**

—— (1911). 'Psycho-Analytic Notes on an Autobiographical Account of a Case of Paranoia (Dementia Paranoides).' *S.E.* **12.**

—— (1912). 'On the Universal Tendency to Debasement in the Sphere of Love.' *S.E.* **11.**

—— (1914). 'Narcissism: An Introduction.' *S.E.* **14.**

# BIBLIOGRAPHY

Freud S. (1916). 'Some Character-Types Met with in Psycho-Analytic Work.' *S.E.* **14.**

—— (1917). 'Mourning and Melancholia.' *S.E.* **14.**

—— (1920). *Beyond the Pleasure Principle. S.E.* **18.**

—— (1921). *Group Psychology and the Analysis of the Ego. S.E.* **18.**

—— (1923). *The Ego and the Id. S.E.* **23.**

—— (1924). 'The Economic Problem of Masochism.' *S.E.* **19.**

—— (1926), *Inhibitions, Symptoms and Anxiety. S.E.* **20.**

—— (1928). 'Humour.' *S.E.* **21.**

—— (1930). *Civilization and its Discontents. S.E.* **21.**

—— (1931). 'Female Sexuality.' *S.E.* **21.**

—— (1933). *New Introductory Lectures on Psycho-Analysis. S.E.* **22.**

—— (1937). 'Analysis Terminable and Interminable.' *S.E.* **23.**

—— (1938). 'Constructions in Analysis.' *S.E.* **23.**

—— (1940). *An Outline of Psycho-Analysis. S.E.* **23.**

Heimann, P. (1942). 'Sublimation and its Relation to Processes of Internalization.' *Int. J. Psycho-Anal.,* **23.**

—— (1952a). 'Certain Functions of Introjection and Projection in Early Infancy.' In: *Developments in Psycho-Analysis* by Klein et al. (London: Hogarth).

—— (1952b). 'Notes on the Theory of the Life and Death Instincts.' *ibid.*

—— (1955). 'A Contribution to the Re-evaluation of the Oedipus Complex.' In: *New Directions in Psycho-Analysis* ed. Klein *et al.* (London: Tavistock).

Heimann, P. and Isaacs, S. (1952). 'Regression.' In: *Developments in Psycho-Analysis* by Klein *et al.* (London: Hogarth).

Hug-Helmuth, H. von (1921). 'On the Technique of Child Analysis.' *Int. J. Psycho-Anal.,* **2.**

Isaacs, S. (1933). *Social Development of Young Children* (London: Routledge).

—— (1952). 'The Nature and Function of Phantasy.' In: *Developments in Psychoanalysis* by Klein *et al.* (London: Hogarth).

Jaques, E. (1955). 'Social Systems as a Defence against Persecutory and Depressive Anxiety.' In: *New Directions in Psycho-Analysis* ed. Klein *et al.* (London: Tavistock).

Jones, E. (1913). 'Hate and Anal Erotism in the Obsessional Neuroses.' *Papers on Psycho-Analysis* (London: Baillière).

—— (1916). 'The Theory of Symbolism.' *ibid.,*—2nd edn–5th edn.

—— (1918). 'Anal Erotic Character Traits.' *ibid.*

—— (1929). 'Fear, Guilt and Hate.' *ibid.,*—4th and 5th edns.

—— (1949). *Hamlet and Oedipus* (London: Gollancz).

Klein, M. [details of first publication of each paper/book are given here;

the number of the volume in which they appear in *The Writings of Melanie Klein* is indicated in square brackets]

Klein, M. (1921). 'The Development of a Child' *Imago*, **7**. [I]

—— (1922). 'Inhibitions and Difficulties in Puberty.' *Die neue Erziehung*, **4**. [I]

—— (1923a). 'The Rôle of the School in the Libidinal Development of the Child.' *Int. Z. f. Psychoanal.*, **9**. [I]

—— (1923b). 'Early Analysis.' *Imago*, **9**. [I]

—— (1925). 'A Contribution to the Psychogenesis of Tics.' *Int. Z. f. Psychoanal.*, **11**. [I]

—— (1926). 'The Psychological Principles of Early Analysis.' *Int. J. Psycho-Anal.*, **7**. [I]

—— (1927a). 'Symposium on Child Analysis.' *Int. J. Psycho-Anal.*, **8**. [I]

—— (1927b). 'Criminal Tendencies in Normal Children.' *Brit. J. med. Psychol.*, **7**. [I]

—— (1928). 'Early Stages of the Oedipus Conflict.' *Int. J. Psycho-Anal.*, **9**. [I]

—— (1929a). 'Personification in the Play of Children.' *Int. J. Psycho-Anal*, **10,** [I]

—— (1929b). 'Infantile Anxiety Situations Reflected in a Work of Art and in the Creative Impulse.' *Int. J. Psycho-Anal.*, **10**. [I]

—— (1930a). 'The Importance of Symbol-Formation in the Development of the Ego.' *Int. J. Psycho-Anal.*, **11**. [I]

—— (1930b). 'The Psychotherapy of the Psychoses.' *Brit. J. med. Psychol.*, **10**. [I]

—— (1931). 'A Contribution to the Theory of Intellectual Inhibition.' *Int. J. Psycho-Anal.*, **12**. [I]

—— (1932). *The Psycho-Analysis of Children* (London: Hogarth). [II]

—— (1933). 'The Early Development of Conscience in the Child.' In: *Psychoanalysis Today* ed. Lorand (New York: Covici-Friede). [I]

—— (1934). 'On Criminality.' *Brit. J. med. Psychol.*, **14**. [I]

—— (1935). 'A Contribution to the Psychogenesis of Manic-Depressive States.' *Int. J. Psycho-Anal.*, **16**. [I]

—— (1936). 'Weaning.' In: *On the Bringing Up of Children* ed. Rickman (London: Kegan Paul). [I]

—— (1937). 'Love, Guilt and Reparation.' In: *Love, Hate and Reparation* with Riviere (London: Hogarth). [I]

—— (1940). 'Mourning and its Relation to Manic-Depressive States.' *Int. J. Psycho-Anal.*, **21**. [I]

—— (1945). 'The Oedipus Complex in the Light of Early Anxieties.' *Int. J. Psycho-Anal.*, **26**. [I]

—— (1946). 'Notes on some Schizoid Mechanisms.' *Int. J. Psycho-Anal.*, **27**. [III]

BIBLIOGRAPHY

Klein, M. (1948a). *Contributions to Psycho-Analysis 1921–1945* (London: Hogarth). [I]

—— (1948b). 'On the Theory of Anxiety and Guilt.' *Int. J. Psycho-Anal.*, **29.** [III]

—— (1950). 'On the Criteria for the Termination of a Psycho-Analysis.' *Int. J. Psycho-Anal.*, **31.** [III]

—— (1952a). 'The Origins of Transference.' *Int. J. Psycho-Anal.*, **33.** [III]

—— (1952b). 'The Mutual Influences in the Development of Ego and Id.' *Psychoanal. Study Child*, **7.** [III]

—— (1952c). 'Some Theoretical Conclusions regarding the Emotional Life of the Infant.' In: *Developments in Psycho-Analysis* with Heimann, Isaacs and Riviere (London: Hogarth). [III]

—— (1952d). 'On Observing the Behaviour of Young Infants.' *ibid.* [III]

—— (1955a). 'The Psycho-Analytic Play Technique: Its History and Significance.' In: *New Directions in Psycho-Analysis* (London: Tavistock). [III]

—— (1955b). 'On Identification.' *ibid.* [III]

—— (1957). *Envy and Gratitude* (London: Tavistock) [III]

—— (1958). 'On the Development of Mental Functioning.' *Int. J. Psycho-Anal.*, **29.** [III]

—— (1959). 'Our Adult World and its Roots in Infancy.' *Hum. Relations*, **12.** [III]

—— (1960a). 'A note on Depression in the Schizophrenic.' *Int. J. Psycho-Anal.*, **41.** [III]

—— (1960b). 'On Mental Health.' *Brit. J. med. Psychol.*, **33.** [III]

—— (1961). *Narrative of a Child Psycho-Analysis* (London: Hogarth). [IV]

—— (1963a). 'Some Reflections on *The Oresteia*.' In: *Our Adult World and Other Essays* (London: Heinemann Medical). [III]

—— (1963b). 'On the Sense of Loneliness.' *ibid.* [III]

Middlemore, M. P. (1941). *The Nursing Couple* (London: Hamish Hamilton).

Money-Kyrle, R. E. (1945). 'Towards a Common Aim: a Psycho-Analytical Contribution to Ethics.' *Brit. J. med. Psychol.*, **20.**

Ribble, M. A. (1944). 'Infantile experience in relation to personality development.' In: *Personality and the Behavior Disorders*, Vol. II (Ronald Press).

Riviere, J. (1952a). 'On the Genesis of Psychical Conflict in Early Infancy.' In: *Developments in Psycho-Analysis* by Klein *et al.* (London: Hogarth).

—— (1952b). 'The Unconscious Phantasy of an Inner World Reflected in Examples from Literature.' In: *New Directions in Psycho-Analysis* by Klein *et al.* (London: Tavistock, 1955).

345

Rosenfeld, H. (1947). 'Analysis of a Schizophrenic State with Depersonalization.' In: *Psychotic States* (London: Hogarth, 1965).

—— (1949). 'Remarks on the Relation of Male Homosexuality to Paranoia, Paranoid Anxiety, and Narcissism.' *ibid.*

—— (1950). 'Notes on the Psychopathology of Confusional States in Chronic Schizophrenias.' *ibid.*

—— (1952a). 'Notes on the Psycho-Analysis of the Super-ego Conflict in an Acute Schizophrenic Patient.' *ibid.*

—— (1952b). 'Transference-Phenomena and Transference-Analysis in an Acute Catatonic Schizophrenic Patient.' *ibid.*

—— (1955). 'The Investigation of the Need of Neurotic and Psychotic Patients to Act out during Analysis.' *ibid.*

Segal, H. (1950). 'Some Aspects of the Analysis of a Schizophrenic.' *Int. J. Psycho-Anal.*, **31.**

—— (1956). 'Depression in the Schizophrenic.' *Int. J. Psycho-Anal.*, **37.**

Winnicott, D. W. (1931). *Disorders of Childhood* (London: Heinemann).

—— (1945). 'Primitive Emotional Development.' In: *Collected Papers* (London: Hogarth).

—— (1953). 'Psychoses and Child Care.' *ibid.*

# INDEX

## Compiled by Barbara Forryan

347

hands, mother's 35*n*, 64, 99
happiness 17, 49*n*, 67, 99, 203, 205;
envy and 180; and identification
with others 259
hatred 4; and love, *see* love
Heimann, Paula 1*n*, 9*n*, 40*n*, 59*n*, 62*n*,
63*n*, 78*n*, 81*n*, 103*n*, 166*n*, 326
heterosexuality 45; unstable 165
homosexuality 162*n*, 164, 165, 252;
female 199, 200; male 201; paranoia 12*n*; *see also* feminine position
in boy; Oedipus complex, inverted
hope, feeling of 75*n*, 196, 233, 305
hospitality 263
*hubris* 280–4, 286, 294
Hug-Hellmuth, H. 122, 338
Hugo, Victor 228
hunger 156 & *n*, 201; alleviation of
63; feeling of 20 & *n*, 64, 206*n*;
*see also* feeding; food
hypochondria 84 & *n*, 243 & *n*; basis
of 63*n*
hysteria 84*n*; and schizophrenia, relation 3
hysterical conversion symptoms 84*n*

id: definitions of 243–4; and ego 57–
60; life and death instincts and 243
idealization 2, 6, 49, 65, 70, 71, 73,
143, 179, 277, 308, 324; of analyst
46; and anxiety, defence against
64; of baby-mother relation 193*n*;
diminution of 305; and envy 192,
193, 216; of the future 311; of
good object 9, 49; of the past 311;
and persecutory anxiety 46, 50, 64,
163, 192, 193, 273, 274, 278; and
positive transference 223; and
splitting, link 7
ideas, flight of 18
identification 259; with good/whole
object 192, 251, 309; indiscriminate 187, 192, 193; by introjection,
*see* introjection; man's, with his
own child 201, 259; with mother,
*see* mother; multitude of 168, 192;
and need for common ground 173;
overwhelming 168; with both
parents 306; and projective processes 13, 142; projective/by projection, *see* projective identification
identity, loss of 12*n*
illness, physical 84, 110

impotence 12, 45, 135, 201, 315, 317
impoverishment, sense of 274
incontinence of urine and faeces 134;
*see also* cleanliness; soiling
incorporation, *see* introjection
independence, spurious 219
indifference to people and toys 104
infant: confusion in 220; depression
in 80*n*, 255; development of object-
relations in 9, 49–50; development
to integration in 14; emotional life
of 50, 61–93, 116, 121, 170, 177,
247, 248, 271, 276, 304; emotions
of, extreme and powerful 64, 71;
feeding difficulties of, *see* feeding
difficulties; helplessness of, in face
of danger 31; love for mother,
earliest 96; mental processes of 236,
248; and mother, *see* mother;
observations on 89, 94–121, 177,
249, 255; —, *instances* 101–5, 107,
111–14; physiological changes in
90; sexual/libidinal organization of
72, 78; states of disintegration in
10 & *n*; states of integration in
34–5; testing of reality by 44; *see
also* baby, suckling
infantile neurosis, *see* neurosis
inhibition(s) 270; instinctual 86; of
one's own gifts 281; in play, *see*
play; in relationships 73
initiative 233
inner world 141, 142; excessive withdrawal to 11; projection of 11; *see
also* reality, inner
insight 232; capacity for, in young
children 132; depression following
212; into psychic reality, *see* reality,
inner
instincts, and phantasy 58
instinctual development 24
integration 6*n*, 69, 72, 118, 231, 268;
and analysis 56; and anxiety,
changes in 93; complete/perma-
nent, impossibility of 233, 274, 302;
dangers of 223; defences against
224; and depression, *see* depression;
and depressive position, *see* depressive position; of ego, *see* ego; fear of
227, 302; of feminine and masculine parts of personality 307; impeded 85*n*; and introjection of
whole object 44; and loneliness